TAKING TOURISM TO THE LIMITS: ISSUES, CONCEPTS AND MANAGERIAL PERSPECTIVES

ADVANCES IN TOURISM RESEARCH

Series Editor: Professor Stephen J. Page
University of Stirling, U.K.
s.j.page@stir.ac.uk

Advances in Tourism Research series publishes monographs and edited volumes that comprise state-of-the-art research findings, written and edited by leading researchers working in the wider field of tourism studies. The series has been designed to provide a cutting edge focus for researchers interested in tourism, particularly the management issues now facing decision-makers, policy analysts and the public sector. The audience is much wider than just academics and each book seeks to make a significant contribution to the literature in the field of study by not only reviewing the state of knowledge relating to each topic but also questioning some of the prevailing assumptions and research paradigms which currently exist in tourism research. The series also aims to provide a platform for further studies in each area by highlighting key research agendas which will stimulate further debate and interest in the expanding area of tourism research. The series is always willing to consider new ideas for innovative and scholarly books, inquiries should be made directly to the Series Editor.

Published:

PIKE
Bridging Theory and Practice

THOMAS
Small Firms in Tourism: International Perspectives

LUMSDON & PAGE
Tourism and Transport

KERR
Tourism Public Policy and the Strategic Management of Failure

WILKS & PAGE
Managing Tourist Health and Safety in the New Millennium

BAUM & LUNDTORP
Seasonality in Tourism

TEO, CHANG & HO
Interconnected Worlds: Tourism in Southeast Asia

ASHWORTH & TUNBRIDGE
The Tourist-Historic City: Retrospect and Prospect of Managing the Heritage City

SONG & WITT
Tourism Demand Modelling and Forecasting: Modern Econometric Approaches

RYAN & PAGE
Tourism Management: Towards the New Millennium

Forthcoming titles include:

SIMPSON
Back to the Future: In Search of an Effective Tourism Planning Model

Related Elsevier Journals - sample copies available on request
Air(line) Transport journal
Annals of Tourism Research
International Journal of Hospitality Management
International Journal of Intercultural Relations
Tourism Management
World Development

TAKING TOURISM TO THE LIMITS: ISSUES, CONCEPTS AND MANAGERIAL PERSPECTIVES

EDITED BY

CHRIS RYAN

University of Waikato, Hamilton, New Zealand

STEPHEN J. PAGE

University of Stirling, UK

MICHELLE AICKEN

Horwath Asia Pacific Ltd, Auckland, New Zealand

ELSEVIER

Amsterdam – Boston – Heidelberg – London – New York – Oxford
Paris – San Diego – San Francisco – Singapore – Sydney – Tokyo

ELSEVIER B.V.
Radarweg 29
P.O. Box 211
1000 AE Amsterdam
The Netherlands

ELSEVIER Inc.
525 B Street, Suite 1900
San Diego
CA 92101-4495
USA

ELSEVIER Ltd
The Boulevard, Langford
Lane, Kidlington
Oxford OX5 1GB
UK

ELSEVIER Ltd
84 Theobalds Road
London
WC1X 8RR
UK

First edition 2005

Library of Congress Cataloging in Publication Data
A catalog record is available from the Library of Congress.

British Library Cataloguing in Publication Data
A catalogue record is available from the British Library.

ISBN-10: 0-08-044644-2
ISBN-13: 978-0-08-044644-8

⊗ The paper used in this publication meets the requirements of ANSI/NISO Z39.48-1992 (Permanence of Paper). Printed in The Netherlands.

Contents

Section 2: Nature-Based Tourism

Section 3: Adventure and Sport Tourism

Section 4: Dark Tourism

List of Figures

List of Tables

List of Maps

Contributors

Michelle Aicken
Michelle graduated with a Bachelor of Commerce and a Postgraduate Diploma in Tourism from the University of Otago. Subsequently she worked in Japan and the United Kingdom in a variety of posts. Currently she works as a consultant with Horwath Asia Pacific Ltd in Auckland while completing her doctoral studies at the University of Waikato, New Zealand. She was a co-organiser of the conference, Taking Tourism to the Limits hosted by the Department of Tourism Management. Michelle is able to claim affiliation with Ngai Tahu iwi of the South Island of New Zealand.

Colin Arrowsmith
Colin is a Senior Lecturer in Geographical Sciences in the School of Mathematical and Geospatial Science at RMIT University, where he teaches physical geography, Quaternary geography and geographical information science. Colin's research interests include impacts of tourism on natural tourist destinations, the spatial behaviour of tourists and the development of virtual tourist environments. He has published in both tourism and cartography journals.

Carl Cater
Carl is a lecturer in tourism at Griffith University, Queensland, Australia. His principal research interests are in the place of the body and emotions in tourist experience, carrying us beyond the limitations of the visual epistemology that is characterised by work on the tourist gaze. In particular he views the growth of so-called special interest tourism as emblematic of a fulfillment of these desires. Consequently he has researched and published work that examines developments in marine tourism, adventure tourism and the nascent astrotourism (space tourism) industry. His Ph.D., completed in the School of Geography at Bristol University, U.K., but with much of the fieldwork conducted in Queenstown, New Zealand, examined the commodification of experience in adventure tourism. He is a fellow of the Royal Geographical Society, a qualified pilot, diver, mountain and tropical forest leader, and maintains an interest in both the practice and pursuit of sustainable outdoor tourism activity.

Prem Chhetri
Prem is currently employed as an Asset and Spatial Information Officer with Brimbank City Council in Melbourne, Australia. Prem's research interests include cognitive mapping, growth modelling and spatial econometrics using spatial information technologies.

Chris Cooper
Chris is Foundation Professor of Tourism Management in the School of Tourism and Leisure Management, Faculty of Business Economics and Law at The University of Queensland, Australia. He has an honours degree and Ph.D. from University College London and before beginning an academic career worked in market planning for the tourism and retail sectors in the U.K. He has formerly held posts at the Universities of Surrey and Bournemouth. Chris has authored a number of leading textbooks in tourism and worked closely with the World Tourism Organisation in developing the status of tourism education on the international stage. He is co-editor of *Current Issues in Tourism*, editor for a leading tourism book series, *Aspects of Tourism*, author of many academic papers in tourism and has worked as a consultant and researcher in every region of the world.

W. Glen Croy
Glen is a lecturer in the Tourism Research Unit at Monash University, Melbourne Australia. He has undertaken research in a number of areas of tourism, though his main interest is in the role of media in destination image formation. Within the media and destination image relationship Glen is particularly focused on the fictional media of film, television and literary works.

Malcolm Draper
Malcolm is a lecturer in sociology at the Pietermaritzburg campus of the University of KwaZulu-Natal, South Africa. His focus is on the interaction between environment and society. Using biographical and other methods, he is exploring the intersections between, amongst other things, environmental history, social theory, ecology, gender, race, identity, nationalism, development, wilderness, wildlife conservation, fly fishing, sustainable agriculture, literature, tourism and indigenous views of the landscape. The scarcity of recruits in the humanities has forced him to cross a few roads and do trans-disciplinary teaching and supervision in the Faculty of Science and Agriculture's Centre for Environment and Development where he is closely involved with the Protected Area Management Programme and teaching Wilderness Concepts and Practice courses. Prior to his academic career he worked in the tourism industry — from taking horse trails in the Drakensberg-Maloti mountains to designing and guiding Zulu-style culture shock at Shakaland. He believes that, if the fluid contemporary world lacks a thing that sociologists called society, then we are, by necessity, scholars of tourism.

Rosaleen Duffy
Rosaleen is a Senior Lecturer in the Department of Politics and International Relations, Lancaster University, United Kingdom. Having completed a Ph.D. on environmental politics in Zimbabwe in 1996, she accepted a position as Research Fellow in the Geography Department Edinburgh University, and then moved to Lancaster University. She has research interests in Sub-Saharan Africa and Central America, and has undertaken field research in Zimbabwe, Madagascar, Ethiopia, South Africa and Belize. The core themes of her research centre on global governance, globalisation, environmental politics, tourism, the politics of development and security/criminalisation. She has written four books: *Killing for Conservation* (James Currey 2000), *A Trip Too Far: Ecotourism, Politics, and Exploitation* (Earthscan 2003), *The Ethics of Tourism Development* (with Mick Smith,

Routledge 2003) and *Global Governance, Conflict and Resistance* (edited with Jan Selby and Feargal Cochrane, Palgrave 2003). She is currently working on an ESRC funded study of global environmental governance and illicit sapphire mining in protected areas in Madagascar.

Shelagh Ferguson

Shelagh is a Senior Teaching Fellow at the University of Otago, Dunedin, New Zealand. Originally an outdoor pursuits instructor working all over the world, this experience provided a context for Shelagh's interest in adventure tourism marketing. After her first degree in Recreation from Heriot Watt, Shelagh became the marketing manager for a Scottish Ski Area. Moving into academia, she took a lecturing post at Wirral Metropolitan College in both Tourism and Business. During her six years in this post she completed a Post Graduate Diploma in Marketing from the Chartered Institute of Marketing and a Masters degree in Marketing. She is currently studying towards a Ph.D. in the area of consumer behaviour in Tourism Marketing.

Tracey Harrison-Hill

Tracey lectures within the department of Tourism, Leisure, Hotel and Sport Management in the Griffith Business School at Griffith University, Queensland, Australia. Wanting to better understand consumers' consumption decisions and behaviour within the service sector industries of tourism, sports and leisure drives her research. Her doctoral thesis focused on tourist decision-making and was entitled "Implications of Long Haul Travel on the Marketing of International Tourism." She has also completed work for the Sustainable Tourism CRC on the Gold Coast Tourism Visioning project, though her more recent research has focussed on decision-making and consumption behaviours of sport tourists.

Leo Jago

Leo is Deputy CEO and Director of Research for the Cooperative Research Centre for Sustainable Tourism and a Professor in Tourism at Victoria University in Melbourne. He was the national Chair of CAUTHE (Council of Australian University Tourism and Hospitality Education) for three years and is a Board Member of a range of public and private tourism organisations. Leo's research interests, whilst eclectic, lie largely in the field of events, tourism marketing, volunteers and small business management. Over the past 18 years, he has owned and operated small tourism businesses largely in the accommodation sector.

Sharon Kemp

Sharon is a Senior Lecturer in the School of Management at University of Western Sydney, Australia. She has a Masters degree in Management and a Ph.D. in Management from the University of Technology, Sydney. Sharon is a Board Member of the European Academy of Management (EURAM), an International Advisory Board member for the Eastern Academy of Management and serves on the editorial board of the *European Management Review*. She has published several articles and conference papers on a number of themes in tourism including the Strategic Management of Tourism, Organisational Culture and Human Resources, Asia Pacific Tourism, the Development of a Regional Identity, and Sustainable Tourism. Sharon is the author of *Management Foundations* (Pearson Education Australia 2002), *Management* (3rd ed.) & *Foundations of Management* (3rd ed.), Video Cases

(Pearson Prentice Hall 2003) and *Management* (3rd ed.) & *Foundations of Management* (3rd ed.), Cases Studies CD-ROM (Pearson Prentice Hall 2003).

Tim Lockyer
Tim started his career by training to become a Chef de Cuisine in London England, working in West End hotels including the Savoy, and then moved on to a number of management positions in and around London. He migrated to New Zealand in 1973 to purchase a restaurant in Wellington. After three years he sold a successful business and left New Zealand to study and work in Hawaii, Hong Kong and China. In 1986 he returned to New Zealand to Massey University to teach Hospitality Management and while there completed a Masters of Management Studies. Three years later he returned to Wellington as Head of the School of Hospitality and Tourism Management at the Central Institute of Technology. In 1997 he became a full time Ph.D. student at the University of Waikato. Having completed that qualification, Tim is now teaching as a Senior Lecturer in the Department of Tourism Management at the University of Waikato.

Robert Manning
Robert is a Professor in the Rubenstein School of Environment and Natural Resources at the University of Vermont, USA. He teaches and conducts research on the history, philosophy and management of parks, wilderness, and related areas. He is Chair of the University's Recreation Management Program and Director of the Park Studies Laboratory. He conducts a program of research for the U.S. National Park Service that examines the impacts of outdoor recreation, carrying capacity, and visitor management. He has spent three year-long sabbatical leaves with the U.S. National Park Service at Grand Canyon and Yosemite National Parks and the Washington Office. Robert has a B.S. degree in Biology and M.S. and Ph.D. degrees in parks and outdoor recreation and conservation. His most recent books are *Studies in Outdoor Recreation: Search and Research for Satisfaction* (2nd ed.), published by Oregon State University Press and *Reconstructing Conservation: Finding Common Ground*, published by Island Press.

Paul Mitchell-Banks
Paul was born in England, but moved as a young child to the north coast of British Columbia, Canada and has spent most of his life in Western Canada. He has a BSc. Honours in Life Sciences at Queen's University at Kingston and a Master of Business Administration from the University of British Columbia. From 1985 he was a commercial and corporate banker, which is where he became concerned about the need to bridge the ecological, social and economic challenges. He resigned from banking at the end of 1989 and established Central Coast Consulting, a firm specialising in the environmental, business, First Nations, community and forestry work. While consulting he completed a Master of Science in Planning at the University of Toronto with a thesis on First Nations and Environmental Monitoring and Enforcement and also a Doctorate in forestry from the University of British Columbia focusing on Forest Economics and Policy with a focus on Community Forestry and Tenures. He was the Program Manager (Senior Government Manager) for the 6.3 million ha Muskwa-Kechika Management Area in Northern British Columbia in which innovative land use management and planning is being developed. Now Paul undertakes research work at a Norway Based Research Institute and teaches at More University College.

Asad Mohsin
Asad has accumulated several years of industry and academic experience working in different countries in the Middle East and Asia Pacific regions including Australia and New Zealand. He is currently a Senior Lecturer and Graduate Convenor in the Department of Tourism Management at the University of Waikato Management School. His research interests include: tourism and hospitality product and service quality assessment; tourism and hospitality customers' perceptions and contemporary trends; attitudes of customers towards holidaying and the backpacker market. He has contributed to several journals including *Tourism Management*; *International Journal of Tourism Research*; and the *Journal of Travel and Tourism Marketing*. His current teaching responsibilities include delivery of Accommodation Management, Hotel and Resorts Operations Management, Food and Beverage Management and International Tourism Marketing and Research. Asad is an Associate Fellow of Catering Institute of Australia and Australian Institute of Management. He obtained his doctorate from Charles Darwin University, Australia in 2003 for a study into multi-ethnic groupings and the demand for tourism product with reference to Malaysia.

Ong Chin Ee
Chin Ee is a graduate student at the Department of Geography, National University of Singapore (NUS). He received his Bachelor of Social Science (Hons) in Geography from NUS in 2002 and subsequently completed his Master of Social Science thesis exploring the geographies of Singapore adventure tourists' motivations. At undergraduate level, Chin Ee benefited from training in geography and sociology. A recipient of the National University of Singapore-Singapore Tourism Board (NUS-STB) Research Scholarship, his research interests include adventure tourism motivations, environmental activism and film tourism. These academic interests have led to fieldwork in various sites in Malaysia, Thailand and Singapore. In addition to geo-graphing and following adventure tourists, Chin Ee enjoys scuba diving, photography and film.

Mark Orams
Mark is currently the director of the Coastal Marine Research Group at Massey University at Albany, Auckland, New Zealand. He holds a Bachelor's degree in natural resource management, a Master of Science and completed his Ph.D. in 1995 at the School of Marine Science at the University of Queensland. This doctoral research focused on the impacts of tourism on dolphin biology and behaviour. Mark continues with this research and conducts additional work on the wider issues of the management of human impacts on marine resources. He has authored or co-authored three books and over 20 scientific papers on the subject.

Stephen J. Page
Stephen joined the Department of Marketing at the University of Stirling in November 2000 as the Scottish Enterprise Forth Valley Chair in Tourism. He is responsible for the development of Tourism Studies within the University as a new initiative funded by Scottish Enterprise and the University of Stirling. He previously worked at Massey University in New Zealand where he held a Personal Chair in Tourism Management and was Director of the Centre for Tourism Research. He holds a number of editorial roles for publishers

including Pearson Education, Elsevier Science and Thomson Learning and is Associate Editor of Tourism Management. He has also been a Visiting Professor at a number of Universities. Stephen has published widely in the tourism literature, being the author, editor or co-author of 15 books in tourism, the most recent examples being *Transport and Tourism* (Pearson Education), *Tourism in South and South East Asia* (Butterworth Heinemann) (with Michael Hall, University of Otago, New Zealand), *Tourism: A Modern Synthesis* (Thomson Learning) and *The Geography of Tourism and Recreation: Environment, Place and Space* and *Managing Urban Tourism* (both with Michael Hall). He maintains an active research interest in tourist health and safety issues which has been the subject of recent studies including the safety and management of the adventure tourism industry and tourist crime and special events with researchers in New Zealand.

Tanaya Preece
Tanaya studied for the degree of Bachelor of Business (Tourism Management) (Hons) at La Trobe University, Victoria, Australia, obtaining her degree in 2002. Her thesis explored the field of dark tourism. Subsequent to graduating with First Class Honours, Tanaya has been employed within the tourism industry. She is currently Marketing Coordinator at Destination Melbourne.

Garry Price
Garry is a lecturer in the School of Sport, Tourism and Hospitality Management at La Trobe University. His research interests include nature-based tourism, regional tourism, entrepreneurship, environmental education, tourism policy and planning and cultural tourism. For over thirty years Garry was employed in secondary education and was a Member of the Australian College of Education (MACE) which "aims to foster educational thought and practice through . . . recognising excellence in educational practice." He also owned and operated an ecotourism business (Top Country Nature Tours). This practical experience helps to provide him with valuable insights into the relationship between theory and practice in tourism.

Linda Roberts
Linda is an Associate Professor in the School of Hospitality, Tourism and Marketing, Head of the Hospitality Discipline Area and Course Director for the Master of Business in Hospitality Management and the Master of Business in Hospitality Management (Professional Practice) at Victoria University, Melbourne. She has thirty-five years of experience as an educator and academic with twenty-seven years in higher education in the hospitality field.

Linda's research interests encompass the areas of: new product development and innovation; new product adoption and the factors affecting decision making in the adoption and purchasing of new products; food and wine tourism; identification of innovative strategies to meet visitors needs in the motel industry; and innovation change management in small and medium tourism enterprises. Her research in recent years has been largely focused on Sustainable Tourism Cooperative Research Centre projects in Australia. Linda is also interested in environmental management and food safety. Her teaching is closely related to her research interests and includes product innovation in hospitality and tourism, catering systems, HACCP and food safety programs, food trends and environmental management for the hospitality industry.

Lisa Ruhanen
Lisa is a Research Assistant with the School of Tourism and Leisure Management, Faculty of Business Economics and Law at the University of Queensland, Australia. She has an honours degree from James Cook University and is currently undertaking a Ph.D. at the University of Queensland looking at strategic tourism planning at the local destination level. She has been involved in a number of research projects in both Australia and overseas. Her research interests are in strategic tourism planning and destination visioning, knowledge management and backpacker tourism.

Chris Ryan
Chris holds a doctoral degree from the Aston Business School, United Kingdom. He is the editor of *Tourism Management*, an elected member of the International Academy for the Study of Tourism and Professor of Tourism at the University of Waikato Management School and Visiting Professor at the Centre of Travel and Tourism, the University of Northumbria. A keen windsurfer Chris manages to mention windsurfing in many of his books that include *The Tourism Experience* (Continuum 2002), and *Recreational Tourism — Demand and Impacts* (Channel View Press 2003) but failed to mention in it his co-authored work with Mike Hall on *Sex Tourism — marginal people and liminalities* (Routledge 2001)! His research interests lie in tourist motives and behaviours, and the impacts that result from these.

Richard Sharpley
Richard Sharpley is Professor and Head of Department of Tourism at the University of Lincoln in the United Kingdom. Previously, having completed an M.Sc in Tourism at Strathclyde University, Richard started his academic career in 1991 at the University of Luton where he helped establish new undergraduate and postgraduate tourism programmes. He also undertook his Ph.D. part-time at Lancaster University, graduating in 1998. In 1997, he moved to the University of Northumbria as a Senior Lecturer in Tourism, subsequently being appointed as Reader in Tourism in 2000. In 2004, he took up a senior academic post at the University of Hull before moving to Lincoln in 2005. Prior to an academic career Richard spent a number of years in sales and marketing, specialising in professional photographic products, managing a department in a major professional photographic wholesaler in London from 1984 to 1986. This was followed by a period of overseas travel and travel photography, which stimulated his initial interest in tourism as an academic subject.

Nell Smith
Nell Smith had a career in industry before starting lecturing in New Zealand. At the time of conducting the research reported in this book she held the post of Lecturer in Tourism Studies at the Waiariki Institute of Technology in Rotorua, New Zealand. She subsequently moved to Dunedin in New Zealand's South Island to commence her doctoral studies at the Department of Tourism, Otago University, where she also undertakes some tutor duties.

Amy Taylor
Amy completed a Degree in Applied Science from the Auckland University of Technology in 2002. Her experience with marine science and tourism led into marine-based filmmaking, and in 2004 Amy completed a Postgraduate Diploma in Natural History Filmmaking

and Communication from the University of Otago. As part of this course Amy made a documentary about Hector's Dolphins, which focuses on the impacts that people are having on the species. Amy continues to be involved in making documentaries and short films, and is particularly interested in projects related to marine conservation.

Sarah Todd

Sarah has been with the Department of Marketing, at the University of Otago since 1989. She teaches mainly in the areas of consumer behaviour, tourism and research methods, as well as being involved in the co-ordination of postgraduate studies in the Department. Sarah is a founding member of the Department's *Consumer Research Group*, which has undertaken several major studies into New Zealand consumers' lifestyles and values, with the most recent being *New Zealand beyond 2000*. She is also a member of the *Tourism Research Group* and is currently researching children's consumption behaviour and their understanding of advertising. Additionally, Sarah has strong interests in the Japanese language and culture. Sarah holds a doctorate from the University of Otago.

Birgit Trauer

Birgit is completing her doctoral studies at the University of Queensland (entitled *Enduring Involvement and Satisfaction within the context of Special Interest Tourism*) having graduated from Griffith University with a B.A. and the University of Waikato with a Post Graduate Diploma in Tourism Management. She has worked for a variety of businesses including Air India and other airlines, as a consultant and for a significant time ran her own fitness business. Her teaching experience includes periods at Lakehead and Queensland Universities. Birgit has published articles in journals including *Tourism Review International*, *Australian Parks and Recreation*, *Tourism Recreation Research* and *Journal of Sport Tourism*.

Dino Zanon

Dino is Team Leader of Visitor Research and Development at Parks Victoria. Dino's research has extended into understanding what the drivers of visitor demand in urban parks are. More recently Dino's research has centred on satisfaction strategies as well as the implementation of mathematical models for the equitable distribution of urban parks in Melbourne and simulation modelling of visitor flows.

Acknowledgments

The editors wish to acknowledge the help received from W. Glen Croy for permission to replicate the papers by Nell Smith and Glen Croy, and Tanaya Preece and Garry Price as companion pieces to the chapter by Richard Sharpley on Dark Tourism. These two chapters emerge from papers presented at the 2002 New Zealand National Tourism and Hospitality Conference. The work of Leonie Pope, administrator at the Department of Tourism Management at the University of Waikato Management School in replicating the diagrams of Smith and Croy is also here acknowledged. Equally the permission of the Aladdin Hotel Las Vegas and the Gaylord Texan Hotel to reproduce their advertisements in Chapter 24 is also gratefully acknowledged.

Chapter 1

Introduction — Conceptualising "the Limit"

Chris Ryan and Michelle Aicken

This book emerged from the conference *Taking Tourism to the Limits* that was hosted by the Department of Tourism Management at Waikato University in December 2003. The theme was an ambitious one and delegates were invited to consider it from a number of perspectives. The potential range of approaches that might be adopted is illustrated by Table 1.1 which lists twelve possible interpretations of the theme. At least two immediate impressions emerge from this list, and they are 1) the apparent paradoxical ones of both how disparate they appear, and 2) just how much they are linked in a dialogic process of questioning and answer. From the perspective of the practical site owner or destination planner, concepts of liminality or the marginal might appear interesting, but abstract, and of limited applicability. Planning is, arguably, to a large degree based upon a modernist, deductive approach derived from the rationalism of the eighteenth century enlightment, and much of the tourism planning literature is still premised within the paradigm, as is illustrated by the work of Gunn (1988, 1993). Deductiveness has maintained its own boundaries, one of which is the distinction between theory and practice; and if there exists any form of duality it is that the purpose of theory is to inform, define and subsequently shape "good practice." The ghost of Bentham and J. S. Mill's utilitarianism survives into the early 21st century even if the advocates of modernism are more reticent about the construction of universal theories.

Yet the issues of social, technological and political change evident in the early twenty-first century cannot be denied and contemporary management texts are no longer those of scientific management but, as evidenced by Gilson *et al.* (2000) in *Peak Performance*, they are redolent with phrases of creativity, imagination, product champions, human empowerment, team work, excellence and even "love marks" (Roberts & Lafley 2004). Empiricism has to meet the challenge that so much of deductive theorising has failed to work at the level of the specific. Tourism has been criticised for its failure to develop well defined paradigms or theoretical structures and what few it has are often found wanting (see, for example Jones 1996; Ryan 1997). Butler's destination life cycle theory is the subject matter of a rich literature which highlights exceptions, problems and differential practices (for example, see Butler 2001). Pearce's tourism career ladder is much cited but is arguably lacking in hard evidence (for example, see Ryan 1998). One response is to develop increasingly complex theorisations and the literature portrays this movement from

Taking Tourism to the Limits: Issues, Concepts and Managerial Perspectives
© 2005 Published by Elsevier Ltd.
ISBN: 0-08-044644-2

Table 1.1: Taking Tourism to the Limits — Conceptualising the Limit.

Concepts of margins, liminalities and ritual in social processes.

Spatial margins and changing physical nature of resorts.

The Pleasure Periphery – the changing social classes and composition of tourist typologies over time in specific tourist destinations.

New products and the use of new technologies as illustrated by space tourism and theme parks.

New definitions of self and discovery of self in succeeding ages and the changing role of tourism – e.g. adventure tourism, extreme sports tourism, the search for adrenalin.

Evolving understandings of stakeholders and political processes – the role of communities, "top-down" vs. "bottom-up" planning, and new understandings of planning approaches.

New "gazes" and processes of globalization, cosmopolitanism, fordism and post-fordism, and the processes of limit dissolution in post-modernistic de-differentiation. The questioning of modernity.

Limits of acceptable change – environmental and social sustainability, site planning, and eco-tourism.

Marginal peoples, indigenous peoples, tourism as a means of legitimizing cultural, social and political aspiration.

Marginal economies, the urban vs. the rural, the status quo vs. new emergent power/economic centres. The changing economic structures of service and experiential industries. Small and medium sized enterprise and their importance vs. the mega corporation.

The existential authenticity vs. the "conventional" cultural authenticities – the questioning of whose authenticity.

Taking experience to the limit of death, disaster, the macabre, to the sites of man's inhumanity to man.

the general to the more particular, perhaps best exemplified by an emergent consideration of chaos and complexity theory in tourism as developed by authors like Faulkner & Russell (2001) and McKercher (1999), or by the increasing use of techniques based upon Artificial Neural Networks software (e.g. Law 2000). As the theories become more sophisticated, so their general applicability becomes more constrained. Even those theorisations that initially challenged the modernist, deductivist and arguably management led tourism literature such as appeals to Foucault and the "gaze" as argued by Urry (2002) have in their turn been found lacking. Examples of critiques include the praise of the corporeal by Veijola & Jokinnen (1994), and Ryan (2001), and Urry's own subsequent work on the processes of globalisation and space-time compression (e.g. see Urry 2000). Consequently, as Pearce (2004) highlights there has been an increasing stress upon the role of qualitative research, even to the extent of perhaps, so he argues, undervaluing the nature of the positivist tradition.

The picture that emerges is thus one whereby tourism research comprises more particularism and contextualisation, of sensitivities to difference and more dynamic understandings that consider temporalities and spatial evolutions — all based upon recognition of significant social change. That social change is in part economic (with generally growing wealth but also evidence of greater disparities of income and wealth) and technological (but evidencing greater differences between those with and without access to information exchanges those technologies bring). Tourism theorising and research reflects these social changes in different ways. Not only does it concern itself with social and political change and aspiration, but also it has become more "technological" as researchers adopt more computer based tools with which to conduct their analyses. Econometric forecasting and textual analysis share, for example, the commonality that increasingly both require the researcher to be conversant with computer modelling but often with a dependence upon only partially understood mathematical procedures. The algorithms of neural networks, backward propogation, co-integration have become part of the language of tourism research.

Consequently, like many forms of social science research, tourism stretches and bends its own boundaries and its own understandings of what comprises its concerns and the means with which those concerns are analysed, defined, measured and interpreted. It overlaps with other discipline areas and fields, such as those of marketing, psychology, environmental sciences, management and transport to name but a few. As a field of enquiry, tourism research like many social sciences faces a tension. On the one hand, there is displayed a greater flexibility in thinking, a greater utilisation of more sophisticated analytical techniques but on the other there is the risk that the work of the academic researcher may become less accessible to the industry or governmental manager who faces the uncertainties of "playful" tourists with constrained resources and possibly ageing asset structures. In practice however, this divide is perhaps more apparent than real with academics being able to address more than one audience (thereby again displaying the skills of adaptability) and practioners increasingly having been exposed to academics through an expansion of higher education. If a characteristic of post-modernism is the de-differentiation of fantasy and fact, history and myth, and the affective and cognitive, then too the boundaries between theory and practice also become blurred to create some hybrid product which often, in tourism, emphasises the experiential. For example Amsterdam without the hypodermic needles is found at Huis Ten Bosch at Sasebo in Japan (see Figure 1.1).

Table 1.1 indicates a number of different interpretations of the "limit." It is not new to state that tourism has often incorporated concepts of limits. The concept of a continually changing periphery is inherent in Butler's destination life cycle because not only does the resort area change its nature over time, but arguably different types of tourists are attracted over time, each type being succeeded by another in a process of resort diffusion. To adopt the language of Rogers (2003), early adopters are replaced by later adopters until eventually laggards discover a resort, by which time it has changed to better meet their needs, thereby ensuring that early adopters have moved on to other thus far undiscovered locations. Cohen's (1972)

Figure 1.1:   Amsterdam in Sasebo, Japan — an example of "de-spacing" place.

drifters become replaced by mass organized tourists, Plog's (1977, 2002) allocentrics submit to the psychocentrics in patterns of geographical discovery and social class encroachment. Historically commentators can point to the locations like the south of France which, even by the late nineteenth century evidenced not only this process, but also highlighted the importance of property developers and planning regimes (e.g. Haug 1982).

The changing nature of the resort complex is well demonstrated by Young (1983) in his article on the touristisation of a Maltese fishing village. Other studies have confirmed the evolving spatial boundaries of place and examples include those of Miossec (1976) and Smith (1992). Tourism is thus, from a spatial and social perspective, not simply taken to the limit, but challenges and stretches spatial and social limits. The challenges presented to the planning processes are social, technological and political. New technologies aid planning, but by their nature infrastructure planning has to incorporate the assets needed to utilise those technologies. For example, contemporary hotels are designed with fibre optic networks to provide rooms with internet access and potentially a whole range of entertainment facilities. The technocrats of planning also increasingly have to involve whole communities, but these communities are not simply those of local residents, but a range of stakeholders that might include global pressure groups with local representation. The "green movement" has given rise to political parties of varying hues of "greenness" as a countervailing power to that of corporate and central government, so that planning is political. Indigenous peoples are brought from the periphery as an interested stakeholder to validate processes, which processes are a means of legitimising their own interests.

The social pressures of the late twentieth and early twenty-first century that create this fluidity in planning also creates on the part of the consumer, new demands and in consequence new products. Products evolve to create new "limits" of that which is possible, tasteful and which represent new forms of escape. The latter part of the twentieth century has seen the emergence of adventure tourism as a mass, commodified product which promises self challenge and escape from an organised world — yet increasingly the product itself is organised and packaged and subject to physical and objective risk minimisation, even while it is signed by promotional images to be life enhancing and free (Cloke & Perkins 1998, 2002). Ryan & Trauer (2005) in this volume present a framework of analysis that argues that image has become so pervasive in the promotion of place that it means that statements that tourism is a search for the unfamiliar have to be modified. They argue that much of tourism today is a search for the enactment of a role made familiar through the media, which role is thought attractive and meaningful to the participant. The adventure tourist wears the t-shirt proclaiming an image of the person as "adventurous" and thereby also identifying the participant to others of like mindedness (as is discussed by Ferguson & Todd 2005 in this volume). Participation is a social as well as an individual act that establishes communities formed upon the shared experience. Wagner (1996: 1) claims, in the formation of what he terms the *Geltung Hypothesis* that human beings are innately programmed to persistently and skillfully cultivate attention, acceptance, respect, esteem and trust from their fellows'. The *Geltung* is recognition and communicating of shared understandings that are signaled in many subtle ways whereby individuals recognise and generate mutual meanings that re-affirm their esteem and prestige of self and other. Ferguson and Todd's analysis of the t-shirt reaffirms this process.

The chapters in this collection all represent different facets of the nature of the limits represented in tourism. The text is divided into five sections. The contributions under the heading of "tourism planning and management" concentrate on planning issues that represent some of the points made above. Three chapters (those of Paul Mitchell Banks, Sharon Kemp and Chris Cooper and Lisa Ruhanen) are about community involvement, multiple uses and the tensions that exist between the requirements of planning and political processes. The fourth illustrates how new technologies can play a research role as Colin Arrowsmith and his colleagues, Dino Zanon and Prem Chhetri report how the use of GIS to track visitor travel patterns within a National Park can provide new understandings of visitor activities.

The use of new technologies is also illustrated by the work of Robert Manning who discusses planning in the Arches National Park in the United States, and indeed it can be said that this chapter could have fitted into the first section. However, it does consider an important component of nature-based tourism, which is the issue of perceptual over-crowding and the way in which that can negatively impact upon the visitor experience. Orams and Taylor's chapter picks up on the theme of education within eco-tourism and explores the degree to which environmental education programmes might impact on a marine mammal tour. But, as is indicated by the above discussion, nature-based tourism and eco-tourism do not exist within vacuums independent of a wider world, and Rosaleen Duffy's paper argues that such tourism does not represent an alternative edge, but rather is a confirmation of the hegemony of capitalist structures.

In the section entitled "Adventure and Sport" the same point is argued by Ong Chin Ee with reference to how the language of sport and adventure is purloined by the Singaporean government to help propagate a new form of entrepreneurial activism that it sees as being appropriate to Singapore's economic well being in the early twenty-first century. Shelagh

Ferguson and Sarah Todd's and Carl Cater's chapters are also about representations of self, and through a self-selected commodisation as participants in adventure products quite consciously want to identify themselves with the product as a statement of who they are. Tracey Harrison-Hill's paper is also about aspects of self and sharing, but reveals how the use of the internet can help shape expectations and anticipation.

Two sections remain. That on accommodation represent a return to the empirical and deductive as Sharon Kemp, Linda Roberts and Leo Jago discuss organisational structures and the need for investment. Asad Mohsin and Tim Lockyer represent a return to the emergent trends of playfulness in their discussion of accommodation as the new entertainment centre. Finally, the irrational and attractiveness of the possibly morbid is discussed in a section on dark tourism. Nell Smith and Glen Croy, and Tanaya Preece and Garry Price provide two examples of sites, those of Port Arthur in Australia and the Buried Village in New Zealand to argue that sites of inhumanity and natural disaster are feasible tourism attractions. Richard Sharpley, for his part provides an analysis of what links and what provides difference among such sites in his framework of various forms of "grey."

Taken as a collection the essays represent some of the current thinking that pertains to varying interpretations of what constitutes as the limits of tourism. The texts are primarily derived, however, from a managerial perspective, as whatever the sociological significance of marginal products, peoples and places, the reality is that they are visited products, peoples and places, and thus the flows of people and their activities need to be managed. Consequently, the second part of the title of the book is important and this needs to be stated to avoid giving false impressions.

Section 1

Tourism Planning and Management

Chapter 2

Tourism Planning and Management

Stephen J. Page

Why Do We Need Tourism Planning and Management?

The provocative title of this book has within it the underlying rationale for tourism planning and management — as a largely private sector-led activity, the inherent search for business opportunities and profit, as the tourism sector has contributed to the development of tourism as a largely uncontrollable phenomenon. As Page (2003) highlighted, tourism has a tendency towards self-destruction, particularly in contexts where uncontrollable growth and development is allowed to progress in spite of attempts to plan and constrain its amoeba like tendencies, where it constantly reproduces (and reinvents) itself by breaking away and replicating itself elsewhere. Few researchers have questioned the need for tourism planning and management, though entrepreneurs and businesses frequently point to the negativity of red tape it creates through the costs imposed by the public sector in seeking to plan and manage tourism and tourism-related businesses. Indeed, if one accepts the general premise widely promoted by industry-led organisations such as the World Travel and Tourism Council (WTTC) that tourism is the world's largest industry and employer, then a degree of planning and management is essential to control the scale, pace and effects of tourism growth and development, unless we endorse the views of the anthropocentric industry worldview discussed in the last section of the book.

Many of the well established texts on tourism planning and management such as Inskeep (1991, 1994) set out all the well rehearsed arguments as to why planning is needed. However, there is a tendency for researchers to focus on western models of tourism, where assumptions are made that tourism is often a complementary tourism activity, rather than being the dominant activity. However, as thoughtful syntheses such as Scheyvens (2002) *Tourism for Development* highlights, tourism is a vital force for developing countries to help modernise their economies, to seek foreign exchange earnings and to provide service-related employment for local communities. Without entering into the dialect of the politicised nature of tourism development and its impacts in less developed countries, it has become an activity which countries now depend upon for economic growth or survival. At a simplistic level, tourism planning and management has a critical, if not reactive and regulatory role in seeking to limit the detrimental impacts which tourism can induce. Yet equally, innovative public

Taking Tourism to the Limits: Issues, Concepts and Managerial Perspectives
© 2005 Published by Elsevier Ltd.
ISBN: 0-08-044644-2

sector agencies can also use tourism as a vehicle for regeneration in rural and urban areas (see Page & Hall 2002), using planning tools and mechanisms to harness investment and opportunities to transform declining communities and localities through appropriate forms of tourism-based development (although this raises the question of appropriate for whom if one reads the literature in this area). The research literature is littered with case studies of this process and the outcomes, though few studies have contextualised such processes in relation to the changing nature of society, particularly the effects of postmodernity. This has meant the public sector has had to retain planning principles and adapt to the changing paradigms in planning, and specifically the demands of tourism.

As Hall (2000) has shown, tourism planning has evolved through a number of phases from an industry approach, boosterism, the land-use approach to a community approach with sustainability being now a dominant paradigm. There remain inherent problems of deriving tangible measures and tools to measure tourism sustainability in locations, highlighting the imperfections in concepts such as carrying capacity and other tools used to calculate tourism thresholds for localities. Despite these problems, sustainability has been operationalised with indicators and measures to ensure that tourism is operated and managed in a more controlled manner, as some notable environments (i.e. the Mediterranean coastline and small historic cities) are saturated and effectively besieged by tourists.

Attempting to delimit the scope and extent of the academic literature on tourism planning and management is an impossible task, once one moves beyond the technical aspects of these tasks (e.g. the planning process and tools to manage tourists such as visitor management). However, what is poignant if one reviews the literature on tourism planning over the last decade is a healthy debate on the scope, extent and who is responsible for planning and management. Inevitably, the range and overlapping responsibilities of agencies now charged with planning and managing tourism in localities is certainly more complex than a decade ago. Whilst the national structures in place to plan and manage tourism (e.g. see Tosun & Timothy 2001), funded by national governments (e.g. NTOs) have been refined and redeveloped in the last decade, to prioritise marketing as opposed to physical planning in many countries, the situation is very different at the local level. The last five years has seen the sustainability paradigm become embedded in a changing public-private sector culture, where partnership working, greater collaboration and co-funding and joint working becoming the norm. This has inevitably seen the range of organisations and bodies created to plan and manage tourism mushroom. In the case of Scotland, Kerr (2003) has actually pointed to strategic failure as a function of flawed public policy to lead and manage tourism at a national level, whilst a large number of quangos and bodies have been developed to assist tourism, contributing towards competing approaches, conflict and a lack of strategic direction. This is often compounded by information overload by hastily commissioned consultant's studies that rarely see the light of day and provide conflicting advice or are so diluted and lack any real teeth to radically transform the existing system, through bureaucratic self-interest protecting the status quo. This situation is not peculiar to individual countries, even where claims of open government and the public interest are cited as reasons for commissioning research and studies. The outcome is a burdensome public policy context for tourism in many countries without the strategic ability to have a vision for tourism and to implement it, due to the multifaceted nature of the interest groups and government agencies seeking to achieve different strategic outcomes. Furthermore, the liaison and information dissemination process to assist the tourism industry at a national level is overcomplicated and problematic (with some cases of agencies refusing to cooperate with each other) and it is certainly a common complaint of the private sector.

What is clear, is that where tourism success has been observed in performance of visitor arrivals and economic growth stimulated by tourism (e.g. Ireland and New Zealand), there is no simple planning model to emulate. Ironically, success creates pressure for localities and one of the key challenges for New Zealand as Page & Thorn (1997, 2003) have shown, is in harnessing local planning structures to address the problems tourism growth and development pose, as national government direct planning to the local level in the absence of a national master plan. Indeed most countries do not have any master plan, preferring to rely upon the status quo or the impact of new infrastructure or transport provision (e.g. the introduction of a low cost airline service) to modify patterns of tourism at a national or regional level. It is usually only at the local level, that local authorities are forced to act where the problems become so overarching that they affect the quality of the tourist experience and the destination image and economy through congestion (e.g. such as small historic cities like Venice, Cambridge, Oxford and York).

What academics have been keen to review are failings in existing planning systems and structures (as opposed to success stories of best practice), where decision-making structures are supposedly designed so that "Planning is the process of preparing a set of decisions for action in the future, directed at achieving goals by preferable means" (Dror 1973: 330). Yet there is the entire area of policymaking as noted above, where the public sector actually decides on the legislative framework for planning, which determines what agencies and bodies are created for and how they should plan for tourism and how they should do it. Yet as Hall (2000: 11) noted from Gunn's (1988) seminal study of tourism planning, a number of assumptions exist related to the value of tourism planning:

(1) Only planning can avert negative impacts, although for planning to be effective, all "actors" must be involved — not just professional planners.
(2) Tourism is symbiotic with conservation and recreation, not a conflicting use with irreconcilability incompatible objectives or effects.
(3) Planning today should be pluralistic, involving social, economic and physical dimensions.
(4) Planning is political, and as such there is a vital need to take into account societal objectives and balance these in the contact of others (often conflicting) aspirations.
(5) Tourism planning must be strategic and integrative.
(6) Tourism planning must have a regional planning perspective — because many problems arise at the interface of smaller areas, a broader planning horizon is essential.
      Source: Hall (2000: 11).

These assumptions highlight the challenge for planning for tourism, since few notable examples exist of agencies which are dedicated to tourism planning. Instead, tourism is normally an activity which is incorporated in urban, regional or local area planning by public agencies like local authorities as part of its legislative requirement to manage the environment. This means that tourism can sometimes get lost in the planning system, although the emergence of stakeholder groups has raised the profile of tourism in many localities so that local strategies and plans have had to be devised. Yet there have also been a greater range of activities associated with planning as Dredge & Jenkins (2003) identified, where place-promotion and destination development have also become functions adopted by different public sector organisations. In some areas, elements of the former boosterism role of tourism in such agencies can be discerned, if not a return to the highly competitive place-promotion role evident in many Victorian and Edwardian coastal resorts in the U.K., in seeking to use tourism to help achieve local economic growth strategies. Interestingly, Dredge (2001) outlined some of the key impediments to tourism planning in local government which included community interest, the resource base, the level of information and research available and commitment to implement policies as well as issues related to the coordination and communication processes aside from technical expertise. It is certainly the case in Scotland that local authorities are an important source of consultancy work for tourism researchers due to a lack of expertise or perceived inability to deal with the technical issues associated with tourism development (e.g. economic impact studies) which is also the case in other countries. And as an innovative study by the Scottish local authorities (SLAED 2002) highlighted not only the innovative and fundamental role that many local authorities play in tourism at the local level, with some of the most significant being:

- Funding the 10 local Area Tourist Boards, providing them with 60% of their £24.2 million of funding;
- As owners of 55% of the Top 20 free visitor attractions in Scotland;
- As a facilitator of applications for external funding from Europe that assist tourism and community development (e.g. European Regional Development Fund and European Social Fund grants);
- Promotion of film tourism locations;
- Operating Convention Bureau Services;
- Sponsorship of events and festivals to stimulate tourism;
- Infrastructure provision related to tourism;
- Signposting;
- Environmental planning and management and providing a safe environment for tourism in the built and natural environment which are functions replicated in many countries worldwide.

Whilst this may illustrate the all-embracing role of local authorities in tourism development and management, it does not imply everything is focused around a core of tourism. To the contrary, the findings of what Costa (2001) observed in a comparative analysis of town and tourism planning is that the latter is heavily reliant upon the former for its theory and practice. The result is that tourism is usually subsumed into wider planning functions and can, in some cases get lost in the wider planning system where there is no specific champion in the agency. Even the sustainability paradigm cannot be a claim for the peculiarity of tourism as a specialist planning function, since this has also been part of a wider development in planning, and so is not unique to tourism, although the obvious implications and application to tourism are certainly evident.

The sustainability paradigm has also seen progress in destinations and environments classified as mass destinations, such as the Mediterranean and specific islands (Coccossis 2002). For example, in a special issue of the *Journal of Sustainable Tourism* edited by Bramwell (2003), sustainable development was being pursued as a means to diversify the industry to promote sustainability, which is evidence of the public sector's perception of the need to actively intervene to manage and direct an industry which developed rapidly around a mass market. Certainly the evidence from many of the tourism planning and management articles being published in academic journals, is a concomitant concern for sustainability in principle. This has led to a greater interest in options, alternatives and opportunities to ensure that less anthropocentric perspectives traditionally promoted by industry stakeholders and entrepreneurs no longer dominate thinking on the future shape and nature of an area's tourism product and offering. It has probably taken the tourism industry two decades to have its horns reigned in within many highly developed destinations, now that global environmental problems emanating from tourism have highlighted catastrophic failures in the planning process. There is also growing evidence that many localities are now being viewed as "destinations" by planning agencies, with a need to recognise joined up thinking in planning terms to understand how sustainability can be integrated into visioning exercises on what tourism will look like in the next decade. Therefore against this background, what contributions do the chapters in this section of the book make to *Taking Tourism to the Limits?*

In many respects, planning helps to set the limits of tourism if it can fully understand the scope and wide-ranging effects on the localities it affects. In the first chapter by Banks, the issue of the effectiveness of planning systems to anticipate, regulate and monitor the impact of tourism is critically evaluated. The case of the Muska-Kechika Management Area is discussed. The lessons of this failed planning and management measures highlights one of the constant features of the tourism literature: the gap between theory and practice, where fundamental failure in certain processes or unexpected dimensions, can cause an entire project to fail.

In many cases, the lack of resources to implement and monitor tourism are cited, not just in the developing world, but across the developed world as politics, changing policy priorities and excessive demands on public sector resources are frequently cited reasons as Dredge (2001) noted. This leads conveniently to the focus of the next chapter by Arrowsmith, Zianon and Chhetri on the monitoring of visitor patterns of use in natural tourist destinations (Eagle & McCool 2002). In theoretical terms, the process of setting up baseline data and then a monitoring system to assist in achieving sustainability goals seems self-evident.

Yet as experience of working with public sector agencies on this very theme shows, the reality is a very different experience. First, the absence of long-term funding to achieve such objectives (even when they feature in strategy documents and local plans) does not necessarily follow the strategic needs. And in the real world, simple monitoring can involve a multitude of agencies and stakeholders due to land ownership and their own strategic needs. Where such monitoring relies on rudimentary technology such as counters, then malfunctions can actually render data meaningless where counters cease working, making the derivation of seasonal and consistent data problematic. Politics, hidden agendas and conflicting goals may mean that organisations who have a statutory requirement to cooperate, may not collaborate making monitoring problematic, as they compete to be the dominant agency for reasons of securing additional public sector resources and to ensure their own survival. Similarly, where visitor surveys are undertaken, inconsistency in the way surveys are developed and implemented, can make longitudinal studies meaningless where comparable data does not get generated or the officers responsible for commissioning do not have a sound grasp of the intricacies of tourism research. Therefore, this chapter raises a very pertinent and operational issue if the limits of tourism in natural areas are to be understood, so planning mechanisms can be put in place. Without effective monitoring, then planning can never be more than a bureaucratic paper exercise.

The next chapter by Ruhanen and Cooper takes this process of place-making a stage further, outlining the process of strategic visioning to establish what type of tourism future a peripheral community will want to see develop. In communities where tourism can be a highly visible and dominant activity, the strategic visioning process is time consuming but critical if community buy-in to tourism development is to be achieved. This is also essential to avoid antagonism, negative attitudes and a sense of loss of control. These last two chapters highlight how the wide ranging remit of tourism planning and management in the public sector is evolving to ensure that the limits of tourism can be understood from the community perspective rather than alienating stakeholders through inappropriate development.

The last chapter by Kemp on developing a place identity for a region highlights the rise of place-making evidenced by the growing literature on this theme in urban tourism (Page & Hall 2002). Seeking to create an identity is a first stage in the planning and development of a destination area, which is a complex process where a multitude of stakeholders are involved. Developing the focus, icons, imagery and market position for a destination region also requires a wide range of skills, and like the initial process, is complex. Furthermore, the process of image development also illustrates that an identity can never be static, since competition and other influences will mean that an identity will need to evolve and develop through time.

Chapter 3

The Muskwa-Kechika Management Area — The Failed Planning and Management of the Serengeti of the North

Paul Mitchell-Banks

Introduction

The Muskwa-Kechika Management Area (M-KMA) encompasses more than 6.3 million hectares of the Northern Rockies and Great Plains in North Eastern British Columbia. The M-KMA is one of the most significant wilderness areas in North America with extensive forests, spectacular geological formations, lakes, rivers, waterfalls, hot springs, subalpine and alpine areas and major wetlands. It is home to a wide variety of wilderness and wildlife. Much of the wilderness is ecologically sensitive and some of the wildlife is threatened or endangered. The M-KMA encompasses large oil and gas reserves, and the energy sector is a major employer in the area. The central and western areas of the M-KMA are high in metallic and non-metallic resources. Exploration projects have been conducted and there is small-scale mining of sand and gravel. Portions of the M-KMA have high timber values, with over 40% of the Fort Nelson (one of BC's most northerly communities) economy driven by the forest sector.

The management model is intended to establish a world standard for environmental and economic stability. The management intent of the M-KMA is to maintain in perpetuity the wilderness values, and the diversity and abundance of wildlife and the ecosystems on which it depends. There is significant ongoing research, inventory, planning, enforcement, education and extension funded by a trust fund that can annually award up to $3.0 million to supplement government base funding in the area. Projects are funded for government agencies, First Nations, Non-Governmental Organisations and the private sector to undertake work directly related to the M-KMA.

History

The M-KMA can be considered a direct result of three Land and Resource Management Plans (LRMPs) which are large regionally based planning processes that involve multiple

Taking Tourism to the Limits: Issues, Concepts and Managerial Perspectives
© 2005 Published by Elsevier Ltd.
ISBN: 0-08-044644-2

stakeholder participation in drawing up a plan that attempts to address the interests of all. The LRMPs can take from 3 to 7 years and involve facilitated multiple round-table meetings at which all participants are encouraged to be involved. The three LRMPs and their completion dates related to the Muskwa-Kechika Management Area were the Fort Nelson LRMP covering 9.8 million ha (October 1997); the Fort St. John LRMP covering 4.6 million ha (October 1997); and the Mackenzie LRMP covering 6.4 million ha (November 2000). Each of these three LRMP processes essentially carved out areas of special significance that were later amalgamated to create the M-KMA (Land Use Co-ordination Office 1997a, b, 2000).

The 6.3 million ha Muskwa-Kechika Management Area is unique within Canada and indeed the world. It is an area of incredible beauty that has been inhabited by First Nations for millennia and has been the home, workplace and recreational area for local residents and international visitors for over a century. The M-KMA is,

> ... One of the few remaining large, intact and almost unroaded wilderness areas south of the 60th parallel. It supports a diverse number of large mammals including moose, elk, mule deer, whitetail deer, caribou, plains bison, mountain sheep, mountain goat, wolves, black bears and grizzly bears in population densities of global importance. Few places in the world match the natural features of the Muskwa-Kechika Management Area in terms of species groupings, remoteness and minimal development. The area is also well endowed with rich energy and mineral resources. In general, oil and gas reserves dominate the eastern portion of the area while a variety of metallic and non-metallic resources can be found in the central and western portions of the area. Valuable timber resources are also present in the southern portion of the area (Land Use Co-ordination Office 1997b).

The 1997 Muskwa-Kechika Management Plan sets out some ambitious objectives to address the unique beauty, biodiversity, cultural importance and resource wealth within the M-KMA, specifying that,

> The management intent for the Muskwa-Kechika Management Area is to ensure wilderness characteristics, wildlife and its habitat are maintained over time while allowing resource development and use, including recreation, hunting, timber harvesting, mineral exploration and mining, oil and gas exploration and development. The integration of management activities especially related to the planning, development and management of road accesses within the Muskwa-Kechika Management Area is central to achieving this intent. The long-term objective is to return lands to their natural state, as much as possible, as development activities are completed (Land Use Coordination Office 1997b).

Legislation

The "roots" of the M-KMA lie within the three approved Land and Resource Management Plans. Specifically however, it was a 1997 Order-in-Council (where ministers in the provincial cabinet approve a decision without going to the legislature) that established the Muskwa-Kechika Management Plan (Government of British Columbia 1997e).

The following year, the government passed *Bill 37-1998, Muskwa-Kechika Management Area Act* that directly addressed the specifics of the Management Area and Plan; the establishment of the Muskwa-Kechika Advisory Board (a public advisory group) the Muskwa-Kechika Trust Fund; and some general issues such as the power to make regulations. Both the Muskwa-Kechika Management Plan and the *Muskwa-Kechika Management Act* address the five required planning processes that are required to be undertaken with the area, namely; Recreation Management Plan; Wildlife Management Plan; Oil and Gas Pre-tenure Plans; Parks Management Plans; and Landscape Unit Objectives (for forestry planning). What was unique about these plans was the requirement for multi-ministry sign-off, which was to assist in ensuring that planning was coordinated and addressed a broad range of issues and not necessarily just those of one ministry. However, with a new government, this was cancelled in 2003 and now the plans are signed off by single ministries, with the Ministry of Sustainable Resource Management deemed to be a "neutral" ministry and responsible for Recreation, Oil and Gas and Landscape Unit Objective Planning. The Ministry of Water, Land and Air Protection is responsible for Wildlife and Parks planning.

Another innovative aspect of the planning is the excellent working relationship between the local government managers who are the statutory decision-makers. There is a team-like arrangement, in which the managers not only focus on their own mandates but also work closely with each other to avoid duplication, conflicting programmes and uncertainty. The government managers and staff also have established close working arrangements with the M-K Advisory Board as a whole, and certain board members who are active participants in various planning processes. While the board participation does not replace public participation, it does provide a greater level of assurance that a wide-range of values is being addressed.

M-K Advisory Board

The Muskwa-Kechika Advisory Board is appointed by the Premier of the province of British Columbia, and has a role to provide advice on the natural resource management in the M-K Management Area. The M-K Advisory Board also identify suitable projects and proposals consistent with the purposes of the trust to receive Trust funding (Minister of Environment, Lands and Parks 1998).

The M-K Advisory Board was originally established with up to 17 members to represent a broad range of interests, including but not limited to: First Nations, environmental, business, labour and Fort Nelson and Fort St. John Land and Resource Management Plan participants (Clark 1988). The current M-K Advisory Board is slightly larger, including: the acting chair; seven First Nations representatives; three local government representatives; two members from the Oil and Gas sector; one mining sector representative; a forestry representative; one labour representative; two environmental representatives; one trapper guide member; a member of the BC Wildlife Federation; a back country tourism representative and the Muskwa-Kechika Program Manager (ex-officio position).

Over the past year, the Strategic Plan as well as the Policy and Procedures Manual for the Board have been approved, and there has been a concerted effort to increase the levels of awareness regarding ongoing issues and concerns. M-K Advisory Board meetings are held a minimum of three times a year, with at least one of the meetings being held deep within the M-KMA to help orient the board members to the issues and to increase their awareness about the Muskwa-Kechika Management Area.

Muskwa-Kechika Trust Fund

One of the unique legislative features behind establishing the M-KMA was creating the Muskwa-Kechika Trust Fund, which has two primary purposes: (1) to support wildlife and wilderness resources of the management area through research and integrated management of natural resource development; and (2) to maintain in perpetuity the diversity and abundance of wildlife species and the ecosystems on which they depend throughout the management area. The trust fund is currently provided annually with $1 million Canadian per year as well as a project fund top-up allowance in which the government will match dollar for dollar contributions, to a maximum of $1,000,000. The base funding as well as the maximum matching creates a maximum annual fund of $3.0 million.

Every fall there is a call for project proposals that are submitted to the Muskwa-Kechika Advisory Board, subject to a number of review processes, with recommendations passed on to the trustee of the trust fund. After the trustee has reviewed and approved the recommended projects, management of the projects is assigned to the Muskwa-Kechika Program Manager who serves as the trust fund projects manager and comptroller. Funding agreements addressing deliverables, reporting and funding arrangements are negotiated and signed. Currently there are five project funding envelopes under the trust fund, namely: building an information base; supporting planning; improving management; advancing applied science (research); and promoting awareness and involvement. Every year the Premier (head of the provincial government) is given a report from the Muskwa-Kechika Advisory Board regarding the activities of the board, and the highlights of the trust-funded activities. There is ongoing research with wildlife and habitat, particularly for certain species such as Grizzly, Moose, Elk, Stone Sheep.

Management Challenges

Of all the activities within the M-KMA, it is the oil and gas sector that is currently the most active, the most visible and which will likely create the greatest management challenges. With the recent sharp increases in both oil and gas commodity prices, there is renewed interest in investing in exploration and development, and this has led to a sharp increase in the number of seismic, drilling, facilities, and pipeline applications (Oil and Gas Commission 1999). The oil and gas rich Western Canada Basin extends into the NE corner of BC and extends west into the M-KMA. While to date the majority of the oil and gas activity is outside of the M-KMA boundaries, given the high prices, there is increasing pressure from industry and a desire by government to complete the pre-tenure planning within the M-KMA and thus open planned areas to oil and gas development. During the fiscal year ending March 31, 1999 a total of 1,801 applications were approved, and for the fiscal year ending March 31, 2000 a total of 2,487 applications were approved — representing a 38% increase (Oil and Gas Commission 2001). Subsequent years have seen an increase in both numbers of applications received and granted. One of the oil and gas exploration initiatives that received a high degree of review and discussion occurred at Chicken Creek in the Upper Sikanni area (one of the Resource Management Zones or management units on the southeast side of the M-KMA). This is an important wildlife area and particular care is being paid to monitor any potential impacts.

Forestry is something of an anomaly within the M-KMA. Whereas the forest sector is one of the province's largest and ubiquitous industries, the Muskwa-Kechika Management Area is unique, in that the timber resources in the M-KMA are relatively limited (Land Use Coordination Office 1997c). Currently (i.e. 2003) there is long-term planning for limited forestry development, with considerations such as road development limitations and costs, haulage distances stand size, density and piece-size all limiting the development potential. It is possible that forestry development will be closely associated with the oil and gas sector and take advantage of roads approved for the oil and gas exploration and development. In the near future, it is quite likely that forestry will initially focus in promising areas located at the south end of the M-KMA in the Graham/North Resource Management Zone.

The vast area of the M-KMA has important mineral resource potential. There is a government funded mineral occurrence database that supports existing tenure holders and exploration and development activity. Historically the area has received limited exploration, but there is significant opportunity for future mine production (Land Use Co-ordination Office 1997d). One of the challenges that mining will face in the area is how to deal with the controlled access to the area — but there are opportunities to explore how to develop mines in conjunction with other industrial activities such as the oil and gas and forestry.

Trapping and guide-outfitting are historically important activities within the M-KMA. While the numbers of employees does not come close to approaching the oil and gas sector, there is still a strong commitment through both legislation and ongoing management and planning to ensure that these activities are supported and have their needs considered amongst all of the industrial activities. Recreationalists, including hunters and fishers, and the back country tourism sector, have historically accessed the area, with users from the local communities as well as others travelling great distances to take advantage of the vast wilderness spaces found within the M-KMA. Obviously wilderness values are important to these users.

Management Challenges

There are numerous challenges in attempting to effectively manage the M-KMA. The most obvious one is the sheer size of the area at 6.3 million hectares. Access is extremely limited (and controlled through Access Management) as directed by the LRMPs — with only a few roads, and trails that are accessed by horseback, snowmobile or All Terrain Vehicles. Government staff makes extensive use of helicopter and jet boat transport to access the M-KMA as ground access is so limited. Fuel often has to be remotely cached for both helicopters and jet boats due to the long distances from staging points and the size of the M-KMA itself.

Along with the huge distances are the extremes in temperature, with seasonal fluctuations of 80 degrees centigrade not uncommon. At minus 40 degrees, equipment is subject to heavy wear and it is trying on the staff as well — particularly if there is a breakdown or incident such as getting stranded. All staff carry emergency survival gear (cold weather sleeping bags, first aid kits, rations, satellite phones, etc.) in their vehicles. I have personally experienced accidentally driving off a remote logging road with temperatures reaching −43 degrees and it was quite a worrying experience and has increased my awareness of the challenges of the northern continental climate.

Another management challenge is the long distance (approximately 1,300 km by road, two hours by air) from the provincial capital and the location of some of the senior government executive managers that are ultimately responsible for the success of the M-KMA. Extra care has to be taken to keep the "southern" managers "up to speed" on the issues and actions being taken by the "northern" statutory decision-makers responsible for government management within the M-KMA. This can be occasionally frustrating for both "southerners" who are more aware of the machinations within the legislature and the "northerners" who are more aware of the local situation.

There is the continuing challenge of attempting to address the overall intent of three Land and Resource Management Plans (LRMPs) in the planning for the M-KMA. The LRMPs tend to deal with generalities and do not give strong direction with respect to operational planning. This lack of specific guidance is further complicated with the five required plans, because the legislation provides no guidance as to what the plans should entail other than the broad activities (such as recreation or oil and gas development) that they are supposed to address. As if that were not enough, there is also the over-riding question of what is wilderness? This is a very hotly debated concept and incorporates issues such as man-made impacts, the presence or absence of people, etc., In the case of the M-KMA, it is a key component of the legislation but is not defined. Wilderness remains an undefined concept four years later in the initiative.

One of the growing challenges for the M-KMA is the growing public awareness and level of expectations about what "could" or "should" occur within the M-KMA. It is difficult to ensure that everything that is planned, or even more challenging — simply decided upon at a political level — can be effectively implemented. The M-KMA, by its very nature of being a new approach to planning and management, demands that the government staff, board members and public participants in the planning process attempt to address every challenge with a set of "fresh eyes" and often innovative approach.

The final, and potentially greatest challenge, revolves around land claims. Treaty Eight was signed over a century ago, and three of the board members represent Bands that signed the treaty. The Kaska Dena Treaty is currently under negotiation and the treaty discussions are wide-ranging and at times very intense. Any legislation, decisions or actions within the M-KMA are "without prejudice" with respect to a future treaty with the Kaska-Dena. Four of the board members represent Kaska Dena Bands (communities). A Letter of Understanding (LOU) was signed in 1997 between the provincial government and the Kaska Dena Council to permit land use planning and other government management initiatives to continue pending the signing of a treaty. The LOU specifically,

. . . Sets out a relationship between the two parties with respect to the planning and management of lands and resources in the LOU Area from the date of signing of this Understanding until such time as it is terminated according to the provisions of this Understanding (Government of British Columbia and Kaka Dena Council 1997).

Planning and management is underway without any future certainty with respect to what lands the Kaska Dena may be awarded in the north and particularly in the Muskwa-Kechika Management Area.

Lessons Learnt to Date

There have been five major lessons learnt to date from the Muskwa-Kechika Management Area initiative.

Lesson One — Adequate Data and Knowledge

The first lesson revolves around the challenges of having or obtaining adequate data and knowledge about the wilderness qualities, wildlife and habitat values, natural resource values and land management challenges. The difficulties stem not only from the 6.3 million ha size but also from the tremendous biodiversity, differences in physio-geography and the problems of access to the area. Many of the Resource Management Zones (management units) are hundreds of kilometres dimensionally and travel by either helicopter (running between $800 and $1,000/hr) or jet boat (time consuming for staff) rapidly consumes limited budget dollars and staff time.

The LRMPs were completed under a previous regime that was not as time or cost conscious as the current government. This has led to challenges when the successor government cut back on staffing and budgets, and so the same challenges remain with fewer resources to address them. A lesson here is to formally commit (through legislation) to adequately following up on unique land management initiatives to ensure their successful implementation. Another strategy is to aggressively use triage and a project management approach to see what are the critical steps in the process that are time sensitive and to focus on those and practice risk management with respect to the budget and timeline. In the case of the M-KMA, this requires co-operation between the Advisory Board and the Government that was not always in place with both parties having differences of opinion with respect to priorities. In retrospect, the government should have mandated that all planning would be completed prior to the expenditures from the Trust Fund being used for any other approved purposes, such as training, extension, non-critical research.

Lesson Two — Accurate and Timely Analysis and Decisions

The second challenge is related to the previous lesson but centres around the challenges of accurate and timely analysis and decision-making. This challenge involves a number of components including translating field data into the Geographic Information System (GIS), and devising adequate tools to verify, correct, analyse, manipulate and map the output. A current initiative underway is determining how to undertake sensitivity analysis and scenario planning to permit the planners and management teams to have a better understanding of potential consequences or outcomes. GIS tools are being explored. GIS staff are in high demand from both the government and private sectors, and we have lost a number of high quality staff as a result of this — which have led to losing institutional geographic familiarity, working relationships, technical skills, process memory and having to repeatedly retrain staff.

There are also the challenges of timing with respect to planning requirements, implementation and ongoing operational management. Politicians and industry can push a timeline to finish planning and create "certainty" that leads to challenges at best, and failure at worst, to complete planning in a comprehensive and integrated fashion. This becomes particularly frustrating with complex landforms and resource values and also heavy industrial and economic development pressure — both of which apply to the M-KMA. Oil and gas development pressure is particularly strong, and remains so, with political instability in other oil-producing areas. A troubled forest economy, and significantly reduced mining and fishing within a staples economy create fiscal pressures on the government who seek to fuel their treasury through oil and gas development.

There are ongoing challenges with respect to out-of-date inventories and missing inventories. Integrated and interactive planning tools, such as Conservation Area Design, are being completed on timelines that do not inform planning from the beginning. Tools have to be creatively shoehorned into the truncated planning timelines — which severely limit the benefits and values that can be obtained from the tool development and application processes. Ideally a Conservation Area Design would be completed before any resource use were contemplated. This is legislatively possible within the M-KMA but due to heavy government and industrial pressures, the planning is accelerated and planners and land managers make the best with what they have and can obtain within the planning timelines. Similarly, incomplete and/or out-of-date inventories can severely constrain the accuracy or value of management decisions and planning. The adage "Garbage in-Garbage out" applies to planning as much as it does to models and simulations.

There are a number of things that would greatly assist accurate and timely analysis and decision-making of the M-KMA and they include:

> Creatively retaining GIS staff through providing them with challenging and intellectually rewarding tasks.

> Take GIS staff out into the field with you, this not only gives them a greater understanding of the challenges but also the pleasure of getting out into the wilderness and an opportunity to see the wildlife as well. Often the expense of doing this is minimal, as the helicopter or jet boat is already paid for and the only cost is staff time. This was discussed with staff and they loved the concept.

Take a project management approach to the planning challenges and be certain to fully address the obvious and potential challenges of political and economic/industrial development pressures.

This not only co-ordinates the activities of staff but also assists in expectation management and assists in establishing an effective communications strategy to keep all of the interested parties aware of progress.

Related to the previous point is the question of effective policy. There needs to be a process to be able to evaluate the short, medium and long-term implications of planning actions or the lack thereof. It is tempting to think short-term and focus on revenue generation, particularly when there are fiscal challenges for the government. Short-term solutions can result in inadequate planning, leading to financial losses through less than satisfactory resource planning (sub-optimal planning for effective use or extraction) or greater costs (associated with environmental restoration and remediation). As importantly, and arguably ethically more so, there is also the potential for species and habitat losses — and there is a strong argument that these should be fully incorporated in the thinking in any policy evaluation, development and implementation/administration.

Lesson Three — Adequate Resource Funding

The third challenge involves obtaining adequate resource funding for travel, sufficient staffing and equipment and resources to effectively manage the area. Related to this is the necessity to be able to address not only ongoing management needs, but to also proactively address anticipated developments — such as oil and gas exploration and development continuing to increase in both scale and scope. Hiring freezes, challenges in finding and retaining staff, particularly those in the GIS area, compound this problem. The Trust Fund provides some security in potential funding, but all government proposed projects seeking trust funding have to be vetted before the Advisory Board and receive recommendations prior to being approved by the Trustee (who is the Minister of Sustainable Resource Management). This has led to some frustration on the part of the Advisory Board as to what are government core responsibilities (which the trust fund is not supposed to give money for) and what are activities incremental to base funding. The frustration is mirrored by government staff who "see" the money being potentially available in the trust fund, but not necessarily accessible for government activities.

There are a number of ways to reduce this occurring, and they include:

When drawing up the initial legislation or policy to establish the area, real attention should have been paid to the future implications and the costs of the planning and management required. In other words, if you are building a Rolls Royce, then budget a lot of resources to successfully do this, if a Volkswagen, then your resource requirements will be less.

Commit to finishing one initiative or related initiatives prior to taking on new challenges. Do not be tempted to spread resources thinly, attempting to do a little bit of everything. This relates to the project management argument — do the things that need to be done first and make certain that they are done well. You do not want to have an elegant planning process established with no data to feed into it for example.

Ensure that there is a clear understanding through legislation and administrative procedure on how funds and staff time can be employed and be consistent with the approach while being flexible to real emergencies and not just 'nice to dos'. The Trust Fund administration was clouded by some uncertainty with respect to how it could be used and more importantly what exactly were the government core responsibilities that were not meant to be funded, but which in reality often lacked funds and were key to making the M-KMA work.

Initiate a fund raising strategy as soon as the area is established or the initiative implemented. Four years into this process, fundraising is only now beginning to be seriously looked at — and it is a case of being very late to start and having lost some very positive media opportunities while the initiative was still new.

Lesson Four — Politics and Agendas

Politics and agendas are the fourth challenge, and are an inherent part of the Muskwa-Kechika Management Area initiative. There are politics in the capital with politicians responding to lobbying and making decisions without consulting government staff — often with very frustrating consequences, as the decisions are often made without any appreciation of the existing situation or resources available to government staff. The Muskwa-Kechika Advisory Board is very political, with every member having a constituency and an agenda to address within the area. Government managers and staff are also political in that they have the mandate of their ministries to fulfil, and there can be clashes between the ministries with their conflicting agendas. One of the most challenging aspects of the Muskwa-Kechika Program Manager's job is to champion the Muskwa-Kechika Management Area initiative and to serve as a liaison between the various groups and promote effective communication, "buying" into a common vision and co-operation. This job plays a keystone role in not only holding the process together but also encouraging it to progressively continue forward.

Politics are always a wildcard. Politicians can be very challenging with respect to how they respond to perceived problems — but their perception is often heavily influenced by either key supporters, effective lobbyists, political assistants or general public opinion. All of these influences often contribute to decisions that do not support effective land use planning. Communication and documentation play a key role in setting the stage and making information and potential scenarios known. It is more difficult for a political decision to be made that is adverse to the land use management if key supporters of the initiative (both within and without government) are aware of the facts and the situation, so that decisions are not made and observed in a vacuum. Management often involves a lot of time explaining to people what is going on and as importantly what might go on.

Lesson Five — Roles and Responsibilities

Roles and responsibilities are the fifth major lesson learnt from this initiative. The Muskwa-Kechika Advisory Board is unique in the province not only for the scope of their advisory and monitoring function, but also in that they are the body that makes recommendations for a multi-million dollar trust fund. Funding has grown increasingly scarce over the last decade, and the trust fund is drawing increasing attention from both within and without government.

In many ways, it is the trust fund that can potentially serve the greatest role in ensuring that the Muskwa-Kechika Management Area is a successful initiative. A requirement for the trust fund to be effective is a healthy appreciation between the Muskwa-Kechika Advisory Board and government staff in how to best apply the fund to complement existing government statutory responsibilities and initiatives. The trust fund is there to advance the Muskwa-Kechika Management Area with a view to maintaining the unique features of the area while also permitting industrial and economic development over three-quarters of the area. This is a daunting, but not insurmountable challenge, but it will require that all parties and individuals involved fully assume their roles and co-operatively work with everyone else to fulfill not only their individual responsibilities but also those of the group as a whole. There needs to be a greater accountability for decisions that are made and a greater attempt to let the general public know how the funds are being spent.

Tourism — The Forgotten and or Ignored Sector

The M-KMA tourism sector is presently predominantly used by two distinct tourism groups (both primarily hunting):

> The first group comprises local residents who invest large sums of money and time to access the area by plane, horse, jet boat, and all terrain vehicle (ATV);

> The second group is composed largely of European and American hunters who pay premium prices to take Stone Sheep, Grizzly Bear, Elk, Moose, and Mountain Goat.

While there is some jetboat based tourism, the bulk of this is dedicated to hunter support, bringing in both people and supplies to the remote areas that provide world class hunting. The fees charged by the guide-outfitters can easily exceed over US$10,000 for hunts involving Grizzly Bears, Stone Sheep and Bison, particularly when the clients opt to hunt more than one species of game. A number of local residents are employed by this sector, with job positions such as camp cooks, factors (people who arrange for supplying and logistical support), assistant guides, pilots, etc. and there are there are over two dozen guide-outfitter operations with interests in the area covered by the Muskwa-Kechika Management Area. The hunting potential for the area is world class, but unfortunately the management of this sector falls far short of what is required, despite the efforts of a number of dedicated government officials and staff.

Despite the noble intent of the legislation and the creation of the Muskwa-Kechika Management Board and Trust Fund, the tourism sector has been largely ignored. Tourism has been overshadowed by the lucrative oil and gas sector. In the wake of the downturn of the forestry sector and the hardships and uncertainty imposed by the ongoing U.S.-Canada Softwood tariff dispute, the oil and gas sector is viewed by the provincial government as a critical economic engine to not only create employment but also generate revenues for the government's coffers.

Dual track tourism (tourists interested in both wilderness and cultural experiences) is a particularly attractive sector as they tend to spend more money and stay longer in their destinations (Central Coast Consulting 2002) and offer an unique opportunity not only for aboriginal communities with their unique cultures but also to non-native communities with their unique "northern way of life."

Tourism can also serve as an economic engine, and if managed effectively, this is a more environmentally benign and sustainable sector than oil and gas or forestry for that matter. To achieve establishing a sustainable and economically meaningful tourism sector, there are a number of ongoing issues that need to be effectively addressed. The next section of the paper will provide details of these issues and a number of potential strategies to more effectively address them.

The Definition of Wilderness

At this time, there is still no accepted definition of the word "wilderness" for the Muskwa-Kechika Management Area, despite the legislation establishing the M-KMA having been drawn up in 1998. As one of the two key values attempted to be maintained by the legislation, this is obviously a fatal flaw in the planning effort. One of the signature values for the area remains nebulous, virtually without any qualitative or quantitative values to serve in the vision, goals, objectives and milestones of effective planning. Planning requires a process that is traceable, accountable and reproducible (Mitchell-Banks 1999), and without a definition of wilderness this is virtually impossible to achieve. Traceable not only refers to a planning process that is documented but involves specific objectives, values, considerations and issues that are addressed. Accountable refers to who is responsible for what, and without a definition of wilderness, the government department/individual manager accountability for this resource remains uncertain. Reproducible refers to being able to retrace or re-enact the planning effort as logical concerns and strategies are documented and continue to be valid if conditions have not changed.

The definition of Wilderness most often cited is that found in *The Wilderness Act 1964* that was established in the United States of America which states that the purpose of the legislation is,

> ... To secure for the American people of present and future generations the benefits of an enduring resource of wilderness (*The Wilderness Act 1964*).

This powerful piece of legislation has globally served as a key conceptual piece of legislation. The legislation addresses the wilderness resource, which as defined under the Wilderness Act, has three equally important characteristics:

It is not controlled by humans; natural ecosystem processes operate freely and its primeval character and influence are retained.

It is not occupied or modified by mankind, humans are merely visitors and the imprint of their work is hardly noticeable.

It offers outstanding opportunities for solitude or for a primitive and unconfined recreation experience (Society of American Foresters).

This definition is limiting in the case of the Muskwa-Kechika Management Area. In the M-KMA there is a deliberate effort to protect wilderness and wildlife values while permitting economic and industrial development to various degrees in both the Protected Areas (tourism and hunting is permitted) and the Special Management Zones (in which forestry, mining, oil and gas development, etc. are also permitted). Nevertheless, this classical wilderness definition can serve as a starting point and can be modified to address the unique nature of the intent and planning of the M-KMA. The first priority to successfully address tourism within the M-KMA is to establish a legislated and regulated wilderness definition that is specific and functional to ensure compliance not only by government officials but also by users of the resource.

Tourism Issues within the Muskwa-Kechika Management Area

Acceptable Limits of Impacts

Tourism offers an opportunity to establish a sustainable economic activity. Badly managed tourism can be extremely environmentally, ecologically and socially destructive. A tourism sector that collapses because of failing to address one or more of these impacts is essentially impossible to revive in a meaningful fashion.

While there has been a Conservation Area Design initiated, it is limited in scope and funding. Furthermore, it commenced well into the planning process and was thus not able to serve as the foundational planning to the other five planning processes (Recreation Management, Wildlife Management, Oil and Gas Pre-tenure Planning, Parks Planning and Landscape Unit Objectives (forestry) planning).

The Recreation Management Plan at this time is completed for only the original two-thirds of the M-KMA (Prior to the 2001 addition of the land from the Mackenzie LRMP). A recreation planning remains to be completed for the additional 1.9 million ha added as a result of the last of the three LRMPs. It should be noted that the Recreation Management Plan only addresses recreation potential, and while this is a very useful exercise, it does not address a co-ordinated tourism planning effort for the entire M-KMA, something which is necessary to ensure a sustainable tourism sector.

The lack of a co-ordinated tourism plan is exacerbated by the lack of clarity about what are the acceptable limits of impacts or more precisely what is the carrying capacity, and what are the ecological impacts and visitor attitudes. Any activities within the M-KMA are going to have an impact, and there is a need to establish what the acceptable impacts are. This has to be determined not only by estimating the carrying capacity (as it is impossible to determine exactly) but also establishing a management system incorporating both monitoring and mediation strategies and plans. The monitoring and mediation strategies and plans will not only address impact management but also serve to continually inform the estimated carrying capacity evaluation. A major failing of the M-KMA management and planning process is the failure of the government to establish sufficient resources and a legislated requirement for managing and monitoring impacts to ensure that carrying capacity is not exceeded, let alone managed to any significant degree. Field evaluations are sporadic and extremely limited, inventories of wildlife are limited in scale and scope and there is little if any meaningful vegetation and habitat assessment.

Measuring the impacts of an economic or industrial activity within the M-KMA are necessary to be carried out in a scientific manner and in a statistically valid manner to carry out effective land use management and planning. Specifically:

> measuring and understanding visitor attitudes, perceptions and the impacts of tourism is vital to understanding the potential capacity of an area to accommodate tourism and how to manage visitor use — especially when it is desirable to maximise tourist revenues (Henry & Western nd).

There needs to be an immediate effort to complete the Conservation Area Design process and scientifically estimate the carrying capacity of the M-KMA for all economic and industrial activities. This carrying capacity would include tourism of all types. This process would establish a legitimate approach to ensure that there is a balanced planning and management approach, which is traceable, accountable and reproducible. The primary intent of the process would be to ensure that wilderness and wildlife values are protected as a first priority with any industrial and economic activities being subservient to those two values.

The failure to carry out the five legislated planning processes in a logical fashion after first having conducted a Conservation Area Design process has led to not only an out of sequence planning effort but also an uninformed one. Conservation concerns (the core concept behind establishing the area) are not effectively addressed for wilderness, wildlife, or even economic and industrial activities such as oil and gas, forestry, mining, or even tourism activities such as guide-outfitting, recreational hunting, wildlife viewing, hiking, camping, etc.

Ideally, what would be done to rectify this would be to immediately halt any new industrial and economic activity within the M-KMA until the completion of the following, and specifically in this order.

(1) Completion of a Conservation Area Design of the entire M-KMA with attention being paid to boundary areas and adjacent issues.

(2) Completion of the Wildlife Plan, and more specifically a plan that focuses on maintaining intact ecosystems and animal populations to ensure ecological integrity — the plan now has an emphasis on big game due to the influence of the guide-outfitting operations and concerns.

(3) Completion of a complete Recreation Management Plan that ensures that the entire M-KMA has been addressed, as well as boundary issue and adjacency concerns.

(4) Completion of the Parks Management Plan for all parks, with a greater number of parks receiving detailed planning rather than Management Direction Statements (MDS) that apply to most of the parks in the M-KMA. These Management Direction Statements are typically a dozen pages or so in length and insufficiently detailed for effective planning. Their original intent was to serve as interim plans pending the completion of a detailed Parks Management Plan, but unfortunately, funding and resources have been curtailed and now these MDS wills effectively serve as the de facto "Parks Management Plans" for the smaller parks. This obviously leads to inconsistent scale and scope management and planning.

(5) Completion of the Landscape Unit Objectives planning process to address landscape planning and effective, ecologically sustainable and economically achievable forestry management, planning and operations.

(6) Completion of the Pre-tenure Planning process to ensure ecologically sound and secondarily economically achievable oil and gas management, planning and operations.

(7) Finally, while completing the five legislated plans, an ongoing tourism management plan would be carried out. This would inform the other planning processes but also ensure that all economic and industrial activities consider each other and specific trade-offs are made to ensure that all activities are accounted for effectively and none are addressed as an "after thought."

This is obviously a rather idyllic and theoretical approach and given the lack of co-ordinated planning to date, it is politically and economically not acceptable to put a halt to oil and gas operations (forestry is virtually non-existent at this time) and tourism activities. The cost of this lack of forethought and commitment to sound planning and management are wilderness, wildlife and ecosystem impacts and a series of conflicts between the various economic sectors.What could be done, is the following:

> Announce a moratorium on any new economic and industrial activities until the planning processes are completed.

> Oil and gas activities would be limited to the one area (The Upper Sikanni Special Management Zone) for which pre-tenure planning (albeit in a cursory and relatively uniformed manner) has been completed. This faulty pre-tenure plan results not from the lack of skill, experience or intent of the planners, but the government's stated 'need' to complete this plan in an inadequate time frame, with limited information and resources and with little regard to how this area functions with respect to the entire M-KMA and surrounding area.

For a time-limited period, allocated additional funding and resources to ensure that the planning is completed in timely and effective fashion. This would not only ensure that the government, M-K Advisory Board and public participation processes were not only completed but more importantly completed in a rational sense. Furthermore, the time-limited effort would also reduce the numerous 'end run' initiatives that have been attempted by not only the provincial government, First Nations the M-K Board and corporate interests in the M-KMA.

Come to a Land Claims settlement not only with the Kaska-Dena Nation but also address the outstanding issues that remain 100 years after the Treaty 8 settlement with a number of First Nations with M-KMA interests.

These actions would require the Provincial Government to reverse a number of policy decisions that have been made not only with the existing government but its predecessor. These policy decisions have severely curtailed the success of the M-KMA initiative and in some cases effectively sabotaged it. A glaring example of this is the blatant favouritism given to the oil and gas sector that has impacted not only the forestry sector but the tourism sector as a whole and undermined the integrated planning and management effort as a whole.

Limits of Experience

There has been no systematic evaluation of the tourism potential and lessons learnt/impacts noted to date, not only in this area, but comparable areas. The M-KMA was established to undertake a unique planning process and to establish a unique management system for an area that is globally unique. That being said, there are many other planning examples throughout the globe that could inform this process, including but not limited to:

The Danube-Carpathian initiative in Central and Eastern Europe
The Eastern Slopes planning initiative in Alberta, Canada
The National Parks in Canada
The large wilderness parks in the United States
The Trans-boundary parks in southern Africa
The Serengeti and associated areas in Eastern Africa

The failures and successes, the lessons learnt and being learnt from these other initiatives need to be systematically examined and reviewed to prevent obvious mistakes being made within the M-KMA and to avoid "reinventing the wheel" — particularly a wheel that is flawed.

Tourism and Marginal Peoples and Economies

There has been no systematic plan or strategy developed to determine how to best use tourism to address the marginal economies of many of the smaller communities in the area, particularly the First Nations communities.

The First Nations people who have resided in the area for thousands of years have very limited involvement in tourism activities. The Blueberry Band do have a Guide Outfitting territory and the Kaska-Dena Nation have an inactive Guide Outfitting Territory effectively reserved for them by the government, but other than this, there is only limited tourism related work in the Guide-Outfitting operations.

There is a need to fully involve the First Nations and non-native communities (Mackenzie, Fort St. John, Fort Nelson and Toad River) in a co-ordinated tourism planning effort (with an emphasis on Dual Track Tourism) that dovetails within the larger tourism planning process that has been proposed. Marginal tourism planning would have to address tourism potential and specifically address potentially limiting issues such as community capacity and financing.

Conclusions

The Muskwa-Kechika Management Area typifies many of the planning problems involved with large tracts of wilderness land that incorporate not only recreational and conservation values but which also possess valuable oil and gas, forestry and mineral resources that continually gain value in economic terms. Planning processes thus possess a *real politick* that runs contrary to the deductive, modernist requirements inherent in planning needs. Planning requires identification of agreed objectives and strategies and the establishment of a technical class of managers who implement these plans in accordance with long term goals and established procedures. The required time frames may be determined by natural processes that might be measured in decades if not centuries. On the other hand, governmental funding is dictated by smaller time-frames, processes of negotiation and outcomes determined by a range of factors including the ability of stakeholders to appeal to wider interests and mobilise support from outside the immediate region which is being "managed." In reality, there is a constant state of "sea change" of the politics and influences under which the planning and management is attempted to be undertaken. While this recipe seems one of potential disaster, it also identifies the importance of Government Management staff inasmuch as they can establish an expertise in the affairs of the region that no other stakeholder can match, while they often have a permanence that is lacking among the political forces that swirl around them. An ability to build upon success and to extend communications and liaisons with interested outside stakeholders becomes a key component in sustaining planning objectives, and the The Muskwa-Kechika Management Area illustrates the importance of good relationships between those with responsibilities for the five legislated plans. That the region is meeting different and often conflicting needs as well as it does is a testament to the skills of those individuals.

Chapter 4

Monitoring Visitor Patterns of Use in Natural Tourist Destinations

Colin Arrowsmith, Dino Zanon and Prem Chhetri

Introduction

Tourist numbers to national parks are expected to increase. In turn this will increase the potential risk from human impacts on natural and cultural resources within these parks. In addition to this increase, there is a corresponding increase in the new types of recreational activities that people pursue within parks, for example mountain biking, rock climbing, scenic flights, horse riding and hang gliding. Each of these new recreational pursuits has its own environmental requirements (Itami & Gimblett 2001). Adverse impacts on the park do not result from tourist visitation itself but rather from the amount of park utilisation, the flows and distribution of people and activities within a region, seasonal use and from the particular leisure activity undertaken (Ziener 2002).

Many of our ecologically sensitive tourist destinations are already experiencing stress from overcrowding (Harris & Leiper 1995). With growing visitor pressure, user satisfaction is diminished and the ecological base for the attractions, which tourists are coming to see, is also actively degraded. In addition to the deleterious impacts associated with overcrowding, there has also been an observed alteration in visitor behaviour in many parks. Arnberger & Brandenburg (2002) noticed that visiting times vary and people's habits will change in an effort to accommodate overcrowding. People have different perceived levels of crowding, and further research into these varying perceptions is required (Arnberger & Brandenburg 2002; Manning 1999). Lawson *et al.* (2002), for example, have applied a simulation model that has estimated numerical values for specific times of social carrying capacities for hikers and vehicles within the Delicate Arch and Arches National Park, Utah, USA. To assist Parks Victoria plan for future service provision, they are currently testing a computer-based simulation approach that uses agent-based modelling for supporting decision-making for their parks and reserves (Itami & Gimblett 2001; Itami *et al.* 2002). The simulator, referred to as RBSim 2 (Recreation Behaviour Simulation) uses computer generated agents to represent humans in a geographic recreation environment. Agents can be programmed to make decisions based on a defined set of rules.

Survey Techniques

Many techniques for monitoring visitor movements and behaviour in national parks have been applied. These techniques range from relatively simple survey methods such as questionnaires administered to a sample of visitors entering parks of interest, to more sophisticated techniques of data collection using GPS receivers and keeping personal journals associated with maps. Tracking of tourists follow methods adopted by Goodchild *et al.* (1993) and Janelle (1997) where participants were required to keep journals on their diurnal movements in urban areas. This technique was adopted by Fennell (1996) to monitor space-time movements of tourists in the Shetland Islands. Four approaches to monitor visitor movements and behaviour are discussed in the following section.

Questionnaire and Interviewing Techniques

Surveys are a commonly used technique applied in visitor satisfaction and behaviour research (Brown & Daniel 1987; Kroh & Gimblett 1992). They have been found to be useful when conducting both qualitative and quantitative research. The effectiveness of visitor surveys is highly dependent upon questionnaire design and its implementation. On-site surveys using questionnaires or detailed interviews have been commonly used to investigate needs, preferences, attitudes, experiences and satisfaction of visitors. Traffic surveys using observers located at strategic locations and automatic traffic counters have been used to collect information of flows and movements patterns of visitors and mode of transport.

Interviewing visitors is another way of understanding visitor behaviour. This technique can be undertaken using either a structured or unstructured format or a combination of both (Ryan 1995). Structured interviews follow a set sequence of questions. Unstructured interviews follow a planned interview led conversation where either the questioner or both parties are aware of the research agenda and are prepared beforehand, but the topics are not necessarily sequenced and can vary from respondent to respondent.

Administering questionnaires have several advantages over other methods of data collection. From a self-administered questionnaire it is relatively easy to determine personal backgrounds of participants along with their anticipated actions and activities whilst in the park. However, the activities people actually engage in are not readily assessable through a questionnaire. Moreover the nature of depreciative behaviour such as walking off designated tracks or annoying other visitors cannot be ascertained via a questionnaire. The use of attitudinal surveys has been suggested (Jackson 1986, 1987; Kiiskilä 2001; Uysal & Jurowski 1994) to understand the hidden nature of visitor travel behaviour where attitudes towards the environment, tourism and other tourists are reflected in their behaviour.

Video Monitoring

Video has traditionally been used in monitoring wildlife behaviour. This technique has been successfully applied in humanistic and phenomenological research in order to acquire an in-depth understanding of people at the individual level. Recently video analysis has been used for collecting vehicle counts. Masoud (2000) proposed a new system for tracking and analysing human motion in using real-time video. Video monitoring in parks has been found to be an effective technique in assessing visitor load over heavily used sites. Recently Janowsky & Becker (2002) have combined the use of different techniques (video, personal interviews and GIS) to monitor specific user groups and identify their needs in urban forests. Data about the number, composition and time schedules of visitors were monitored using video, and then their needs and conflicts with other user groups were determined through personal interviews. The technique has, however, been seen as an intrusion into visitor privacy and is therefore subject to ethical issues. Nonetheless video cameras can be set up in such a way that will not identify individual visitors and therefore protect their anonymity.

The predictive and forecasting capability of this technique is rather limited at the present time despite rapid technological advancements. One of the advantages of video monitoring is its capability to vary the size of the observed area to enable capturing aberrant behaviour from a distance. Other tools such as zooming, panning, sound recording are useful in examining social stress at sites that are heavily used. However, maintaining visitor anonymity, as well as the expense and limited geographic coverage are seen as limitations with video monitoring.

Detectors and Sensors

Detectors are useful for counting vehicular traffic in transport research. Detectors are generally categorised as being either active or passive. Active detectors transmit and receive electromagnetic radiation. The distance of the intercepted target can be determined by measuring travel time of the reflected signal. Detector types include microwave detectors, active infrared detectors and ultrasonic detectors. Passive detectors use environmental radiation (for example passive infrared detector and video cameras) rather than emitting their own radiation. Detectors can also be classified as static or dynamic wherein the former can detect fixed objects whilst the latter can detect moving objects.

Mat detectors enable detecting the presence of visitors within a confined area. These devices use pressure plates that detect the pressure of a passing visitor. Keßel *et al.* (2002) notes that there are two types of pressure sensitive mats. The first is comprised of piezo-electric coaxial cables embedded in rubber mats. An electric voltage is generated when pressure is exerted such as people standing on, or walking across the mat. The second detects change in the optical properties of glass fibres. There are also other detectors that use laser (infrared) and radar (microwave) scanners for detecting, counting and measuring the distance of a target by computing travel distance. Mowen (2002) has used inductive loop encounters to estimate recreational visitor numbers. Inductive loops are commonly used in collecting data from moving cars where a signal is collected by a computer every time the inductive loop is triggered by a moving car. McKenzie & Katic (2002) have used a combination of active and passive trail counters and remote photo stations along with observational reporting for monitoring frequency and intensity of recreational trail use in Banff National Park.

One of the disadvantages of using sensor mats in detecting visitor movements and flows, is its inability to determine walking speed and direction as well as the sequence of visitor movements. These parameters are significant in visitor management research particularly for agent-based studies.

Global Positioning Systems (GPS)

Another approach to monitor the spatio-temporal dimensions of visitor movements in parks is to use global positioning systems or GPS. GPS is one such technology that allows a user to capture the positioning of visitors to a park both spatially and temporally. Information is transmitted through a network of satellites orbiting in space around the Earth. For location positioning at least three satellites are required. Altitudinal information requires a fourth satellite. Continuous collection of data enables measurement of both speed and travel direction.

Acquiring tourist movements in time and space with GPS has the potential to provide both arrival and departure times, as well as record the nodes visited, the sequence or order in which those nodes were visited and walking speed and direction. Forer (1995) believes that movement data can be analysed to understand the decisions made by tourists as they walk along tracks in a park setting as well as provide detailed information on how tourists interact with the environment. Further, demands for additional location based services (LBS) to provide real-time contextual information including guidance and support can also be based on GPS recorded location.

There are two fundamental limitations of GPS. First, it is necessary to have at least four satellites for three-dimensional locations to be determined. Canopy cover can restrict the number of satellites required for high positional accuracy. Second, GPS recorded locations alone are not capable of interpreting the nature of visitor behaviour.

A Study into the Effectiveness of GPS for Tourist Tracking

In 2002, a pilot project was undertaken to assess the utility of GPS combined with on-site surveys to identify behaviour patterns within a park setting. One of the outcomes from this study was to develop a library of visitor types to specific parks. This library of visitors would then be used to characterise agents for input into Parks Victoria's Recreation and Behaviour Simulator (RBSim2) for future scenario building.

Specifically the project objectives were to:

(1) Identify typical behaviour sequences within a park site; including where visitors were going and how long visitors were spending at each location.
(2) Examine the relationship between these behaviour sequences and visitor characteristics including demographic and attitudinal measures.
(3) Utilize this information to develop a typology or library of day visitors.
(4) Examine the proportion of visitors that exhibit depreciative behaviour, i.e. walking off designated paths.

Study Area

Loch Ard Gorge within the Port Campbell National Park (PCNP) was selected as an appropriate study location for three key reasons:

- the site is heavily visited, exhibiting pressures from overcrowding and environmental stress, particularly at peak tourist times;
- Parks Victoria has expressed a desire to plan new infrastructure to support tourism at Loch Ard Gorge; and
- a complex existing network of walking tracks enabled some of the decision-making processes by tourists to be ascertained.

Parks Victoria manages more than 3.8 million hectares of parks and reserves, which equates to approximately 16% of the total land area throughout Victoria. The total number of visits to Victoria's parks and reserves are estimated to be 42.8 million per year. This comprised 27.6 million to national parks and 15.2 million to metropolitan parks (Parks Victoria 2002). Current research shows that there has been a significant increase in tourist numbers to Port Campbell National Park (PCNP). The PCNP and Bay of Islands Coastal Parks Management Plan (Parks Victoria 1998) estimated a 5.7% growth rate in the number of visits to the area. The PCNP Management Plan (Parks Victoria 1998: 25) has identified a higher concentration of visits to several sites in PCNP including the Twelve Apostles, Loch Ard Gorge and Port Campbell foreshore. These concentrations of visitors have been noticed during the summer and autumn seasons when visitor numbers often exceed existing parking and trail capacities (Parks Victoria 1998). This has resulted in traffic and park management problems at the Twelve Apostle and Loch Ard Gorge where there are 970,000 and 620,000 annual visits respectively, representing 54% of the 2.96 million visits to all sites at Port Campbell National Park.

PCNP is one of the most important tourist destinations in Victoria. The park is located along the Great Ocean Road in southwest Victoria situated approximately 250 km from Melbourne. The Twelve Apostles and Loch Ard Gorge are well known tourist sites due to their outstanding coastal scenery and spectacular geomorphology. PCNP was established in 1964 as a result of the National Parks Act (Victoria) 1964 and has since been assigned IUCN Category II status of the United Nation's list of National Parks and Protected Areas (Parks Victoria 1998). The park forms a narrow coastal strip that consists of steep, often vertical and even overhanging or precipitous cliffs up to 70 metres high. The park's geology is composed of a series of calcareous silts (marls) up to 150 metres thick, and fine-grained sandy limestone that were laid down in the sea during Miocene period between 10 and 25 million years age (Bird 1993: 64). Coastal processes have produced numerous shoreline features such as cliffs, natural arches and stacks, blowholes, caves, coastal gorges and beaches that now have become a tourist icon for their scenic value (Figure 4.1).

In addition to the natural attractions of Loch Ard Gorge, the site is an important cultural/historic site and was the location of a nineteenth century shipwreck, where a cemetery was established for those bodies recovered from the tragedy.

Figure 4.1: Coastline — Port Campbell National Park — Mutton Bird Lookout.

Study Approach

The research approach adopted used a combination of GPS and visitor surveys to ascertain visitor movement. Survey participants were recruited using an on-site random intercept method, where people were approached in their cars entering the Loch Ard Gorge site. Where groups of people were encountered, one person was asked to complete the questionnaire. The questionnaire was used to acquire basic socio-demographic data including age, gender, level of education, lifecycle classification, group visitor characteristics and activities to be undertaken. The same participants were given a Garmin eTrex GPS receiver and were requested to carry this during their visit to the park. They were then requested to return the GPS receiver at the end of the trip.

The GPS receivers were tested several times prior to the actual surveys and showed reasonable spatial accuracy of between four to eight metres. It was found that the landform and land cover characteristics of the Loch Ard Gorge site were conducive to using hand-held GPS because of the relatively flat terrain and low-lying vegetation cover.

Inventory Development

For registration and analyses of GPS recorded locations, it was decided to use a geographic information system (GIS). Base digital data were supplied by Parks Victoria including the 1:25000 Land Victoria digital topographic data comprising contours, road networks, major

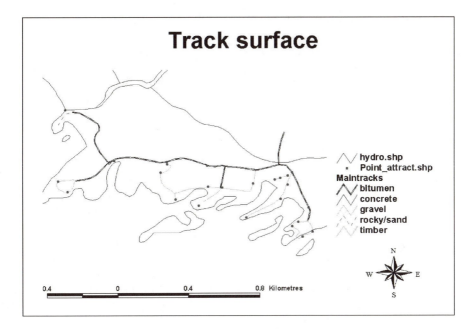

Figure 4.2: Roads and walking tracks at Loch Ard Gorge.

tracks and hydrology for the region. Additional geographic features such as missing tracks, track width, surface type, slope, and key attractions were field surveyed, using GPS, and input into the GIS prior to visitor surveys commencing. Figure 4.2 shows the locations of key tourist attractions and track layout for the Loch Ard Gorge site. Table 4.1 lists key attractions located in the GPS survey.

Visitor surveys were conducted over a weekend period in May 2002. Each GPS receiver continuously recorded time-stamped locations as signals were received from contributing satellites. These occurred approximately every five to eight seconds but did vary up to 60 seconds between logged locations depending upon ground conditions and signal strength. A total of 13,146 locations points representing the movements of 102 people (that is individual surveys) were recorded and used in the analysis. Results from the 102 participants were initially downloaded onto a field laptop before being edited and transferred to the GIS. Each GPS survey was assigned an unique code (survey-id) so that these could then be matched against socio-demographic surveys completed in the field. Figure 4.3 shows an aerial photograph for the site with GPS recorded locations. Attributes stored for each recorded GPS location are shown in Table 4.2.

Leg lengths, times, speeds and bearings were recorded with logged locations within the GPS. These refer to the individual line segments traversed immediately prior to the logged location. Figure 4.4 shows the relationship between the leg attributes and the individual logged location.

Lines connecting each of the recorded points were generated purely to give an indication of visitor movements along walking tracks.

Table 4.1: List of attractions at Loch Ard Gorge GPS survey data.

Attraction_id	Attraction_type	Name
1	carpark	Carpark 1
2	lookout	Loch Ard View
3	lookout	Limestone Curtain
4	lookout	Cliff lookout
5	lookout	Razorback
6	lookout	Razorback
7	lookout	Loch Ard lookout to beach
8	lookout	Razorback
9	lookout	Loch Ard Point — The Wreck
10	lookout	Top of Stairs — The Survivors
11	sign	Loch Ard story
12	carpark	Carpark 2 — The Cemetery
13	lookout	Mutton Bird Island
14	lookout	Cliff lookout
15	carpark	Carpark 3
16	lookout	Blow Hole 1
17	lookout	Blow Hole 2
18	lookout	Over cliffs
19	intersection	to Blow Hole
20	lookout	Thunder Cave
21	lookout	Broken Head West
22	intersection	to River
23	cemetery	Loch Ard Cemetery
24	lookout	Broken Head East
25	river	Sherbrooke River
26	beach	Loch Ard Beach

Spatial Data Analyses

In order to spatially classify and describe behaviour using the GPS observations 13 separate "regions" were generated for the Loch Ard Gorge site. Within a number of these regions, sub-regions were generated for particular point attractions, in order to ascertain times in and out and durations of stay for each of these sub-regions. A total of 27 sub-regions were delineated. These are shown in Figure 4.5.

Boundaries for each of the regions were delineated in a manner that enabled GPS observations to be encapsulated, and separated according to walking track surface and point attraction location. The purpose of the regions was to assist in describing behaviours for different locations throughout the Loch Ard Gorge site. Each lookout and walking track segment was assigned to a separate region. Using regions it was then possible to ascertain

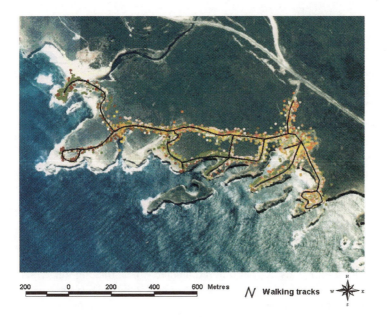

Figure 4.3: The study site at Loch Ard Gorge showing the road and track network with GPS recorded locations.

fundamental behaviour statistics including maximum, minimum and average walking speeds as well as duration of time spent within each region. Duration was determined by calculating the entry and exit times into each region.

Maps showing walking speeds and duration of visit for the 27 different sub-regions are shown in Figures 4.6 and 4.7, respectively.

Table 4.2: Attributes stored against GPS recorded locations.

Attribute	Units
Point_id	integer
Survey_id	integer
Easting	AMG66 metres
Northing	AMG66 metres
Date	dd/mm/yyyy
Time	hour:min:sec
Altitude	metres
Leg_length	metres
Leg_time	seconds
Leg_speed	kmph
Bearing	Whole degrees

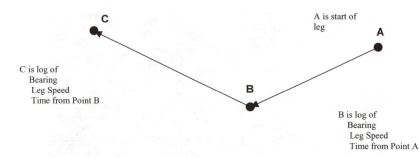

Figure 4.4: Relationship between leg attributes and individual logged location. Leg speed, time and bearing recorded at point C refers to the line segment between B and C. Leg speed, time and bearing recorded at point B refers to the line segment between A and B.

Topological relationships for spatial information include orientation, adjacency and connectivity.

Networks are defined as a "set interconnected lines making up a set of features through which resources can flow" (Heywood *et al.* 1998: 123). If we consider that these interconnected lines link a series of locations and that people can travel along each of these interconnected lines, then the series of walking tracks that form the Loch Ard Gorge site can be considered a network.

Locations that are connected include attractions, endpoints of walking tracks or connectors between alternate paths. From Figure 4.2 a simplified topologically correct

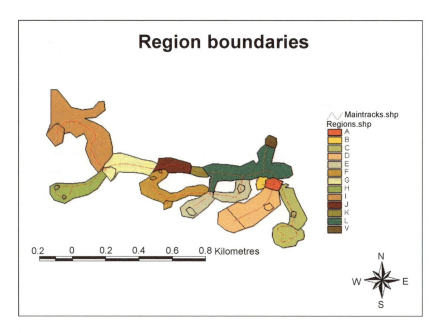

Figure 4.5: Region boundaries for the study site.

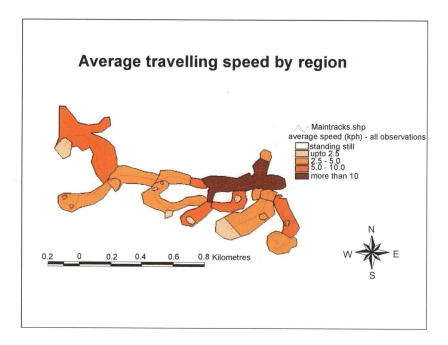

Figure 4.6: Average travelling speeds by region.

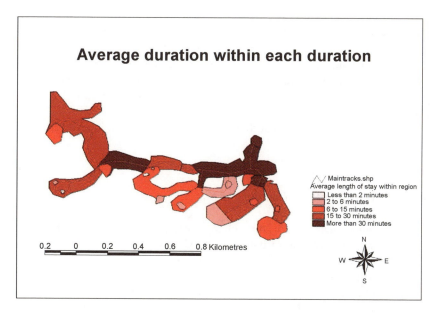

Figure 4.7: Average length of stay within each region.

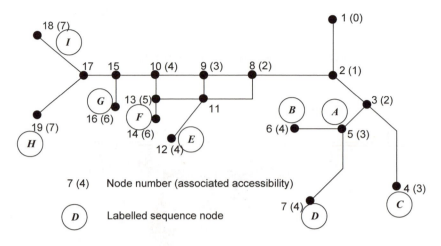

Figure 4.8: Topological network diagram for Loch Ard Gorge with associated numbers. The labelled sequence node was used for determining visitor sequence patterns.

network diagram was constructed (Figure 4.8). Visitors will traverse along one or several of these links commencing at one of the nodes and passing through one or more of the other nodes. For example, all surveyed recipients commenced and finished, after passing through several of the other nodes, their GPS surveys at node number 1.

To ascertain movement patterns of visitors it was important to determine the order, or sequence, in which they moved through the path network. To assist in determining their movements, it was useful to label each track endpoint or key node through which they passed, with an alphanumeric character. These have been termed "sequence nodes." Beside each node is its associated number which is the topological distance that node is from node number 1. The associated number gives a measure of the relative accessibility of that node (Campbell 2001: 197).

From Figure 4.8 it can be seen that there are 19 separate nodes, interlinked by 20 paths or links.

Sequential Movement Patterns Through the Site

To enable spatial movement patterns through the site to be described, it was decided to label each node marking the endpoint of the network (C through to I) as a "labelled sequence node" or as a node in which participants passed through (A and B). These are shown in Figure 4.9 and Table 4.3.

From Figure 4.9, for example, out of the total of 102 participants, 61 individuals (or 60%) chose to visit node A (the Loch Ard story board) then moved to node B (the beach at Loch Ard Gorge). Of those moving from A to B, 28 of the 61 chose then to visit node D (Loch

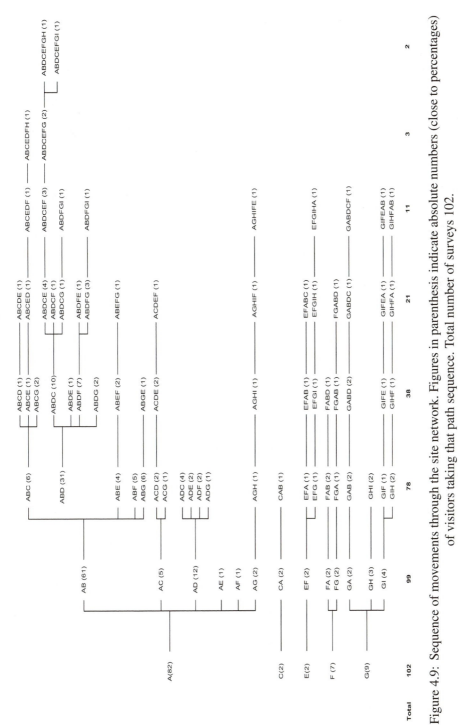

Figure 4.9: Sequence of movements through the site network. Figures in parenthesis indicate absolute numbers (close to percentages) of visitors taking that path sequence. Total number of surveys 102.

Table 4.3: Location description for sequence nodes.

Sequence Node	Location Description
A	The Loch Ard Storyboard
B	Loch Ard Gorge beach
C	The Razorback loop
D	The Loch Ard Lookout
E	Muttonbird Island Lookout
F	Cliff lookout
G	Thunder Cave
H	Broken Head loop
I	Sherbrooke River

Ard Lookout) next. It is interesting to note that out of 102 participants, only one elected to visit all nodes.

By summing the numbers in parenthesis downwards the total numbers of sequence nodes visited by individuals can be ascertained. By subtracting sums of visitation from sums of visitation of increasing numbers of sequence nodes visited, it is possible to determine how many individuals visited a particular number of sequence nodes. For example, out of the 102 participants who visited at least one sequence node, 99 of them went on to visit a second sequence node. Hence, 3 participants only visited one sequence node. Of the 99 participants visiting 2 sequence nodes, 77 of them went on to visit a third sequence node. That is 22 of them only visited 2 sequence nodes. The average number of nodes visited was 4.5, and the average length of stay at the Loch Ard Gorge site was 65 minutes.

Non-Spatial Data Analyses — Developing Tourist Typologies for the Site

The third research objective was to...*utilise* [behaviour sequence and visitor characteristics] *to develop a typology or library of day visitors* [to the study area] .... From the socio-demographic survey results a cluster analysis was undertaken. Four clusters were determined from this analysis. Output from the cluster analysis is detailed in Table 4.4.

From Table 4.4 four clusters or typologies of visitors have been identified. These were classified as "the single groupie," "the international couple," "the elderly couple" and "the local family."

Visitor Typology 1 (The Single Groupie)

This cluster or tourist typology comprised of generally young local (i.e. Australian) visitors, mostly in the 18 to early 20 s age group, having completed primary and secondary education. They are young and single, but travelling as a group of friends and therefore will tend to stay longer and travel more widely once at the site. On average they will travel to six attraction nodes. Figure 4.10 shows a plot of the locations this typology visited whilst at Loch Ard Gorge. The total number of visitors within this typology was 13.

Table 4.4: Cluster analysis output from SPSS.

Final Cluster Centers.

Cluster	AGEGRP	DURATION	EDUCATIO	GROUPTYP	LIFECYCL	NODESVIS	PEOPLNUM	TRIPTYPE
1	1.0000	4.6923	1.2308	5.0000	1.1538	6.0769	3.8462	2.9231
2	1.2222	3.1852	2.8519	2.2222	1.6667	3.0741	2.1111	2.5185
3	2.7941	2.2059	2.3529	2.1765	5.8529	2.7353	2.0000	2.0588
4	1.8929	3.0357	2.2143	4.3571	3.3929	3.5000	3.7500	1.3214

Cluster	VISITNUM	GENDER	RESIDENC
1	1.0769	1.0000	1.0769
2	1.5926	1.8148	1.5556
3	1.0294	1.3824	1.0588
4	1.7500	1.8571	1.1071

Distances between Final Cluster Centers.

Cluster	1	2	3	4
1	0.0000			
2	5.1262	0.0000		
3	7.4956	4.7218	0.0000	

Number of Cases in each Cluster.

Cluster	Unweighted Cases	Weighted Cases
1	13.0	13.0
2	27.0	27.0
3	34.0	34.0
4	28.0	28.0
Missing	0	
Valid cases	102.0	102.0

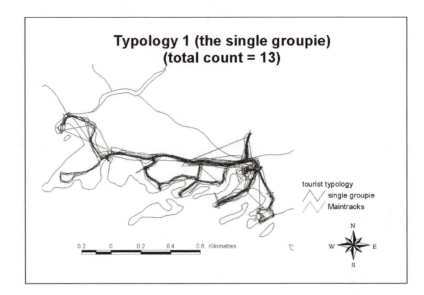

Figure 4.10: Tracked events for the single groupie.

This category of visitors largely comprised of tertiary educated male/female couples predominantly from overseas, who are likely to stay for longer than average (from 50 to 70 minutes), visiting in the order of 3 attraction nodes. They are generally young, predominantly within the 18 to 29 year age group. There were 27 cases that fitted this typology (Figure 4.11).

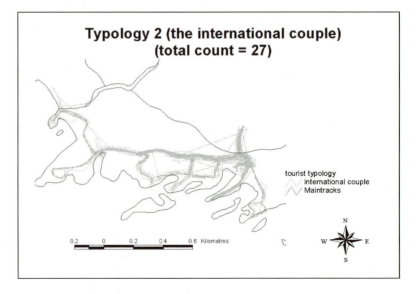

Figure 4.11: Tracked events for the international couple.

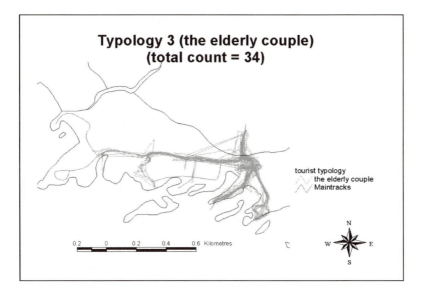

Figure 4.12: Tracked events for the elderly couple.

This third group of visitors are largely those local tourists who are elderly citizens, 60 years or older, on an extended holiday who are perhaps passing by the location on their way to somewhere else. Their visits tend to be shorter with fewer nodes visited (less than 3). Their stay at Loch Ard Gorge also tends to be shorter (in the order of 30 minutes) (Figure 4.12).

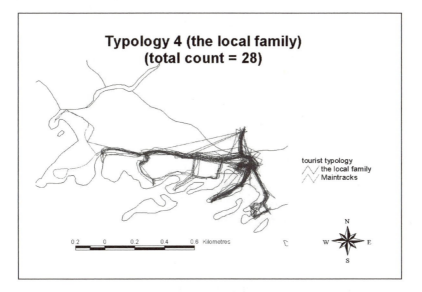

Figure 4.13: Tracked events for the local family.

This final grouping of visitors is primarily comprised of the Australian middle-age family travelling to Loch Ard Gorge as part of a longer holiday. They stay an average of 50–70 minutes and visit 3–4 attraction nodes (Figure 4.13).

Discussion

In general, people tend to follow a pre-determined sequence of nodes. Of the surveyed participants 82% commenced their visit at the same node (the Loch Ard Story Board) and 61% then travelled on to Loch Ard Beach. This regularity should provide data for future planning for Parks Victoria. In addition, knowing the average length of stay (65 minutes) and average number of nodes to be visited (3.5) should assist in planning for vehicular parking.

At Loch Ard Gorge, four tourist typologies were identified from basic socio-demographic variables using cluster analysis. When plotted, their spatial movements at the site showed certain identifiable characteristics. By far the most adventurous tourist type was the "single groupie." This person is likely to be travelling within a group comprised of young people. They tend to travel widely once at a given destination and will spend longer than their counterparts. The second group is made up of what have been called "international couples," who are young and generally well educated. This tourist type will stay longer than average and will visit in the order of three attraction nodes. Elderly citizens are represented in the third tourist group, the "elderly couple," and tend to stay at tourist destinations for a shorter duration than average. They also tend to restrict their visitation to concentrated locations near the entry and exit points to a destination. The final typology is the "local family." This group tend to visit an average number of attraction nodes at a given destination. Their duration of stay ranges from 50 to 70 minutes.

The final objective was "*. . . to examine the proportion of visitors that exhibit depreciative behaviour, i.e. walking off designated paths*." However with a GPS recorded spatial resolution of between 5 and 10 metres, it was felt that this objective was largely unmet. Whilst the GPS surveys observed in this study did show recorded locations away from the marked tracks it could not be determined with certainty whether this was an artefact of the spatial resolution of the GPS and recorded position, or an actual incident of depreciative behaviour. In addition it is likely that by merely participating in the survey, a participant might modify his or her behaviour to conform to what is considered to be acceptable behaviour. This is a difficult issue, since visitors are more than likely to modify their behaviour if they feel park managers are observing them. We did observe several instances of depreciative behaviour where visitors were leaving marked pathways to take photographs, despite warnings of cliff instability. Videoing visitors raises concerns regarding invasion of privacy, costs associated with setting up observation points, and susceptibility of equipment to vandalism. The mere presence of park rangers will also result in modified behaviour of visitors, so straightforward observation by park management will be difficult, as well as time consuming and expensive.

Conclusions

This paper reviews a research project that investigated the patterns of behaviour and movements of tourists throughout the Loch Ard Gorge site within Port Campbell National

Park. Data were collected via on-site questionnaires to ascertain the socio-demographic characteristics of visitors to the site. These data was supplemented with GPS surveys that monitored the movement patterns of the surveyed participants. Using the GPS recordings with a spatial database or geographic information system, it was possible to investigate the movement characteristics for different tourist types.

This project has shown that spatial technologies such as GPS can be used to ascertain movements of visitors through national parks. These movements can be input, displayed and spatially analysed within the assistance of GIS. However it still remains largely unknown how visitors interact with their environmental surroundings and how decisions in the field by these visitors are actually made. For example, we do not know how biophysical variables such as vegetation, path construction and signage influence how visitors made decisions when confronted with bifurcation points along a pathway. At this stage these decisions can only be inferred from the GPS observations recorded using hand-held receivers. It is proposed that future research should be undertaken to adopt spatially referenced personal digital assistants (PDAs) to acquire decision making processes in real-time through location based surveys. Location based service provision is currently being researched in the Department of Geospatial Science at RMIT to investigate the utility of providing visitors with supplementary park information via mobile devices (including mobile phones or PDAs) as they move through a national park (Hadley *et al.* 2003).

The study has also shown that for a selection of alternative track routes open to tourists, more than half commenced their visit at the same location, i.e. the Loch Ard Story Board adjacent to the first carpark, before moving on to the Beach at Loch Ard. About half of these then moved on to the Loch Ard Lookout. The average number of nodes visited was 3.5 and the average length of stay was 65 minutes.

Further research into examining how visitors from differing socio-demographic backgrounds make decisions is required. We need to understand whether visitors from different cultural backgrounds or within different age groups respond differently when posed with alternative pathways. We need to research whether these visitors will respond differently to biophysical variables and social contexts. For example are visitors from one cultural background more or less comfortable with crowding? Will crowding alter visitor behaviour when visiting a particular location such as a lookout at a national park?

This study has made limited attempt to explore and understand the relationships between visitor characteristics and the sequence of movements made by those visitors. Simple analysis of numbers of nodes visited, and the spatial extent of visitation for four types of tourists have been reviewed in this study. These four types were determined from cluster analysis based on the survey responses for the 102 participants in the study. More extensive surveys are required to validate these tourist types, and to provide a more rigorous set of parameters for the RBSim2 simulator in order to determine generic agent parameters for a wide range of national park settings.

The typologies identified as part of this study can be used as the basis for characterising agents within agent-based models such as the RBSim2 simulator. However given the small number of participants (102), it is suggested that the study be repeated for a similar park site at the Port Campbell National Park initially, and then to extend the surveys to other parks with different characteristics (for example the Grampians National Park).

Acknowledgments

This research was undertaken with the assistance from many people. However, we would like to specifically acknowledge the assistance we received from the following organizations and individuals. Firstly we would like to acknowledge the financial support received from Parks Victoria (Visitor Research) and from RMIT University (Research and Development). Thanks are also extended to the rangers from Port Campbell National Park, and in particular John McInerney who provided much needed assistance in conducting the surveys for which we are most grateful. Finally we would like to acknowledge the many nameless people who participated in the field survey and provided the data as the basis for this research. Their efforts are very much appreciated.

Chapter 5

The Use of Strategic Visioning to Enhance Local Tourism Planning in Periphery Communities

Lisa Ruhanen and Chris Cooper

Introduction

Tourism has had a profound impact upon destinations worldwide, and although this impact has been positive for many destinations, there are numerous examples where tourism has adversely impacted upon the environment and social fabric of the destination community (Coccossis 1996; Murphy 1985). The negative impacts of tourism have been attributed, among other things, to inadequate or non-existent planning for development (Gunn 1994; Hall 2000). This has led to increased calls for tourism planning to offset some of the negative impacts that tourism can have on the destination community. While a number of approaches have been advocated, a collaborative philosophy, based on the principles of sustainability, is more likely to result in acceptable and successful policies and programmes for tourism destinations (Farrell 1986; Jamal & Getz 1995; Maitland 2002; Minca & Getz 1995). Such an approach focuses on cooperation and broader based participation in tourism planning and decision-making between stakeholders to lead to agreement on planning directions and goals, with one of the primary objectives of collaborative arrangements being to develop a strategic vision for a destination (Bramwell & Lane 2000).

The aim of strategic visioning is for stakeholders to be involved in determining appropriate forms of development, through a publicly driven process based on shared values and consensus. Although there are few examples where strategic visioning has been applied to date, empirical evidence from a visioning process conducted for the Gold Coast in Queensland, Australia, suggests that this process may be an emerging best practice benchmark for collaborative tourism destination planning. While strategic visioning can be considered a useful mechanism for achieving a coordinated strategic approach for any type of tourism destination, whether urban or regional, it is often destinations within peripheral regional areas where the impacts of tourism are felt most acutely. It is therefore proposed that peripheral destination communities could derive considerable benefits from this type of strategic planning.

Taking Tourism to the Limits: Issues, Concepts and Managerial Perspectives
© 2005 Published by Elsevier Ltd.
ISBN: 0-08-044644-2

This chapter will examine the relatively recent emergence of the strategic visioning concept for tourism destinations. To illustrate the benefits of such an approach, the peripheral tourism destination of the Tweed Shire will be examined. The Shire is beginning to experience increased levels of interest in its tourism product, with growing numbers of visitors and new infrastructure developments. The Tweed Shire's tourism stakeholders are dissatisfied with the planning efforts of authorities and wish to be actively involved in guiding the future of tourism development, and have identified the strategic visioning approach as a means for achieving this. Building from the limited literature on strategic visioning and the Tweed Shire example, several benefits of adopting the process for periphery destinations will be proposed including: improved decision-making capability, an emphasis on the future, and broader based collaboration among stakeholders groups.

Tourism Destination Planning

Tourism has undoubtedly had a significant impact on destinations all over the world. Coccossis (1996) claims that in some areas it has revitalised local economies whilst in others it has destroyed them; in some areas it has reinforced local identity whilst in others it has destroyed customs, traditions and social relations; in some areas it has helped protect environmentally sensitive areas whilst in others it has wrought havoc with local ecosystems and resources. The economic optimism that followed World War II saw many nations and communities lured into the tourism business, encouraged by the highly publicised positives of the industry as an economic sector. However, this once positive picture did not take long to be revised as the environmental and cultural impacts of tourism on host communities became increasingly apparent. As Murphy (1985) finds, tourism was seized upon with little forethought concerning a viable tourism product, the social and environmental consequences of development, or the spill over effects in surrounding areas. Where tourism planning did occur it was seen as a process of simply encouraging new hotels to open, ensuring there was transportation access to the area, and organising a tourist promotion campaign. Such an approach was based on the optimistic assumption that tourism was an industry with few costs and considerable economic benefits (Young, Richins & Rugimbana 1993). While this approach may have been successful for developing individual hotels and resorts during this period; it was hardly sufficient to manage the unprecedented rapid growth of tourism and the impacts it had on destination communities. Unfortunately many destinations are still paying the social and environmental consequences of the rapid tourism development following World War II and have been forced to implement remedial actions for failing to plan and control tourism development (Inskeep 1991). Therefore, Hall (1998) quite rightly states that tourism cannot be allowed to progress in an ad hoc manner without an overall guiding framework and predetermined strategies toward development objectives. This is necessary as it is often too late to reverse or redirect unwanted development once it has become established in a destination and these destinations will always suffer from environmental and social problems that are both detrimental to tourists and residents (Gunn 1994).

The need to plan for tourism to mitigate the environmental and social impacts of tourism on host communities became increasingly apparent throughout the 1970s and 1980s.

Tourism's potential as an economic force had been seized upon by government at all levels, but the result was centralised top down planning and promotion that left destinations with little control over their own destinies and local residents often received few if any of the promised positive effects of tourism (Bramwell 1994; Murphy 1985). The dangers of this approach have since been realised for what they are, and as Akis, Peristianis and Warner (1996: 481) reflect, ". . . governments, perhaps persuaded by foreign entrepreneurs' assurance of streets paved with gold, took little trouble to consult with local residents." As the numbers of tourists grew it was eventually acknowledged that tourism was having irreversible and damaging effects to the communities and cultures that were exposed to tourism and that alternative planning and management was needed to develop more socially acceptable guidelines for tourism expansion. This realisation led to an explosion in the academic literature with authors claiming that the involvement of the community in the planning and decision-making process for tourism is pivotal to offset some of the negative social impacts (Blank 1989; Burr 1991; Haywood 1988; Keogh 1990; Murphy 1983, 1985). This "community approach" to tourism planning and decision making can be described as a form of "bottom up" planning, where residents are regarded as the focal point of the tourism planning exercise rather than the tourists, and the community, which is often equated with a region of local government, is regarded as the basic planning unit (Hall 1998). Proponents of the community approach argue that residents of the area should be given the opportunity to express their views on the type of community in which they live (Hall 1998). The aim of the community approach is to seek appropriate tourism development which ideally will lead to improved living standards and economic benefits for the community; infrastructure, facilities and services for residents and visitors alike; development that is in keeping with the cultural and social norms of the community; all of which will ultimately result in resident and visitor satisfaction (McIntosh & Goeldner 1986).

Collaborative Destination Planning

Despite the need to integrate community residents into the tourism planning process, the community approach is a rather narrow view when the dynamics of tourism destinations are considered. While the perceptions and attitudes of residents towards tourism development is an important planning and policy consideration, the community approach does not account for the broad range of stakeholders in a destination community. Tourism destinations involve a variety of stakeholders, including: the government (national, regional and local); governmental departments with links to tourism; tourism organisations (national, regional and local); tourism developers and entrepreneurs, tourism industry operators; non-tourism business practitioners, and the community, including local community groups, indigenous people's groups and local residents (Freeman 1984; Roberts & Simpson 2000). Within the organisational context it is widely acknowledged that failing to incorporate participation from all stakeholder groups will result in the failure of an organisation (Clarkson 1995; Sautter & Leisen 1999). Therefore the need to integrate all destination stakeholders in the tourism planning process has been advocated because decisions about tourism development should not be left to a few politicians, government officials or tourism entrepreneurs who may not consider the full gamut of issues (Bramwell & Lane 2000). One approach for integrating the various destination stakeholders into the planning process is the notion of stakeholder collaboration. Collaboration theory is a useful process when autonomous stakeholders who share a common problem domain engage in an interactive process to address issues related to the problem domain and seek solutions, which go beyond their own limited vision of what is possible (Gray & Wood 1991). Collaboration essentially is an emergent process where groups learn to manage their changing environments with joint ownership of decisions and a collective responsibility for progress (Jamal & Getz 1995). It can also help stakeholders appreciate their common interests and realize the advantages to be gained by working together as opposed to competing with each other (Williams, Penrose & Hawkes 1998). It is claimed that the "go-it-alone" policies of the past are giving way, as government and public agencies in many developed countries endorse stronger cooperation and collaboration (Bramwell & Lane 2000; Gunn 1988; Jamal & Getz 1995; Potts & Harrill 1998).

A collaborative approach can be considered a more comprehensive approach to planning and management in tourism destinations than other forms of ad hoc planning. Such collaboration aims for cooperation in tourism planning and decision-making between stakeholders to lead to agreement on planning directions and goals. This is a vital principle and challenges the typical planning process where stakeholders (often community residents) are consulted minimally (if at all) near the end of the process, which leaves little opportunity for meaningful input. The tourism industry is widely acknowledged as being highly fragmented, so it should not be surprising that a diverse range of attitudes often exist toward future development (Cooper 1995). Therefore, a wide range of stakeholder opinion should be canvassed in relation to future tourism development to address the diversity of attitudes (Smith 1984). Collaboration is also seen as a process through which parties who see different aspects of a problem can constructively explore their differences for solutions that go beyond sectional visions of what is possible (Gray 1989). As Bramwell & Lane (2000) state, one of the primary objectives of implementing a collaborative arrangement is to develop a strategic vision for a tourism destination.

Strategic Visioning for Tourism Destinations

The concept of strategic visioning has recently emerged as an extension of the collaborative planning process for tourism destinations (Bramwell & Lane 2000; Ritchie 1999). Vision, as defined in the business strategy literature, is a practical and achievable picture or description of the nature of the organisation's business as it is intended to be at some time in the future, which should motivate people to come together in an alignment of purpose and from which point strategic plans are developed (Hussey 1999; Korac-Kakabadse & Kakabadse 1998). As Vogel & Swanson (1988) find, traditional strategic planning methodologies are being revised to include a "visionary" phase, as leaders are recognising the importance of thinking about the future, developing goals and coming up with realistic strategies to achieve those goals; commonly referred to as strategic visioning. Essentially, strategic visioning is a form of democratic, bottom-up, grass roots collaboration, which reverses the traditional strategic planning and management structures.

This process is illustrated by the way strategic visioning has been used in communities throughout Canada and North America, where it is perceived as a process for empowering community residents (Walzer 1996). In this context, strategic visioning occurs through public involvement; where a group of people seek to identify their purpose, core values and vision of the future. These are then transformed into a manageable and feasible set of goals, action plans and/or strategies (Department of Rural Sociology n.d.). The concept has been used to address general community issues such as economic development, housing, transport, education, public safety and the environment. However, strategic visioning as a planning practice has only recently been extended to tourism destinations.

Based upon Canadian experience, Ritchie (1999) considers strategic visioning for tourism destinations as a new but important extension of the more common process of strategic planning in tourism. Even though the direction for tourism development is implicit in strategic planning, strategic visioning has a stronger emphasis on bringing together the views of the many organisations and individuals of both the industry and the destination community through collaborative and participative processes. The underlying philosophy of this approach is to nurture appropriate forms of development, through a publicly driven process based on stakeholder values and consensus (Ritchie & Crouch 2000).

It is thus argued that a well-articulated vision that has been developed through a consensual process between relevant stakeholders can subsequently provide the focus for the strategic planning process (Faulkner 2003). Therefore, strategic visioning for tourism destinations essentially formulates a framework that provides broad guidelines as to the kinds of major facilities, events and programs that the community finds most consistent with their values and aspirations for the long-term development and well being of the community (Ritchie 1993). The vision developed for a destination will define the nature of long term major developments, many of which are irreversible, so the choice of vision is absolutely critical, as it will set in motion the development of the destination for many years to come (Ritchie 1993; Ryan 2002). A strategic vision also provides a means for ensuring that day-to-day decisions are informed by a longer-term perspective, as opposed to the *ad hoc* decision-making which is often prevalent in destination communities.

It is thus apparent that an important caveat to the strategic visioning concept is the notion of collaboration and cooperation between destination stakeholders. Strategic visioning requires *all* destination stakeholders to work together to develop a vision of the desired future of the destination (Ritchie 1993). Both process and objective are thus the same in that consensual decision making is both an objective and means, and is normally facilitated through a publicly driven process based on stakeholder values as opposed to a dictated future, disseminated by a higher authority and/or based solely on market forces.

As has been discussed, strategic visioning can be considered a useful means for achieving coordinated strategic planning for tourism destinations. It has been argued that a re-iterative and mutually reinforcing process occurs, where the act of participation itself begins to identify first, commonality of concerns and then second, build consensus of objectives and means. Faulkner & Noakes (2002) argue that developing a vision for a destination can define the nature of the tourism product and its future development and so assist in building collaboration among stakeholder groups.

Generally, Calgary, Canada is recognised as the first destination to use the visioning process in the early 1990s in an attempt to provide both direction and support for future tourism development (Ritchie 1993). Ritchie (1999) also reports on the use of visioning for the Canadian tourism icon of Banff National Park, Alberta, where the various stakeholder groups sought to identify the environmental, economic and social future of the park. Getz & Jamal (1994) also illustrate with reference to Canmore the notable attempts by Alberta to utilise community driven processes for planning purposes. Similarly, Johnson & Snepenger (1993) report on the use of a visioning process with park and forest managers of the Greater Yellowstone Region in an attempt to improve the management of the region.

In the Australian context the most comprehensive tourism visioning project that has been undertaken to date is the Gold Coast Visioning Project. This three year project was undertaken and funded jointly by the Gold Coast City Council, the Cooperative Research Centre for Sustainable Tourism and the local tourism industry. Faulkner & Noakes (2002: i) report that, "the Gold Coast Tourism Visioning Project articulates a set of core values and principles that underpin a preferred future for the sustainable prosperity of Australia's leading tourism destination in the medium to longer term (10–20 years). It challenges destination Gold Coast to move from a past *ad hoc* approach to tourism to one that integrates economic, social and environmental dimensions to evolve new patterns of managing and growing tourism in a more systematic and dynamic way in this new century. Tourism is a key component of the inevitable transition to sustainable development strategies in advanced western democracies such as Australia (Figures 5.1 and 5.2)."

Although a strategic visioning process is a useful mechanism for achieving a coordinated strategic approach for any type of tourism destination be it urban or regional, it is often destination communities within peripheral regional and rural areas where the impacts of tourism are felt most acutely. It is therefore proposed that such destinations can derive considerable benefits by incorporating strategic visioning into their tourism planning. To illustrate the potential of this process, the Tweed Shire will be used as an example of how strategic visioning can assist tourism destinations in peripheral areas address some of their challenging planning and management issues. These challenges often include isolation from planning authorities, changing economic structures and local governments inexperienced in dealing with a sector such as tourism.

The Tweed Shire, New South Wales, Australia

The Tweed Shire is located in the far northeastern corner of New South Wales, and borders the growing southeast Queensland capital city of Brisbane and the regional city of the Gold Coast; however, the Shire's own state capital is located over 800 kilometres south of the Shire in Sydney. In recent times, the Tweed Shire has seen considerable population growth and new economic sectors such as tourism supersede the traditionally agricultural based economy. Although the region as a whole does not offer a sophisticated tourism product, the area is popular for its coastal beaches and villages; the World Heritage listed rainforests, and registered club industry. Recent infrastructure developments such as an international resort and upmarket residential developments on the pristine (but vulnerable) coastal foreshore have seen the area attract increasing attention from tourists, investors and developers, eagerly supported by the current "pro-development" local council. Public

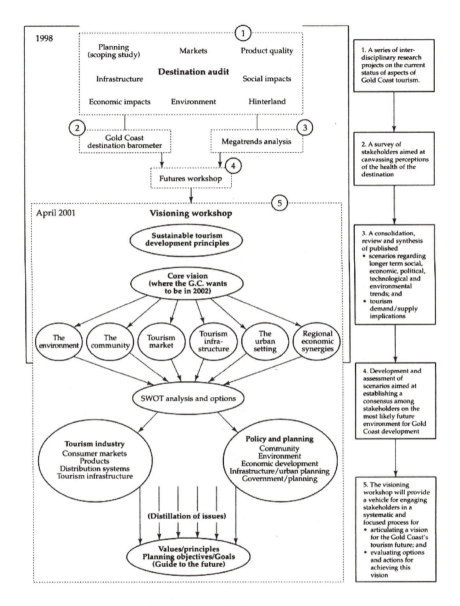

Figure 5.1: The Gold Coast destination visioning process. *Source:* Faulkner (2003).

consultations on new developments are rarely entered into aside from some tokenistic efforts on an *ad hoc* basis. Public involvement is more likely to be a confrontational display by disgruntled community members. Therefore it is not surprising that there is considerable concern amongst stakeholders regarding this unprecedented level of tourism and residential development. As Richins (1995: 177) finds, "it is not unusual for concern to arise among the local population during periods of rapid development, and in order to minimise the potential

> In summary, the Destination Vision as articulated by stakeholders participating in the Gold Coast Tourism Futures and Tourism Vision Workshops is:
>
> "The Gold Coast will become one of the great leisure and lifestyle destinations of the world. The region will be renowned for the sustainable management of its natural and built environment, its sense of self-confidence, the vibrancy and depth of its service economy, the continuing well being of its community and its unique sense of place as a thriving and dynamic resort city.
>
> The destination will be safe, clean, well serviced and uniquely Gold Coast in style. The region will have leading edge organisational, management and marketing structures, which will be underpinned by new partnerships between business, community and government. It will have developed a brand and market awareness which positions destination Gold Coast as a market leader in targeted domestic and international markets. The Gold Coast will set the pace as the lifestyle and leisure capital of the Pacific Rim."

Figure 5.2: The Gold Coast vision. *Source:* Faulkner & Noakes (2002).

negative impacts of increased tourism, recreational home and residential development, people living in these areas have looked for long term solutions".

The desire for such long term solutions became evident during a study conducted in the Tweed Shire in 2001 with over 30 tourism stakeholders, including local government officials and private sector tourism providers. While the study primarily sought to explore tourism stakeholder's views on the development potential of their region (see Murphy & Cooper 2002), what was uncovered were some concerning planning and management issues. The overwhelming majority of stakeholders who participated in the study were concerned that although tourism (and residential) development is quickly progressing in the Shire there are no planning and management mechanisms in place to ensure this happens in a sustainable manner or that the benefits of tourism return to the local community. The majority of respondents categorically stated that they were not aware of any tourism planning in the Tweed Shire. The lack of planning controls were primarily attributed to the parochial nature of the local council who have little understanding or experience of the dynamics of the sector, or appreciate the importance of strategic planning and management for tourism development. The local council, typical of the Australian governmental system, is generally regarded as the agenda-setter and leader in such issues yet the study participants were of the opinion that there is little chance of the council acting to remedy the situation. There is also concern that the local council have tunnelled their economic interests into the rapidly expanding coastal residential developments in the Shire, encouraged by the developers and investors cashing in on the "sea change lifestyle developments," which are beginning to proliferate the east coast of Queensland and New South Wales. Adding to this problem is the Shire's geographical separation from the state government in Sydney. Respondents claim that this "dislocation" has seen the area overlooked by the state government and the state tourism authority in terms of planning and management, with the local council being somewhat left to their own devices.

Following on from the survey, a workshop forum was held with the participating stakeholders to discuss the issues uncovered in the study and attempt to develop a consensus on the way forward for tourism in the Tweed Shire (see Murphy & Cooper 2002). The stakeholder respondents overwhelmingly agreed that the development of a shared strategic vision was the first step in securing the future of tourism in the Tweed Shire. As the Tweed Shire neighbours, the Gold Coast, the Tweed's stakeholders are well aware of the visioning project recently completed and consider that such a process would be of benefit to their Shire. A strategic visioning exercise is seen by the stakeholders as desirable because it would allow for an overall framework to guide the future of tourism in the Tweed Shire which would then set the guidelines for other issues of concern such as destination development, planning strategies, product development, marketing and destination management. It was considered vital that the strategic vision for the Shire is in fact a "shared strategic vision," thus necessitating consultation and involvement between governments at all levels, the tourism industry, the private sector and community residents. This was considered an ideal solution to the current problems in the Tweed, as not only would the vision set the agenda for future development but the council would be bound by the agreed direction in approving developments, and could not make the ad hoc development decisions which have been prevalent to date. Therefore, if the vision for the Tweed were, for example, to maintain its low-density coastal infrastructure, a development application to the council for a high-rise apartment building on the coastal strip would not be permitted, as it would not be in keeping with the shared vision for the Shire. Essentially, the stakeholders viewed the strategic visioning process as providing the opportunity to expand upon the traditional decision making structure and give both industry stakeholders and the local community a role in deciding the most appropriate future of the Shire.

Discussion

Although the concept of strategic visioning in a tourism destination context is relatively new and has yet to be explored in detail in either theory or practice, empirical evidence from its application in destinations such as the Gold Coast suggest that it may be an emerging best practice for achieving a coordinated strategic approach to planning for tourism destinations. While acknowledging the difficulties of public participation and other grass roots initiatives (Haywood 1988; Tremblay 2000), a strategic visioning process should be considered a preferable to some of the narrower approaches that have been advocated in the past, such as government disseminated planning or development decisions based solely on the desires of the local community.

As the Tweed Shire example demonstrates, the implementation of a strategic visioning programme allows for the expansion of traditional decision making structures and aims to give both industry stakeholders and the local community a stake in deciding the most appropriate future of the destination. In the Tweed situation it is seen as a vital mechanism for dismantling the traditional decision makers whose development decisions are not considered to be in the best interests of the community, and also to compensate for the fact that the state tourism authorities have (in the stakeholder's opinion) overlooked the area due to its geographical location. This situation is unlikely to be unique to the Tweed Shire.

Strategic visioning can potentially benefit regional and peripheral destinations, which face a number of specific challenges. Similar to the Tweed Shire, these destinations may be geographically isolated from decision making authorities, have changing economic structures and, if like the Tweed, the future of the destination is in the hands of an inexperienced local government who are unsure of (or unwilling) to manage and plan for such change. Similarly, Buhalis (1999) finds that the economic and political systems within peripheral destinations often make the area more vulnerable to external interests such as those of developers. Keeping in mind these challenges, several key benefits of strategic visioning for periphery tourism destinations are proposed, including the improved decision making capability, the emphasis on the future and the broader based collaboration among stakeholders.

Firstly, a strategic visioning process can assist local governments who have little or no experience in planning for a sector such as tourism. In Australia, primary industries have been the mainstay of rural and regional areas, but as these economic sectors face decline and tourism rises in importance, local government will have to rechannel its planning and management skills to cope with a sector such as tourism. Although local government should be the most appropriate body to plan and manage for tourism, this does not necessarily mean that they have the skills, capacity or resources to make the best decisions. Therefore a broader base of decision makers with a variety of experiences, knowledge and understanding of the tourism sector, could collectively solve a problem which could not be solved individually.

A second benefit of strategic visioning is the emphasis on the future. This is particularly important for destinations where tourism is an emerging economic sector that has the potential to change the structure of the community. As Getz & Jamal (1994) find, any type of development requires a plan, which clearly delineates the type and pace of tourism development, capacity and growth management policies, socio-cultural and environmental considerations as well as supply/demand parameters. Strategic visioning encompasses these issues by proactively looking to the future through the development of a vision and identifying the desired states of the destination before developing strategies to achieve those desired states.

Thirdly, strategic visioning is a mechanism for achieving the collaborative approach to planning and management discussed previously. One of the major appeals of strategic visioning is the emphasis the process places on stakeholder collaboration and participation in decision making to determine the future development of the destination. While the process of broader based decision making has often been impeded by traditional decision-makers who see it as a threat to their power, incorporating participation by the various destination stakeholders can lead to greater acceptance of tourism development. Therefore a collaborative approach where all stakeholders become party to, and share decision making responsibility for destination planning is more likely to result in acceptable and successful policies and programs, which in turn will lead to a successful tourism industry (Farrell 1986; Maitland 2002; Minca & Getz 1995).

Conclusion

This chapter has examined the relatively recent concept of strategic visioning for tourism destinations. Empirical evidence from strategic visioning programs conducted to date suggest that it is a useful means for achieving collaboration and consensus between the various destination stakeholders. Strategic visioning is a planning process, which although could benefit any type of destination planning, may be a particularly useful tool for peripheral destinations which face a number of specific challenges including geographical isolation from decision making authorities, changing economic structures and local governments inexperienced in dealing with tourism. Using the Tweed Shire to illustrate the applicability of the concept to peripheral regions, it can be seen that the process has the potential to lead to improved decision-making capabilities, an emphasis on the future and broader based collaboration among all stakeholders. However, future research into the application of strategic visioning will inevitably determine its success in practice.

Chapter 6

The Development of a Regional Identity for the Macarthur Region

Sharon Kemp

Introduction

The Macarthur region is a part of the Greater Western Sydney Region and comprises three local council areas, namely Camden Council, Campbelltown Council and Wollondilly Council. The areas of Camden and Campbelltown in the period prior to 2004 have been undergoing major economic, social and environmental changes that require a sustainable response (DOTARS, March 2002). The region suffers from regional unemployment, a population with significant representation from disadvantaged groups and negative perceptions by residents and non-residents.

The Australian Government Department of Transport and Regional Services has indicated that a sustainable response for regions experiencing major economic and social changes must: (a) strengthen the regional economy and create employment in the region; (b) transform vocational capabilities and labour force skills; (c) improve social conditions and make the region a desirable place to live, work and pursue leisure and recreational activities; (d) create closer community interaction by fostering new ideas and harnessing community energy, drive and self reliance; and (e) transfer knowledge and skills and utilise an action learning approach.

A number of studies to develop a strategy for parts of the Greater Western Sydney region have been completed over the last ten years including *A Tourism Action Plan for Greater Western Sydney* (Dwyer *et al.* 1995) and *A Tourism Strategy for Campbelltown* (Dwyer, Edwards & Valerio 1997). Each of the studies indicates that Western Sydney, and the Macarthur region in particular, has a negative image and lacks identity, but none indicates what action should be undertaken to rectify these shortcomings. Arguably a region lacking a positive image or distinctive identity cannot effectively compete with other regions and areas and therefore, regardless of its assets, the region will not fulfil its tourism potential. A further issue of critical importance is community and stakeholder involvement: to date none of the studies develop a community-based vision and strategy for regional development. This chapter outlines a research component of the "*In Our*

Own Backyard" project which was developed in order to remedy these shortcomings by addressing both issues of regional identity and a community-based vision and strategy. This research has developed an unprecedented coalition between community, business, university and government stakeholders within the Macarthur region. An important outcome to date has been the effective mobilisation of stakeholder energies to provide a basis for creating a sustainable tourism industry in the region.

It was considered that the first step should be to determine the character of the Macarthur region. The identity of a tourist destination is a major determinant of tourism flows and subsequent economic impacts on business sales, household income and employment. The identity of an area affects the hosts' levels of civic pride and its perceived desirability by guests. According to MacInnis & Price (1987) the strength of a region's identity pervades the whole consumption experience. Identity can entice consumption and beckon repeat consumption. Understanding the "drawing" effect that identity can have is valuable, enabling the salient attributes of the destination's identity to be incorporated into the tourism planning process and destination strategic marketing (see Selby & Morgan 1996). A positive, strong identity can be used to increase remembered satisfaction and encourage repeat visitation behaviour. Meanwhile the discovery of a negative and/or weak identity provides a basis for remedial and corrective action.

A second step in this research was to determine the assets and strengths of the Macarthur region. A good knowledge of the region's tourism assets, and the extent to which they match visitor needs is essential for tourism planning and marketing. At the time the study commenced there were no specific strategies in place to identify the Macarthur Region's cultural, natural and heritage sites of interest for either local residents or potential tourists. A number of tourism operators had been undertaking their own promotional activities in conjunction with their local council tourism offices but there was no unifying and integrated strategy to promote the wealth of tourism destinations and opportunities that many stakeholders believe the Macarthur region has to offer.

During preliminary discussions with a range of stakeholders in the Macarthur region it was identified that the region could be divided into eight distinctive segments in which the community have significant assets and experience of use as a basis for developing a new regional identity. The market segments are: (1) Culture/Heritage; (2) Rural Tourism and Nature based Tourism; (3) Food and Wine; (4) Adventure; (5) Accommodation; (6) Special Events; (7) Corporate Market-functions and Conferences; and (8) Industrial Tourism. Several of these themes were previously identified in the Tourism Plans developed for Greater Western Sydney and Campbelltown (Dwyer, Edwards & Valerio 1997; Dwyer *et al.* 1995). Although there are differences between these segments and those identified by Ritchie (1993) in his seminal attempt to develop a tourism vision for Calgary, the process he used for identifying the assets and strengths of Calgary was applied to this study. Ritchie developed "wheels" indicating the facilities, events or programs that:

- were already in place and required additional support to improve their recognition and quality;
- were proposed by stakeholders and were currently under review; and
- suggestions for new projects.

Figure 6.1 illustrates the concept and is derived from Ritchie (1993).

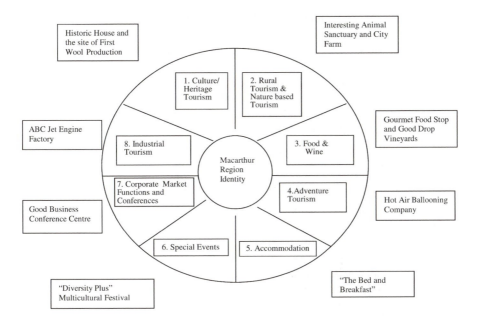

Figure 6.1: Ritchie's conceptualisation of "wheels" applied to the Macarthur Region.

The "wheels" provided a basis for the third step of this research, which was to conduct a visioning process for the future of the Macarthur region. What was already in place and suggestions for new projects were linked to the desired identity of the Macarthur region as decided by the community consultation processes. A research literature has emerged on how best to facilitate the development of tourism. One view, drawing heavily on the economic literature, argues that tourism and its associated entrepreneurship opportunities are best developed by helping and creating individual businesses and then letting them compete in the marketplace (see Eadington & Redman 1991). This view, however, has been criticised because: (1) it views tourism and tourism-related businesses as isolated from the larger community and its issues; (2) it does not recognise the interdependence of the various sectors and actors involved in tourism; and (3) most small tourism businesses, especially those in regional areas, do not have the individual resources to promote either themselves or the community as a tourist product (Gunn 1988; Murphy 1985; Palmer & Bejou 1995).

Opposing this view is the community approach to tourism development and entrepreneurship (Murphy 1985). As its name implies, the approach argues that tourism is a community product and that, along with entrepreneurial skills and the presence of tourist businesses, it is also necessary to have the community and local capabilities (e.g. local leadership, formal and informal networks) directly involved in tourism development and promotion effort (Murphy 1985). CEDA (1991) reinforces this view stating that "Resident responsive tourism is the watchword for tomorrow: community demands for active participation in the setting of the tourism agenda and its priorities for tourism development and management cannot be ignored". While the community approach may be an effective way to develop and promote tourism, creating the necessary inter-community cooperation and collaboration is a complex and difficult process. Businesses are asked to share resources while simultaneously competing. Local governments may see collaboration to develop tourism as risky, or they may be worried about losing control over local decision-making (Huang & Stewart 1996; Jamal & Getz 1995). Because of these problems, various researchers have noted that research on collaboration and those factors that allow for community development of tourism is a priority (e.g. Jamal & Getz 1995).

It can thus be argued that what is still largely missing from the literature is an identification of those factors and processes that help regional communities successfully develop tourism and entrepreneurship opportunities. There is a need for a best practice model that can be widely adopted in regional settings. The model should provide industry with broad guidelines as to the kinds of major facilities, events and programmes that members of the community find most consistent with their values and aspirations for the long-term development of their area and their own well-being.

This need for approaches to translate the concept of community participation in development into reality was recognised by Ritchie (1993). Ritchie (1993) refers to the writings of Mintzberg and his colleagues to draw the distinction between strategic planning and strategic visioning. As noted by Mintzberg (1990), strategic planning can be described as prescriptive in orientation, and is often a controlled conscious process of thought for which ultimate responsibility lies with the Chief Executive Officer of the organisation involved in strategy development. On the other hand "Visioning," according to Westley & Mintzberg (1989), is the envisioning of an image of a desired future organisational state that, when effectively communicated to followers, serves to empower those followers so they can enact the vision. Visioning is a dynamic, evolving process in which strategies take form as a result of learning over a period of time. Ritchie (1993) developed a community-based process to craft a "Vision" for the long-term development of tourism in the city of Calgary, Canada. After hosting the XVth Winter Olympic Games in 1988, Calgary needed to plan for the future diversification of the economy. While that desire was driven primarily by economic motives, it also reflected a desire to develop a broader range of activities and interests for residents to make the city a desirable and more vibrant place to live. A number of other authors have also pointed out the desirability of providing a broad-based citizen input into tourism-related policy and development decisions (Keough 1990). Additionally, a range of approaches for obtaining consensus, or at least unbiased input into the decision-making process, has been developed and tested (Ritchie 1988). However Ritchie's process for the crafting of a vision for tourism destinations is considered as ground breaking. Whilst it is acknowledged that other cities and regions have undertaken similar economic renewal initiatives, most have not emphasised the visioning process in tourism, based on meaningful citizen involvement, to the same extent. Ritchie's community-based process for crafting a vision for tourism has not, hitherto, been applied in Australia. His process was, however, considered an exemplar of best practice for tourism development in an area or region and was adopted in this research for application to the Macarthur region.

There is a strong and growing recognition that a greater balance needs to be struck in weighing the desires of visitors against the wellbeing of their hosts. There is a need to recognise that tourism must benefit the local community and that there must be broad-based participation in tourism development decisions at the community level. There is a realisation that while tourism enhances community life; it can also threaten the well being of residents as well as the values they hold, hence the need to solicit broad-based community input into tourism development.

The fourth step of developing goals for the Macarthur region involved tourism operators and other stakeholders in formulating goals for each of the eight market segments using the vision and the previously identified assets and strengths of the region.

Methodology

Mintzberg's visioning process was carried out using a focus group methodology. According to Echtner & Ritchie (1991) the failure of most studies to address the holistic components of destination identity is related to the methods used by researchers. In the tourism literature there had been a strong preference for structured methods that concentrate on the attribute component of destination identity. The use of structured methods, such as Likert and semantic differential scales, requires an individual to rate a set of pre-determined attributes subjectively, or to characterise stimuli using standardised rating scales. Because this type of procedure involves a priori list of attributes to which an individual is supposed to respond, it might be relatively unreliable (Timmermans *et al.* 1982: 191). The weakness in the structured method is that some or all of the attributes might be totally unimportant to the individual, or important attributes may be missing. The elicitation of constructs from respondents through qualitative research minimises the danger of forcing respondents to react to a standardised framework that may not be an accurate representation of their image.

Focus groups were used to overcome the methodological weaknesses discussed above. In the groups participants discussed the Macarthur region's current identity, the strengths and weaknesses of the region and the broad parameters within which tourism development should take place. The examination of these issues exposed participants' values and what they desire as an identity for the region. Extensive notes were taken during the focus groups, and then the important dimensions, constructs and attributes were extracted. The categorization process needed to be transparent to avoid the researcher's own biases being imbued in the results. To ensure transparency the research team[1] documented the development of the categorisation system using a process of constant comparison, revision and modification to identify and code the specific dimensions and themes contained in the field notes.

Preliminary discussions with key stakeholders and members of the community identified eight possible tourism themes for the Macarthur region. Some of these themes were identified in the Tourism Action Plan for Greater Western Sydney (1996). Participants were invited to join the tourism theme that was most relevant to their experience and interests. Each "tourism theme group" had its own focus group conducted. Focus groups were used to obtain in-depth information regarding community member's (residents, businesses and other key stakeholders) views as to the strengths and assets of the region as well as their views and attitudes regarding the range of initiatives considered appropriate for the process

---

[1] Team members assisting in various aspects of the research study were: Damien Battisson, Lyn Davey, Roger Golding, Tracy Gordon, Neva Gregory, Melinda Harley, Roderick Kemp, David Mason, Rebecca Sheraton, Kevin Williams.

of tourism development in the region — i.e. those that will fit with the identity they desired for the region (Agar & McDonald 1995; Milman 1993; Morgan 1988). As Dean (1994: 342) noted, a "focus group is an informal, small-group discussion designed to obtain in-depth qualitative information" and is an excellent method to study processes. Members of the Macarthur community were invited through a range of media announcements, and mailing lists provided by the region's Tourist Information Offices to two meetings regarding "Tourism Development in the Macarthur Region." One meeting was held in Campbelltown and one meeting in Camden, as it is these two local government areas that have the largest numbers of residents. Attendees were asked to provide details of how they would like to receive future contact to the researchers. The purpose of the project and the visioning method was explained to the meeting. Attendees were invited to express an interest in being involved in the focus groups and the tourism themes/market segments they had an interest in. The contact information supplied was used to notify arrangements for focus group discussions.

The first round of group sessions for each theme were conducted to establish a benchmark of what tourism assets currently existed in the Macarthur region that required changes and or additional support in order to meet the quality standards (key result area indicators) perceived by focus group members to be appropriate for the Macarthur Regional Tourism Strategy. Information already known was used (Dwyer *et al.* 1995) but it needed to be updated, since the Dwyer *et al.* study was already eight years old. A second round of group sessions was conducted to suggest new projects and initiatives that flowed logically from the vision for the Macarthur region.

Care was exercised in selecting focus group participants and writing the questions for the focus groups. However, the project leader was present at each focus group session. The focus groups used the tourism theme groups already identified in the Macarthur region. The number of participants per focus group was set at eight, to ensure a deep level of discussion to fully explore issues and suggestions. The average length of the discussion in the focus groups was 40 minutes.

Different sets of questions/focus group protocols were developed for each of the tourism theme groups. These were developed by the study team and piloted to practice and fine-tune the moderation skills needed for conducting the focus groups. The project team then reviewed and revised the questions and probes. The questions and probes were then pre-tested and further revised.

The study team also developed a set of focus group procedures that helped to increase reliability and consistency across the focus groups. Debriefings were conducted and field notes were made as soon as possible after each focus group.

Discussion

According to Mayo (1973) and Crompton (1979) regional image and identity are important because they influence the decision-making behaviour of potential tourists. Identity is a critical factor in a tourist's destination choice process. It is important that the projected identity match reality because action proceeds on the basis of subjective reality and assumes that the identity is a true representation. According to MacInnis & Price (1987) image and identity pervades the whole touristic consumption experience. Understanding the various

Table 6.1: Attributes of the Macarthur Region.

Scenic/natural attractions
Hospitality/friendliness/receptiveness of people
Costs/price levels reasonable
Sports facilities/activities
Shopping facilities
Personal safety
Interesting cuisine
Restful and relaxing environment
Accessibility/not too far from Sydney
Historic sites and museums
Accommodation facilities
Tourist sites and activities
Local infrastructure/transportation
National parks and wilderness areas
Interesting architecture and buildings
Uncrowded
Cleanliness/tidiness
Opportunities for adventure
Facilities for information/tours
Atmosphere
Family or adult oriented
Opportunity to increase knowledge
Quality of service
Fairs/exhibitions/festivals
Extent of commercialisation
Degree of urbanisation
Friends and relatives
Wildlife
Sophistication
Interesting
Busy/exciting
Local people
Small towns
Authenticity
Quality of merchandise
Water activities
Wide open spaces
Diversity/different culture

images that visitors and non-visitors associate with a destination is invaluable, enabling the salient attributes of the naive image and the more accurate re-evaluated image to be taken into account in marketing strategy and re-positioning exercises if necessary. What is important to note, according to Jenkins & McArthur (1996) is that each person's image of a particular place is unique, comprising their own memories, associations and imaginations of a particular place. A region's identity may be supplied to the market place in a uniform and planned way but its consumption and decision- making regarding visitation will be fragmented at the level of the individual. The focus groups identified the attributes shown in Table 6.1.

The most commonly mentioned attributes of the Macarthur region were in order of frequency: accessibility/not too far from Sydney, wide open spaces, restful and relaxing environment, friendliness and hospitality of local people, the extent of commercialisation (appropriate, not too much), historic sites and museums, interesting architecture and buildings, and opportunities to increase knowledge.

Those attributes that were mentioned in a negative context were: lack of accommodation facilities/little variety in accommodation offerings, tourist sites and activities are not linked or themed, the standard of cleanliness/tidiness was below what would be expected by a visitor, there is a lack of sophistication about the area and its people, and there is a lack of fairs/exhibitions and festivals compared to surrounding tourist areas to keep people coming back to the region.

The process revealed the Macarthur region has some significant attributes upon which to base its identity. Equally the negative attributes were items that could be successfully countered with well-planned strategies. It can be observed that Macarthur is a newer region with a growing population and so aspects of infrastructure such as accommodation, which are demand driven, would not be expected to be as well developed as those found in well established tourist destinations nearby such as the Blue Mountains or the Southern Highlands. The perceived sub-standard level of cleanliness and tidiness could be targeted by the three local councils in the region as a special project. The Environment Protection Agency has had past successful campaigns which they can launch and relaunch when needed to remedy problems of littering. The local councils in the region could tailor their clean-up campaign to complement the EPA's anti-litter campaign launch. A lack of sophistication is not necessarily a negative. If the region wants to develop an identity as a place where visitors "get away from it all" to enjoy the "wide open spaces" and the "friendliness and hospitality of local people" then a relaxed "down to earth" approach is more in keeping with these attributes than sophistication and slickness. Fairs, exhibitions and festivals are important to many regions; however such major events require significant planning and investment of resources and undertaking financial risk. Without a guarantee of visitor numbers it would be unwise to expand the number of events staged until there was an indication that attendance numbers were consistently increasing at existing events. Tourist sites and activities are not presently linked or themed in the Macarthur region. This fact does not necessarily represent a negative attribute of the Macarthur region; it can be seen as an opportunity. The identification and classification of the region's assets, using Ritchie's wheel applied to the eight segments that were previously identified, will contribute to addressing this attribute.

After formulating strategies to address the perceived negative attributes of the Macarthur region, a number of themes that capture the desired regional identity for the Macarthur region were identified from the focus groups. The themes in descending order of mention included:

A Breath of Fresh Air — Take in Macarthur
Rediscover Real People and Real Places
Wine, Wheat and Wool — Where it All Began
Simple Pleasures
Delight Your Senses in the Macarthur Region

From the above themes one can argue that what focus group respondents' value above all is the fact that the Macarthur region is accessible from a number of areas within Sydney, that it has wide open spaces and is a destination that tourists can visit for the purpose of rest and relaxation. Macarthur is seen as a pleasant contrast with the perceived busy and crowded environment of Sydney. In the Macarthur region tourists are able to escape the hustle and bustle of everyday life by literally taking a breath of fresh air in the wide open spaces of the Macarthur region.

The focus group respondents were also proud of the fact that there is a high level of hospitality, friendliness and receptiveness shown to people living and working in the Macarthur region that is also extended to visitors. There is a sense of community that draws people together and creates a pleasant atmosphere in the region. The other attributes of authenticity and quality of merchandise and quality of service indicates that the people of the Macarthur want their environment to "stay true to itself" and not compromise the standard of its offerings or merchandise. Commercialisation and erosion of standards may increase the amount of income generated from tourists in the short term but be detrimental to the region in the longer-term.

The focus group respondents also felt that the history of the Macarthur region was an important contributor to the region's identity. Focus group respondents specifically mentioned historic sites, museums, interesting architecture and buildings. The Macarthur region has an extensive register of historic buildings, cottages and churches as well as historic sites relating to industry and agriculture. Some of the earliest sites of wine grape production, wheat breeding and wool growing in Australia are located in the Macarthur region.

Conclusions

Previously conducted studies of the Greater Western Sydney region have identified the poor image of the Macarthur region and its lack of distinctive identity as a major barrier to tourism development. They have not indicated what action should be undertaken to rectify these shortcomings. This paper has detailed the process of involving the community and other stakeholders in developing a collaborative vision, goals and strategies to develop a distinctive identity for the region to underpin a regional tourism strategy. An action learning process was embedded in the project's methodology and approach. Central to this approach was local stakeholder participation which created a sense of ownership of the identity which was collaboratively developed with the research team. A sense of ownership of the regional identity was seen as important to ensure ongoing commitment from the community to the "In Our Own Backyard" project.

The research study adopted a strategic approach to "visioning" the future for the Macarthur region. A number of steps were undertaken. The first step was to determine the current identity of the Macarthur region. The second was to determine the assets and strengths of the Macarthur region. Ritchie's "wheels" provided a basis for the third step of this study, which was to conduct a visioning process for the future of the Macarthur region. What was already in place and suggestions for new projects were linked to the desired identity of the Macarthur region as decided by the community consultation processes. The fourth step of developing goals for the Macarthur region involved tourism operators and other stakeholders in formulating goals for each of the eight market segments using the vision and the previously identified assets and strengths of the region.

One outcome of this research study is the development of a best practice model for the development of a regional identity that can be widely adopted in other regional settings elsewhere. The four step process combined with an action learning approach engendered wide community involvement and an important sense of ownership of the regional identity. It is suggested that the process should provide industry with broad guidelines as to the kinds of major facilities, events and programs that members of the community find most consistent with their values and aspirations for the long-term development of their area and their own well-being.

Section 2

Nature-Based Tourism

Chapter 7

Nature-Based Tourism

Stephen J. Page

Tourism and Nature: Three Propositions

The conference theme of *Taking Tourism to the Limits* is both an appropriate and topical focus for an industry which trades upon the basic premise — that the earth's resources can be used for human enjoyment through leisure and tourism activities. With a growing environmental consciousness among some sections of modern society, tourism raises many philosophical issues if one considers the conference theme. Among the questions this raises, are:

- Should tourism be allowed to take the earth's resource base to its limits?
- How does the tourism industry view the world and what world views exist?
- What are the implications for natural areas, given the continued growth in niche markets such as ecotourism?

If the role of the academic is to pose critical views and to question prevailing assumptions and critiques of society, tourism academics have a duty to act as a counterbalance to the profit-led, short-term and global power of the tourism industry rather than simply endorsing their views. Tourism has a long tradition of academic questioning of the way the industry seeks to take tourism to the limits of the resource base which natural areas can cope with, as reflected in seminal studies such as Krippendorf (1987). Whilst such studies are informed by scholarly activity, they have highlighted a fundamental distinction which exists in the world views held by different components of the tourism industry.

Essentially, Page & Dowling (2002: 3) observe that "the two most common [world views] vary according to whether or not they are human-centred as opposed to environment focused" which are two opposing paradigms, located along a continuum ranging from the anthropocentric (dominant human-centred world view) through to the ecocentric view as shown in Table 7.1. In essence, the human-centred view typifies the traditional tourism industry perspective, prior to the rise of environmentalism, where people are the dominant species on the planet, and that the earth has a limitless supply of resources to meet all human needs, including tourism. The use of technology and science has enabled the earth's limits

Taking Tourism to the Limits: Issues, Concepts and Managerial Perspectives
ISBN: 0-08-044644-2

Table 7.1: The dominant worldview (anthropocentricism) and ecocentric view.

Dominant Worldview	Ecocentric View
Dominance over nature	Harmony with nature
Natural environment as a resource to be exploited by humans	All elements of nature have intrinsic worth
Economic development is necessary for human development	Humans have simple material needs
The reserves of resources are plentiful	The earth's resources are finite
Technology will provide solutions to environmental and resource-related problems	Appropriate technology is needed which is in balance with nature
Consumerism	Recycling
National/centralised community	Minority tradition

Source: Page and Dowling (2002: 3).

to be explored and exploited for tourism. In contrast, the minority view, a life-centred one which respects the biodiversity of the earth and the harmony which exists between man and nature, has received less attention, particularly by the tourism industry (even among supposed proponents of green tourism). Yet if tourism is a resource-dependent industry, where tourism activities are based upon the concept of attractivity (Page 2000), then the earth is a delicate series of ecosystems which are interdependent and tourism can easily destroy the delicate balance which exists, and environmental problems can arise, since the earth has a finite range of resources. Environmental problems induced by tourism normally occur through mass intervention in these delicate ecosystems.

In a thought-provoking review of this tension between the dominant anthropocentric views of the tourism industry and the growing importance of the ecocentric view, Yeoman (2000) pointed to the global environmental problems related to tourism and rise of ecological ethics. This highlighted the inter-connectedness of different environmental systems and the principle that humans are an important species but are not superior to other species. Yeoman also pointed to the concept of intrinsic value, where every living thing has a right to live and is not determined according to their value to humans. Yeoman argued that sustainability was another important concept, where biodiversity and preservation were key reasons for achieving a balance between competing users of resources. However, the principle of inter-generational equity also highlights the need to leave the earth in the same shape as one finds it, if not better. Many societies, and indigenous people practised (and still do practise) these principles. Yet as Devall & Sessions (1985) suggest, humans dominate other species as wildlife-based tourism has highlighted in less controlled settings, often using marketing labels such as ecotourism, green tourism and environmental tourism to promote their products. Tourism as an industry therefore has a tendency to exploit the earth and its resources and the dominant world view has a continuous quest for the next niche market and its potential using these new labels and rebranding exercises to seek higher profits. Therefore, with these issues in mind, how have academics approached this controversy?

It is not surprising to find that tourism academics have embraced the natural environment as one of the trendy subjects to research in the 1990s. A cursory evaluation of Leisure, Recreation and Tourism Abstracts in February 2004 found 641 abstracts featuring "ecotourism" for the period 2002–2004 which also include items on natural areas. Research activity in this area has multiplied since the reviews by Page (2000) and Page & Dowling (2002). The research is being published across a wide range of subject areas including tourism, recreation, environmental science, forestry, planning, geography, politics, economics and other areas of social science. Among some of the recent syntheses published of this rapidly expanding literature are Newsome, Moore & Dowling (2002), with its explicit focus on natural areas from an environmental perspective. One of the most wide-ranging reference works to appear is Weaver's (2003) *Encyclopaedia of Ecotourism* although this is less of an encyclopaedia, but a simple collection of essays on specific themes produced as a handbook. This does, however, provide an overview of current thinking in the area. Other contributions on policy and planning exist (Fennell 2002; Fennell & Dowling 2003) with a focus on the less developed world (Weaver 1998) and the all-essential descriptive set of case studies (Buckley 2003) along with texts such as Fennell (1999), Wearing & Neil (1999) and Page & Dowling (2002). In the wider natural world context a range of monographs focused on National Parks and protected areas have also appeared (e.g. Butler & Boyd 2000).

This collection of texts and monographs certainly demarcates the ecotourism and natural world as key themes in both the teaching of tourism and in research. Yet the research activity is probably out of balance in tourism studies as one overriding theme now driving the research agenda. However, critics of this viewpoint would argue that if the sustainability paradigm is considered, as a way of approaching tourism, then ecotourism and natural areas are a sub-set of this approach to tourism which involve a philosophical stance on tourism as something to permit, albeit in balance with nature (if this can ever truly be achieved). In this respect natural areas and ecotourism cannot be pigeon-holed from the other dimensions of sustainability, such as planning and development (also discussed later in this book in the next section). Whether one endorses or rejects this argument, the quality of the research activity generated by this explosion in the number of publications on this theme is telling. This is a highly subjective issue and certainly open to varying interpretations. In the ecotourism field, the number of textbooks now published highlights the problem of agreeing definitions, working propositions and criteria which researchers can agree on to progress the field. To the contrary, it seems that each new book wishes to reinvent the wheel, by claiming a unique approach that has universal validity, which makes progress in knowledge in this area problematic. Not surprisingly, many of the journal articles are also descriptive case studies of particular places, projects or themes which may provide empirical data, but this does not generate a cohesive body of knowledge. To the contrary, taking stock of where knowledge is at any point in time is problematic because one has to wade through so many studies that only add a limited number of new insights. The proliferation of this area of research has also been supported by the launch of a *Journal of Ecotourism*. Consequently, in any literature review of this area of research, the same seminal studies are cited by researchers as a core of knowledge, with dedicated researchers working in this area as opposed to the "dabblers" who make forays into what is seen as a trendy and popular theme. As Weaver (1998: 1) rightly acknowledged, "terms such as sustainable tourism, alternative tourism and ecotourism, which were not even in the lexicon 20 years ago, are now the objects of intense scrutiny, debate and controversy. At present, there is no consensus at all surrounding the use of the term ecotourism." Weaver's assessment is as valid today as it was in 1998. It is not surprising that researchers keep referring back to seminal studies such as Boo's (1990) *Ecotourism: The Potential and Pitfalls* and the work of Weaver, Wright, Fennell, Lindberg, Eagles and Dowling together with the seminal environment-tourism nexus studies which highlight the delicate balance which exists from an ecocentric perspective. Therefore, if knowledge is to make significant advances in this area, a greater philosophical debate on the natural area and ecotourism relating to epistemology (see Jaakson 1997) and ethical issues (see Malloy & Fennell 1998) are necessary. Whilst empiricism is certainly the easy option for many researchers, more philosophical and theoretical debates are now needed, perhaps by engaging researchers from outside of tourism and environmental studies to generate fresh ideas, new perspectives and to infuse a new critical perspective of where this research domain is going.

Therefore, how do the papers in this section of the book fit with the wider development of knowledge on this burgeoning area of research?

The first chapter by Orams and Taylor is a contribution from a leading marine tourism researcher, Orams, who has worked on this area, cultivating a specialism in much the way that some of the leading researchers listed above have done. Orams and Taylor focus on one of the most controversial and contested areas of ecotourism — the viewing and involvement of humans with mammals. This goes right to the roots of the anthropocentric-ecocentric debate, as to whether humans should be interacting with mammals, and if they do, how this interaction is managed. The more scrupulous and ethical ecotour operators working in this area have highlighted the environmentally educative value which ecotourism can offer. As Page & Dowling (2002: 67) suggest, "environmental education and interpretation are important tools in creating an enjoyable and meaningful ecotourism experience . . . . Ecotourism education can influence tourist, community and industry behaviour and assist in long-term sustainability of tourism activity in natural areas." Therefore, Orams and Taylor's chapter is a valuable contribution in highlighting how well-thought ecotourism can be, rather than being exploitative.

The next chapter by Duffy examines what is a neglected theme, the politics of ecotourism. At different spatial scales and in different environments, the politics of tourism are often a hidden element of tourism. The political dimension is frequently overlooked, yet it invariably determines what happens when, why and where. Indeed, ecotourism raises many ethical issues for communities and can become extremely political when the competing needs of stakeholders at the local level are examined. Add to this the wider political agenda of local politicians and national governments seeking to drive tourism employment and revenue generation, then the politicisation of ecotourism become a complex issue. Yet understanding the political dynamics of ecotourism, as Duffy's chapter shows, is far from an easy theme to address. This is very much reiterated in the seminal tourism: public policy monograph by Kerr (2003) which introduced many of the theoretical issues which researchers have to grapple with in understanding the politics literature, particularly concepts and theoretical propositions on political philosophy.

In the next chapter, Draper reviews many of the issues raised by ecotourism encounters, that of authenticity and how such experiences are viewed. This reveals the importance of the initial debate on ecotourism and dominant worldviews vs. a more ecocentric perspective, since Ryan *et al.* (2000: 161) acknowledged that "ecotourism has its own anthropology of symbols and signifiers ... ecotourism is not simply another form of consumerism whereby the tourists legitimises the act of consumption ... in a nutshell, to return to an earlier statement, tourists tour for reasons of change and relaxation — rarely are they lay anthropologists, botanists or environmental scientists. As consumers of tourism, their choice of the tourist product is akin to the consumption of other products." This commentary by Ryan *et al.* (2000) reinforces the dilemma inherent in such ecotourism encounters, in both the provision of an experience (i.e. if it is ecocentric in focus and in the way it is developed) but also in the way tourists engage in such encounters, which may not have anything to do with conservation, environmental education and appropriate tourism development. To the contrary, it may be seen as the latest "must have" fashion accessory which highlights the status-laden nature of many environmentally-related holidays. Therefore, this chapter raises many of the fundamental philosophical and ethical issues raised at the outset in this review.

The last chapter in this section by Manning, examining the limits of tourism in National Parks and Protected Areas and is both a useful conclusion to this section of the book and a lead into the next section on planning and development. Ecotourism exploits natural areas and this chapter poses many of the critical issues related to the ability of such areas to absorb tourism and what the real limits to development are before they are destroyed. Sustainability is a critical concept in this debate, although there is also an argument raised by such a focus — that is, should all areas be developed and exploited for tourism?, or is there a case for leaving areas to be free of human intervention, which highlights the importance of philosophical debates raised in this review, the politics of development and what happens when ecotourism is allowed to develop. This chapter therefore raises many critical issues which are explored further elsewhere in this book.

Chapter 8

Making Ecotourism Work: An Assessment of the Value of an Environmental Education Programme on a Marine Mammal Tour in New Zealand

Mark Orams and Amy Taylor

Introduction

The rapid growth of ecotourism has been widely reported (Weaver 2001). Accompanying this growth has been an increasing focus on ecotourism as a specialist area within the wider tourism management field. The recent establishment of the *Journal of Sustainable Tourism* and the *Journal of Ecotourism* and the publication of a variety of books on the subject (e.g. Page & Dowling 2002; Weaver 2001) reflect the growing body of literature that focuses on the subject. It is now generally excepted that ecotourism should include three major components; that it is focussed on a nature-based tourism attraction in a natural setting, that it is managed in a sustainable manner and that it includes an educational component for the tourists (Valentine 1990; Weaver 2001).

One of the most dramatic examples of the growth of ecotourism has been the increase of cetacean (whales, dolphins and porpoises) based tours. Hoyt (2000) completed an overview of the industry worldwide and concluded that that by 1998 nearly 500 communities and almost 100 countries or territories were involved in dolphin and whale based tourism. He also estimated that the worldwide economic impact derived from whale and dolphin watching activities in 1998 totaled more than US$1 billion.

In association with this growth has been a growing concern regarding the potential impacts of this industry on the targeted animals (Beach & Weinrich 1989). A variety of studies have been directed at quantifying these impacts (for example, Acevedo 1991; Barr 1997; Bejder & Dawson 1998; Bejder, Dawson & Harraway 1999; Constantine 1999, 2001; Constantine & Baker 1997; Corkeron 1995; Kruse 2000; Nowacek 1999) and developing management strategies to minimise negative impacts (for example, see Curran, Wilson & Thompson 1996; Lusseau & Higham 2004). By comparison, there is a general lack of research into how cetacean-based tourism affects the participating tourists (notable exceptions include,

Amante-Helweg 1996; Neil, Orams & Baglioni 1996; Orams 1997). In particular, there has been little consideration of the educational value of these tours for the participants. This is somewhat surprising because the incorporation of education into ecotours is held to be an essential component of ecotourism (Weaver 2001) and also because the great majority of cetacean-based tourism operators do attempt to include education and interpretation as part of their service (personal observation, first author). What is even more significant is that, in New Zealand, the Marine Mammals Protection Regulations (1978: Section 6h) state that "the commercial operation should have sufficient educational value to participants or to the public." This requirement contains wording which, at the least, implies that educational services should not only be offered but should have "educational value." Thus, it is surprising that no research in New Zealand (to date) has attempted to assess this issue and clarify whether this regulation is being met.

As a result of the lack of attention to this area, a study was designed to assess the value of the education program offered onboard a permitted marine mammal tour operator (Dolphin Explorer Ltd) operating in the Hauraki Gulf, Auckland, New Zealand. More specifically the following research objectives were set:

(1) To evaluate the educational services offered by Dolphin Explorer, and to assess the value (impact) of those services on the participating tourists.
(2) To consider how the tourist's experience onboard Dolphin Explorer affects their knowledge, understanding, attitudes, and intentions to change behaviour.

Methods

Study Site and Setting

A survey was conducted during the 2001/2002 summer period onboard Dolphin Explorer, a 20 metre GRP passenger catamaran powered by twin Scania nine litre (300 kw) diesel inboard motors. The vessel has a capacity of 100 passengers but restricts numbers to less than 85 for marine mammal tours. It operates daily (conditions permitting) from the ferry terminal in downtown Auckland. Trips typically are four to five hours in duration and (primarily) focus on viewing common dolphins (*Delphinus delphis*) in the Hauraki Gulf (see Map 8.1). Dolphin Explorer's marine mammal tour permit also allows them to conduct "swimming with dolphins" (adult common dolphins only) as part of their marine mammal tour, however, swimming occurs infrequently, primarily because the majority of common dolphin groups in the Hauraki Gulf contain juveniles and calves (New Zealand Marine Mammal Protection Regulations expressly forbid swimming with dolphins of these age classes). In addition, the operator is permitted to view other marine mammals when they are encountered. The species most frequently seen (in addition to common dolphins) are Bryde's whales (*Balaenoptera edeni*). Bottlenose dolphins (*Tursiops truncatus*), Sei whales (*Balaenoptera borealis*) and Killer whales (*Orcinus orca*) are also sometimes seen.

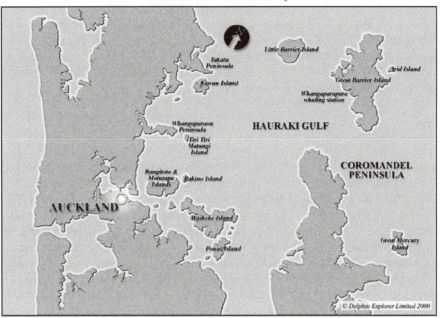

Map 8.1: The study region.

Research Design

Eleven trips were randomly selected for surveying during the summer (austral) of 2001/2002. A researcher accompanied each of these voyages (with the support of the operator) and administered a self-reply questionnaire to passengers onboard the vessel. After an introduction to the researcher and the research project over the vessel's public address system, all passengers over 15 years of age were approached and requested to complete a matched two-part self-reply questionnaire. This questionnaire contained a cover letter advising the respondent of the objectives of the project and containing statements guaranteeing their anonymity and the confidentiality of their responses (these guarantees are required for all research carried out under the auspices of Massey University).

Respondents completed part one of the questionnaire soon after departure from the embarkation point on their way out to the area where dolphins were usually sighted. These responses constituted the "before trip" data set. Respondents were then asked to complete the second part of the questionnaire on the return voyage after departing from the dolphin viewing area (in the inner harbour area soon before leaving the vessel at the end of the tour). This part (two) of the questionnaire constituted the "after trip" data set. With the exception of socio-demographic data, questions were matched (identical) in both part one and part two of the questionnaire, thus a comparison of responses from before the experience with after the experience was possible.

Questions of both an open and closed format were used in order to maximise the range of responses received and to allow for both quantitative and qualitative comparisons to be made (Orams & Page 1999). Questions were designed to assess respondents' knowledge, attitudes toward the natural environment and behavioural intentions. Thus, the study was designed to replicate the question format used by Orams (1997) in a previous study where he assessed the effectiveness of an environmental education programme in prompting more environmentally responsible behaviour in tourists.

The Question of "Value"

While the New Zealand Marine Mammals Protection Regulations (1992: Section 6h) require "sufficient educational value" there has been no clarification regarding what this "value" constitutes. To date, this regulation has not been tested in a legal sense. The New Zealand Department of Conservation (responsible for administering the regulations) has adopted an "advocacy and support" approach toward marine mammal tour operators rather than a prescriptive approach and, as a result, no definition of "value" in this context is available. Thus, for the purposes of this study the question of what is "sufficient value" is interpreted in terms of published literature on ecotourism and the purpose of educational services associated with the ecotourism experience. Orams (1995) argues that ecotourism management strategies should attempt to move ecotourists from a state where they simply minimise their impact on the host natural environment (attraction) to a state where they actively contribute to the health and viability of that environment. He argues that this transition is (or should be) the purpose of educational services offered as part of the ecotourism experience and that participants' knowledge, attitudes and intentions to change their behaviour are suitable indicators of this transition. For the purposes of this study these indicators were chosen to be a suitable means to assess the "educational value" of the marine mammal tour.

Results

Knowledge

In an attempt to gain an insight into learning pertaining to knowledge of cetaceans, respondents were asked to rate their knowledge about whales and dolphins before the trip, and were also asked how much they thought they had learnt about whales and dolphins as a result of the trip. Most respondents thought they had "average" knowledge (34%), "below average" knowledge (28%), or "very little" knowledge (33%) about cetaceans before the trip (see Table 8.1).

The majority of respondents also indicated they considered that they had learnt "some" (42.8%), 32.9% thought they had learnt "a lot," and 17.5% thought they had learnt "a little." Only 1% of all respondents thought they had learnt "nothing" from the trip, and 6% thought they had learnt "a huge amount." A χ^2 test showed that the amount the respondents' considered that they learned did not depend on their assessment of their prior knowledge ($\chi^2 = 5.807$, df $= 6$, $p = 0.445$).

Table 8.1: Self-assessment of knowledge of cetaceans before trip and amount learnt during trip.

% Within Personal Rating of Knowledge of Cetaceans (Before Trip)	Personal Rating of Learning About Cetaceans from Trip (After Trip)					Total
	Nothing (%)	A Little (%)	Some (%)	A Lot (%)	A Huge Amount (%)	
Personal rating of knowledge of cetaceans (before trip)						
Very little	1.0	19.6	41.2	28.9	9.3	97
Below average		20.7	39.0	35.4	4.9	82
Average	2.0	14.0	50.0	30.0	4.0	100
Above average		8.3	25.0	66.7		12
Excellent				100.0		1
Total	1.0	17.5	42.8	32.9	5.8	292

Table 8.2: Percentage of correct answers for true/false questions (before and after trip).

Question: (T = true, F = false)	% Correct Before	% Correct After
• Dolphins are always friendly towards people (F)	39.7	50.7
• Common dolphins are usually found in larger groups than bottlenose dolphins (T)	29	58.7
• Common dolphins are found in close family groups (F)	3.3	10.7
• In adult Common dolphins, males are usually larger than females (F)	18.3	26.3
• There are no porpoises found in New Zealand waters (T)	6.7	15.3
• Brydes whales are only found in New Zealand (F)	18.7	24.7
• Brydes whales use echolocation or sonar to find food (F)	5.3	6.3
• The scientific name given to all whales, dolphins and porpoises is "Cetaceans" (T)	33	59.3

Thus, the majority of passengers onboard the tour considered that they had average, below average, or very little knowledge of cetaceans before the trip, and assessed that they had learned "some" or "a lot" from the experience onboard the vessel.

In order to provide a more independent assessment regarding learning respondents were asked to answer eight matched true/false questions before and after the trip. These questions tested a range of knowledge issues relating to cetacean biology and behaviour relevant to the tour (both of a general and specific nature). Results (Table 8.2) showed a significant increase in the number of correct answers for all questions answered after the trip ($z = -3.08$, $p = 0.001$). However, the number of correct answers for some questions remained surprisingly low (Table 8.2).

Attitudes Toward the Natural Environment

Respondents were asked to indicate the level to which they agreed/disagreed with three statements about the environment. Each of these statements was designed to assess respondents' attitudes towards important environmental conservation issues relevant to a marine mammal tour in this location. In addition, each statement was "personalised" in an effort to render the statement relevant to the respondent's own personal attitude (as opposed to a response that might reflect a general societal attitude or socially desirable response). Statement 1: "*Pollution of the sea has little to do with me as it is primarily caused by industry*" showed little change between the before and after trip data sets ($\chi^2 = 7.254$, $df = 5$, $p = 0.202$). However, 30% of respondents strongly disagreed with the statement before the trip, and 33% respondents strongly disagreed after the trip (see Figure 8.1).

The second statement "*when dolphins or seals cause a reduction in the amount of fish available for humans, a 'cull' (reduction) of some of those dolphins or seals is justified*" also resulted in small increase in the "correct" response (i.e. a response reflecting an

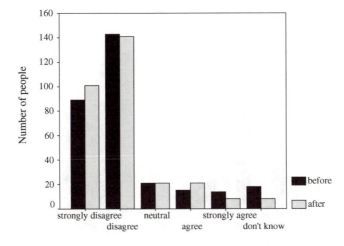

Figure 8.1: Pollution of the sea has little to do with me as it is primarily caused by industry.

environmentally sound attitude), 40% of respondents strongly disagreed with the statement before the trip, whereas 49% respondents strongly disagreed after the trip (see Figure 8.3). This change was not significant ($\chi^2 = 10.671$, df $= 5$, $p = 0.058$).

There was a significant change in the responses to the third statement from before to after the trip ($\chi^2 = 122.402$, df $= 5$, $p = 0.000$). Seventeen percent of respondents strongly disagreed with the statement "*it's better to swim with young (juvenile) dolphins because they enjoy it more*" before the trip, compared to 53% after the trip (see Figure 8.2). In addition, there was a large decrease in the number of respondents who selected "don't know" before the trip (36%), to after the trip (7%).

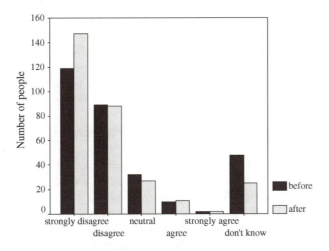

Figure 8.2: When dolphins or seals cause a reduction in the amount of fish available for humans a "cull" (reduction) of some of those dolphins and seals is justified.

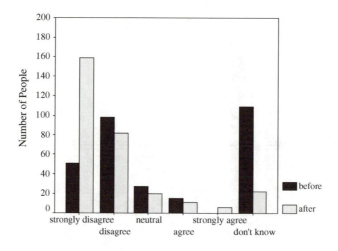

Figure 8.3: It's better to swim with young (juvenile) dolphins because they enjoy it more.

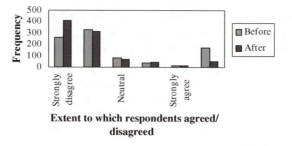

Figure 8.4: Total results from environmental attitude statements.

The largest difference in response to the environmental attitude statements was that the majority of respondents who selected "don't know" before the trip, changed to selecting "strongly disagree" (the "correct" response after the trip (see Figures 8.3 and 8.4).

Behavioural Intentions Relevant to the Environment

Prior to the trip respondents were asked how certain "behaviour" relevant to environmental conservation applied to them. After the trip they were asked about the same behaviour, and if their experiences on the tour had influenced their intentions with regard to that behaviour. The first statement asked respondents to consider their usual behaviour when seeing litter at a beach and to select whether they would either "always," "frequently," "sometimes," "seldom" or "never" pick up that litter. The question preface also asked respondents to be "please be as honest as you can." A significant change was evident in the results from before and after the trip with regard to this statement ($\chi^2 = 50.574$, df $= 5, p = 0.000$). The

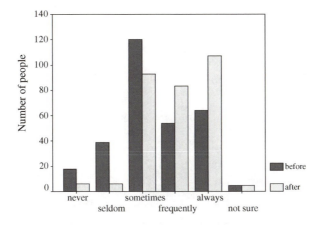

Figure 8.5: Picking up litter at the beach.

number of respondents who indicated that they would "always" pick up litter when at the beach increased from 21 to 36%, and the number of respondents who selected "frequently" increased from 18 to 28% (see Figure 8.5).

A similar change occurred with regard to the statement "*I get (will get) involved with environmental activities*" ($\chi^2 = 80.845$, df = 5, $p = 0.000$). The largest difference for responses before and after the trip was for the "sometimes" option; before the trip 36% of respondents indicated they would sometimes get involved in environmental activities, compared to 52% after the trip (see Figure 8.6). "Frequently" also increased, from 12% before the trip, to 20% after the trip, and 8% of respondents indicated they would "always" get involved in environmental activities.

Results from the responses to the statement "*I make (or will make) a donation for an environmental cause*" also showed a significant change ($\chi^2 = 47.122$, df = 5, $p = 0.000$). Again, the largest difference in responses before and after the trip was

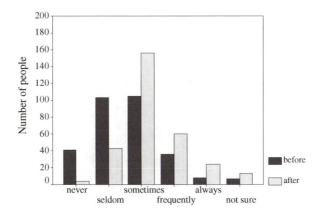

Figure 8.6: Getting involved in environmental activities.

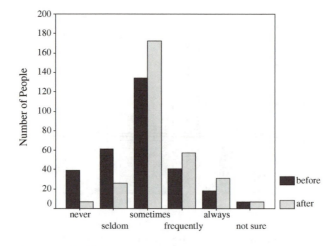

Figure 8.7: Making donations to environmental causes.

for the "sometimes" option; before the trip 45% of respondents indicated they would make a donation for an environmental cause, compared to 57% after the trip (see Figure 8.7). "Frequently" increased from 14 to 19%, and "always" increased from 6 to 10%.

The number of people who indicated they would "always" consider environmental issues when voting increased from 23 to 37%, and the number of people who selected "frequently" increased from 22 to 24% (see Figure 8.8). Once again, the overall change is significant ($\chi^2 = 26.258$, df $= 5$, $p = 0.000$).

The pattern of responses to this section of the questionnaire is consistent, respondents consider themselves more likely to behave in an environmentally responsible way after the trip (see Figure 8.9).

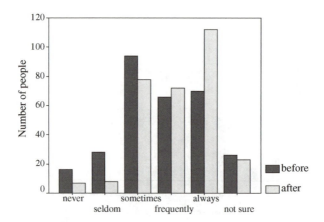

Figure 8.8: Considering environmental issues when voting.

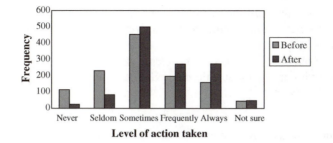

Figure 8.9: Total results for environmental behaviours and intentions.

Table 8.3: Age structure.

Age Group	Percentage of Respondents
15–29 years	34
30–49 years	47
50–69 years	16
70 years and older	3

Demographic Characteristics of Respondents

The majority (56%) of respondents were female. Of the four age classes, greatest representation was in the 30–49 year age group (47%), followed by 34% in the 15–29 year age group (see Table 8.3).

Results from Open Ended Questions

Three open-ended questions were included in the after-trip questionnaire. Each of these provided some information relevant to the educational programme, as well as other aspects of the experience onboard.

A question that asked respondents what they enjoyed most about the experience produced responses that can be categorised under five general themes. These were (from most frequent comments to less frequent comments):

(1) Seeing dolphins: so close; for the first time; in their natural environment (not captive) and seeing baby dolphins, dolphins being curious about people and the opportunity for children to see dolphins.
(2) Learning about dolphins: Learning about dolphin behaviour, general information about dolphins, the educational aspects of trip (informed viewing), learning how to find dolphins and seeing grandchildren learning about dolphins.
(3) Seeing whales: for the first time.

(4) The crew (staff) onboard the vessel: Great atmosphere created by crew, the friendly attitude of the crew, talking with crew/interacting with crew and talking with the crew about marine life.
(5) Other: Being out on the water, scenery, seeing gannets diving, information about birds, swimming (with and without dolphins), almost swimming with dolphins and taking photos.

A further question asked for specific "feedback on the educational talks given onboard." Comments on the content of the talks included that they were "wide ranging," "interesting," "knowledgable," "comprehensive," "informative," "useful," "enlightening," and that they "helped to increase awareness of environmental issues." Respondents also commented that the educational talks "added a huge amount to trip," that they "encouraged further reading" and they had "learnt about local marine environmental issues" and that they considered that they "now knew more than before."

Additional comments of interest were related to the delivery of the talks. These included that it "makes a difference if you can understand what you are seeing and what to look for," that the talks were "appropriate to what was happening at the time" and that the staff were "friendly and approachable," "humourous," "light-hearted" and had a "relaxed style." One respondent complimented the crew by stating that the "passion displayed by crew motivates us to be part of the solution," however, another thought that the environmental message was overdone and stated that the "Green Party propaganda was annoying" (the Green Party is a political party in New Zealand that advocates a strong environmental message). A number of respondents wanted more educational material including more brochures, more information on dolphins and on whales.

A further open-ended question asked respondents to comment generally on any aspect of the trip (comments, criticisms or suggestions). A number of responses were complimentary of the overall approach of the trip, for example, one stated that the "crew made good judgement calls about when to leave the dolphins alone (the dolphins needs were made a priority over the tourists)" while another commented that it was a "very dolphin/eco-friendly trip." Criticisms included those who "wished the ride was less bumpy" (seasickness) and some who wanted to reduce the length of the trip, while others wanted to "spend more time with the dolphins." One respondent was "wondering/worried about negative impacts on dolphins from tourism" and another wanted the "option to donate to environmental organisations on the boat."

Summary

Respondents showed a consistent increase in knowledge (at least pertaining to the questions asked) from before to after the trip, however, while attitudes showed an improvement from before to after the trip, these changes were not statistically significant ($p = 0.05$ level). Respondents' intentions to conduct environmentally positive behaviour did improve from to before, after, data sets. Qualitative data provided some additional evidence that passengers derived value from the educational programme offered onboard.

Discussion

The challenges of eco-tourism education programs are many and varied, and include such factors as a limited time-frame, a diverse range of ages, educational backgrounds, cultures and languages, and often the unpredictable nature of the trips themselves (International Fund for Animal Welfare 1997; Orams 1997). Despite these challenges, results from this study suggest that significant improvements can be made in tourists' knowledge, attitudes and behavioural intentions as a result of an ecotourism experience. Thus, this study adds to the evidence that the use of environmental education in ecotourism is an important way to manage tourists' interactions with the natural environment and contribute to effective ecotourism. This is important because, as Russell (2002: 485) states, "while the educational value of whalewatching has often been proclaimed, there has been little research on the topic." Similarly the International Workshop on the Educational Values of Whale Watching concluded that "there has been no serious investigation of what education is" or what effect it has in a whale-watching context (International Fund for Animal Welfare 1997: 1). This study represents an important contribution, therefore, by providing empirical evidence that education can be effective in a marine mammal tourism situation.

Knowledge

Despite the relatively specific nature of the questions used to test knowledge of respondents in this study, these indicators revealed a consistent pattern of improved knowledge as a result of the tour. This is encouraging because the education programme offered onboard the vessel was not specifically targeted at providing answers to the questions posed on the questionnaire. Questions were selected by the researchers on the basis that they were representative of the kind of knowledge that could reasonably be expected to be learned after a trip of this nature (researchers' own judgment). It was noted, however, that collaboration amongst respondents when completing the questionnaire did occur (despite requests for respondents to complete the questionnaire individually). It was not possible to quantify whether collaboration was different between both data sets and thus, it is assumed that the effect was not significantly different between each data set.

It is important to recognise that while this study did show that significant learning occurred, overall, respondents had limited knowledge (at least as tested by the questions posed) regarding cetacean behaviour and ecology both before and after the trip.

A further interesting observation made during the study was that a number of respondents tended to overestimate their knowledge of cetaceans initially, and after completing the true/false questions on the second question of the questionnaire, would go back to the first question and change their self-assessment of knowledge to "below average" or "very little" from their prior higher rating. This demonstrates that before the trip some respondents seemed to think that their understanding of cetaceans was more comprehensive than perhaps it actually was. Dolphins and whales are popular animals, and are frequently portrayed in the media, which may cause people to overestimate their knowledge about them. However, what is portrayed in the media and what is fact can be completely different, and many misconceptions exist (International Fund for Animal Welfare 1997). The questions posed in the questionnaire may have induced a change in respondents' perception of their own knowledge.

Attitudes

Environmental interpretation has been shown to improve tourists' attitudes towards the natural environment (Olson *et al*. 1984; Ministry for the Environment 1996). It is a little disappointing that the testing of respondents' attitudes in this study did not provide clear evidence to that effect. However, the results of this study may, in fact, be influenced by the respondents' understanding of the "socially desirable" answer to the question and not truly reflect the attitude of the respondent. This "social desirability" influence has been shown to be influential in other studies (Orams & Page 2000).

Intentions to Change Behaviour

The assumption that tourists will adopt more environmentally responsible attitudes and behaviour through ecotourism experiences is not necessarily correct (International Fund for Animal Welfare 1997). Behaviour change is a complex process affected by a variety of influences and, as a result, behavioural modification is difficult to achieve (Hammitt 1984). In addition, in ecotourism settings few education programs are actually structured to attempt to induce behavioural change (Orams 1997). However, studies have shown that it is possible for ecotourism education programs to prompt more environmentally responsible behaviours (Orams 1997; Orams & Hill 1998; Russell 1994). The results from this study suggest that the education program and experience onboard Dolphin Explorer may be succeeding in doing this. What should be remembered, however, is that intentions to change behaviour may not necessarily lead to an actual change in behaviour (Hungerford & Volk 1990) and this study did not test for this. It is reasonable to assume that a certain degree of redundancy would exist and that actual behaviour change would be less than that indicated as intended by respondents.

Demographics and Qualitative Results

The results from the gender and age sections of the questionnaire are consistent with the generalisation that wildlife based activities tend to be dominated by older age groups, and by females (Shackley 1996).

Not surprisingly, the majority of respondents indicated that the most enjoyable aspect of their experience onboard Dolphin Explorer was actually seeing dolphins. However, it is also important to note that open-ended questions also revealed that learning about the dolphins was also highly valued, as was interacting with the Dolphin Explorer crew in an educational context. There was a majority of positive comments made about the educational talks, and it is obvious respondents rated them of a high quality. An important point to note is that seasickness and language differences had an impact on the response to the educational talks, this is, of course, a challenge not unique to this marine tour operator (for example, see Forestell & Kaufman 1990).

The Question of "Value"

The educational programme offered onboard Dolphin Explorer has produced a number of desirable outcomes. It has promoted learning at a number of levels, passengers show an increased understanding of and appreciation for the dolphins and marine environment that provided the focus for the tours. In addition, some passengers showed a tendency toward improved attitudes toward the environment and, more significantly, a number of passengers indicated that they were intending to become more environmentally "friendly" and "responsible" in their behaviour in the future. This is encouraging because this is one of the main aspirations and potential contributions of the ecotourism industry (Orams 1995). The evidence provided by the research reported in this study does allow the reasonable conclusion that the education provided does have "sufficient educational value" as required under the New Zealand Marine Mammals Protection Regulations. What is perhaps more important here, however, is that the operator surveyed does not conduct their educational programme in order to simply meet a requirement of their marine mammal tourism permit, but that they do so because they appear to strongly believe in taking advantage of the opportunity to maximise the benefit of the tourism experience for their patrons. Moreover, the passion and dedication of the staff onboard the vessel revealed a deep commitment to marine conservation and a genuine compassion for marine mammals and their future. It is this, rather than the regulation requirement, that is the most important contribution toward making ecotourism work in this case.

Conclusions

The role of environmental education is receiving increasing attention in the ecotourism literature. This attention is deserved and overdue because it has been long recognised and advocated that education has a central role in advancing the lofty aspirations of ecotourism to represent a new enlightened use of natural resources. It appears, however, that many ecotourism operators and management agencies naively assume that by simply providing information in an entertaining manner that this will somehow, magically, produce ecotourists who are environmentally aware and responsible and that this will negate the potentially negative consequences of tourists interacting with nature. Even a cursory understanding of educational psychology would reveal that this assumption is flawed. Changing human behaviour is notoriously difficult and the reality is, at the moment, the vast majority of so-called "ecotourism" operators are simply offering information and entertainment and not environmental education. Fortunately, there are some operators who are working extremely hard to make the most of the opportunity provided by nature-based tourism experiences to (through those experiences) contribute to the health and viability of the natural ecosystems on which their business is based. This study reports on one such business. It is hoped that the research reported here (supported and encouraged by the operator) may contribute to the fledgling impetus for ecotourism operators to take environmental education more seriously.

Acknowledgments

The authors wish to acknowledge the assistance of Dolphin Explorer Ltd. in conducting the research reported in this paper. In particular, the authors wish to acknowledge the vision and enthusiasm of the late Stephen Stembridge who established the operation in 1999. Thanks also to the crew onboard the vessel who were very supportive of this research project. The support of staff at both Auckland University of Technology and Massey University at Albany was also appreciated. Finally, thanks to all the people onboard Dolphin Explorer who willingly gave of their time and thoughts in filling out the questionnaires.

Chapter 9

The Politics of Ecotourism

Rosaleen Duffy

Introduction

Ecotourism is often presented as a politically neutral form of development that ensures the conservation of natural resources. However, this chapter will explore the political dimensions of ecotourism in developing countries through an examination of the inter-relationship between it and globalisation. One of the main strands of globalisation is the expansion of market oriented systems, and for the purpose of this text, ecotourism is one example of that. Developing states are increasingly encouraged to utilise their comparative advantage in sun, sea, sunshine, adventure and landscape through the expansion of ecotourism. Ecotourism is promoted by organisations as diverse as the World Bank, the United Nations, the World Tourism Organisation and NGOs such as Tourism Concern as a possible pathway through a seemingly intractable problem of environmental conservation with development for the South. Ecotourism is equally recommended as a "politics" free option that is purely about raising hard currency for the developing world. However, this chapter will focus on the politics of ecotourism, and in particular the notion that ecotourism fits neatly within the political and economic changes brought about by globalisation, and more specifically the global liberalisation of the post Cold War order (see McGrew 1992; O'Brien, Goetz, Scholte & Williams 2000; Rosenau 1990).

In order to explore these issues, this text will focus on the development of ecotourism in Madagascar. Madagascar has been identified by global organisations such as the UN, the World Bank and Conservation International as being in particular need of sustainable development that conserves the environment as well as generating hard currency. Its national parks have formed the centrepiece of Madagascar's ecotourism development strategy, and thus this paper concentrates on the politics of ecotourism in protected areas. Madagascar can be seen as a key site for global environmental governance, where global level ideas of good conservation practice have been transmitted through the operation of a donor consortium. This paper will examine the role of the consortium and how it works with the Malagasy government to determine priority areas for receipt of aid. Due to the unique and highly biodiverse nature of the Malagasy environment, it has become a key area for donor intervention. In particular, ecotourism has been identified an especially appropriate form of development for Madagascar. With such a unique set of flora and fauna, Madagascar is defined as having a global comparative advantage in wildlife based ecotourism. As such this study will investigate whether ecotourism does offer a radical eco-centric policy for developing countries, or if it is a non-radical option that fits with existing global political and economic structures.

Globalisation, Neoliberalism and Tourism as Development

The increased interest in embracing tourism as a development strategy is part of the global re-emergence of neo-liberalism expressed through global governance and the shift towards a "liberal peace" (for further discussion see Fukuyama 1989, 1992). The interest in tourism can be related to neo-liberal theories of modernisation and their emphasis on the importance of internal factors as facilitators or inhibitors of business-oriented development. The ideological basis of development through tourism growth reveals that tourism is very much a political process and part of a global shift towards political and economic liberalism, rather than a private or individualised activity (Matthews & Richter 1991). For further discussion and critiques of neoliberal development see Escobar (1995) and Hoogvelt (2001).

The renewed emphasis on outward oriented growth and the rise of neo-liberal development strategies has focused attention on tourism as a potential growth sector. The central core of neo-liberal development strategies is an emphasis on economic diversification, particularly a commitment to non-traditional exports, such as tourism (Brohman 1996; also see Reid 2003). This approach has also been favoured by the international lending agencies such as the World Bank and IMF, and by bilateral donors, which have made loans available in return for reforms favour market-oriented growth (World Bank 1994).

Supporters of tourism as a development strategy also point out that it snugly fits in with neo-liberal strategies of basing economies on comparative advantage. Advocates of this position argue that each state should concentrate on exporting goods that it is "naturally" best at producing (Amsden 1990; Porter 1990). For example, in the Caribbean, tourism was actively promoted in order to diversify away from the diminishing profitability of banana production in the 1990s (Pattullo 1996).

Developing countries are considered to have a comparative advantage in tourism since they attract tourists from the First World who seek sunshine, beaches and other natural and cultural attractions found in the Third World. Governments in these latter countries, facing financial problems and an end to secure markets for their goods in former colonial metropoles, have looked to tourism as an answer to their problems (Lynn 1993). Most governments, regardless of their political ideology, have viewed tourism as economically important and so it has been an area for significant levels of state intervention. This is unusual for business, which is primarily regarded as a matter for private enterprise (Hall 1994). National tourism policies tend to be geared toward the generation of economic growth and the concept of tourism development is almost synonymous with economic growth, westernisation and modernisation for governments, since tourism means employment, balance of payments, regional development and foreign exchange (Fukuyama 1992; Hall 1994; Harrison 1992; Huntington 1971; Rostow 1991).

Tourism development is also closely involved with the private sector at the local, national and global level. Many governments are keen to couch public sector tourism development in terms of a pro-business rhetoric and policy (Matthews & Richter 1991). Tourism development has proved particularly attractive to local elites in developing countries, whether they are involved in government or private sector. Elites tend to favour tourism for much the same reasons as businesses in the developed world and global lending agencies (Hall 1994). Modernisation theorists view elites as the modernisers within a developing society. The activities of international tour operators create new economic opportunities within developing countries, and this in turn means that local entrepreneurs with existing businesses are able to take advantage of new tourism developments. As a result of these new opportunities elites tend to promote tourism because the profits from it flow towards them (Fukuyama 1992; Harrison 1992; Huntington 1971; Rostow 1991; Van de Berghe 1995). As a part of this liberal global governance process, tourism is clearly a highly politicised policy choice. It is essentially political because the pursuit of tourism development raises questions about the economic, political and social dimensions of the development process. Tourism also means that overt and covert development objectives are pursued at the expense of other objectives, and the selection and implementation of certain political and economic values will depend on the winners and losers in the development of tourism (Hall 1994).

Often tourism is credited with being a major provider of employment in developing states, often in areas where there is little other opportunity for waged labour. Tourism provides employment in direct and indirect ways. Direct employment is provided within the services and industries that comprise the tourism industry, including hotels, tour operators and casinos. Indirect employment is provided in sectors that are affected by tourism, such as local transport, craft production, restaurants and bars used by locals and visitors alike. However a great deal of direct and indirect employment that is created by tourism is in the informal sector. In the informal sector, local people provide services to tourists on a casual basis, such as selling local crafts as souvenirs (Abbot-Cone 1995; Hitchcock & Teague 2000; Pattullo 1996). However, the extent of employment creation in the informal sector is unquantifiable, even so such opportunities can make a significant contribution to household finances in developing countries (Pattullo 1996). It is clear then that tourism is inter-related with one particular strand of globalisation, namely the extension of development ideas and policies that are informed and defined by neoliberalism. This chapter will now turn to the role of neo-liberalism in the environmental debate.

Tourism and the Sustainability Debate

The idea that environmentally sustainable tourism can contribute to development in developing countries is clearly related to neoliberalism. Yet, while there is an emphasis on various forms of environmental management and an attempt to develop resources (and while not degrading a policy of ecotourism) they do not challenge existing political, economic and social structures. Instead, the "blue-green" strategy of ecotourism operates within current norms and crucially, within existing business or market logic. Ecotourism also relies on the individual exercising power through choices about consumption rather than acting as a citizen engaged in collective and organised protest (Duffy 2005). In this way ecotourism, as a subset of the global tourism industry, is firmly embedded in green capitalism, where the individual bears responsibility for environmental conservation or degradation rather than governments or private industry.

One of the challenges facing the tourism industry is how to develop without destroying the environment. Tourism in developing states is often reliant on the environment as the attraction for western tourists, and so mitigating the impact of tourism in that key attraction is critical to its continued survival. The environmental problems caused by conventional mass tourism development have provided a clear example of how tourism can be the cause of its own demise. The impacts associated with mass tourism development, including building infrastructure such as roads, airports, hotel complexes and restaurants, have led to calls for a more small scale and environmentally friendly form of tourism.

The vastly differing ideas that collectively form the environmental perspective, range from those who do not challenge the existing global structures to those who advocate a fundamental reorganisation of society on every level. In terms of political ideology, the environmental perspective can be divided into three strands. These varying environmental ideologies can be characterised as "blue green" (or "light green"), "red green" and "deep green," and each perspective leads to differing policies designed to protect or manage the environment. It is clear from the divisions in the environmental movement that what is known as the environment is constructed through social, cultural, economic and political ideas. In turn these ideas determine, for each interested party, perceptions as to what constitutes sustainable strategy for environmental care and development.

"Blue greens" can be defined as the conservative or right wing end of the environmental spectrum. "Blue greens" are also often associated with concepts of weak sustainability or light green policies intended to ensure environmental protection within existing social, economic and political structures (Beckerman 1994; Dobson 1996; Miller 2000). "Blue green" thought has varied historical antecedents in the writings of Bacon, Malthus and Darwin and draws heavily on the writings of Adam Smith and John Stuart Mill (Beckerman 1994; Mill 1963, reprint 1987; and Smith, 1776, reprint 1970). First, it is reformist, since many "blue greens" suggest that environmental care is possible within existing structures. This reflects a commitment to conservatism, which leads to preservation of the status quo. This is translated into ideas about the natural balance in society, economics and politics. It also relies on the idea that man-made capital is a perfect substitute for natural capital (Dobson 1996).

"Blue green" methods of environmental care are drawn from utilitarianism, liberalism and free market principles. The utilitarian principle of the greatest good to the greatest number has been translated into methods of environmental management (Mill 1963, reprint 1987). Environmental economics relies on the idea that the free market is the most efficient allocator of resources, which will maximise pleasure for the greatest number of people (Pearce, Barbier & Markandya 1990; Sagoff 1994; Winpenny 1991). "Blue green" notions of sustainability have proved particularly popular with the business community, and have been adopted by the International Chamber of Commerce as the guiding principles for sustainable development in the future (Eden 1994). "Blue green" ideas certainly constitute the reformist side of the environmental movement. A commitment to weak sustainability does not require a fundamental reorganisation of social, economic and political structures, but rather it assumes that sustainability can be achieved within existing structures.

There is no single definition of ecotourism, but in general, ecotourism should satisfy conservation and development objectives (Lindberg, Enriquez & Sproule 1996). It is often defined as travel to natural areas that conserves the environment and improves the welfare of local people. Defining ecotourism is particularly difficult, and as a result it has become a loose, catch all term for tourism that is concerned with visiting and experiencing some aspect of the environment, be it wildlife, rainforests, coral reefs or even beaches. One definition of ecotourism is provided by Boo (1990) who broadly defines it as nature tourism that consists of travelling to a relatively undisturbed or uncontaminated natural area with the specific object of studying, admiring and enjoying the scenery and its wild plants and animals as well as existing cultural manifestations in the areas (Boo 1990; also see Bottrill 1995). Along similar lines the Ecotourism Society defines it as responsible travel to natural areas that conserves the environment and sustains the well-being of local people.[1] Furthermore, ecotourists themselves are also a relatively difficult type of global traveller to categorise. However, in general ecotourists can be described as vacationers with an interest in outdoor pursuits, who are financially comfortable, well educated, older people with free time to travel (Ballantine & Eagles 1994).

Neoliberalism, Ecotourism and Madagascar

In keeping with neoliberal development and environmental strategies tourism has been identified as a critical sector for Madagascar. The unique cultures, flora, fauna and landscapes means that in terms of neoliberalism the country has a "comparative advantage" in nature, adventure and cultural tours. Madagascar has a unique environment, and in terms of recognition as a "brand" in the global tourism market, it has the great benefit of the highly charismatic and instantly recognisable lemurs. The "lemur factor" in Madagascar means that it can compete with other African destinations on the basis of wildlife and the exotic habitats in which they live. In fact, the Malagasy environment and wildlife tourism "product" has no equivalent competition. Where Madagascar fails to compete in the global tourism industry is in terms of facilities for visitors and price when compared with other African and Indian Ocean destinations. It has also begun to develop its profile as a diving destination that offers pristine coral reefs, and the solar eclipse "event" in mid-2001 served to raise its profile to potential visitors.[2] In addition, the Ministry of Tourism has begun developing plans to co-market Madagascar with Mauritius to make the destination more cost effective and attractive. This would allow Madagascar to offer a nature/culture tour, followed by a beach stay in Mauritius.[3] Just over half of Madagascar's visitors are French, with most

---

[1] See http://www.ecotourism.org/.Accessed 12.08.03; also see http://www.ResponsibleTravel.com. Accessed 20.08.04; and Denman (2001).

[2] Interview with Lala Randrianarivo, Chargee de Mission, Ministry of Tourism, Antananarivo, 21.08.01; interview with Jose Ravelonandro, Chef de Volet Ecotourisme, Isalo National Park, Ranohira, 29.08.01; and Guardian (UK) 27.08.02 *Survey reveals risk to reefs*.

[3] Interview with Lala Randrianarivo, Chargee de Mission, Ministry of Tourism, Antananarivo, 21.08.01.

others from elsewhere in Europe and a very small number from South Africa.[4] Furthermore, in 2003 ANGAP, Conservation International and a Malagasy NGO, Fanamby, launched a 14 minute film, entitled "A Cry for Hope" in an effort to attract international tourism. The film focused on Analamazaotra Special Reserve and Ranomafana National Park and their contribution to conservation and ecotourism. In particular, as part of the film launch the new Malagasy President Marc Ravalomanana met with the Director of Conservation International, Dr. Russell Mittermeier to discuss the use of ecotourism as a means of conserving biodiversity.[5]

Madagascar has also experienced a boom in conservation and tourism related activity by international organisations. For example, the World Bank provided funding for a National Environmental Action Plan with a pledge of US$100 million. In addition, in 2003 the new Malagasy President, Marc Ravalomanana, announced that Madagascar was to triple the area under protection to create a 6 million hectare network of terrestrial and marine reserves to protect its unique biodiversity and to turn Madagascar into a regional leader in ecotourism.[6] As a result Madagascar has financially benefited from a proliferation of relationships with multiple global donors since the mid-1980s that are all interested in funding environmental conservation programmes. The result for Malagasy people is an increase in foreign funded projects that aim to halt what they define as the human (or more specifically Malagasy) induced spiral of destruction (Kull 1996: 50, 53).

Madagascar has become a key site and nexus of global interest in conservation and ecotourism partly because it contains high levels of biodiversity (also termed megadiversity), high rates of endemic species and is well known to have severe environmental problems.[7] Alfredo Scheller Tsaramody, Chief of the Environmental Support Service in the Ministry of Industry, has highlighted a number of environmental problems including erosion, deforestation and habitat destruction which are claimed to be the result of slash and burn (*tavy*) agricultural techniques, land degradation from cattle grazing and industrial pollution from mining and textile industries.[8] While all new industries and businesses require an environmental impact assessment before they can move from the planning to the implementation stage, Tsaramody suggested that the environmental laws were poorly

---

[4] Interview with Lala Randrianarivo, Chargee de Mission, Ministry of Tourism, Antananarivo, 21.08.01; interview with Jose Ravelonandro, Chef de Volet Ecotourisme, Isalo National Park, Ranohira, 29.08.01; precise Figures are impossible to obtain, these general figures are estimates.

[5] *"Madagascar Banks on Biodiversity to Rebuild Tourism Industry"* (04.02.03) http://www.conservation.org/xp/news/press_releases/020403.xml (Accessed 03.11.03). Also see interview with Serge Rajaobelina, Director, Fanamby, Antananarivo 26.03.04.

[6] Interview with Dr. Helen Crowley, Country Director, Madagascar Programme, Wildlife Conservation Society, Antananarivo 25.03.04; interview with Bienvenu Rajohnson, Senior Environmental Policy Adviser, World Bank, Antananarivo, 26.03.04; and see *"Madagascar to Triple Areas Under Protection"* (16.09.03) http://www.conservation.org/xp/news/press_releases/020403.xml (Accessed 03/11/03).

[7] For further discussion of threats to biodiversity in Madagascar see http://www.bbc.co.uk, *"Madagascar Biodiversity Threatened"* (16.01.02). Accessed 08.02.02; and Financial Times, 15.05.01, *"Madagascar's jewels of nature under threat."*

[8] I am aware that the identification of slash and burn techniques and cattle grazing as the source of deforestation, soil erosion and habitat destruction is highly contested. Here I am suggesting that local agencies placed the blame on such activities rather than arguing that this was actually the case. For further discussion of contested narratives of environmental degradation and local agricultural practices see Leach and Mearns (1996).

enforced and full environmental assessments were rarely carried out.[9] The idea of an environmental crisis in a megadiverse and extremely poor country means that Madagascar has been identified by donors, NGOs, International Financial Institutions and others as a place that demands global attention, and more importantly, global action.

Ecotourism and conservation policy in Madagascar indicate a partial resurgence of the fortress conservation narrative. Brockington (2002) argues there is a specific vision of the African environment that has driven conservation. The premise is that people have harmed the environment, a view supported by scientific interpretations of environmental change, a romanticised view of a stunning wilderness and an aura of extraordinary biodiversity. Consequently, to many donors, global environmental NGOs and others, saving African environments means that they have to become denuded of people. While this narrative has been challenged by influential work on the need to integrate people and environments for conservation (see Hulme & Murphree 2001; Leach & Mearns 1996), the vision of the human free African wilderness remains a powerful one. For example, USAID has been involved in developing biological corridor projects in Madagascar that aim to ensure that environmental resources that link protected areas are governed in a sustainable way.[10] Part of the biological corridors project is to ensure that human activities do not reduce biodiversity in the area, prevent the movement of wildlife populations or frustrate the expansion of ecosystems (such as forests or savannah) between protected areas. This means that areas that fall outside the boundaries of national parks are subjected to forms of governance that will generally place restrictions on the activities of companies, government organisations and more importantly local people. Similarly, WWF and Conservation International arranged US$8 million worth of debt for nature swaps, which released funding for conservation initiatives such as training park rangers and conserving the Zahamena Natural Integrated Reserve. The debt for nature swaps do not relieve debt *per se*, but instead the revenue released by such schemes is specifically tagged for conservation activities (Tucker 1994).

The active involvement of global donors in environmental management and protected areas in Madagascar has assisted in the transmission of preservationist ideas. Furthermore, that preservation narrative coexists alongside a neo-liberal discourse that promotes the introduction of market-oriented strategies through reliance on ecotourism to ensure that conservation pays its way. In particular, ecotourism is promoted as a strategy to secure conservation and promote development for all levels of society from local communities through to the Malagasy state. Conservation International, a Washington-based NGO with global reach, has been involved in directly running protected areas in Madagascar. The Zahamena National Park is run by Conservation International as it develops the institutional capacities of the state run national parks agency (ANGAP) by training game guards. There has been some interest in community involvement in managing the national park, such as

---

[9] Interview with Alfredo Scheller Tsaramody, Chief of Environmental Support Service, Ministry of Industry, Antananarivo, 21.08.01; interview with Hery Zo Rakotondrainbe, Office National Pour l'Environnement, Antananarivo, 29.08.01; and interview with Josette Rahantamalala, Conservation International, Antananarivo, 20.08.01.

[10] Interview with Holisoa Rasamoelina, Chef de Service Suivi et Communication, Project d'Appui a la Gestion de l'Environnement (PAGE), Antananarivo, 28.08.01.

drawing trainee game guards from the surrounding area and educating people to ensure that they live sustainably, or "correctly" as a Conservation International representative put it.[11] Similarly, the Managing Director of the Ministry of Water and Forests stated that the environmental challenge was to fight against traditional local practices, such as grazing, slash and burn agriculture and hunting. She suggested that the Ministry was involved in developing alternative strategies for forest use such as collection of raffia and medicinal plants or ecotourism to generate income for local communities.[12] The emphasis on community involvement and integrated conservation and development projects was clear amongst donors, local NGOs and local state agencies. This is in part a reflection of how the community conservation discourse has entered into the consciousness of donor and recipient alike. However, this community conservation narrative was very much at odds with other more preservationist environmental priorities. Organisations are clearly capable of simultaneously holding multiple contradictory views of how best to conserve or preserve Madagascar's natural resources. While individuals in each organisation may well favour one view over another it is clear that organisations have to speak at the same time to a number of different agendas. They must simultaneously attempt to satisfy multiple audiences that may favour preservation, economic development initiatives, poverty reduction, education, community-based conservation, sustainable use and many more. For many local organisations, they are aware that funding will not be forthcoming without at least some acknowledgement of the "local people" factor. In many ways the promotion of ecotourism satisfies all of these competing and overlapping agendas in one neat neo-liberal package.

This cross cutting and contradictory discourse on preservation and community conservation is also interspersed with a clear commitment to neo-liberal principles that equally suit donor agendas, and very quickly become part of the local agenda. As with many programmes in protected areas, much of the discussion about saving the environment becomes intimately tied up with the idea that eventually conservation would have to pay its own way. Again, a common argument put forward by donors and local organisations alike is that once the environment is secured or "saved" it will attract global business in the form of ecotourism or adventure tourism.[13]

Donors certainly have a high profile in national environmental organisations, regardless of whether they are in the public or private sector. Donor organisations have been especially keen on promoting market-oriented mechanisms for environmental management and economic development. Hery Zo Rakotondrainbe, of the Office National de l'Environnement, indicated that donors were operating together in a consortium. The principal funder for the Office National de l'Environnement is World Wide Fund for Nature, but others are involved, specifically USAID, Japan, France and Switzerland, but the key

---

[11] Interview with Josette Rahantamalala, Conservation International, Antananarivo, 20.08.01.

[12] Interview with Fleurette Andriantslavo, Managing Director, Ministry of Water and Forests, Antananarivo, 30.08.01; also see interview with Lantoniaina Antriamampianina, Director Of The Terrestrial Programme, Wildlife Conservation Society, Antananarivo 24.03.04.

[13] Interview with Lala Randrianarivo, Chargee de Mission, Ministry of Tourism, Antananarivo, 21.08.01; and interview with Josette Rahantamalala, Conservation International, Antananarivo, 20.08.01.

lynchpin of the donor consortium is the World Bank.[14] The World Bank funds all three phases of the Charter for the Environment. The Charter for the Environment was established in 1991 and was expected to run for 15 years (in 5-year segments). The Office was to be the key organisation to oversee and implement the Charter.[15] Similarly, the agency responsible for managing protected areas in Madagascar, ANGAP, is run and funded by a group of donors, International Financial Institutions and Malagasy state agencies. As a kind of private organisation that runs a public utility, ANGAP has received funding from Conservation International, The World Bank, WWF, USAID, the German development agency GTZ, and the French and British Governments. The Board of Directors is drawn from government ministries, such as the Ministry of Tourism and the Ministry of the Environment, but donors such as the World Bank and WWF also have seats on the board.[16] One of the responsibilities of ANGAP is to provide tour guide training to assist the development of ecotourism in the protected areas that they control. There is a clear community conservation rationale in this policy, since ANGAP is in charge of a number of protected areas. For example, tour guide training is provided for members of local communities only in order to provide a local incentive to co-operate with conservation programmes in the national parks. In areas outside ANGAP control individual tour agencies provide training to guides. ANGAP is the only national organisation that offers tour guide training, but its primary role is to act as an environmental management organisation.[17] This indicates the ways that neo-liberal market-oriented strategies such as ecotourism development are intimately bound up with environmental policies in Madagascar.

Rakotondrainbe suggested that during the initial phases of the Charter for the Environment the Malagasy people were suspicious of donor intentions. It seemed that the Consortium of Donors had simply picked an area of Madagascar and taken control to govern it for conservation purposes with little thought of the impact on local people. It was felt that the donors were carving up the environment in Madagascar between themselves, so that USAID selected a national park to be their own and WWF did just the same. For example, Ranomafana National Park was regarded as "the American place" because of Stony Brook's lemur conservation project, the Peregrine Fund's programme and the large numbers of American students working in the park. Consequently, there was a clear perception that there was no concern about how such conservation programmes might benefit or seriously disadvantage local people, instead the focus was on the need to save landscapes and wildlife. Rakotondrainbe argued, however, that this perception has now begun to die away, as people were becoming more aware of the need for environmental management and conservation in Madagascar.[18]

---

[14] Interview with Bienvenu Rajohnson, Senior Environmental Policy Adviser, World Bank, Antananarivo, 26.03.04; and interview with Dr. Helen Crowley, Country Director, Madagascar Programme, Wildlife Conservation Society, Antananarivo, 25.03.04.

[15] Interview with Hery Zo Rakotondrainbe, Office National de l'Environnement, Antananarivo, 29.08.01; and Tovondriaka Rakotobe, Coordonnateur General, Office National de L'Environnement, Antananarivo, 31.03.04

[16] Interview with Parfait Randriamampianina, Director of Parks, ANGAP, Antananarivo, 21.08.01.

[17] Interview with Lala Randrianarivo, Chargee de Mission, Ministry of Tourism, Antananarivo, 21.08.01.

[18] Interview with Hery Zo Rakotondrainbe, Office National de l'Environnement, Antananarivo, 29.08.01. Also see (Walsh 2002a).

Market vs. Market: Ecotourism or Gemstones?

The reliance on the global market in ecotourism to pay for conservation faces multiple challenges. In particular the notion that conservation must pay its way through ecotourism, and the heavy reliance on the market as an efficient allocator of resources that will ensure environmental protection, is very problematic. A significant difficulty with the political position that the neo-liberal market is best placed to provide environmental management is that an uncontrolled market may well mean that environmental damage is more highly valued than protection. In essence, ecotourism must compete with the production of other commodities in the neo-liberal market, and in this instance, that competing commodity is sapphires. One of the most pressing local level problems is sapphire mining, especially close to Isalo National Park in southern Madagascar. In effect, sapphire mining is reliant on one type of "free" market, namely the global (and often illegal) trade in gemstones. This directly affects the capacity for neo-liberal forms of development which are equally dependent on the global market place that is ecotourism.

Isalo National Park is a key protected area in Madagascar, in terms of conservation and ecotourism development. It is one of Madagascar's most visited protected areas, and the number of tourists rose from approximately 15,000 in 1998 to 20,400 in 2000.[19] Isalo National Park is an important part of Madagascar's conservation estate. It comprises 81,000 hectares and is the country's most visited park. It contains numerous different species of lemurs, but a particular attraction is the sifaka (endemic to southern Madagascar). It is also the site of a number of ancestral graves and sacred landscapes that are spiritually significant to the local Bara people.[20] Lala Randrianarivo, of the Ministry of Tourism, suggested that there was a need to develop eco-lodges in the area, and as a result the ministry was offering ground rental to foreign investors to develop appropriate accommodation to develop environmentally sustainable tourism in the area. She argued that foreign investors were vital because first, they could develop international standard facilities and second, because local investors did not have access to the levels of capital needed for such developments. Unlike many other emerging tourism destinations in the developing world, the Malagasy Government does not require foreign investors to work with a local partner.[21]

In line with the discourse on community oriented conservation through ecotourism development, ANGAP had pursued a policy of attempting to bring local Bara people into managing the protected area. ANGAP has an agreement with the local community that 50% of the gate fees go to them. For example, Bara people were given priority when jobs as tour guides and game rangers arise. In return, the Bara had to provide assurances that they would not undertake a variety of proscribed activities within the park boundaries, such as

---

[19] Interview with Jose Ravelonandro, Chef de Volet Ecotourisme, Isalo National Park, Ranohira, 29.08.01.

[20] Interview with Parfait Randriamampianina, Director of Parks, ANGAP, Antananarivo, 21.08.01. Parfait Randriamampianina, Director of Parks at ANGAP, was the Manager of Isalo for 6 years, and his term covered the period before and after the sapphires were discovered.

[21] Interview with Lala Randrianarivo, Chargee de Mission, Ministry of Tourism, Antananarivo, 21.08.01; and interview with Jean Jacques Rabenirina, Ministre de la Culture et du Tourisme, Ministry of Tourism, Antananarivo, 30.03.04.

grazing cattle, burning grasslands and hunting.[22] These revenues have then been used for community development projects such as building schools and clinics. ANGAP also runs education programmes to raise awareness about their conservation programmes in the park, but it can be argued that the success of these efforts have worked partly because they intersect with pre-existing local ideas about appropriate uses of sacred landscapes.[23] Moreover, this community involvement in environmental management did not falter because of a lack of understanding between the community and the parks authorities, like so many others that are covered in the literature (see Hulme & Murphree 2001). Rather the Bara and ANGAP were and are allied together in their attempts to resist a common problem: the miners and gem dealers of Ilakaka and their links to global networks of national and international political and economic elites.

During the late 1990s Ilakaka town sprang up after the discovery of high quality sapphires. It was estimated that the population of Ilakaka town increased from 30 to 100,000 between 1998 and 2000.[24] The sapphires are considered to be of the highest quality and if gem mining and trading were properly regulated then Madagascar has the potential to be a very rich state. However, the sapphires have been mined in a haphazard and disorganised way and the stones are mostly exported illegally to Sri Lanka, Thailand, Democratic Republic of Congo and Europe. The sapphires are found in alluvial deposits, which means that an organised and commercial mining operation is not necessary to extract them. Instead, alluvial gem deposits are particularly accessible to any individuals who want to take a spade and dig. The case of Madagascar stands in stark contrast to the successes of the gem mining sector in Botswana. Since the Government and private companies have been able to capture the revenue from diamond mining operation in Botswana, it now has the fastest growing economy in the world. Unlike foreign gem dealers, the diggers are primarily poor Malagasy who have travelled from all over the country in the hope of striking it rich. The stories and rumours of sapphires the size of footballs and of fortunes made in a single day have meant that Ilakaka has proved irresistible. Since Ilakaka is close to Isalo National Park, the state run parks department (ANGAP) and the other donors involved in the area became concerned about the impact of illegal mining and its rapid expansion into the park. The discovery of sapphires has had multiple environmental impacts, ranging from cholera outbreaks to miners collecting wood in the park as a source of fuel for heating and other purposes. As a result ANGAP has tried to run education campaigns to encourage the diggers to stay out of the park, but these have had limited effects. One of the key cultural and political impacts in the local area is the growing conflict between the local Bara and the gem miners in Ilakaka. The Bara have felt insulted by what they regard as the sacrilegious behaviour of the gem diggers. Sapphire hunters have begun to dig for sapphires within the park boundaries and in areas that are considered as sacred landscapes. Even breaking the earth within these landscapes is regarded as an insult to the Bara and their ancestors. Bara people have then become embroiled in conflicts with the diggers in their attempts to prevent

---

[22] Interview with Parfait Randriamampianina, Director of Parks, ANGAP, Antananarivo, 21.08.01; and pers comm Emison Jose, ANGAP guide, Isalo National Park, 25.08.01.

[23] Interview with Jose Ravelonandro, Chef de Volet Ecotourisme, Isalo National Park, Ranohira, 29.08.01.

[24] Financial Times, 18.08.00, "*Big hopes for Madagascan sapphires*"; and interview with Tom Cushman, Manager/Adviser, Institut de Gemmologie de Madagascar, Antananarivo 18.03.04.

what they see as desecration of the landscape, and clashes with the sapphire diggers have even led to deaths.[25] The ANGAP authorities in Isalo also have had to call in the national army and the police to guard the boundaries of the park and keep diggers out. This heavy law enforcement around the park led to inevitable clashes with diggers trying to get into the park.[26]

The difficulty is that now it is believed that the area immediately around Ilakaka has been exhausted of the best sapphires, and the rumour amongst the diggers is that the national park contains bigger stones of even higher quality. Parfait Randriamampianina, the former director of Isalo National Park also suggested that the diggers and gem dealers believed that the Government knew this and that was why the area had been listed as a national park in the first place. A personal threat also existed in that the illegal miners also believed that he, as the park director, knew the location of the biggest and best sapphire deposits. Consequently, his life had been threatened on a number of occasions, and he was transferred to the ANGAP office in the capital as a precaution. The Malagasy sapphire miners were not the only problem either. As rumours of big deposits spread, it was found that foreign tourists were also entering the park with spades and starting to dig for gems. ANGAP responded with a stipulation that all visitors to the park had to be accompanied by a licensed ANGAP guide.[27]

The expansion of illegal mining in Ilakaka has also caused significant social, health, cultural, economic, environmental and political problems outside the park boundaries. First, the mining is mostly illegal, unregulated and untaxed. As a result increasing numbers of individual diggers have arrived in Ilakaka and dug large holes. One concern for conservation authorities in the area is what will happen to these holes. The ANGAP park managers were worried that once the area is exhausted of gems, the mining will have left a highly visible and unappealing scar on the landscape. Consequently, the development of tourism and ecotourism in the park and surrounding area would be jeopardised by the old mining area because tourists would be put off visiting the area by stories of how the gem mining had damaged the landscape.[28]

Sapphire mining presents real hazards to the diggers too. Numerous diggers have been buried as the holes and tunnels they are working in have collapsed. Since the digging is unregulated, deaths amongst the miners go unrecorded and unnoticed.[29] Apart from these direct risks from the mining itself, the sapphire boom in Ilakaka has also created significant public health problems. Each year the mining area suffers from a cholera outbreak due to lack of adequate sanitation and contaminated water supplies. The only visible organisation

---

[25] Interview with Parfait Randriamampianina, Director of Parks, ANGAP, Antananarivo, 21.08.01.

[26] Interview with Parfait Randriamampianina, Director of Parks, ANGAP, Antananarivo, 21.08.01; also see interview with Beatrice Olga Randrianarison, STD and AIDS Unit Head Catholic Relief Services — Madagascar, Antananarivo, 30.03.04; interview with Tiana Razarimahatrata, CARE Madagascar Antananarivo, 21.04.04.

[27] Interview with Parfait Randriamampianina, Director of Parks, ANGAP, Antananarivo, 21.08.01.

[28] Interview with Jose Ravelonandro, Chef de Volet Ecotourisme, Isalo National Park, Ranohira, 29.08.01; also see interview with Josoa Razafindretsa, Environmental Policy Specialist, USAID Madagascar, Antananarivo 22.03.04.

[29] Interview with Beatrice Olga Randrianarison, STD and AIDS Unit Head Catholic Relief Services — Madagascar, Antananarivo, 30.03.04; interview with Tiana Razarimahatrata, CARE Madagascar Antananarivo, 21.04.04; interview with Parfait Randriamampianina, Director of Parks, ANGAP, Antananarivo, 21.08.01; Financial Times, 18.08.01, *"Blue dreams in a world of red clay"*; and Focus, August 2000, *"Sapphires in the Sand."*

in Ilakaka, the Catholic Relief Services, runs a project aimed at preventing cholera, but the overcrowding around Ilakaka means that cholera remains a problem.[30]

The growth of the mining and dealing sectors has created further public health and social problems. When miners achieve a "good" find, the sale of the stones gives them instant access to wealth. Walsh (2002a) has observed that in Ambondromifehy, another sapphire town in northern Madagascar, young male sapphire miners earn and spend a great deal of what they call "hot money." The miners engage in conspicuous consumption with the money that they define as "hot" so it cannot remain in a person's hands, it must be spent. Such conspicuous consumption by sapphire miners and the gem dealers is evident in Ilakaka, with such hot money being spent on prostitutes, drinking and gambling. The increasing rates of HIV/AIDs and other sexually transmitted diseases has also caused alarm amongst the park authorities, fearing that it will deter tourists travelling to the area. The brothels and bars are also sites of violence, and are identified as extremely dangerous at night. The illegal nature of the gem mining and dealing has created an industry centred on protection and extortion. It is usual for dealers to have hired armed protection, which in turn means that violence in the bars can easily erupt into shootouts between rival dealers and their bodyguards.[31]

The sapphires have also attracted gem dealers from around the world, who have set up shops in Ilakaka town such as Congo Gems, Colombo Gems and Sri Lanka Saphir. The names of the shops provide an indication of the ways that Ilakaka is intimately linked up with transnational trading routes and broader processes of globalisation. A World Bank Study in 1999 found that US$100 million in gems was smuggled out of Madagascar in that year alone.[32] It is impossible to place a precise value on the stones that are traded in Ilakaka each day, but one rough estimate was that US$4 million worth of stones changed hands each day in 2001. Despite this massive cash flow in southern Madagascar, the Malagasy franc continued to fall against the U.S. dollar. Rather than making its way into the formal economy, the income generated from the gem sector remains in an informal and illegal economy populated by gem dealers, criminal organisations, protection racketeers, miners and individuals in the Malagasy elite. While the top traders are foreigners, rumours have abounded that top Malagasy officials have been able to siphon off large profits from the illegal gem sector.[33] The ways that Ilakaka is linked through local elites to the global market place presents real challenges for the long term development of ecotourism in the area. The illicit market in gemstones is one form of globalisation that directly and adversely affects another form of globalisation, ecotourism, and its capacity to provide a framework in which to secure conservation and development.

---

[30] Interview with Beatrice Olga Randrianarison, STD and AIDS Unit Head Catholic Relief Services — Madagascar, Antananarivo, 30.03.04; interview with Tiana Razarimahatrata, CARE Madagascar Antananarivo, 21.04.04.

[31] Interview with Parfait Randriamampianina, Director of Parks, ANGAP, Antananarivo, 21.08.01; and pers comm Emison Jose, ANGAP guide, Isalo National Park, 25.08.01; also see Financial Times, 03.02.01, "*Prospectors and poverty mar an island paradise.*"

[32] Focus, August 2000, "*Sapphires in the Sand.*" For further information on the World Bank reports on Madagascar and the sapphire sector see http://www.worldbank.org/afr/wps/wp19/1.pdf; and http://www4.worldbank.org/afr/poverty/pdf/docnav/03298.pdf (Accessed 05.09.02); also see interview with Tom Cushman, Manager/Adviser, Institut de Gemmologie de Madagascar, Antananarivo 18.03.04.

[33] Anonymous interviewee; also see Financial Times, 18.08.01, "*Blue dreams in a world of red clay.*"

Conclusion

In this chapter it has been argued that ecotourism is not a radically different political free option for sustainable development. Rather ecotourism is firmly located within the neo-liberal discourse and the globalisation of neo-liberal development policy and practice. It relies on the idea of the developing countries trading globally on its comparative advantage in wildlife, sunshine, sea and sand. In this way ecotourism links with philosophical debates that suggest environmental conservation is possible within the existing capitalist system. As such ecotourism is a highly political option that does not challenge the existing political and economic order in anyway, rather it supports it. Furthermore, examining local level case studies such as protected areas and ecotourism in Madagasar, reveals that reliance on the market place to provide conservation is very much more complex than the neo-liberal discourse suggests. The ways that different neo-liberal market formations (legal ecotourism, illegal sapphire mining) cross cut, compete and contradict one another indicates that a reliance on ecotourism and the market may not provide along term conservation or development strategy.

Chapter 10

African Wilderness® Pty Ltd: An Authentic Encounter with the Big Five, Death and the Meaning of Life

Malcolm Draper

> It is very evident what mean and sneaking lives many of you live, for my sight has been whetted by experience, always on the limits . . .
>
> Henry David Thoreau 1854[1]

Introductory Sketch

According to a glossy eco-tourism magazine, the absence of wall-to-wall development in Africa is the only hope for overcoming poverty and competing in the global economy: "probably the safest prediction that one can make is that shortly the world's fastest-growing market, tourism, will be chasing the world's fastest shrinking product: wilderness" (*Getaway*, November, 1996). We also read in the *National Geographic* that 'South Africa may be the continent's best hope for preserving wildlife in a wild land' (July, 1996). Such was the thinking soon after a democratic South Africa emerged from civil strife and global isolation. The country has since enthusiastically embraced global trade and is well aware of the importance of its wildlife resources in attracting tourists and foreign exchange, colonial conservation legacy notwithstanding. Predictably this scenario has generated unprecedented tourist packages, products and places as the process of commodification has gathered momentum. Whilst privatisation has been a cornerstone of government neo-liberal policy, much effort has been directed at ensuring that the fruits of such industry do not bypass local African communities. It is, however, not the intention of this chapter to consider the economics and equity of wilderness where the limits of acceptable change are most strictly policed, but rather the idea of limit in the wilderness experience itself. As a geographical space or protected-area category, wilderness has a formal definition laid down by the IUCN. Like the National Park concept, it has North American roots that have spread around the world. The idea of wilderness first made African policy in the

---

[1] By the limits here Thoreau (1995: 3) meant as an outsider scratching a living. Or to use Bauman's formulation introduced later in this essay, a tourist who deliberately chose to live like a vagabond.

Taking Tourism to the Limits: Issues, Concepts and Managerial Perspectives
© 2005 Published by Elsevier Ltd.
ISBN: 0-08-044644-2

Zululand game reserves after the Second World War. From there, through the visionary efforts of Anglophone and Zulu conservationists responsible for taking the idea to heart, and saving the white rhinoceros from extinction, it became a global movement in the form of the World Wilderness Congress. From 1977, this platform dramatised concerns about wildlife and wild places. More significantly, it centre-staged indigenous people and their plight in the face of modernity. This is ironic when we recall that it was the height of apartheid. The intertwined narratives of key figures of the Congress are examined: Ian Player, Magqubu Ntombela, Laurens van der Post, Credo Mutwa and Linda Tucker. A common, central and formative theme of rebirth after a brush with a deadly animal in the wilderness is uncovered. An indigenous person plays a role as both saviour and spiritual guide in the experience which thoroughly decenters the eurocentric perspective and launches white subjects onto a mythological journey of discovery. The fabled African Big Five derive from a 19th-century white hunter's classification of the five most dangerous animals to stalk. Since risk and death are so fundamental, Foucault's notion of the limit experience explains the subjective state better than Maslow's peak experience, but such ecstasy is limited by conservative politics. While myth and adrenaline are fundamental to the intrigue of African wilderness, tourist products dare not promise the real risky thing. Yet Zululand wilderness trailists are often hopeful about a rhino charge and disappointed when no such encounter occur, and a private safari lodge's popularity soars after a tourist is eaten by a lion on her way to bed one night.[2] It is argued that while tourist operators need to embrace such expectations and manage them optimally, it places them at the ethical limit.

The Sky is Not the Limit: The Launch of an Afronaut

"A Foreign Spring": So ran a headline in the *Pretoria News* reporting the South African government's declaration as alien and undesirable the tree so symbolic of our political capital affectionately dubbed "Jacaranda City." It also served as a literary device revealing the anxieties of the Petra, the protagonist in *An African Grey*, Simone Opperman's winning fiction story in a local youth culture magazine. Petra's white middle-aged disenchantment not only applies to the political landscape but the industrial wasteland, and her marriage to an embittered metal worker recently tossed onto the economic scrap heap. The competition judge, Ashraf Jamal, says that we readers "are uncomfortably implicated in an uneasy, on-going question concerning who and what we are as so-called South Africans. The bird at the centre [The African Grey] is the ventriloquistic vehicle through which the writer accesses the unconscious" (*Student Life*, May 2003).

---

[2] These points are derived from conversations over years with KwaZulu-Natal Wildlife wilderness trail guides such as Mike Reid who now is in the publicity division. At Phinda Private Resource reserve in 1992 an elderly Durban woman, Grace Strous, was killed by a lioness when she left the boma (outdoor dining area) during supper to return to her bungalow. The company was fined R20,000 after pleading guilty to a charge of culpable homicide. My interviews with staff who asked not to be named revealed that Conservation Corporation Africa paid gladly given the subsequent groundswell of demand for the Phinda product.

This discussion shares such issues of identity, indigeneity and the mediation thereof through landscape identification, the agency of animals and the unconscious in the process of a re-orientation of white Eurocentric identity. Most importantly, it emphasizes the importance of travel stories and their tellers in such transformations which Laurens van der Post (1990) called *metanoia* after the original Greek denotation of a change of mind and heart, a revision and transformation consciousness so profound it is as if a metamorphosis has taken place. Essentially these stories are of the mystical experience of travel and rebirth whereby imperial history is not denied so much as reversed when settlers and tourists "go native," identify with the landscape and set out to preserve rather than cultivate it in their own image. The stories vary but common denominator is the setting of a wilderness of malevolent nature rendered homely by indigenous spiritual wisdom provided by a local guide.

But, first, a disclaiming caveat. The animal-bush genre has no monopoly over such trips and resulting metamorphoses. The story of Mark Shuttleworth the "Afronaut" provides a counter example. After buying a ticket for a rocket ride from the proceeds of entrepreneurial maneuverings in the virtual realm,[3] Africa's first man in space celebrated his return to the country by jiving with President Thabo Mbeki at a hi-tech reception in his honour in Pretoria. Mbeki thanked Shuttleworth for all he had done for South Africa and the African continent:

> There is an indigenous African saying: 'Please hold the sun where it is, so it doesn't set'. Mark's statement to the world is — Here we are, a country and continent that are being reborn, on which the sun will never set. He has shown us that the stars are accessible to us. We are grateful that he had the courage and vision to do what he did (*The Star*, June 03, 2002).

Shuttleworth exclaimed that he was filled with pride walking to the rocket with a badge of the South African flag on his spacesuit. "It is truly wonderful to be back. During this experience I noticed two beautiful things — seeing Africa from space and seeing Africa as I came in to land on a 747." This privileged view qualified him to make pronouncements on the continent's renaissance and African entrepreneurship whilst basking in the ensuing glow of media attention (*The Star*, June 03, 2002).

Shuttleworth's patriotic pronouncements at his reception in Pretoria contrasts harshly with Opperman's "Foreign Spring" of purple prose, ominous Jacaranda blossoms and fears of a symbolic chainsaw massacre. Deliberate or not, Opperman's title plays on Rachel Carson's *Silent Spring* (1962) which signaled the birth of the environmental movement of the 1960s and beyond. As Jean and John Comaroff point out, Mbeki had the most portentous words when in 2000 he avowed that alien plants "stand in the way of the African renaissance." In a pub fraternized by the lower strata of white Pietermaritzburg the proprietor has a jar for tips marked "Fuck the Whale. Fuck the Rhino. Save the White Man!!" Similar bumper stickers are sported on vehicles and serve as a plain example of what the Comaroffs call the naturalisation of existential anxieties about national belonging which, they argue, are particularly acute in this country's current postcolonial condition.

---

[3] Shuttleworth sold his internet security company, Thawte Consulting, to the U.S. company, Verisign, for U.S. $575 million in 2000.

Through taking a self-indulgent trip to the limits, our Afronaut inadvertently discovered that the envelope of national identity could be pushed. He accomplished this through inanimate technology, but such mediation to new frontiers is not, theoretically speaking, distinct. So has the work of Haraway shown: from apes in space illustrating *Primate Visions* to her "Cyborg Manifesto" cheekily published in the *Socialist Review*, and now her *Companion Species Manifesto* (2003) which implicates non-human agency in human history. Further conceptual framing is provided by Zygmunt Bauman's work on tourism and globalisation which describes the two worlds of the "haves and have nots" as "globals and locals" or "vagabonds and tourists." Life for both in our consumer society is a "magic wheel of temptation and desire" but, for the tourists, the wheel turns faster and faster with no obvious end point:

> The very notion of the 'limit' must need temporal/spatial dimensions. The effect of 'taking the waiting out of wanting' is taking the wanting out of waiting. Once all delay can in principle be flattened into instantaneity, so that an infinite multitude of time-events can be packed into the time-span of human life, and once all distance seems to be compressed into co-presence so that no space-scale is in principle too big for the explorer of new sensations — what possible meaning could the idea of the 'limit' carry (1998: 79)?

Following Mathieson's critical extension of Foucault's panopticon to the synopticon of the digital age, Bauman emphasizes how vagabonds and tourists never really meet:

> Segregated and separated on earth, the locals meet the globals through the regular televised broadcasts of heaven. The echoes of the encounter reverberate globally, stifling all local sounds yet reflected by the local walls, whose prison-like impenetrable solidity is thereby revealed and reinforced (1998: 54).

In this essay I seek to look for exceptional stories of tourists who have found a new edgy sensation in the wild and, in so doing, transcended the digital divide and made real connections with locals who changed their lives forever. I take up the attraction of the pearly portal gates and the possible meaning of the limit. To pervert Bauman I want to interrogate a particular genre of writing from the postmodern inverted frontier — the line of wilderness being held out against civilisation — and ask: when do globals begin really trying to think like locals? Or, to put it another way, when do tourists empathise with vagabonds? Whilst Bauman sketched the rule, I am concerned with the exceptions who step out of their matrix of social power and let go of their Eurocentric gaze. This is perhaps what Mamdami calls the "survivor's justice" which can work at answering his question; "When does a settler become a native?" (1998: 14). To do so, I show herein, they must flirt with what Foucault recognised as the ultimate release from power: "death is power's limit, the moment that escapes it" (1996: 138). Such an experience heightens the limit attitude as never before and the extreme adrenalin-based tourism industry bears testimony to the global demand for travel as tripping. The states that travel promises to explore are not always national or geographic, but are frequently altered. As Fabian points out,

There is overwhelming indirect evidence that European travellers seldom met their [African] hosts in a state we would expect of scientific explorers: clear minded and self-controlled. More often than not, they too were 'out of their minds' with extreme fatigue, fear, delusions of grandeur, and feelings ranging from anger to contempt. Much of the time they were in the thralls of 'fever' and other tropical diseases, under the influence of alcohol or opiates (laudanum, a tincture of alcohol and opium, was the principal drug used to control acute and chronic dysentery), high doses of quinine, arsenic, and other ingredients from the expedition's medicine chest . . . I thought there might be interesting material in these travelogues for a paper to be titled 'Travel as Tripping' (2000: 3).

It is not contemporary commodified manifestations of adventure tourism that I am concerned with here. While Swarbrook (*et al.* 2003) explore the industry as "the new frontier," the novelty lies in the more safely packaged adrenaline products sold in a post-frontier world. As I have argued elsewhere, wilderness adventures when cloaked in the sacred mantle of conservation take place on an inverted frontier of the wild pushing back the boundaries of civilization (Draper 1998). It is debatable whether or not the interactions dealt with here are merely "anti-conquest" maneuverings in a "conquest zone" called wilderness — whereby travellers proclaim their innocence vis-à-vis the "travellees" and the land whilst continuing to assert their hegemony (Pratt 1992). Beinart (1998) has called for a more fluid approach to such a history after revisiting some of Pratt's travel writing sources and uncovering evidence to the contrary. Here I further confound Pratt by featuring a female protagonist who cannot be dubbed a "seeing-man" — her "admittedly unfriendly label for the European male subject of European landscape discourse — he whose imperial eyes passively look out and possess." It is also a further exploration of what Pratt calls "transculturation" — a phenomenon of the contact zone. Ethnographers have used this term to describe how subordinated or marginal groups select and invent from materials transmitted to them by a dominant or metropolitan culture. Pratt recognises that the transmission goes both ways and "treats the relations between colonised and colonisers, or travellers and 'travellees' not in terms of seperateness and apartheid, but in terms of co-presence, interaction, interlocking understandings and practices" (1992: 6, 7).

So this is a hopeful excavation of the limits of the *Tourist Gaze* (Urry 1990) recognising that tourism is the edge (Ryan 2002), and arguing that the wild cuts at the sharp point. Some of my previous work (Draper 1998) and the analysis offered here about the issues of identity in question, are greatly enriched through scholarship coming out of New Zealand and Australia. Comparisons between African and antipodean experiences are fruitful. My mission here is to extend Adrian Franklin's "zoological gaze" (1999: 62–83) to the limit of life itself, to plumb the deathly depths of darkest tourism (Sharpley 2005) and darkest Africa. The "eco" in tourism must alert us to the biological, the birds and the bees, the cycles of life that have made the world go around for eternity: birth, sex and death. Setting aside reflection for the time-being, come with me and encounter the animal adventures which are the basis of this exploration.

Metanoia: Travel and Transformation

Animals have long been intimately bound up with identities and patriarchal power in Africa as they are elsewhere. Kiwis clash with Wallabies and Lions and post-apartheid attempts to get the South African Springbok rugby team renamed after a flower (the Protea) failed. A praise name of the Zulu King is *Wena Wendlovu* (You the Great Elephant), only royalty may don the hide of the leopard and many clans have animal names and traditionally show respect to their namesake fauna. Animals have been the literal engines of new identities for settlers — the Afrikaner's "Great Trek" away from British imperialism could only have taken place with ox power and their strength in the Anglo-Boer war lay in their horse power.[4]

Perhaps the most widely known South African travel writer is the late Laurens van der Post who made much of his Afrikaner and African identity. Yet, like Mark Shuttleworth and John Aspinall, van der Post's "white Zulu" plutocrat zoo keeper friend, the South African travel author resided in Great Britain resided in Great Britain (Draper & Maré 2003),[5] Van der Post was inspired and befriended by the German psychologist Carl Jung. Van der Post argues in the foreword of Saayman (1986) that the Great Trek, like the conquest of the American frontier, was driven by an extroverted attempt of Europeans trying to avoid introversion and reappraisal of their history. This reiterated his thesis made in *The Dark Eye of Africa* three decades earlier that "since the Reformation European man has been increasingly at war with himself . . . the natural man within us not only has had very little honour but wherein also his rich intuitive and instinctive promptings have been thrown out of the courts of reason; just as the aborigines of our time have been despised and rejected by western man" (1955: 4).

Van der Post saw apartheid as having a similar genesis in the sick and fragmented soul of western modernity, but introduces gender to his schema: "It is a man's idea, coming not from the feminine but the masculine side of human nature, which out of its addiction to logic and ideology can break things up" (in Saayman 1986: xiii). Whilst van der Post and company saw the problem of apartheid and modernity being bound up with masculinity, he appeared to have seen the solution in even more masculinity, urging "our bureaucrats" to "stand up manfully and say to their people. 'We're sorry. We've made the most terrible mistakes. Forgive us.' " (in Saayman 1986: viii). The course desired by van der Post was eventually embarked upon and the Truth and Reconciliation Commission has extracted post-apartheid apologies.[6]

Van der Post's credibility was recently damaged by JDF Jones's official biography *Storyteller* (1991). His claim to be the first indigenous South African to have spoken out

---

[4] An innovative Zulu eco/cultural destination called Simunye (we are one) transports tourists to the location by ox wagon or horseback. Upon arrival, the host Vincent Sikakane welcomes them with the greeting "welcome home!." Home is the which emerges repeatedly in affirmative discourse about an authentic African wilderness experience.

[5] John Aspinall perhaps best illustrates boundary crossing with animals (see Franklin 1999). J. M. Cotetzee was proudly claimed by the government as a son of South Africa when he was awarded the Noble prize for literature in October 2003, but lives abroad in Australia. The portrayal of South Africa in Coetzee's novel *Disgrace* was earlier deemed unpatriotic by the government.

[6] The collaboration of Player, van der Post and Aspinall's Zulu allies with the apartheid regime has been well demonstrated but they have given no remorseful satisfaction. The Zulu King is only a political figurehead but the Kingdom is the official tourism marketing strategy for my province (KwaZulu-Natal) after which my university was recently renamed.

against Apartheid may not be true, but he certainly was a most prominent white critic of Apartheid. Like AT Bryant (1949) the Zulu linguist and missionary ethnographer, he firmly believed that most white settler South Africans were deficiently endowed with soul. In his Rousseau-like view, this has been prime mover behind the deadly encounter between western modernity and noble cultures and natures throughout the world. Conservation of both felt van der Post, requires an about-turn in consciousness and identity — a metamorphosis he claimed would only come about through contact with wild nature and natives. To this end he threw his weight behind the efforts of the South African wilderness movement associated principally with Zululand game rangers Ian Player and Magqubu Ntombela. Player appropriated American ideas of strict principles of wilderness management and stringent limits of recreational experience excluding mechanical access to designated zones. By 1977 their efforts at a local level post World War II had reached global level proportions with their initiation of the World Wilderness Congress in Johannesburg. It was, according to van der Post, "one of the most remarkable occasions of the many of its kind that I have attended. I know of course that, as a native of South Africa, my judgment could be very easily be biased . . ." (1977: 3).

Van der Post's writing inspired Player to explore Jung's work. They became friends and collaborated over the World Wilderness Congress, the Wilderness Foundation and the Cape of Good Hope Centre for Jungian studies. The volume which captures such deliberations is *Modern South Africa in Search of a Soul: Jungian Perspectives on the Wilderness Within* (Saayman 1986). The book offered idealist psychological explanations of the crisis of apartheid which, not surprisingly, did not enjoy a wide currency in the materialist intellectual climate of struggle prevalent at the time.

It was at that congress that van der Post told of an experience during WW II in Java where he was dropped, eventually falling into the hands of the Japanese who intended an execution which ultimately never came. He experienced great relief the night which he thought his last when a storm reminded him of the powers that man cannot control. He goes on to tell how an encounter in "virgin jungle" near the great volcano of Krakatoa, in Indonesia with an immense tiger turned from terror to ecstasy when his guide went down on his knees and prayed to "Taun Tiger" — "Lord Tiger" and the animal's aggression dissipated: "a moment even came when the ghost of what I can only describe as a smile flickered across the tiger's face and the tiger turned about and walked off in the opposite direction" (1977: 9). Jones triumphantly holds up this story as proof of van der Post's Hemingway-like mythomania — the blurring between fact and fiction animating his life and literature and which "must have bewitched his Prince" — Prince Charles was his confidant (Jones 2001: 400). The publication of Jones's biography *Storyteller* caused a huge stir and is the most reviewed book I have dealt with. I must confess to having only read a purposive sample of the multitude of reviews. Some observed that Jones wielded the hatchet quite unfairly and never got to the heart of the man and his magic. None of the commentators I have read, thus far, have picked up on Jones's failure to properly deal with the tiger incident, including David Attwell (2003) who insightfully observed that the moral of the story had something to do about "whites seeking home in Africa." Van der Post lived out his days in England, not Africa, yet he claimed a transcendental African identity and manipulated his influential friends in an attempt to direct South Africa towards a right-wing post-apartheid path of ethnic balkanization. The storm in Java reminded him of Africa, only in African wilderness did he feel at home (van der Post 1996), and he could not imagine Africa without homelands (Jones 2001). So whilst he was the first prominent white to openly come out against apartheid, he was a dyed-in-the-wool believer in separate development, the ideology of the apartheid government. In the last decade of his life he "presided over a nexus which brought together Wilderness, the Cape Town Jungian Centre, and in due course, right-wing support of Zulu federalism" (Jones 2001: 4001).

However Jones's treatment of the tiger story reveals a weakness of his biography. He found it in an undated memorandum on Indonesia from van der Post's last years (1989) and maintains that he "never told this story before or since. Even as a fantasy it has the authentic van der Post power." It is covered in a chapter on "My Prince" (Charles of Wales) (Jones 2001: 400). Jones has a chapter on wilderness, but neglected to read his subject's foreword in the proceedings of the first World Wilderness Congress where the story is told. Nor did he notice that it appeared almost word-for-word and again some two decades later in an anthology called *Wilderness and the Human Spirit* by van der Post with Player (1996). Of course some details differ between the embellished wilderness version and the memorandum. Significantly, a "futile pistol" disappears. (Player maintains that a firearm can come between the true communion between man and beast that is a "peak" wilderness experience. (Pers Comm. 2002).[7] The tiger's stare only "relaxed and his face went benign" (Jones 2001: 400), there is no anthropomorphic smiling. Nevertheless, the point is that Jones never recognised that this experience cannot be abruptly dismissed given the parallel resonance with several others set out below. Because he neglected to come to terms with his subject's near-death experiences, he failed to understand and satisfactorily convey his life. The dust jacket of the Congress Proceedings, *Voices of the Wilderness* (Player 1979) has a famous quotation from Henry David Thoreau's *Walden 2* (1854):

> I went to the woods because I wished to live deliberately, to front only the essential facts of life, and see if I could not learn what it had to teach, and not, when I came to die, to discover that I had not lived.

A similar incident to van der Post's Tiger story that occurred between Player and Ntombela in the late 1950s is set out in Player's book about their relationship (1997: 171–186).

In the Zululand bushveld in Mfolozi Game Reserve in 1952, a young cadet game ranger, Ian Player, met game guard Qumbu Magqubu Ntombela, who had begun his career in 1914. It was the beginning of a profound friendship between a black and white man that took them along rhino, elephant and hippo paths, across the black and white Umfolozi Rivers and into the domain of the ancient Zulu kings, Dingiswayo, Shaka and others. Their association involved battling against poaching gangs, initiating the internationally famous capture and translocation of the white rhino, setting aside the first wilderness area in southern Africa, leading the first wilderness trails which led to them conceiving and pulling together the World Wilderness Congress. The adventures and experiences of these two men have been

---

[7] A South African born doctor includes wilderness travel therapy in his medical practice in California and has published a text which sets out what the peak experience is about (Cumes 1998). Although very much a product of the history discussed in here, Cumes does not mention Player at all. Cumes has a company called "Inward Bound" which leads journeys of discovery and healing.

the subject of television documentaries and thousands of newspaper and magazine articles which made them household names.

Player describes how his life was changed by a dramatic confrontation with a black mamba (Africa's most venomous snake) after he had initially refused a request by Ntombela to respect African custom and the spirits of the ancestors by spitting on a stone and adding it to an *isivivane* (stone cairn). He finally did after Ntombela became passively mutinous and the snake which towered over them further up the path let them pass. Ntombela was sure that, had Player not complied, the outcome would have been very different. This led to a subtle shift in the relationship between the two men and the Zulu subordinate became Player's teacher and mentor. Magqubu Ntombela introduced Player to the natural mysteries of the wild animals, the plants, the birds and the insects of his native Zululand. Player called this a rebirth and Ntombela the midwife. But to reborn one has to die, or come as close as can be:

> Magqubu and I stood motionless, the black mamba hovering above us. We knew that one movement on our part meant death. I have never been so terrified. The black mamba can strike with chilling swiftness, and we would soon have died on this mountain slope because after our strenuous climb the blood was rushing through our veins, and the venom would quickly have been carried to the heart. Mamba poison attacks the nervous system, a most unpleasant way to die (1997: 181, 182).

Before he died of old age in 1995, Ntombela told of his visions when being bitten and ultimately surviving a green mamba bite. This was then analysed by a Jungian psychologist (see Saayman 1986). When Player is done, Ntombela is valorized into a legend hallowed with the magic of a shaman. For more detailed analysis of this history see Draper (1998) where the politics of the story is analysed in the framework of the emerging gender scholarship around men and masculinities. These are, after all, boys' stories. Nelson Mandela has endorsed the view in the publicity blurbs that this is a story of great significance in modern South Africa because it is about how two men of entirely different walks of life became inseparable friends on the same path while revealing the interdependence of man, the landscape and the wild life, and suggests that the healing power of wilderness can transform a nation. The book is marketed thus as more than just a wildlife conservation story.[8]

Since then, the latest to join the ranks is a woman: enter Linda Tucker. A Cape Town and Cambridge-educated scholar of Jungian dream psychology and symbolism, she returned to South Africa and commenced a study of the spiritual significance of white lions and an initiation into African lion shamanism in 1994. This was catalysed an incident in 1991 when, on safari in the Timbavati, she and her group were saved from the jaws of death by "lion queen" and "Shangaan shaman woman," Maria Khosa, who directed her to seek the counsel of controversial prophet, shaman and 'great lion priest, Credo Mutwa

---

[8] Player's *Zululand Wilderness: Shadow and Soul* was published in the USA by Fulcrum Press as *Zulu Wilderness*. The Mandela endorsement appears in their catalogue which was collected at the World Wilderness in 2001.

(Tucker 2001). Although Ntombela was no longer around, at the World Wilderness Congress in 2001, Player had kept the magic alive by having Mutwa at his side and Tucker sharing their limelight by introducing their marathon elder's "fireside" story-telling late into the night. Player called her *Children of the Sun God* "a phenomenal book that comes at a critical time in African environmental history" (http://www.whitelions.co.za).

Tucker's story is worth a read. Essentially her predicament with the lions was brought about by a young macho game ranger's disrespectful use of mechanical power to intrude on the privacy of a cubbing pride of lions. Yet unlike the other stories dealt with here, it is contemporary and can be corroborated by several witnesses. She relates it to van der Post's tiger tale:

> This was an astonishing story yet it harmonised with my own experience and with other documented material I had begun to uncover. I would have reason to recall Van der Post's description of the tiger's face becoming 'filled with light' when I uncovered the phenomenon of the great cats as symbols of enlightenment-bearers across the globe . . . Respectful communication, in this case prayer, proved to be the key to preservation. According to van der Post, the feline priest was 'protected' from the jaws of death not by 'contrived armour' in the manner of the feline hero, but through mutual respect which provided spiritual armament. While such an approach to predators was absolutely beyond my personal understanding at the time of my own brush with death, contact with lion shamans such as Maria gradually introduced me to a different way of seeing, which would ultimately become second nature (Tucker 2001: 41, 42).

Going Home: A Different Way of Seeing

For Player the most powerful lesson he learnt from the Zululand wilderness with Ntombela as his guide was that of respect (Draper 1998). The lesson was such a tough one that it took none less than the grim reaper to drive it home. When asked about what ecotourism in Africa should be about, Player replies that ideally it should provide soulful revelations of being at home in the cradle of humankind and teach respect for nature and indigenous cultures. It should, in other words, disorient western attitudes which have been lording around the world from the imperial age.[9] Player's Wilderness Leadership School has run programmes for both school children and parliamentarians who have had such life-turning experiences well documented in the Wilderness Leadership Schools publications over several decades. More broadly, a visit to the websites of Africa's adventure and adrenaline capital, Victoria Falls, will reveal reports that this natural wonder of the world leaves one feeling humbled by nature's majesty. Waterfall's notwithstanding, it is still textbook orthodoxy that "our ancestry lies among a group of apelike animals living in Africa" and that the best place to

---

[9] Ian Player (Aspinall's friend) interviewed at his Farm in the Karkloof, South Africa, 20 May 1999 by Malcolm Draper and Keyan Tomaselli.

begin a study of human culture is with the primates most closely related to us. (Haviland 1999: 74). Travellers such as Aaron Latham (1991) go into Africa in the hope of discovering a strand that might inspire and root them more firmly into the earth and the cosmos. All this speaks of a deeply decentred tourist gaze. As a case study Franklin (1999: 62–83) has extended Urry and Rojek's concepts into the zoological realm using the zoo-keeping practices of John Aspinall, the eccentric English-gambling-plutocrat. This we traced to Africa through Aspinall's close connections with Zulu leader Chief Mangosuthu Buthelezi, Ian Player and Laurens van der Post (Draper & Maré 2003).

These prominent figures are extreme cases, but perhaps their stories give us a sense of something give us a sense of something distinctive about African ecotourism and why "the Big Five" are the most compelling draw cards in marketing the continent as a destination. The Big Five are thus called not because of their size, but because of an aggressive capacity to turn the tables on human hunters, to invert the relationship between the hunter and the hunted. According to Tucker's review of the archaeological record, coupled with African oral sources, our World Heritage Site, the Cradle of Mankind at Sterkfontein Caves, contains the bones of the drama of the about-turn from being the hunted to the hunter that marks humanity's evolutionary relationship with lions (2001: 75–84). Humans used to be dragged into caves by felines and dined upon and, at some vague point, figured out how to oust the lions from the dining room except as food — a particularly sweet meat hunters tell me. There is no doubt a fascination with evolution that brings tourists to Africa. *Africa Geographic* regularly features the apes who share such a close DNA relationship to us and trekkers are drawn to harmless creatures such as gorillas for this reason. That magazine also regularly focuses on battle field tourism, for the British have a similar morbid fascination with the sites where their forefathers fell in battle or butchered the Zulu who gave the empire their most decisive defeat at Isandlawana in 1879. A veritable heritage industry has sprung up around this history. I am not wanting to detract from the fact that other ways of dying are important. Admittedly, other continents have lethal charismatic megafauna, but not as many. The film *The Edge* (1998) has an instructive moral to its tale: An aeroplane accident in Alaska followed by the drama of a rich man of advanced years emerging from the wilderness, after being stalked by a bear as the sole survivor with his status vindicated and his power legitimated. Yet I am not merely arguing that these are stories of hegemony being shored up through adventure in the wilderness.

Zane Gray popularised New Zealand as a world trout fishing destination and *Stalking Trout* (Hill & Marshall 1989) — albeit exotic introduced game — can lead to an identification with nature and a concern with conservation, natural history and wilderness, both in South Africa and New Zealand (Draper 2003). Nevertheless, Americans travelled initially to Africa to hunt animals. This can lead to them hunting their own "dark hearts" as Latham's autobiographical musings, *The Frozen Leopard: hunting my dark heart in Africa* (1991), suggests. In the foreword, Morris maintains that when Hemingway wrote his parable *The Snows of Kilimanjaro*, with its epigraph concerning a frozen leopard found near the House of God, he was making an admission:

> Mighty hunter that he was, the epitome of literary and physical *machismo*, he was conceding that there was more to Africa than killing animals and

drinking whiskey. It was a mystical story that he was writing, and inherent to its plot was the idea that the experience of the Dark Continent can take one nearer to things first, ultimate and finite (1991: xi).

Lennon and Foley's *Dark Tourism* (2000: 9) is quite Eurocentric in focus. Whilst mentioning how film can portray "realistic" accounts of events, including *Apocalypse Now*, they fail to point out that the movie owed its literary inspiration to Conrad's *Heart of Darkess* set in Africa. As Hall says of "The legend of the Lost City" the theme park neighbour of Sun City (popular destinations for the world when sanctions made South Africa out of bounds):

> The world only has one role for Africa — as a destiny for other people's expectations, "and as the home of 'dark forces. Rider Haggard, Wilbur Smith and Sol Kerzner [Sun City and Lost City's Sun International founder] have all seen this point — and have become wealthy (1995: 198)."

As my title somewhat facetiously suggested, this is an excavation of these expectations as demand and supply, as crude commodification — in the tourist industry's own words, 'packages.' But I also wanted to suggest a more sincere dimension and suggest that we suspend for a moment the materialistic view of the all consuming tourist gaze. Take Clint Willis's volume *Wild* (1999). It is subtitled as *stories of survival from the world's most dangerous places*. It is published under the "Adrenaline™" with a cover blurb maintaining that "Like the wilderness itself, *Wild* is about death as well as life." Yet the book carries chapters by writers such as Edward Abbey and Bill Bryson whose stories are about the corrupt nature of consumer society rather than danger and heroic survival.

So too should we look for a silver lining around the dark thoughts of white men and women who have stared death in the face in Africa. In other words, the Biblical beast lumbering towards Bethlehem may have an important message. There is hope and evidence that the imperial attitude becomes positively decentered and some of my biographical work shows this leading to a willingness to, if not relinquish, then at least share power. Elsewhere I have used the concept of hegemonic masculinity, developed by the Australian gender sociologist and historian Bob Connell, to argue that it is by no means straightforward (Draper 1998). Connell drew on Phillips's seminal work on the making of the New Zealand white male which shows how significant the frontier experience was:

> Colonising elites nearly always like to see their role in history as bringing civilization to a wilderness. Their corresponding fear is that the wilderness might prove too powerful, and that men far from the constraints of ordered society might give way to their lower impulses. They might descend to the level of the beasts, or as in New Zealand, they might go native and live the 'savage' existence of the Maori (1987: 47).

As Beinart and Coates show, frontiersmen in both the United States and South Africa learnt much from indigenous people and adapted to the natural environment. 'The South African "trek boer" (mobile pastoral farmer) . . . was viewed as semi-barbarised by visiting Europeans' (1995: 111). We must of course remember that it was the trek of the Dutch

East India Company to which New Zealand owes its name. Trading of goods often leads to the trading of identities. Tourists can become vagabonds and visa versa. If this was so in the nineteenth century, how much more so in the twentieth century on a postcolonial inverted frontier of wilderness for men who empathised with both nature and the "natives?" Looking across to Australia, Connell's "Whole New World" (1990) study of new men in the environmental movement, there is much to hope for in the closing of the gap between tourists and vagabonds. Crocodile Dundee might yet go soft on us.

Ian Player, the African wilderness man of global import, has. He encourages my students to read Tacey's *Edge of the Sacred* which he feels is a brilliant assessment of our spiritual future and reconciliation between wilderness and civilization. Tacey sees this as the future for white settler reconciliation with Australia's indigenous peoples. He recounts his experiences of living in Central Australia as especially "heavy," a spirituality unknown to many Australians who perch on the edge of the huge continent in an attempt to avoid the spiritual potency of the Australian landscape. Another connection is travel writer Bruce Chatwin, whose book about Australia, *The Songlines* (1988), is a big influence on Tucker.

African Wilderness: the Limit of Maslow's Peak

Big Five aside, Africa is no exception and to assert that in whichever form of adrenalin chosen to take to try and get near it, tourists are fascinated by death. If animal agency is introduced into the drama, however, the mystical seems to switch on more readily. 'Foucault's concepts of the "limit experience" is more useful than Maslow's notion of the "peak experience", suggesting as it does issues of social power and history, rather than a de-politicised psychological model of therapeutic self-actualisation. The negative aspects of ecotourism are frequently dubbed 'egotourism', but the therapeutic or transcendental literature recognises that 'it is the place beyond the ego that the wilderness effect occurs' (Cumes 1998: 37). This chapter has sought to assert the importance of a brush with death as central to this effect. Stanford's *Heaven: a traveler's guide to the undiscovered country* (2002) shows that the idea has a long history and makes a plea for the re-establishment of myth. Whilst recognising the value of such an experience, I have argued that it is limited and can be dangerously conservative in political effect. At one extreme, ecotourism represents a desire for release from power and the modern forms of knowledge that sustain it. This is very retrospective for as Foucault points out in his *History of Sexuality*, since the French Revolution in the Western world at least, death was "ceasing to torment life so directly" (1976: 142): "The pressure exerted by the biological on the historical remained very strong for thousands of years; epidemics and famine were the two great dramatic forms of this relationship that was always dominated by the menace of death."

It may be an obvious point that the "eco" in tourism implies the biological, the birds and the bees. But not always realised is the importance of death in these cycles of life. Nor is it something that tourists will realise that they consciously seek. People may not readily admit to their drives in this industry. Thus sex tourism can be understood with similar tools as those used to unpack the wild and the wet. Indeed, Africa's adrenaline capital at Victoria Falls is the oldest such safari destination on the continent and has a flourishing sex industry in spite of all the dangers of HIV Aids so rampant in Africa.[10] The novel and film *The Beach* (2000) shows that paradise on earth cannot last. Westerners pollute and ultimately destroy the very sanctuary they seek. Nature always bites back and when tourists meet the vagabonds and try to live like them, they are soon stalked by the grim reaper. Death is no longer the taboo subject it once was, but analysis of the mystical is still not an easy task for an empirical secular scholar. Meaning, like wilderness, has become increasingly privatized. If tourism is an edge, then wilderness is the edge. The issues of identity it raises are more transcendental than national and it was the transcendentalist nature philosopher Henry David Thoreau who made the point about travel, wilderness, civilization and limits one and a half centuries ago in 1854 — two years before David Livingstone put Victoria Falls on the map:

> At the same time that we are earnest to explore and learn all things, we require that all things be mysterious and unexplorable, that land and sea be infinitely wild, unsurveyed and unfathomed by us because unfathomable. We can never have enough of nature. We must be refreshed by the sight of inexhaustible vigor, vast and titanic features, the sea-coast with its wrecks, the wilderness with its living and its decaying trees, the thunder-cloud, and the rain which lasts three weeks and produces freshets.We need to witness our own limits transgressed, and some life pasturing freely where we never wander ([1854] 1995: 205).

When van der Post maintained that "wilderness is about a crisis of meaning in the modern world" (1996: 10), he was talking about what the sociologist Peter Berger (*et al.* 1973) called the *Homeless Mind* of modern culture. In their chapter on "the limits of de-modernization" they lump concern for wilderness preservation with the search of the counterculture for spiritual values and alternative lifestyles in the "Third World." Although stoical in conclusion, the Bergerian analysis conservatively prefigures Bauman's tourists and vagabond formulation of the post-modern global encounter. Turning back to the search for home and identity in travel, when van der Post went on a solo African wilderness retreat after returning from the second world war, upon sighting the first animal (a kudu bull),

> I looked at him with a tremendous feeling of relief. I thought 'My God I'm back home! I'm back at the moment when humanity came in, when everything was magical and alive, quivering with magnetism.' Gradually, through the animals, I was led back to my own human self. All the killing and death dropped from me, and only then could I go home and greet my own mother (1996: 12-13).

---

[10] I owe this observation to a black African horse safari guide at Victoria Falls National Park who, in 2002, got me close enough to a Bull Elephant for it to mock charge and me to take fright. I pressed him about his job and he confessed to being highly sought after by white female tourists who tip well, but claimed he avoided their advances. Local black women exchange their favours openly for money. When I presented this paper in Pietermaritzburg in 2004, Duncan Hay, a former game ranger from at Mala Mala, an exclusive game reserve, said it resonated with his experience where the tip was commensurate with the adrenaline rush. While he had claimed no experience of it, game rangers are preyed upon by female clients. My university lost a good zoologist who worked there to a tourist from Texas. This is common at Victoria Falls according to my guide and several others questioned in 2002.

For Foucault, Africa and animals were never elements of what he called the "limit experience." But he reached for sex, drugs, the danger of Aids and limit ideas. When he had an experience with LSD at Death Valley's Zabriskie Point in 1975, it was comparable to van der Post's. Nature an animated universe, the transcended self, and home are all also present in his ecstatic report. Indeed it was this limit experience that redirected his study of sexuality towards the self (Miller 1993: 251).

This chapter has also sought to push the limits of gendered analysis on this subject. According to Chilla Bulbeck, whose book *Facing the Wild: ecotourism, conservation and animal encounters* (2005) was published after earlier drafts of this essay were written; "Where the Western woman's path to the other lies through New Age spirituality or ecofeminism, men are more likely to find their wild selves through wilderness experiences, whether hunting or saving national parks. These activities also have their resonances with the imagined native, the "original ecologist" who hunts his game with awe and reverence" (2005: 145). While Bulbeck's analysis creatively moves past many dualisms, it is limited by an essentialist grasp of gender. Award-winning writer Jay Giffiths's book on time concludes with a chapter on "wild time" which led to her current project on wilderness. "Sex, drugs, rock 'n' roll: Play, nature, and the sacred" is the title of a recent article about wild time reiterating her thesis in her *Sideways Look at Time* (1999) written by an English woman too confined in a tame and long-enclosed land:

> For years I have wondered what it feels like to be deep in the wilderness. Then, on a trip to the Taku River watershed of Alaska, I found out. Wilderness is a ferocious intoxication that sweeps over your senses. It is an untouched place that leaves you elated, awed, and changed. It is an aphrodisiac, a place of furious, ripe fullness (2003).

"Timeless" is a word we frequently encounter on lyricism about wild Africa promising relief from from the stifling regime of modern time. There is much more for scholars of tourism to explore in African wilderness, yet with caution, for the edge that we must walk carries great risk of scholarly slippage from the sublime. Yet, at one level, the form of travel considered here seems to be about spiritually homeless tourists at the end of their modern tethers seeking risky transcendental homes in wilderness. Such demand pushes tourist operators managing the desired encounters to the ethical limit, especially when animals come into play. As John Urry points out, tourism is about places *to play* and places *in play* with one another for network nexus in the tourism growth industry (2004). Globalisation has always meant getting into the ring with the gloves off, and southern students of the industry need to know the fluidities of the wealthy northern market intimately and engage with theoretical developments such as Urry's mobilities paradigm. If the globe can cope with all the jet fuel burnt by tourists and if they are sensitively managed, perhaps we can play our way to a bright future: "Wild time is playful. A sense of play, serious play — in Indian mythology, is the deepest energy in creation. The manifestation of this energy is called Nature — Prakriti" (Griffiths 1999).

This chapter has asserted the importance of death in the play of nature. This point, and Africa as the ultimate dark eco-tourism destination, has been overlooked by the emerging scholarship from the antipodes on the zoological gaze (Bulbeck 2005; Franklin 1999). The literature dealing with the management of visitor experience does not sufficiently deal with death, and the ethical limits stretched by the contradictory desires of tourists to be at once safe and at risk (Manfredo 2002; Shackley 1996).[11] This essay is a call for work on ecotourism to be spiced up and take full account of what intrigues visitors to Africa. Latham wrote of wildlife-viewing experience in *Hunting My Dark Heart in Africa*: 'The scent of Africa, red and peppery, was intensified by the water. Enlarged, underscored, magnified, it finally identified itself: the smell of death' (1991: 308). Paradox and contradiction might well be the order of the day. Africa's big five have always been the major travel attraction of the continent and from hunting to conservation, their fate has hinged on the changing tourist gaze. As much as roads and cars might be anathema to formal wilderness management we must remember that the king of the African wilderness and the largest of Africa's predators, the lion's prospects did a somersault when game wardens gave up shooting and began protecting Leo in the 1930s. It was their rising demand as a spectacle for tourists that drove the about turn and facilitating this new zoological gaze was Henry Ford and the mass production and consumption of the internal combustion automobile. The Jeep® logo, which has spread all over the outdoor wear market, is as follows: "Since 1941, Jeep has been a symbol of freedom and capability . . . Jeep products are created for living life without limits."[12] Conservation, on the other hand, is about setting and enforcing limits. So the wildcard in the nature-culture game often turns up trumps and the kisses of life and death can be hard to tell apart.

---

[11] Cage diving operators who lure sharks with bait have come under the ethical spotlight, but the risk is not to their clients but other unprotected divers. Michael Manfredo's collection (2002) deals with the North American situation, but Kodiak Bears do sometimes stalk people and give wilderness experiences an edge qualitatively different to that provided by the extremes of climate. Myra Shackley's global study has much to offer, but does not convey the full flavour of the African experience.

[12] This is quoted from a tag of a shirt with the Jeep brand and logo 'Live life without limits'.

Chapter 11

The Limits of Tourism in Parks and Protected Areas: Managing Carrying Capacity in the U.S. National Parks

Robert Manning

Introduction

As the name suggests, national parks are resources of national and, increasingly, international significance. The United States national park system, for example, contains natural and cultural resources of great importance to the nation, and in many cases, the international community. Given the significance of this resource base, tourism demand to see and experience these areas should not be surprising, and data on national park visitation in the U.S. dramatically support this premise: the national park system now accommodates nearly 300 million visits annually. These data are only one manifestation of global tourism trends in national parks and protected areas.

The increasing popularity of national parks presents both an opportunity and challenge. The opportunity is to fulfil the mission of the national parks "to provide for the enjoyment of the people" as required in the 1916 Organic Act of the U.S. National Park Service. The accompanying challenge, of course, is to fulfil the complementary component of the national park mission "to conserve the scenery and the natural and historic objects and the wildlife therein." This can prove difficult under conditions of high tourism demand. Implicit in this dual mission of national parks is the issue of the quality of the visitor experience. The quality of visitor experiences must be maintained at a high level for national parks to contribute their full potential to society. Moreover, high-quality visitor experiences are more likely to develop public appreciation of, and support for, conservation of national park resources.

It is ironic that one of the greatest threats to national parks is commonly seen as their increasing popularity. To many observers, national parks, at least in some places and at some times, are crowded, and this detracts from the quality of the visitor experience. Moreover, natural and cultural resources can be degraded by excessive visitor use. In both formal and popular terms, use of some national parks, or portions thereof, have exceeded their carrying capacity (Manning 1999, 2001; Mitchell 1994; Shelby & Heberlein 1986; Stankey & Manning 1986; Wagar 1964; Wilkinson 1995).

Taking Tourism to the Limits: Issues, Concepts and Managerial Perspectives
Copyright © 2005 Elsevier Ltd.
ISBN: 0-08-044644-2

This chapter explores the theory and application of carrying capacity to national parks and related areas. Emphasis is placed on development and application of Visitor Experience and Resource Protection (VERP), a framework developed for managing carrying capacity in the U.S. national parks. The first section briefly traces the theoretical development of the carrying capacity concept, including development of the VERP framework. The second section describes application of VERP to Arches National Park and other units of the U.S. national park system. A final section suggests that the conceptual framework underlying VERP and other contemporary approaches to carrying capacity can be applied to a variety of parks and protected areas, but that this will require a commitment to park planning, management and research.

The Concept of Carrying Capacity

The question of how much tourism use can ultimately be accommodated in a national park or related area is often framed in terms of carrying capacity. Indeed, much has been written about the carrying capacity of national parks. The underlying concept of carrying capacity has a rich history in the natural resource professions. In particular, it has been applied in wildlife and range management where it refers to the number of animals of any one species that can be maintained in a given habitat (Dasmann 1964). Carrying capacity has obvious parallels and intuitive appeal in the field of park management. In fact, it was first suggested in the mid-1930s as a park management concept in the context of national parks (Sumner 1936). However, the first rigorous applications of carrying capacity to park management did not occur until the 1960s.

These initial scientific applications suggested that the concept was more complex in this new management context. At first, the focus was placed on the relationship between visitor use and environmental conditions. The working hypothesis was that increasing numbers of visitors causes greater environmental impact as measured by soil compaction, destruction of vegetation, and related variables. It soon became apparent, however, that there was another critical dimension of carrying capacity dealing with social aspects of the visitor experience. An early and important monograph on the application of carrying capacity to parks and related areas reported that it was:

> ... initiated with the view that carrying capacity of recreation lands could be determined primarily in terms of ecology and the deterioration of areas. However, it soon became obvious that the resource-oriented point of view must be augmented by consideration of human values (Wagar 1964, preface).

Wagar's point was that as more people visit a park, not only can the environmental resources of the area be affected, but so too can the quality of the visitor experience. Again, the working hypothesis was that increasing numbers of visitors cause greater social impacts as measured by crowding, conflict, and related variables. Thus, as applied to national parks, carrying capacity has two components: environmental and social.

The early work on carrying capacity has since blossomed into an extended literature on the environmental and social impacts of outdoor recreation and their application to carrying capacity (Graefe *et al.* 1984; Kuss *et al.* 1990; Lime & Stankey 1971; Manning 1985; 1999; 2000; Shelby & Heberlein 1986; Stankey & Lime 1973). But despite this impressive literature base, efforts to determine and apply carrying capacity to areas such as national parks have sometimes failed. The principal difficulty lies in determining how much impact, such as soil compaction and crowding, is too much. Theoretical development, backed up by empirical research, generally confirms that increasing use levels can lead to increased environmental and social impacts (Hammitt & Cole 1998; Manning 1999). But how much impact should be allowed in a national park? This basic question is often referred to as the "limits of acceptable change" (Frissell & Stankey 1972; Lime 1970). Given substantial tourism demand for national parks, some decline or change in the quality of park resources and the visitor experience appears inevitable. But how much decline or change is acceptable or appropriate before management intervention is needed? How much use and associated impacts are too much?

To emphasize and further clarify this issue, some writers have suggested distinguishing between descriptive and evaluative (or prescriptive) components of carrying capacity (Shelby & Heberlein 1984; 1986). The descriptive component of carrying capacity focuses on factual, objective data. For example, what is the relationship between the number of visitors entering an area and the number of encounters that occur between groups of visitors? Or what is the relationship between the level of visitor use and visitor perceptions of crowding? The evaluative or prescriptive component of carrying capacity concerns the seemingly more subjective issue of how much impact or change in resource conditions and the quality of the visitor experience is acceptable. For example, how many contacts between visitor groups are appropriate? What level of perceived crowding should be allowed before management intervention is needed?

Recent experience with carrying capacity suggests that answers to the above questions can be reached through development of management objectives and formulation of associated indicators and standards of quality (Graefe *et al.* 1990; Manning 1997, 1998; Shelby *et al.* 1992; Stankey *et al.* 1985; Stankey & Manning 1986). This approach to carrying capacity focuses principal emphasis on defining the degree of resource protection and the type of visitor experience to be provided and maintained. Each might be said to comprise the following:

> *Management objectives* are broad, narrative statements that define desired future conditions: the degree of resource protection and the type of visitor experience to be provided. They are based on review of the purpose and significance of the area under consideration. Development of management objectives may involve review of legal, policy and planning documents; consideration by an interdisciplinary planning and management team; historic precedent; local, regional, national or international context of the park; and public involvement.

> *Indicators of quality* are more specific measurable variables that reflect the essence or meaning of management objects; they are quantifiable proxies or measures of management objectives. Indicators of quality may include elements of both the resource and social environments.

> *Standards of quality* define the minimum acceptable condition of indicator variables.

An example of management objectives, indicators and standards may be helpful. Review of the U.S. Wilderness Act of 1964 suggests that areas of the national park system contained in the National Wilderness Preservation System are to be managed to provide opportunities for visitor solitude. Thus, providing opportunities for solitude is an appropriate management objective and desired future condition for most wilderness areas. Moreover, research on wilderness use suggests that the number of visitors encountered along trails and at campsites is important to wilderness visitors in defining solitude. Thus, trail and camp encounters might be key indicators of quality and help to make operational the general management objective of providing opportunities for solitude. Further research suggests that wilderness visitors may have standards about how many trail and camp encounters are acceptable before the quality of the visitor experience declines to an unacceptable degree (Heberlein *et al.* 1986; Manning *et al.* 1999a, 1996b; Roggenbuck *et al.* 1991; Shelby & Vaske 1991; Vaske *et al.* 1986; Whittaker & Shelby 1988). Such data may help to define standards of quality.

By defining indicators and standards of quality, carrying capacity can be determined and managed through a monitoring and management program. Indicator variables can be monitored over time and management actions taken to ensure that standards of quality are maintained. If standards have been violated, carrying capacity has been exceeded. This approach to carrying capacity is central to contemporary park and outdoor recreation planning frameworks, including Limits of Acceptable Change (LAC) (Stankey *et al.* 1985), Visitor Impact Management (VIM) (Graefe *et al.* 1990), and Visitor Experience and Resource Protection (VERP) (Manning 2001; National Park Service 1997), recently developed by the U.S. National Park Service.

Application of VERP

The VERP framework noted above comprises nine steps or "elements" and was initially applied at Arches National Park, Utah, USA (Belnap 1998; Hof *et al.* 1994; Manning 2001; Manning *et al.* 1995, 1996a). The purpose of this application was to refine the VERP framework (as shown in Table 11.1) and provide a model for the rest of the national park system. Planning and research aimed at formulating indicators and standards of quality for the visitor experience are described in this section. Complementary research addressed indicators and standards of quality for natural resource conditions such as soil disturbance and compaction and destruction of vegetation (Belnap 1998; National Park Service 1995).

Arches National Park comprises 73,000 acres of high-elevation desert with outstanding slick rock formations, including nearly 2,000 sandstone arches. Many of the park's scenic attractions are readily accessible through a well-developed road and trail system. Tourism to Arches has been increasing rapidly, and the park now receives over three-quarters of a million visits annually.

Following the VERP framework, an interdisciplinary project team was created, comprising planners from the National Park Service's Denver Service Center, Arches National Park staff, and NPS scientists and consultants (Element 1), and a public

Table 11.1: The visitor experience and resource protection (VERP) framework.

Elements

1. Assemble an Interdisciplinary Project Team
2. Develop a Public Involvement Strategy
3. Develop Statements of Park Purpose, Significance, and Primary Interpretive Themes; Identify Planning Constraints
4. Analyze Park Resources and Existing Visitor Use
5. Describe a Potential Range of Visitor Experiences and Resource Conditions
6. Allocate the Potential Zones to Specific Locations in the Park
7. Select Indicators and Specify Standards for Each Zone; Develop a Monitoring Plan
8. Monitor Resource and Social Indicators
9. Take Management Action

involvement strategy was developed (Element 2). Workshops were conducted to develop statements of park purposes, significance and primary interpretive themes (Element 3). Authorizing legislation and the current General Management Plan provided important reference sources. Park resources and existing visitor experiences were then mapped (Element 4) and a spectrum of desired resource and social conditions was constructed using a matrix format (Element 5). Based on this analysis, a system of nine zones ranging from developed to primitive was created and overlaid on the park (Element 6).

Element 7 requires selecting indicators of quality and specifying associated standards of quality for each zone. This required a research program that was conducted in two phases. Phase I was aimed at identifying potential indicators of quality (Manning *et al.* 1992). Personal interviews were conducted with visitors throughout the park. In addition, focus group sessions were held with park visitors, park staff and local community residents. Findings from Phase I research suggested several social and environmental indicators of quality for the park, including the number of people at frontcountry attraction sites and along trails, the number of visitor groups encountered along backcountry trails and at campsites, the number of vehicles encountered along roads, the number of social trails and associated soil and vegetation impacts, the level of trail development and visitor knowledge of regulations regarding off-trail hiking.

Phase II of the research program was designed to gather data to help set associated standards of quality (Lime *et al.* 1994). A survey of park visitors was conducted, covering all nine park zones. The survey was administered to a representative sample of over 1,500 park visitors by means of both personal interviews and mail-back questionnaires. Five indicator variables received special attention: (1) the number of people at one time at major front-country attraction sites; (2) the number of people at one time along frontcountry trails; (3) the amount of environmental impact caused to soil and vegetation by off-trail hiking; (4) the number of visitor groups encountered along backcountry trails and at campsites; and (5) the number of vehicles encountered along unpaved roads. The first three of these variables were addressed by a series of photographs that illustrated a range of impact

Figure 11.1: Representative photographs of Delicate Arch showing a range of visitor use levels.

conditions (Manning *et al.* 1996b). Photographs were developed using a computer-based image capture technology (Chenoweth 1990; Lime 1990; Nassauer 1990; Pitt 1990). Base photographs of park sites were taken, and these images were then modified to present a range of impact conditions (e.g. number of visitors present, amount of environmental impact). A set of 16 photographs was developed for each major attraction site and trail, presenting a wide-ranging number of visitors present. Representative examples of photographs for Delicate Arch are shown in Figure 11.1. An analogous set of photographs was developed for a range of environmental impacts caused by off-trail hiking (Figure 11.2). Respondents rated the acceptability of each photograph on a scale of –4 (very unacceptable) to +4 (very acceptable). Questions regarding encounters in the backcountry and along unpaved roads were asked in a more conventional narrative and numeric format.

Earlier in this paper, it was noted that park visitors may have standards (or norms) for judging the appropriateness of park conditions. Methodological techniques have been developed and refined to measure such norms of park visitors (Heberlein *et al.* 1986; Manning 1985; Manning *et al.* 1999a, 1999b, 2001, 2002a, 2002b, in press; Shelby & Heberlein 1986; Shelby *et al.* 1992; Vaske *et al.* 1986; Whittaker & Shelby 1988).

The research program at Arches National Park was based on these techniques. Findings from Phase II research provided data to help formulate standards of quality for each of the nine park zones. Where appropriate, at least one resource and social indicator of quality was chosen for each zone and standards of quality were set for each indicator variable. For example, the "pedestrian" zone of the park contains several of the most prominent attraction sites in the park, including Delicate Arch. Visitors reported that the number of

Figure 11.2: Representative photographs of a trail at Arches National Park showing a range of environmental impacts.

people at any one time at such attraction sites was important in determining the quality of their experiences. Thus, the number of people at one time (PAOT) at Delicate Arch was selected as an indicator of quality for that zone. Moreover, findings from the series of 16 photographs of Delicate Arch (as shown in Figure 11.3) suggested that visitors generally find up to 30 PAOT to be acceptable. (It can be seen from the figure that the line tracing visitor evaluations of the 16 photographs crosses from the acceptable range into the unacceptable range at about 30 PAOT.) Based on these findings, 30 PAOT was selected as the standard

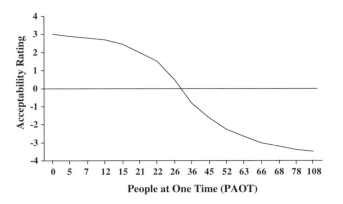

Figure 11.3: People at one time (PAOT) framework.

Table 11.2: Indicators and standards of quality identified and addressed in selected units of the U.S. National Park System.

Park	Indicator Variable
Canyonlands National Park	Encounters with other boats
Statue of Liberty/Ellis Island National Monuments	Waiting time to enter Statue Waiting time to purchase ticket Waiting time to get on ferries
Golden Gate National Recreation Area	PAOT on Alcatraz Island
Grand Canyon National Park	PAOT on trails
Appalachian National Scenic Trail	Encounters with other hikers Encounters with other campers
Boston Harbor Islands National Recreation Area	PAOT at attraction sites Encounters with other hikers Encounters with other campers Trail impacts Campsite impacts Waiting time for ferries Litter Graffiti
Yosemite National Park	PAOT at attraction sites PAOT along trails Encounters with other hikers Encounters with other campers Campsite impacts
Mesa Verde National Park	PAOT at attraction sites Size of tour groups Length of tours
Kenai Fjords National Park	PAOT at attraction site
Hawaii Volcanoes National Park	PAOT at attraction sites PAOT on trails Walking time from parking lot
Blue Ridge Parkway	Automobile traffic PAOT at attraction sites
Sagamore Hill National Historical Park	Size of tour group Length of tour

Table 11.2: (*Continued*)

Park	Indicator Variable
Arches National Park	PAOT at attraction sites
	PAOT on trails
	Trail impacts
	Trail development
Acadia National Park	PAOT on carriage roads
	PAOT at attraction sites
	Trail impacts
	Trail development
	Automobile traffic
	PAOT on trails
	Social trails
Yellowstone National Park	Encounters with snowmobiles
Isle Royale National Park	Campsite sharing
Haleakala National Park	PAOT at attraction sites

of quality. Indicators and standards of quality were set for all zones in a similar manner. A companion set of resource-based indicators and standards of quality was formulated based on a program of ecological research (Belnap 1998; National Park Service 1995).

A monitoring program focused on indicators of quality has been designed and is now being implemented in the park. This will allow park staff to address Elements 8 and 9 of the VERP framework. This monitoring program will determine the extent to which standards of quality are maintained. The VERP framework requires management action if standards of quality have been, or are in danger of being, violated. Primary management actions being undertaken at Arches include adjusting the size of trailhead parking lots, issuing backcountry camping permits, and educating visitors about the impacts of off-trail hiking.

Computer simulation modeling of recreational use can be employed as a substitute or complement to monitoring (Lawson *et al.* in press a; Wang *et al.* 1999). Such models can be developed to estimate PAOT at attraction sites, the number of encounters between recreational groups along trails, or other indicators of quality. Moreover, such models can estimate the maximum number of visitors that can be accommodated within a park or protected area without violating standards of quality. A computer simulation model of recreational use was developed for Arches National Park and was used to estimate the maximum number of vehicles per day that could enter the park without violating the standard of quality of 30 PAOT at Delicate Arch (Lawson *et al.* 2002, in press b; Wang *et al.* 2000).

Following its initial application at Arches, VERP has been applied at a number and variety of areas contained in the U.S. national park system. A concerted effort has been made to address the diversity of environments and issues within the national park system.

For example, indicators and standards of quality have been established for both crowding and conflict on the carriage roads of Acadia National Park (Jacobi & Manning 1999; Jacobi *et al.* 1996; Manning *et al.* 1997, 1998, 1999b). These indicators and standards of quality address both the number of visitors using the carriage roads and visitor behavior. The carrying capacity of this system of multi-use trails has been estimated using a computer simulation model of carriage road use (Wang & Manning 1999). Indicators of quality identified and addressed in selected units of the national park system are shown in Table 11.2.

Conclusion

Over 30 years of research and experience has led to development of several frameworks for analyzing and managing the carrying capacity of parks and related areas. All of these carrying capacity frameworks rely on a similar series of steps or elements. VERP is specifically designed to identify and manage carrying capacity in the U.S. national park system. Carrying capacity is managed by defining desired resource and social conditions by means of a series of indicators and standards of quality. Indicator variables are monitored over time to ensure that standards of quality are maintained. If standards of quality are violated, the VERP process requires that management action be taken. VERP provides a theoretically sound and rational process for analyzing and managing carrying capacity in national parks and related areas. It provides a structured framework within which to conduct a systematic, thoughtful, traceable, and defensible carrying capacity analysis. An associated research program can provide a strong empirical foundation for applying the VERP framework.

VERP has been applied in a number of units of the U.S. national park system. These applications have resulted in development and implementation of carrying capacity plans for these areas, the first such carrying capacity plans in the U.S. national park system (e.g. Jacobi & Manning 1997; National Park Service 1995). A VERP handbook has been developed (National Park Service 1997) along with a workbook of management actions designed to support the VERP framework (Anderson *et al.* 1998). Additional applications of VERP in the national park system are on-going.

Despite development, testing and refinement of VERP and related carrying capacity frameworks, application across the U.S. national park system and related areas will be challenging. The number and diversity of parks suggests that a wide variety of indicators and standards of quality will have to be formulated. This will require a substantial investment in park planning and related natural and social science research. It will also require a long-term program of park monitoring and a commitment to implementing management actions designed to maintain standards of quality.

Acknowledgments

A number of people inside and outside the U.S. National Park Service have been involved in the development and application of the VERP framework. VERP was initially developed by a group of planners at the NPS Denver Service Center, including Marilyn Hof, Jim Hammett,

Gary Johnson, and Michael Rees, and associated scientists, including Dave Lime of the University of Minnesota, and the author. Several NPS staff at Arches National Park were instrumental in the initial application of VERP, including Noel Poe, Jim Webster and Karen McKinlay-Jones. Park staff and researchers who made significant contributions to other applications of VERP described in this paper include Charlie Jacobi and John Kelly (Acadia National Park), Terri Thomas (Golden Gate National Recreation Area), Dave Wood and Bruce Rodgers (Canyonlands National Park), Linda Jalbert (Grand Canyon National Park), John Sacklin (Yellowstone National Park), Diane Dayson, Cynthia Garrett, and Richard Wells (Statue of Liberty National Monument), Marjorie Smith (Sagamore Hill National Historical Park), Gary Johnson (Blue Ridge Parkway), Rita Hennessey (Appalachian Trail), Patty Trap (Mesa Verde National Park), Bruce Jacobson (Boston Harbor Islands National Recreation Area), Russell Galipeau, Jan van Wagtendonk, and Laurel Boyers (Yosemite National Park), Jeff Troutman and Shannon Skibeness (Kenai Fjords National Park), Ann Mayo Kiely (Isle Royale National Park), Kerri Cahill (NPS Denver Service Center), Dave Lime (University of Minnesota), Jeff Marion (U.S. Geological Survey), Yu-Fai Leung (North Carolina State University), Alan Graefe (Penn State University), Gerard Kyle (Clemson University), David Cole (Aldo Leopold Wilderness Research Institute), William Stewart (University of Illinois), Martha Lee (Northern Arizona University), Jonathon Taylor (U.S. Geological Survey), Darryll Johnson and Mark Vande Kamp (University of Washington), Wayne Freimund and William Borie (University of Montana). Staff and graduate students in the Park Studies Laboratory at the University of Vermont were instrumental in conducting this program of research, and include William Valliere, Steven Lawson, Peter Newman, Megha Budruk, Benjamin Wang, Daniel Laven, and James Bacon.

Section 3

Adventure and Sport Tourism

Chapter 12

Adventure Tourism and Sport — An Introduction

Chris Ryan and Birgit Trauer

A number of commentators have observed the growth of adventure tourism and its associated recreational pursuits. Indeed, for some specific locations adventure tourism products are a significant part of the total tourism product. For example, Queenstown, New Zealand, has sought to be the "adventure capital of the world" (see http://www.resortrentals.co.nz/queenstown.htm and http://www.kanes.co.nz/1zones/52AD.htm as two examples). The core components of adventure tourism are generally held to be risk taking, uncertain outcomes and generally a natural setting. For example Ewert & Jamieson (2003: 68) define adventure tourism as:

> A self-initiated recreational activity, typically involving travel and overnight stay component, that usually involve a close interaction with the natural environment, structurally contains elements of perceived or real risk and danger, and has an uncertain outcome that can be influenced by the participant and/or circumstance.

This definition additionally draws our attention to the fact that outcomes can be influenced by "the participant and/or circumstance" and thus it can be argued that such influence includes the control exercised by management. Consequently the adventure experience can be engineered and that such "engineering" is consistent with notions of commodification that have been advanced in the literature, for example by Cloke & Perkins (1998; 2002). Increasingly adventure tourism products have to adhere to various safety regulations, whether externally imposed or voluntarily accepted by the operator. Examples of such regulations are provided by those to which New Zealand's white water rafting companies have to adhere in agreement with New Zealand's Maritime Safety Authority (see www.msa.govt.nz — part 80 of Marine Rules that apply to Marine Craft involved in Adventure Tourism); which arrangements were instituted after the drowning of overseas tourists in the 1990s.

Paradoxes thus abound. While adventure implies risk taking, the "objective" risk may be comparatively small even while the psychological challenge may be significant. One

Taking Tourism to the Limits: Issues, Concepts and Managerial Perspectives
© 2005 Published by Elsevier Ltd.
ISBN: 0-08-044644-2

example is bungy jumping, where the number of fatalities as a percentage of those who jump is almost miniscule, yet the sense of achievement by many who jump is intense in its emotional state. For example, Ryan *et al.* (2003) note one respondent in their survey of "peak experiences" saying of bungy jumping.

> (It was) exhilarating — I have photos and a video so it will live in the memory (Bungy jumping).

while another respondent stated with reference to skydiving that:

> It was the first time I had ever thrown myself out of plane, and I never thought I could do it! I overcame a fear of flying.

as evidence of categories of "a sense of achievement" and obtaining "the adrenalin high" that found in their sample.

For their part Cloke & Perkins (1998, 2002) argue that adventure tourism products of this nature are increasingly manufactured experiences of adventure, a commodity of adrenalin that can be purchased and which appear exciting because of the affective responses they elicit even though the level of risk taking is low. The implication of this analysis is that levels of adventure exist, and it has become feasible to analyse products along a continuum of soft to hard adventure. At the soft end the duration of the experience may be short, as in bungy jumping. Alternatively, if longer, the tourist may be little more than a passenger as in jet boating. Little requirement is demanded of the tourist in terms of either skill or stamina. On the other hand such demands may be significant, as in mountain climbing expeditions that may last several weeks. Yet even in these latter cases it might be argued that today, with satellite positioning and digital communications the "explorer" is less at risk than his or her counterparts a century or more earlier. Additionally discomfort levels due to better clothing and more easily carried provisions are much less than those experienced by earlier generations of explorers.

One possible consequence is that the limits of adventure recede to differences of type and degree. On the one hand, the tourist experiences the limits of technology, as arguably is the case in space tourism; but the tourist is little more than a passenger (or financial benefactor) and as the technology improves the technology increasingly provides comforts for the passenger. Alternatively, the adventure becomes the means of a psychological testing of limits of self, whereby the mind might logically know the risk is minute, but nonetheless the act defies ingrained senses of self preservation, as in bungy jumping. A third aspect is that limits of competency are continually explored as the participant engages in increasingly risky forms of recreation made "safe" only by the continuous acquisition of skill. This position is represented by many adventure recreational pursuits such as climbing, mountain biking, snowboarding, windsurfing, sky diving, skate boarding and the like, where increasingly "extreme" conditions are sought. Additionally, those who commit themselves to such extremes also commit themselves to subcultures. Skateboarders, surfers, climbers and divers adopt the language, clothing and other signs of "belonging" associated with such sub-cultures. Values are thus signified to not only each other, but also to non-participants.

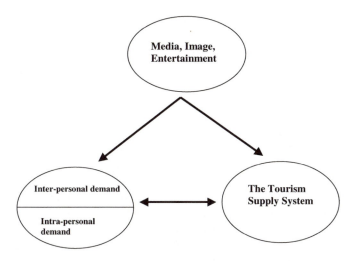

Figure 12.1: A modified tourism system.

Consequently, the process of the commodification of adventure is not solely that of product design, but also the production of accessories that sign the product and the nature of those who participate as being "adventurous." Following the logic of this it becomes possible to modify the tourism system as expounded by Leiper (1990). This is illustrated in Figure 12.1. In the original system Leiper defines a spatial relationship between the tourism generating zone and the tourism receiving zone or destination. Between the two lies the transversed space, or the travel zone. In the modified system the tourism generating zone is replaced by the tourism supply system, which may partially lie in both geographical zones as the distribution chain links both the actual product and the agencies through which it is sold. Indeed, in the early twenty-first century the distribution chain also resides in hyper-space and thus is arguably geographically free. The tourism receiving zone is now replaced by the tourist demand system comprising two components, the intra-personal and inter-personal; thereby representing the intrinsic and extrinsic needs. These are met by the product provided in the tourist receiving zone, but today, as argued by Harrison-Hill (2005) a component of the tourist experience is delivered through expectation generated again through the use of the internet.

The major modification to Leiper's tourism system is the addition of the media, entertainment and image industries. This has several roles, including the signage of tourism product and the conveyance of images, values and roles associated with a product. The representation of adventure through television (particularly perhaps cable and satellite television stations such as the *Discovery* and associated Channels) and magazines that cater for various levels of enthusiasts has made many of the recreational and adventure images familiar to tourists. Indeed, it can be argued that the very pervasiveness of the image is now affecting tourism to the degree that no longer is tourism a search for the unfamiliar but increasingly it is becoming a search for the desired role made familiar through the media. Tourism has become part of the entertainment industry and tourists have become as actors seeking roles with which they can identify; and in that acquisition of identities seek to explore part of themselves.

A key component of the search for self then lies with the degree of commitment that is made to the activity. Some tourists are simple collectors of different adventure roles, who taste activities in pursuance of adrenalin highs or as collectors of places and activities. Other tourists may commit to an acquisition of expertise in order to test themselves in increasingly more challenging environments. The adventure industry is also familiar with the media imagery, and contributes to those images, and subsequently uses those images to attract the very clientele it wants. A symbiotic relationship exists between activities, places, operators and tourists that reinforces a mutual process of identifying each as being pertinent to the other.

This is mode of thinking leads to the framework shown in Figure 12.2 and which is adopted from Ryan & Trauer (2004). The basis of the model lies in the two continua of first, that lying between "soft" and "hard" adventure, and second relating to the degree of involvement to which the participant is committed. What the original Ryan and Trauer framework perhaps fails to capture fully is the nature of involvement, which can be divided into two categories. These are the situational and the enduring. Enduring involvement relates to the long-term commitment to skill and knowledge acquisition relating to a specific

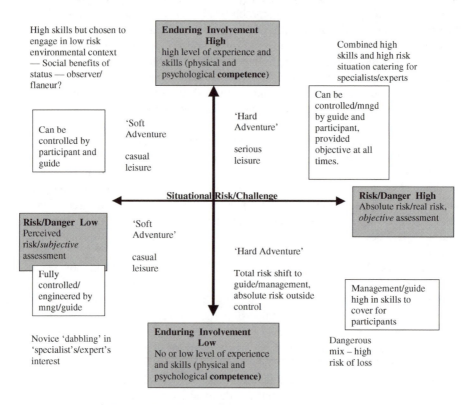

Figure 12.2: Dimensions of adventure tourism.

activity, whereas situational involvement pertains to the affective and cognitive state at the time of doing the activity. The current framework shown in Figure 12.2 attempts, partially, to capture this difference by locating the situational within the horizontal dimension originally labeled "hard-soft" by Ryan & Trauer (2004) but here labeled risk/danger with an attempted distinction between the subjective and the objective. It is admitted the diagrammatic representation does not wholly capture this nuance, but it is sufficient to indicate four different cells that highlight different degrees of management and experiences that tourists might have.

Various degrees of evidence for the framework is provided by the four chapters that follow, and equally the proposed framework indicates one way in which the chapters link with each other. Ferguson and Todd and Cater both indicate the importance of signs through the clothing industry. Apparel has various ways of signing. Souvenir t-shirts indicate the activity done and signals the nature of the person to others as an "adventurous" person. More specialized clothing such as wetsuits, cycle shirts, or casual clothing with specific logos signal degrees of commitment, expertise and enduring commitment. The wearing of such clothing arguably bestows psychological benefits of self-esteem and prestige, including also affective rewards of being "recognised" as an adventurous person. Ferguson and Todd also demonstrate how attitudes toward the wearing of the souvenir shirts is situational dependent upon which sub-culture one belongs. Cater (2004) has also shown how important clothing is, noting that economic power can be derived from the value of its sales to such an extent that it enables the sporting wear manufacturers to become an effective political stakeholder in U.S. policies pertaining to the classification of natural areas and the economic consequences that subsequently flow from such categorization. Harrison-Hill also indicates how aspects of adventure that appear incidental to the main activity nonetheless can influence how the activity is experienced. The search for information, the identification of interested others with whom one can share an enthusiasm and exchange knowledge about venues and activities seemingly helps build expectations prior to participation. These expectations are important because they shape subsequent behaviours.

The final paper, by Ong Chin Ee also signifies the relationship of signage, symbols and values that exist between adventure products and society — but in an unusual but interesting manner. The premise of his chapter is that the adventurous person who commits to sports like diving displays exactly those characteristics required by the new economic realities of Singapore. In an attempt to create innovative, risk taking individuals, Ee argues that the Singaporean government has sought to use the adventure tourism commodity to encourage the development of the required skills.

Chapter 13

Acquiring Status Through the Consumption of Adventure Tourism

Shelagh Ferguson and Sarah Todd

Introduction

Much has been written on the attractiveness of adventure to the general population. Ewert (1989) cites the example of an advert placed in the London Times in 1906 that sought volunteers for a polar expedition. It emphasised the expected emotional and physical hardship and the distinct possibility of not returning, yet the advertisement attracted over 5,000 responses. The lure of adventure appears not to have diminished over time. Adventurous activities appear regularly on Sky Sports channels and have been the subject of several films, including *Vertical Limits* and *Point Break*. These media representations of adventure add to its allure. As Mayo & Jarvis (1981) note when writing on the Ulysses factor, adventure and excitement are intrinsically satisfying in themselves.

Adventure is central to New Zealand's positioning as a tourist attraction within most tourist markets. Key activities such as bungy jumping, northern hemisphere summer snow sports, white water rafting and paragliding are positioned prominently as key aspects of the New Zealand brand (New Zealand Tourist Board 2001). Although not unique to New Zealand, they have come to epitomise adventure tourism in New Zealand, particularly bungy jumping through the A. J. Hackett brand. Adventure tourism in New Zealand continues to grow and generate significant income, despite recent world events that have negatively affected other destinations (New Zealand Tourist Board 2001).

Background Literature

Academic research into the consumption of adventurous tourism is relatively limited. However there is a body of work that has explored specific activities such as mountain biking, white water rafting or skydiving (e.g. Arnould & Price 1993; Celsi, Rose & Leigh 1993; Dodson 1996; Holyfield 1999). Such studies have mostly been set in an American context and adopted a psychological perspective but there has been some New Zealand based adventure tourism work (e.g. Berno, Moore et al. 1996; Cloke & Perkins 1998).

Taking Tourism to the Limits: Issues, Concepts and Managerial Perspectives
© 2005 Published by Elsevier Ltd.
ISBN: 0-08-044644-2

In the wider tourism literature, the study of the motivation to consume tourism has a long history (Cohen 1972; Dann 1981; Krippendorf 1984; Turner & Ash 1975). There has been a strong focus on differentiating between motivation towards a destination (pull) and motivation away from the pressures of everyday life (push) using a sociological or psychological perspective (Dann 1981).

According to Krippendorf (1984), a popular motivation to consume tourism was centred on the need to escape and research has revealed that this can act as the major motivator to consume such diverse products as sun worshipping in a purpose built Mediterranean resort and sex tourism in Northern Thailand (Krippendorf 1984; Mayo & Jarvis 1981). According to Mayo & Jarvis (1981), people from similar backgrounds with similar family situations should make similar tourism consumption choices. A comparison with similar profile acquaintances tells us that this is not true! Mayo & Jarvis (1981) account for this difference through consistency and complexity theory that influence an individual's set of motivations. The amount of variety that one seeks is proportional to what is missing from their life, complexity in tourism to balance consistency in home life or vice versa. These would appear to be very broad brush strokes to cover consumers' motivation for many different and essentially individualistic activities. So a relevant question must be, how can a better understanding be gained of this motivation to consume tourism, and adventure tourism in particular?

More recent work has moved away from a segmentational approach, understanding consumer behaviour through socio-demographic, economic or life stage criteria, towards an understanding of consumption based upon a more individualist, post-modern perspective (Gonzalez & Bello 2002; Urry 2001). Urry (2001) specifically discusses his perception that we are all tourists most of the time and tourism is so culturally bound that tourism and culture are inseparable. He then goes on to build upon Campbell's (1987) argument that daydreams are culturally defined and heavily media influenced, to the extent that they are central to modern tourism consumption. The daydream forms the aspiration that the consumption attempts to emulate. The daydream that is central to the motivation to consume is both constructed and sustained by non-tourist practices in popular culture, films, magazines, TV and video. Urry (2001) argues that intensely pleasurable anticipation is derived from reliving these daydreams and this forms the basis upon which consumption decisions are made.

A post-modern sociological perspective on tourism consumption can give an insight into an individual's desire to consume certain types of tourism, the need to be an individual or to de-differentiate themselves from others. This expands upon the argument that modernism is "structural differentiation" in cultural terms between various cultural spheres, therefore the de-differentiation of post modernism involves the breakdown in the distinctiveness of these spheres until they implode (Lash 1990). This latter perspective would appear particularly relevant to gaining an understanding of the consumption of adventure tourism in the specific context of this research, as it is a commonly held belief that a primary motivation to consume for status associated reasons would be closely linked to the need to differentiate oneself from others.

Although Krippendorf clearly identifies the consumption of tourism as a status associated activity, he describes it in relation to either the loss of face or "a need to keep up with the Jones" (Krippendorf 1984: 18), thus giving the motivation to consume both a negative (loss of face) and a positive (an opportunity to gain status) aspect in relation to status. The consumption of a specific tourism experience can therefore create jealousy and/or admiration among one's neighbours in relation to these positive or negative aspects. Several authors comment upon tourism consumption as a positive status marker utilising a sociological perspective (Feifer 1985; MacCannell 1999; Pearce 1982; Turner & Ash 1975; Urry 2001) although Krippendorf (1984) specifically warns that this influence should not be overestimated. The adoption of a more sociological/societally driven perspective reflects the importance of status in the current environment, thus Krippendorf's caveat appears dated in today's society.

Therefore if we accept that a prime motivation to consume tourism is concerned with status aspirations, it seems reasonable to conclude that consumers could acquire more status from the consumption of some types of tourism than others — relative to the value that this type of tourism has with the consumers' immediate aspiration group. For example, certain cruises have more status than others among those choosing a more sedentary or passive type of tourism, so if a cruise is consumed it could ascribe status to that consumer in accordance with the norms and values of the aspirational group by being particularly expensive, or an exotic location or oversubscribed (perhaps with a long waiting list such as cruises to Antarctica). This research focuses upon status acquired from the consumption of adventure tourism and the group of consumers who use the consumption experience to acquire status from their aspiration group, according to the group's norms and values.

Therefore if the consumption of adventure tourism is considered from a similar perspective, within a specific aspiration group the consumption of certain types of adventure tourism will ascribe more or less status to a group member as governed by the group's norms and values. Adventure has certainly been commodified in popular media and representations of extreme sports have been applied to a wide range of products in attempts to appeal to youth consumers. Adventure is sexy to the MTV generation (Keen 2002). This is reflected by the popularity of events such as the X Games and films such as *Vertical Limits*. It is argued that adventure is an aspirational activity and this acts as a powerful consumption motivation. Popular culture relevant to our aspirational group has a significant influence on our likes and dislikes, opinions, world-view and the consumption choices that we make (Solomon 1992). Segments such as Generation Y are said to be constantly seeking the next big thing or to be as "cool" as it gets and this influence of consumption depicted in popular culture is central to the formation of aspirational groups (Russell & Puto 2000) and, currently, adventure is cool!

An important concept relevant to the process of status acquisition is the role and structure of aspiration groups. Schouten & McAlexander's (1995) work on the subculture of Harley Davidson owners describes in detail the aspirations of these motorbike owners and the process that moves towards fulfilment of these aspirations in relation to other group members. For example, the owner of the most modified motorbike with respect to other group members' bikes gains the most status. These aspirations are unwritten but clear to everyone within that group (Schouten & McAlexander 1995). Similarly, brand communities form cohesive groups that share consumption practices through shared values reflected in a certain brand (Cova 1997).

A key tool in the acquisition of status is the process of narration and central to the quality of this narration is the use of props or artefacts that represent the symbolic consumption of these experiences. It is commonly accepted in the marketing literature that consumer choices are not driven solely by the actual functional utility of the goods or services but also by their meaning (Levy 1959). Product meaning can be symbolic and communicate information about some aspect of the consumer (Levy 1959), and is in turn heavily influenced by popular culture (Solomon 1992). The post experience narration of tourism consumption utilising symbolic artefacts can be central to an individual's attempts to "narrate identity" within their aspirational group (Torun 2001). Mathlein (1998) found that within some aspiration groups the consumption of terrifying or dangerous experiences as part of a tourism experience could become the most status enhancing to an individual.

Methodology

To complement relevant work already done in the area from a psychological perspective, a sociological multi method approach is proposed. The choice of methodology evolved during preliminary research and has been moulded by initial findings and continuous reference back to the relevant literature. This type of inductive methodology matches the perspective and the exploratory nature of the research problem. In order to identify a community with strong membership bonds that would facilitate interaction between members, the researcher immersed herself into various communities. These bonds proved essential to the narration of consumption experiences and ascribing of status within the community.

The research suggested that consumers of adventures bond tightly and form a subculture of consumption as defined by McAlexander & Schouten (1993), such as these found by Arnould & Price (1993) in the white water rafting fraternity or Celsi *et al.* (1993) in sky diving. An initial proposition investigated whether consumers of adventure tourism experiences created a closely bonded group that allowed status to be acquired by an individual in a meaningful way. Two communities were initially tested, namely a "backpacker" subculture interacting in the social areas of backpackers' hostels and resort workers' communities. Through preliminary investigation it was found that the "backpacker" subculture exhibited strong social links and interaction on occasions but not on a regular, replicable or predictable basis. Itinerant ski field workers in Queenstown, New Zealand were clearly defined as a community by employment and geography but, due to their shift work patterns, it was very difficult to gather group interaction information. They are sociable and located in proximity to many adventurous activities, giving them the opportunity to consume these experiences, but capturing the narration of consumption was too irregular and contrived.

Searching for accessible aspiration groups with strong social links that consumed adventurous activities led to groups of university students living in shared accommodation. These groups were investigated within their household and interaction was recorded providing rich, detailed and naturally occurring data. The method adopted was focus group interviews using broad questions, asking participants to narrate their adventurous experiences. The transcribed data was then analysed with reference to literature to identify key emergent themes for wider testing. These emergent themes are reported below and will later be tested on a broader section of the aspiration group to investigate their validity and reliability. The most relevant of these emergent themes will be investigated in depth, using a case study approach.

Findings

Two main themes emerged from discussions with all groups and the contrasting views add depth to the emergent topic of status and the means by which it is acquired.

Theme 1. Hard and soft core consumers dictated by the knowledge level of the subculture.

There appears to be a hierarchy of 'cool' associated with adventure tourism consumption that is acknowledged by the consumers, or, more descriptively, a "hard" and "soft" core. Consumers actually use the words "hard" and "soft" core to describe themselves in relation to their adventures. Fox (1987) originated the concept in relation to her work on punks and it describes a simple concentric social structure based on the relative status of individual members. Adventure tourism consumers appear to divide into two groups where behaviour is modified by their environment. Some types of behaviour are acceptable for the soft-core consumers, to the extent that they believe it will ascribe status to themselves, whereas the hard core regard the same behaviour as reducing their status within their aspiration groups. For example, backpackers who are travelling on an extended trip to several countries will wear their A. J. Hackett bungy t-shirts immediately and with pride. Several commented on the increased attention from fellow backpackers that it attracted but Queenstown locals would consider this "naff."

The backpacker community were gathering experiences to retell to their significant others during and after their travels, but were also willing to re-tell their experiences to other immediate groups such as those encountered in backpackers' hostels. This implies that these experiences are consumed not only for internal satisfaction but for the ability to re-tell post consumption, in search of social approval. Members of the other communities of temporary workers and New Zealand residents admitted that they would not consume an adventurous experience alone, as the real enjoyment was in sharing the experience and the re-telling post experience, particularly the crashes and injuries. It was also deemed "cooler" by the student group to have someone tell your experience for you, "rather than front up and tell it yourself." Crashes and reckless behaviour appear to have the highest status for this subgroup and often instigate questions allowing consumers to re-tell their experience. One group of university students, who have consumed several adventurous experiences together, were re-telling their experiences of jumping off a cliff and everyone could clearly remember who went first and who had the biggest bruises.

Theme 2. Symbolic consumption of T-shirts.

A key factor in the use of symbolic props (particularly t-shirts as these created the most spontaneous narration opportunities) was the knowledge level within the subculture that the experience would be narrated to. Backpackers were proud to wear their t-shirts. Conversely respondents who were working temporarily in Queenstown or were New Zealanders would not wear their t-shirt in public, rather it was most commonly worn to bed. This phenomenon is commented upon as examples of hard and soft-core behaviour in an earlier theme. Some respondents indicated they may consider wearing a t-shirt if it represented completion of the Nevis bungy jump (the highest and most exposed bungy jump in New Zealand) but felt anything else was "too common and touristy."

One female had participated in Mad Dog river boarding and bought the t-shirt post experience and wore it "into holes and is still probably used for dusters," as she said no-one knew what Mad Dog river boarding was and the t-shirt had those words and cool paw prints all over it and it solicited lots of questions. Thus, if the experience is relatively unknown within the subculture, the t-shirt is cool! In contrast, most New Zealanders, and especially Queenstown locals, would recognise an A J Hackett bungy t-shirt immediately and it was seen to most likely attract derogatory comments and be "uncool." Therefore it is proposed that the t-shirt not only symbolises the experience but also acts as a prompt to enquiries to facilitate narration of the experience. In subcultures where the knowledge base is higher (hard core) and an adventurous experience such as bungy jumping at Kawarau Bridge would not be considered cool, risk taking behaviour and injuries create these similar opportunities for narration within these more knowledgeable subcultures. The hard-core group are more likely to move towards a novel experience and find "cool" by being the first to experience something others have not.

Conclusions

Further research is required to develop these themes by investigating how props are used to create opportunities to acquire status. At this stage, there are some obvious overlaps between the themes to emerge to date. However, it is also evident that consumption of adventure tourism is motivated by individuals' desire to achieve status within a particular group. As well as purchased "markers" such as t-shirts, physical evidence of the consumption (e.g. bruising) instigates opportunities to discuss the consumption with one's aspirational social group. Shared consumption of adventure appears to act as a form of social bond and this was observed both among "looser" groups such as the backpacking community as well as more tightly formed groups such as university flatmates. The findings to emerge to date from this exploratory research indicate that adopting a sociological perspective and appropriate methodology have the potential to contribute much to our understanding of why people participate in activities which may seem, at best, reckless if not downright dangerous.

Chapter 14

Looking the Part: The Relationship Between Adventure Tourism and the Outdoor Fashion Industry

Carl Cater

Performance

Performing various roles in public space are the dominant way that individuals make sense of their worlds and, especially, of their own bodies. As Denzin suggests, "performance is interpretation...a performance is a public act, a way of knowing, and a form of embodied interpretation" (1997: 97). Furthermore, these embodied performances shape, and are shaped by, the spaces that they inhabit. "The body is entangled with fantasy and discourse; fantasy mobilizes bodies and is expressed through discourse; and discourse, well, discourse is disrupted by fantasy and interrupted by the body. And all of these relations are articulated spatially; their performance articulates space" (Rose 1999: 258). As Adler states, each new tourist practice, however seemingly new, is built upon earlier travel traditions, and in this sense, tourism itself may be seen as an inherently performative act;

> In effect, travel may owe some of its cultural prestige, as well as its importance to persons' lives, to the fact that, in carrying a performer beyond the world of routine home life, it yields observations, encounters, and episodes that are free to function as relatively abstract signifiers. Like 'important' cultural texts, travel experiences can provide enduring referents for thought whose interpretation remains open to change. Once inscribed in memory, photographs, or journals, a single travel performance may always be interpreted as saying something new in response to a new emotional need or cognitive query (Adler 1989: 1369).

Adventure as Performance

Nowhere are these observations more clear than in the burgeoning adventure tourism industry. Whilst grounded in a long history of adventurous tourist practice, adventure

Taking Tourism to the Limits: Issues, Concepts and Managerial Perspectives
© 2005 Published by Elsevier Ltd.
ISBN: 0-08-044644-2

tourism is clearly about an active participation involving the body. The inability of tourist metaphors such as Urry's "gaze" to capture this enacting body has been highlighted in previous work (e.g. Cater & Smith 2003; Cloke & Perkins 1998). Drawing on earlier work by MacCanell (1976, 1992) and others, it may be argued that the body is an authentic site of consumption in a way that solely visual experience is not. As Urry suggests, the other senses may offer us a "more direct and less premeditated encounter with the environment" that contrasts with "the abstractive and compositional characteristics of sight" (1999: 41). The construction of the recreational body is thus important in understanding participation in adventure activities.

This chapter seeks to demonstrate how the "dressing up" involved in many adventure tourism activities is a central part of their performative nature, as there is often the requirement to feel that the participant is wearing suitable attire for the experience. Costumes, such as lifejackets, help participants get into their roles as adventurers, even when their use is not strictly necessary. The discussion shall focus principally on the manner in which these issues are negotoiated in places where adventurous activity takes place. Following this, the narrative will highlight the other end of the spectrum, in terms of multinational clothing manufacturers seeking to use themes of adventure to sell their products. The text concludes with an illustration of the considerable power that this lobby wields in the spaces of adventure themselves. The material for this chapter comes largely from the author's experience of adventure tourism management in Queenstown in New Zealand.

Earning the T-Shirt

Quite clearly it is the performance of adventurous activities *in situ* that is most relevant to this discussion. To begin with it is worth highlighting that the participants seem to be fully aware of the roles expected of them in their enacted role. A frequent comment in interviewing is the desire to achieve the perfect form, particularly where the activity is captured on film or camera. In bungy jumping this may be a perfect swan-dive, in other activities the look of confidence and domination in the frame. The look is one of harmonic conquest of the environment, embodying the adventurous ethic itself. As Schibe states "The *right stuff* as a concept is bound up with vertigo and transcendence in the escape from earth's bondage. If you have the right stuff you are in harmony with the sublime" (1986: 142). Respondents are undeniably aware of the desire to bring this expression of having the "right stuff" into their performances;

> I jumped off a bit harder and a bit further, tried to make it look slightly better, instead of just falling off!' Adam, U.K., 15–25, The Ledge Bungy (Second Jump).

Looking the Part

Tied into these conceptions of looking good are notions of "looking the part," the classic adventurer. It is clear that in the performance of adventure there is often the requirement to feel that the participant is wearing suitable attire for the experience. Thus the donning of specific *costumes*, or in some case the removal of more "ordinary" ones, as in the relatively common practice of bungy jumping naked or just in underwear, is a clearly performative aspect of the practice.

> The lifejackets are really just for the photos, I mean yes they would make you float if you did fall out of the boat, but we don't let people fall out of the boat. So the lifejacket is part of the . . . It's part of the experience you know (Nick Flight, Marketing Manager, Shotover Jet).

It is clear that the donning of costumes is as much about stripping, metaphorically, as it is about the wearing, since adventure is about reclaiming a more suspended, liminal identity. Clearly "the performances characteristic of liminal phases and states often are more about the doffing of masks, the stripping of statuses, the renunciation of roles, the demolishing of structures, than their keeping and putting on" (Turner 1986: 107).

The fleeting nature of these costumes also bears identification, since these are characteristic of the quick-fix activities under examination, and this corresponds to many other performative genres. As Shields (1991: 269) contends, the "wearing of different hats" is central to the articulation of the agency of the body. In the way that actors may change costumes several times during a play, tourists likewise may don different guises during a holiday. Market sectors such as adventure tourism are particularly notable for the handover of responsibility from the individual to the operator, which includes the issue of all of the costumes required and expected from the activity. As Buckley (2003: 129) states, "outdoor recreation is now treated much more as a purchasable short-time holiday experience than as a gradually acquired life-time skill with its own set of social rewards and responsibilities."

Performing for an Audience

Active participation, however, is nothing without an audience. As Adler highlights, "the audiences for whom travellers perform are crucial to any travel world, and anticipations of their responses, as well as their direct interventions, play a constitutive role in the production of journeys" (1989: 1378). A. J. Hackett are acutely aware of the importance of viewing platforms, shown by changes they made to the Ledge bungy after acquiring it from a previous operator;

> The whole system was wrong, so what we have done is twisted it into the hill more and shortened it, so there is a lot more viewing, with the hanging viewing decks (Ian Leech, Marketing Manager, A. J. Hackett).

Quite often it may be the presence of an audience, possibly one where there are peers and relations that is the catalyst for perfomance.

> It was scary, I thought I was going to die! If there hadn't been people watching I wouldn't have done it (Franco, Sweden, 15–25, Pipeline Bungy).

Denzin (1997: 101), discusses the fluidity of the participant/audience boundary; "Audiences are neither pure voyeurs of nor passive recipients of performance events ... (they) interpret and live through performances — they are performers of their own interpretations and witnesses of the performed ... the audience is an interactive structure. Although members bring their own interpretative frameworks as audience members to a performance, the audience-as-a-performer can also enact its own performance aesthetic. In this way, the audience is both inside the performance and observer of its performance."

Company Performance

In addition the performance of the guides is clearly an integral part of the experience. The participants have an expected idea of the person who will lead them through the activity, typically active, outdoorsy, knowledgeable and larger than life, acting as the "exemplars of the bodily habitus expected of and desired by tourists" (Crang 1997: 151). This is obviously enhanced by the company advertising, in fact one of the most blatant found was one for a jetboat ride which positions their drivers as being "personality plus," clearly referring to their distinctive auras, enhanced by company dress. Evidence suggests that adventure operators seek individuals that conform to a particular kind of look that corresponds to tourists expectations;

> If they have experience on ropes and karabiners and that, we would like that, but we choose a person on how they communicate at the end of the day, and if they are on to it. But communicating with people if they are liked, **just the look**, it plays a huge factor in it, because if you are tying a person up then you have got to look confident. They can't be way over the top though, so we have to be selective on appearance and how they communicate with people (Matt, marketing manager, Pipeline Bungy).

Often this picture is enhanced by the very organisation of the adventure trips, and on several occasions of being briefed by the guides whilst being bussed along dirt tracks wearing our "gear" to the activity sites seemed to remind one of various war movies as the troops are being briefed for battle whilst in their transport (for example scenes reminiscent of those in *Aliens* or *Platoon*). Clearly this enhances the feeling of entering *into* an adventure. In addition, the guides undoubtedly enhance the desire to "look good" during the practice of the activity. For example on a river surfing trip, "participants were told that the most important thing was to *try to look cool* whilst walking down to the river suited up in a wetsuit" (Personal account, Serious Fun river surfing). The last thing that most participants hear before a bungy is the jumpmaster telling them to look out and give a good swan dive.

In addition the adventure companies must perform to specific criteria to support their adventurous credentials, although this may be somewhat at odds with commercial practice. The founders of Pipeline bungy left A. J. Hackett precisely because they felt that the company had moved too far away from its adventurous, "fun" and personal roots to follow an overly corporate ethos;

> We wanted to get back to the fun on the bridge you know, none of this big corporate international scene with management structures and that. Just a good team around us, who we knew were the right kind of people, and focussed on keeping it simple and giving the customers a good time and developing more of a relationship with them basically (Andrew Brindsley, founder, Pipeline bungy).

It is interesting to consider the ramifications of such an acknowledgement for the expansion of adventure tourism operations. Is it possible, at least outwardly, for adventure tourism operators to exist as part of a large tourism operation? It is suggested that, from a principled viewpoint, commercial interest and adventure are opposed, and careful masking of such relationships takes place. This leads to the situation where "operators of alternative adventurous sites will *both* wish to distance themselves from the hegemonic imagery and style of Disney *and* adopt tried and tested techniques of branding, marketing, pricing, ancillary product sales, safety, staff performance and the like" described by Cloke & Perkins (2001: 6). As Buckley states, the links between the two may not be "immediately apparent to consumers and tourists; but a glance at corporate financial figures tells the story loud and clear" (2003: 133).

Adventure Spaces

Theming the various activities is recognised as a highly important process, particularly in an environment that has become as competitive as Queenstown, the self-styled "adventure capital of the world" in New Zealand. A clear theme helps to identify an activity from its competitors, and this can be seen in the success of "Catching the Canyons" with Shotover Jet, or the clear branding of the Pipeline bungy jump. Where the latter is concerned, the rebuilding of a fake pipeline across the gorge to hark back to a sluicing pipe that was in the area a century before defines the frontier gold *rush* element to the Pipeline experience. So successful has this piece of adventure architecture become, that few participants realise the actual inauthenticity of this icon. It was interesting to observe the emergence of a new activity in the form of the A. J. Hackett Nevis bungy, which the company was attempting to push as taking the experience to another level;

> Theme is super-important, its going to be particularly strongly themed (Ian Leech, Marketing Manager A. J. Hackett).

Such a process may be presented as a grassroots example of the invocation of what Hollinshead (1998) terms a "distory" in tourist practice, the selective presentation of history in a commodified and manipulated fashion, characterised by the processes of historical appropriation by the Disney corporation. Such practices enable "a postmodern seizure of useable storylines from the past which are decontextualised and romanticised and thereby turned into nostalgia which can decorate, and be purchased, but are frequently much diminished in connected meaning" (1998: 80). Whilst it is important to recognise that this process is unlikely to have the rigidly authoritarian delinination seen in McDisneyization

(Ritzer & Liska 1997), the close personal networks detailed previously and below, combined with a hegemonic touristic focus in Queenstown, may propogate a similar phenomenon, albeit of a more subversive nature.

Indeed it seems that, perhaps unsurprisingly, the industry is a step ahead of academia, for while Weber (2001: 374) suggests that careful diversification of the product may allow access to previously untapped markets without alienating operators' existing customer base, this strategy can be clearly already observed on the ground. For example, AJ Hackett's instigation of historical tours of the Kawarau bridge and provision of related information clearly captures a wider market, as well as extending the attraction for the existing customers. Likewise, Shotover Jets' "history-added" Goldfield Jet and "nature-added" Dart River Jet may be observed as part of the same process.

For bungy jumping, one of the clearest identifiers of an individual jump is its height, and this forms an important part of the attraction for a significant proportion of participants;

> I was deciding that if I was going to jump I wanted to do the 71m, I didn't
> want to do a small one, if I jump I want to JUMP! I wanted something higher
> so it would mean something (Naya, Israel, 15–25, A. J. Hackett Bungy).

This process may also be observed in the other activities, for example the attraction of rafting the Shotover river, normally grade 5, as opposed to the grade 3 Kawarau.

Been there, got the T-shirt

This theming of the activities often translates into the performance of the activities through apparel worn off-site. Frequently the icons and numbers previously mentioned are used to heavily brand the adventure activities and also produce merchandise that reinforces the perfomative iteration. What is important to recognise, however, is the manner in which "such place meanings not only change the ways in which places are represented and experienced, they also influence the ways that those places are managed. Seen in this way, advertising isn't just simply a technique for attracting business; it is a medium through which places and experiences are made in order that particular interests are served and others downplayed" (Cloke & Perkins 1998b: 271). The circuit continues, for these interests then translate into particular senses of place, for whilst "place is a negotiated reality, a social construction by a purposeful set of actors . . . the relationship is mutual, for places in turn develop and reinforce the identity of the social group who claims them" (Ley 1981: 215).

The availability of heavily branded souvenirs have served to strongly reinforce this reputation. It is interesting to see how, for the adventure tourism operators, souvenirs, such as T-shirts, are positioned just as much a form of advertising, and therefore product reinforcement, as they are a business venture in themselves;

> Advertising is the main thing with the merchandise, there isn't a great markup
> on the t-shirts to be honest, because they get seen around the world and people
> go 'oh what is that?' . . . it sells for us' (Matt, Marketing Manger, Pipeline
> bungy).

Queenstown Rafting's selection of a fern as their symbol has both been reinforced by, and reinforces the existence of the fern as a New Zealand icon, and has also resulted in a wide range of branded merchandise. Again this is as much for brand recognition as it is to generate profits. Over a third of respondents asked confirmed that they intended to purchase some form of adventure merchandise. The sheer effectiveness of such branding processes in Queenstown is shown by this respondent's categorisation of the resort when asked about his main reason for visiting Queenstown;

Scenery, Adrenaline, Partying (Gordon, U.K., 31, River Surfing).

Of interest is the manner is the way in which non-participants in adventure can still buy into the mythology of adventure through such conspicuous consumption. This is somewhat parallel to Buckey's (2003) discussion of the manner in which Surf-style clothing has penetrated the streetwear market.

New Media

Of further significance is the fact that the performance of adventure is *not* confined to the geographical boundaries of the space in which it takes place. The fact that the experience is available in a number of media formats to take away with the participant is important. Of the respondents from the Queenstown sample, over 80% confirmed that they intended to purchase either a video or photos from the adventure operator. In this way the experience goes on acting and confirming through this, achieving the sort of added value discussed above;

Do you think the experience represents value for money?

Ah man that is such a good question, such a relevant question. So it was seventy bucks, probably not. It will be worth it going home and talking about it and showing the video to my friends though. But the jump itself, probably not (Rachel, U.S., 48, Kawaru Bungy).

This quite clearly demonstrates the intrinsic value held in such souvenirs, highlighted by Schiebe (1986).

This continued reinforcement is not limited to the photos and videos alone, however, as with the conspicuous consumption of everything, from key-rings to clothing, identifies with the performance. It is a rare week that I do not see someone wearing some T-shirt proclaiming success of having done some adventurous activity. Jazzy designs and eye-catching colours ensure that everybody knows that they are a performer.

I am going to get a jacket to show I have done it, he promised me one! And the photos! (June, Australia, 36–45, Shotover Jet).

Big Business?

All of this discussion is also important in a consideration of the manner in which adventure has been used to sell fashion from a global perspective. Of course the consumption of these goods is not wholly defined by the adventure itself. The consumption of consumer goods related to an adventurous ethic is explained by Riley (1995: 634), as the need to engage "in ideal rather than utilitarian consumption; the burgeoning phenomenon of fashion-oriented consumption; and an increase of interpreted symbolism from consumptive displays." Thus a huge consumer goods industry has grown alongside the tourism itself, with the adventure tourist being able to assert their identity as such through the carrying of the badges that denote such a lifestyle, with goods that "possess qualities beyond their functional purpose" (Riley 1995: 634). Johnston and Edwards demonstrate how the activity of mountaineering has become progressively commodified;

> Corporate sponsorship has shaped mountain experiences and even the fantasy of a mountain experience in order to sell commodities to a consuming culture. (As a result,) . . . many more well-equipped, stylishly dressed holiday consumers are travelling to mountain regions . . . sent by an ever-growing legion of adventure travel companies who advertise their services in (a also growing number) of 'Adventure Travel' magazines and guides. They arrive carrying clothing and equipment purchased at outdoor shops staffed by adventure enthusiasts; and they are guided through their mountain adventure by mountaineers turned tour guides' (Johnston & Edwards 1994: 468).

It has been estimated that the level of expenditure on the latest skiwear in Britain every year, for which there are relatively good statistics, amounts to some £44 million alone (Mintel 1996, quoted in Holden 1998). It is suggested that expenditure on "adventure clothing" is at least equal to this, perhaps more so given the current vogue for adventure design in urban lifestyles. This latter point highlights that it is possible to confirm the ideals of an adventurous lifestyle through the display of such consumption, without even partaking, and the superficial nature of this consumption bears investigation. It is interesting to see how the adventurous ideals of the Royal Geographical Society both reinforce and are reinforced by their corporate sponsors, Land Rover and River Island (Phillips 1997: 184).

Consequently, because of the fact that adventure sells, multinational clothing companies are eager to push their credentials in this area. The vogue for "outdoor style" in fashion is dominated by identifying with an ethic of adventure. Nike have been particularly active in promoting the sales of their "All Conditions Gear" brand (and consequently the entire product range) through sponsorship of adventure sports competitions. One example is the extreme sports week held in Voss, Norway every year, which has emerged as one of the premier global showcases for these pursuits, partly on the back of the corporate funding received from Nike. In turn the Nike and ACG logos get to adorn everything from parachutes to kayaks and media interest circulates these symbols to a global audience. Nike are certainly not alone in this sort of brand promotion, as many other clothing groups have used similar strategies, as do other companies, particularly motor manufacturers seeking to establish their adventurous credentials. The links between adventure, clothing and new media highlighted here reinforce Buckley's suggestion that "adventure tourism may have grown from outdoor recreation, but both have now become inseparable from the clothing, fashion and entertainment sector" (2003: 133).

The Politics of a Fashion

This phenomenon is paralleled and related to the increasing size of the adventure clothing industry itself. The Outdoor Industry Association (OIA), a body "representing the 4000 or so companies that clothe and equip the more than 149 million Americans that like to hike, bike or roam the great outdoors," estimates the industry is worth some $18 billion annually in the U.S. alone (OIA 2003). Thus a huge consumer goods industry has grown alongside the tourism itself, of increasing political as well as societal significance. In the summer of 2003, the OIA was closely involved in lobbying for the protection of wilderness areas in Utah (Economist 2003).

Following a closed deal between the Utah state government and the department of the interior, whereby wilderness protection was removed for some 2.6 m hectares of state land, the OIA threatened to move its annual trade fair out of Salt Lake City. This annual event was estimated to bring in some $24 million into the capital, and its significance to the local economy was far from small. Initial protests from environmentalists fell on deaf ears, but when the OIA joined in the argument, the outdoor recreation industry began to realize that it had real clout. It might seem that companies of the likes of Nike and the green lobby are somewhat unlikely bedfellows, but in the case of preservation of wilderness areas for adventure recreation, they have some common ground.

In conclusion therefore, a mutual synergy exist between participants, fashion wear, the adventure tourism industry and conservation interests, in that the symbols are indeed a signing of roles that possess economic advantage as is suggested by Ryan and Trauer in their introduction to this section of the book.

Chapter 15

Getting into the Spirit: Using Internet Information Search to Heighten Emotions in Anticipation of the Sport Tourism Experience

Tracey Harrison-Hill

Introduction

This chapter explores Internet information search behaviour by sport tourists. It focuses on external search behaviour that takes place in an online environment. In particular it is interested in online search behaviour where consumers are making conscious efforts to acquire information that will assist specific sport tourism related product and service decisions. While many of the studies on consumer information search behaviour are intertwined with research on consumer information processing and choice behaviour, this study is interested only in exploring how and why sport tourists are using the Internet to collect information regarding their sport vacation. In particular, what needs are these consumers trying to satisfy through using the Internet in relation to vacations? This focus serves to enable marketers operating within the sport tourism sector to gain greater insight into how the Internet might be utilised within the promotional mix and essentially within the inception of their product offering.

Consumer behaviour research has traditionally focussed on the cognitive aspects of information search. Initially economic concepts such as benefits and costs within a process of logical decision making have been prominent. Information search was seen as a stage within the rational activity of purchasing the "right" product. Subsequently, in the 1980s the concept that consumption and information search might be driven by enjoyment and motivated by a desire for fun was suggested (e.g. Hirschman & Holbrook 1982; Holbrook & Hirschman 1982). This perspective treats the entire consumption process, including the search for information, not as a problem that the consumer is trying to solve, but rather as an experience in which the consumer tries to maximize their positive feelings.

This approach led to the recognition that the information search can occur purely for pleasure. Bloch *et al.* (1986) defined ongoing search as activities that are independent of a recognized and immediate purchase problem. Ongoing search processes that consumers undertook for the pleasure of keeping up to date in a particular area of interest were also

Taking Tourism to the Limits: Issues, Concepts and Managerial Perspectives
© 2005 Published by Elsevier Ltd.
ISBN: 0-08-044644-2

strongly linked to enduring involvement (Bloch & Bruce 1984) and were considered to be motivated by needs extending beyond immediate functional needs.

As an information source the Internet is ubiquitous and has been shown to accommodate both functional product-specific search and ongoing search (Hoffman & Novak 1996). Among the characteristics possessed by the Internet are two key features that facilitate consumers' search activities, namely the extensive availability of information and its interactivity and associated retrieval methods. The Internet incorporates various mediums of information including, among others, an array of web pages that embody the World Wide Web, discussion groups, listservs, bulletin boards, emails and instant messaging. It also possesses the capability to support and facilitate several forms of interaction including one-to-one, one-to-many, and many-to-many communications through these information sources. This vast information network is made retrievable, and hence valuable and usable, through efficient and constantly evolving search mechanisms including browsers, search engines, recommendation agents and shopping bots.

The reasons underlying consumers' information search behaviour on the Internet are still being explored as this phenomenon continues to grow (Peterson & Merino 2003). Recent research has demonstrated that the Internet is being searched for purchase-specific information as well as providing information more generally for those who are searching for the intrinsic enjoyment of the task (Hawkins 1996; Hoffman & Novak 1996; Shim, Eastlick *et al.* 2001). Hoffman & Novak (1996) distinguished between these two types of online search behaviour. Purchase specific search was extrinsically motivated and was characterised as reflecting situational involvement and seeking utilitarian benefits. On the other hand, general information search was seen as being intrinsically motivated and was further differentiated from purchase-specific search by being more likely to reflect enduring involvement and the quest for more hedonistic benefits.

Online purchases for tourism products have been recognised as one of the largest sectors on the Internet (World Tourism Organisation Business Council 2001). Managerial research on the content of online tourist information has largely focussed on the functional and utilitarian aspects. Similar to consumer behaviour research though, it has been found that there are many tourists who are seeking social and hedonistic benefits from their Internet search activities (Cano & Prentice 1998; Wang & Fesenmaier 2003; Wang, Yu *et al.* 2002).

These studies reflect the earlier findings by Vogt & Fesenmaier (1998) that not all consumers who collect tourism information actually intend to travel. These authors stress the need to recognise that consumers searching for tourism information are driven not just from a functional perspective but also from social, hedonic, aesthetic, innovative and symbolic perspectives. Functional needs are seen to include the need for knowledge about a destination including attractions, prices, and value. It also incorporates the need to use information to reduce risk and encompasses the desire for efficient use of time in searching for information. Innovative needs are seen to include searching for information about new places and to ensure creative solutions for vacation choices. However, hedonic needs involve searching for information to enjoy sensory pleasures and to heighten excitement through information acquisition. Hedonic needs also encompass the desire to search for information to "experience" the local culture and to better understand "the personality" of a destination. Quite similar to hedonic needs are aesthetic needs. These include searching for information to build fantasies of the destination and to appreciate the beauty of a place. The final need the authors identified was sign or symbolic needs. These generally refer to how consumers search for information to be able to better advise others and so demonstrate their knowledge and identity as an active traveller.

Vogt & Fesenmaier's (1998) research demonstrated that tourism information is largely collected and used for functional reasons and was closely related to planning tips. The other information needs, however, clearly existed but were less important in the time period leading to a vacation. These needs for information were also found to exist beyond the traditional "information search" phase of travel decisions. Vogt & Stewart (1998) demonstrated that information was indeed collected prior to travel but also importantly that it was collected, consumed and recalled throughout the duration of vacations.

The Study

This study is interested in the needs sport tourists' are attempting to satisfy by conducting information search using the Internet and the nature of those searches. A convenience sample was derived from participants within four sport-related email newsgroups. Each group was international in membership and had over 200 members and over 2000 messages for 2002. With the permission of the newsgroup owners, archives from these groups were analysed for the preceding twelve months to identify list members who had discussed travel and/or intentions to travel for sport purposes. This process revealed 130 potential participants. These members were then contacted through email and consenting participants were interviewed utilising instant messaging. Where a common instant messaging software was unavailable, the email group's public chat room was used to conduct the interview and transcripts downloaded. Interviewing via the chat software was challenging. The researcher found it more difficult to establish rapport with participants without the use of body language and eye contact.

The resultant sample consisted of 51 usable interviews with participants from 10 countries. Participants were encouraged to consider the most memorable sport tourism occasions that they could recall that had them travelling away from home for a minimum of one night within the past 12 months. Sport tourism was defined for the participants as travel whose primary purpose was to participate within, or spectate at, a sport occasion or visit a sport attraction. The role of the Internet within information search regarding those sport vacations was then investigated.

Sample Characteristics

The participants were primarily female comprising 71% of the sample. This was not surprising, as the sports selected were female-dominated sports including dressage, agility, softball and netball. There was a spread of ages from 22 to 73 years of age. Respondents were also internationally dispersed as can be seen in Table 15.1. All participants felt that they were highly involved in their sport. This was also evidenced within the type of sport tourism in which the participants were involved. In the twelve-month period of

Table 15.1: Respondents' country of residence.

Country	Number of Participants
USA	16
Australia	11
Canada	9
New Zealand	7
England	3
South Africa	1
Malaysia	1
Ireland	1
Belgium	1
Brazil	1

2002, 92% of participants (47) had been involved in active sport tourism, and two had travelled internationally to participate. Participants also travelled for the primary purpose of spectating at a sports event, with 35 of the participants travelling domestically for such purposes and three having travelled internationally.

Findings

A major theme emerging from the interviews was that of seeking information to heighten the emotional anticipation of the forthcoming sport vacation. Participants reported that they searched for information for both purchase-specific reasons and for more intrinsic reasons, but searching for information to help them "... get into the spirit of the vacation" as one participant suggested, was a recurring theme. When this idea was further explored a number of participants identified an event marker that triggered a change in their search patterns. The event marker led to the finalisation of the decision and subsequent booking of the vacation. The nature of this process varied slightly for different participants. For those independent travellers who were doing the planning, booking and purchasing of their entire vacation themselves through online means, this event was more arbitrary than for those booking through an agent. An independent traveller described the feeling as:

> I suddenly felt that was it! It's all in place now! Then I felt a little sad and thought what have I got to search for now. That was when I started looking for more of the little things to build the hype. I added the weather and clock from Dortmund to my homepage with this javascript countdown thing so that each day when I went online I could see it and get more excited...

Those who were booking through an agent were able to identify this marker quite succinctly and these participants expressed the change as very deliberate. They moved from making sure they were getting good value to searching to help build the excitement and anticipation. As one participant expressed, they now went online with the purpose of "getting emotionally charged." Discussion between list members was also seen as part of this process with a number of participants discussing how the interaction between members that were going to the same event helped build the anticipation through sharing.

> . . . Sue from Perth kept us in touch with what the weather was like so we knew what to pack. It was all exciting. Some of the emails were really short, like — do you think I'll need XYZ? We had our own thread happening, those not going were very quiet at that time, just saying they wished they could go and stuff like that.

For one participant the tour organisers precipitated the sharing via a newsgroup.

> They (tour operators) set up an email list for those going on the tour, we all got to know each other before we even got on the bus — it was great. Those that used the list tended to hang out more together on the trip too.

Other participants also expressed the desire, post-booking, to get to know more about the history of the event as well as the destination they were visiting. A "softballer," who was travelling as a sport participant, described the process of becoming more involved with the event in this way: "Each night I'd sit there for hours looking up info on the teams . . . I think I was a walking encyclopedia by the time of the trip . . . ."

A participant who was travelling to spectate also expressed the desire to be more involved with the destination.

> Once I knew I was going I started to want to know more of the detailed stuff like about the people, the culture, like what is their average day, what do they eat, what do they do, stuff like that to make me feel like I know the place.

So the needs of the participants changed during the pre-consumption period. During the planning and before the booking they were mostly concerned with functional information, particularly in getting good prices, organising flights or transport, and other utilitarian information.

> My first stop now when looking for anything, a camera, a hotel, whatever, is a couple of key words in google . . . I often use my own search results to compare with travel agent or brochure information.

Similarly:

> The Internet was great in helping to compare hotels — we decided which hotel from info on the net as well as using the maps to work out the best location for us, central to the various venues we wanted to go to.

Yet once they felt the planning was finalised, needs changed to become more hedonistic. In this phase participants both sought and shared information to help build their emotional excitement about their forthcoming vacation. They sought significant information about the event, the destination, the date and the venue. One participant who was putting together an international holiday itinerary based around spectating agility events throughout England wrote about a venue:

> I was so excited about Olympia — where it all started. I was searching for as much info as I could get so I would be informed when I got there.

Participants' needs in this post-booking phase were also often satisfied through online sharing of information, primarily through the email newsgroups but also on a one-to-one basis. As this netballer wrote, "Sherry and I kept emailing new things we'd found out."

Two participants also expressed the view that their search motivations had three different stages. Both were planning to attend an annual event that they had been to before and their discussions revealed that they went through an early pre-planning stage that was about keeping excited but also concerned reminiscing. Then there was a planning stage followed by an excitement stage.

> . . . nothing specific, just keeping in touch to stay interested. Looking at last year's web page and stuff like that. Then it got closer and I started searching for flights and hotels and checking prices. . . . Then when it was all planned I helped others organise theirs by telling them different stuff I'd found.

An agility spectator also expressed this cycle:

> Sometimes when I had some time to kill online, I'd look up the stuff on Dortmund or search on the world champs, and read people's personal pages about the championships. It just helps me to remember what a good time I had, and I like to read other people's stories about it too. That all stopped when this year's got closer. Suddenly it all seemed rushed and I didn't feel prepared. But once the tour was booked that stress turned into full-on excitement.

So while searching and sharing information to build anticipation is a strong theme, it is also evident that there is a cycle of changing needs that drives different search strategies.

Discussion

The findings suggest that participants are engaging in an ongoing search for information within a purchase-specific process. This is somewhat different from Hoffman & Novak's (1996) findings in the consumer behaviour literature that suggest that product-specific search and ongoing search are independent constructs. This research suggests that these two constructs can form part of one cyclical experience. For these participants the delineation made between product-specific search and ongoing search is blurred. The decision to travel is established and the major components of the vacation purchased and extrinsic needs have been satisfied, but consumption has not yet occurred and still these consumers continued their online search behaviour to satisfy more intrinsic needs. Furthermore, a number of participants identified an event marker that they suggested pinpointed the changing orientation of their needs.

The cyclical nature of these online information search needs is not surprising given the nature of the participants' enduring involvement with their sports. Furthermore Vogt & Fesenmaier's (1998) typology of tourist information needs suggests that these needs can co-exist within one vacation period. Where the findings differ in this research is that the participants placed more emphasis on the hedonic and symbolic needs than the functional in their discussion of the role the Internet played in their information search. This research also suggests that the importance of needs changed at different phases of the vacation planning. These phases were distinguished by the event marker of finalising vacation plans. This has important implications for marketers and managers of sport, tourism and indeed online communities. If the changing needs can be identified then information that satisfies these needs can be delivered in a timelier manner. Additionally, in this instance where a number of the vacations were to specific sporting events that were at a fixed time and place, the point at which tourists finalise their plans may be better generalised providing a timeline for marketers to change their online information emphases. By catering online information to the hedonic needs of heightening excitement and the phenomenology of the experience, further purchasing and opinion leadership may be stimulated.

These findings have implications for existing frameworks of information search and sequentially depicted decision processes within the literature. The research supports more robust models of information search that incorporate hedonistic and symbolic needs in addition to the traditional functional needs. They also support a more holistic perspective on the collection of information as an ongoing activity. Even when information search is driven by a specific purchase, the collection and consideration of information are not discrete phases within a decision process but rather integrated throughout the decision. The research also supports the notion that emotional and experiential needs are particularly relevant within tourism information (Goossens 2000).

However, this research project has a number of limitations that should be discussed. The sampling frame for this research was skewed toward females. This should be addressed in future research designs; particularly as previous research has suggested women may be more predisposed to hedonic and aesthetic needs. This research has also reported that a temporal cycle may occur with respect to needs, yet the research has been conducted after the event and is relying on the memory of participants. Future research designs should consider in-situ methods within the pre-travel phase to more accurately capture any change in information needs.

Acknowledgments

The work of Ms Karen Miller is acknowledged. Her Honours research project in 2001 provided the impetus for this distinct research project.

Chapter 16

Adventurism: Singapore Adventure Tourists in "Soft" Capitalism

Ong Chin Ee

Introduction

> The real lessons of life are more likely to be learnt on the icy slopes of a
> mountain than the air-conditioned comfort of a lecture theatre.
> > Dr. Vivian Balakrishnan in *The Knowledge Enterprise, January 2003.*

> In many ways, mountaineering has similarities with different facets of our
> lives, at work and in society. It teaches us discipline, sensitivity and humility
> — some of the core attributes of leaders across many fields.
> > Ee Khong Lean, Fourth Year Arts Student of the National University of
> Singapore and participant of the Make It Real Programme in *The Knowledge
> Enterprise, January 2002.*

> More than learning how to organise and execute expeditions, our students
> had first hand experience working as a team and leveraging on each other's
> strength to triumph over adversity. The MIR Programme is a students'
> adventure of learning and discovery, testing character, endurance and the
> spirit of enterprise.
> > National University of Singapore (NUS) President and Vice Chancellor
> Professor Shih Choon Fong in *NUS Press Releases*, "Launch of Make it Real
> 2003 Student Mountaineering Programme," 26 Nov. 2002).

Launching the *Make it Real (MIR) Student Mountaineering Programme* of 2003,
Dr. Vivian Balakrishnan, Singapore's Minister of State for National Development and
MIR Patron, proclaimed that "timeless qualities" of "courage, discipline, determination,
ingenuity and teamwork" can only be actualised if Singaporean citizens, particularly the
National University of Singapore (NUS) students to whom he was speaking, (ad)venture

Taking Tourism to the Limits: Issues, Concepts and Managerial Perspectives
Copyright © 2005 by Elsevier Ltd.
All rights of reproduction in any form reserved
ISBN: 0-08-044644-2

beyond the geography of their cosseted lives — the way MIR participant Ee did. The Vice Chancellor of the National University of Singapore (NUS), Professor Shih, agreed that adventure has visions beyond the planning and practice of expeditions and that it has more to do with workplace ethics and ideals — endurance, enterprise and the ability to triumph over adversity — and the ability of adventure in realising these attributes.

Dr. Vivian, Professor Shih and MIR participant Ee each demonstrate the existence of a specific discourse that can be termed "adventurism" which, broadly speaking, aligns capitalist workplace aspirations with adventure. Neither of these entities alone is static, and the ways in which they have become aligned involve essentially geographical processes that create significant spatial consequences. These are the concerns of this chapter.

As a concept, adventurism is, firstly, a discursive realm which produces specific rationalities and practices in the spaces of work and adventure. First, it brings about the adoption of adventure ideals in the new capitalist workplace. Second, it does the converse: an adoption of work ethics in adventure. As a result, the two spaces have moved closer, imaginatively, discursively and materially, for adventurism concerns not just imaginings but possesses material and embodied manifestations. This is evidenced by the formation and proliferation of adventure parks, outward bound, leadership and team bonding courses conducted by outdoor adventure specialists, and also includes motivation talks delivered by professional adventurers and popular adventure publications, programs, game-shows and an increasing demand for adventure tourism.

The objectives of this chapter are three-fold. The first is to investigate the transformation of workplace aspirations and appropriate worker selves in Singapore's labour force. Drawing upon Foucault's (1999) thesis of governmentality, the chapter examines the tensions of the changing governmentality of Singaporean labour and the myriad citizen selves that are desired and realised. Attention is paid to the role that a stable and orderly landscape in Singapore plays in the realisation of a disciplined but allegedly unimaginative workforce. The second objective is to highlight the emergence of adventurism and a new form of Singaporean labour governmentality. This concerns itself with what is termed the "adventurer-citizen," as a new breed of Singaporean citizens and workers is required by the current economic situation of "soft" capitalism (this concept of "soft" capitalism will be elaborated later in the chapter). The concept of the "adventurer-citizen" demonstrates the incorporation of adventure ideals in work. The third goal is to look at how some of these Singaporean workers attempt to escape from work and its ethics by adventure training and scuba diving in Peninsula Malaysia. Yet it is argued that while they seek freedom from work, they are nevertheless governed by it in their attempts to realise self conceptions as "adventurer-citizens." Hence, the manifestation of "adventurism" in the practices of adventure tourism by Singapore adventure tourists is examined. Of relevance here is how the leisure time and space away from Singapore in the forms of adventure landscapes are no longer just avenues for "rest and relax" but are transformed as "outdoor gymnasiums" providing "scheduled workouts" in Singaporeans' adventure tourists' travels. The final section of the chapter will summarise the argument and consider adventurism's broader implications for freedom, social equity and/in "soft" capitalism.

Within the argument exist three caveats. First one should not dismiss adventurism as merely some "brainwashing" Singapore state propaganda for the so-called "knowledge-based economy." While its most unrelenting promoter remains the ruling People's Action Party (PAP), the Singapore-specific workplace aspirations in adventurism have been disciplined by international business, particularly the notions of "knowledge-based" economy and the formation of what Nigel Thrift (1998) observes as "soft or knowledgeable capitalism." Furthermore, while adventurism resembles a discourse perpetuated by the business and political elite largely unaffected by economic difficulties, its promotion and circulation have broader implications. Second, while the analysis of governmentality employs landscape to examine the subjectification of the Singaporean worker, it is not to be seen as a form of landscape determinism. Landscape is investigated not for its cultural "essence" but to problematise it because landscapes "naturalise" power relations (see Berger 2003; Cosgrove 1984; Matless 1998; Williams 1973). Landscape for "new" cultural geographers (see for example Bunnell 2002; Matless 1998) is understood as both the "work" of culture and that which "does work" (Mitchell 2000: 94). The manner in which Singaporean workers preserve and reform themselves through their landscapes and how these landscapes get reconfigured is crucial to the analysis. Third, the thesis of "adventurism" is not a claim that all adventure is aligned with all workplace ethics and vice versa. Not all adventure tourists subscribe to "adventurism" and not all workers see the need to become "adventurer-citizens." The alignment of work and adventure in "adventurism" is not absolute and perfect.

Before discussing the changing governmentality of Singapore labour, it is necessary to briefly note some methodological concerns. The research is derived from differing sources including various published sources, attendance of an adventure/economy public seminar and participant observation of both a PAP-affiliated adventure training course and Singaporean scuba divers travelling with commercial/capitalist ventures.

Landscape and the Changing Governmentality of Singapore Workers

Why talk about governmentality of workers when this paper is concerned with, first and foremost, adventure tourists? Yet the context of the phenomenon is one in which Singaporean workers have been subjected to specific forms of work ethic endorsement since the formation of a PAP-led Singapore. Currently a process exists whereby the governance of Singapore workers is changing from the post-separation survival ethics to those that entwine old "Asian Values" and new "neo-liberal" strands in an emergent knowledge economy of "soft" capitalism workplace ethics. These are the ethics the workers think they are escaping from when they go on an adventure tours. While not all workers go on adventure tours, their numbers are increasing, particularly among the young tertiary educated professionals.

Notions of survival underpinned the post-separation (of Singapore from the Federation of Malaysia) work ethics (Savage & Kong 1993). Successful urban planning also created an orderly space (Koolhaas 1995; Savage 1997, Savage & Kong 1993) — one free from communist insurgency and union unrests and one conducive for "footloose" foreign capitalists to invest in. The docile, disciplined, cheap but unimaginative Singapore workers realise themselves in the orderly, efficient and safe landscape jointly configured by the PAP and themselves.

When the threat of communist insurgency and economic failure petered away, an "Asian Values" discourse was created to promote communitarian ethics crucial for restraining "western indiscipline and excesses" and lend an ideological edge for the continual shaping of "docile" Singapore workers. The "Asian Valued" worker, however, was too costly for foreign capitalists. Hence, "Asian Values" proved adequate as a source of work ethics for Singapore's workers for, when facing global competitions, they needed to be "flexible." Variable components were created in the wage structures as the labour force also faced competition from the more "flexible" (in terms of wage and numbers) foreign workers who migrated to Singapore, who, indeed, were sometimes actively encouraged by governmental policies (Coe & Kelly 2000). This need for workers capable of surviving global terrains — via flexible demands and enterprising outlook — was emergent in this first stage, but became an aspiration that intensified in the next stage.

Additional to programmes of flexible wages and the intensification of worker training and industry technology upgrading (Coe & Kelly 2000: 415), a program of regionalization was also implemented whereby Singapore relocated lower-end production to neighbouring regions while retaining higher end facilities (Yeung 1998; 1999) for its still costlier workers. Organisations and measures were created to support Singaporean workers to venture and actualise themselves as intrepid expatriates in the less certain but potentially lucrative business landscape of the region. Furthermore, the PAP advocated a "letting go" and Singaporean workers were, and continue to be, urged to go entrepreneurial (*Straits Times* 5 June 2003). It is here that tensions were created as neo-liberalism, "enterprising self" and adventurism arrived in a developmental state. This process, according to Yeung (2003), possesses a uniquely strong institutional capacity to manage financial markets and workers in (spite of) the global economy.

Enterprising Self, Adventurism and the Adventurer-Citizen in "Soft" Capitalism

In their report presented to the Prime Minister, the Economic Review Committee (ERC Report 2001) described a new economic terrain:

> Singapore is going through a major economic transition, possibly the most far reaching since independence in 1965. The economy is maturing. The environment has changed radically. Globalisation, the emergence of China and the problems of South East Asia all affect us. In addition, we have not yet fully recovered from the 2001 recession.

This Economic Review Committee (ERC) report is instructive for it represents the views of the elite in Singapore, some of whom include important Cabinet and Parliamentary members, and claims to include more than 1000 Singaporeans and expatriates residing in Singapore and abroad. The stated common goal is a "globalised knowledge economy" and the strategies include, most notably "a creative and entrepreneurial nation willing to take risks to create fresh businesses and blaze new paths to success." The earlier part of this paper assumed the emergence of a new avatar of capitalism — the kind described by the

ERC. This new form of capitalism, argued Coe & Kelly (2002: 368), is disciplined by the rhetoric of the knowledge-based economy and the rise of "soft or knowledgeable capitalism" (Thrift 1998: 28) in the broader realms of international business. By soft capitalism, Thrift is not talking about something gentle and caring but a form of capitalism — dominated by information, software technology and high performing business managers and workers. It replaces the more secure material accumulation with the vulnerable position of perpetually managing new knowledge. In such a capitalist environment, managers and workers are under the constant stress of high-performance and super (self) exploitation as they seek to realise themselves in accordance with a fickle and fast-changing knowledge based workplace, environments and ethics. Far from being soft, "soft" or knowledgeable capitalism is treacherous (Bauman 2000) and not only do individual bodies need to be " 'lean', 'fit', 'flexible' and 'autonomous' ," so too must collective bodies, institutions, corporations and states (Lemke 2001: 203). This resonates with the kinds of business environment the ERC is seeing or anticipating.

Such "soft" capitalism rhetoric also brings about the alignment of workplace ideals and conduct with adventure, or what this chapter terms "adventurism" in Singapore. While adventure pursuits and adventure tourism have long been practised by Singapore's citizens, the intensity with which they have been adopted by or co-opted into workplace rhetoric and vice versa, is new. Adventure metaphors have been used considerably in themes such as recession, investments, skills upgrading, retrenchment, retraining, pay cuts and so on. Workplace ethics such as self-improvement, team work, enterprise, creativity and leadership have similarly made their way into adventure pursuits and adventure tourism. Singapore's Prime Minister, Goh Chok Tong, is a convert to adventurism. On top of his metaphors of bungee jumping and his promise of legalising the once banned adventure pursuit of bungee jumping and its even more adrenalin pumping cousin — reverse bungee jumping — in the once "safety-obsessed" Singapore (*Straits Times* 5 June 2003), Prime Minister Goh advocated that Singapore citizens become adventurers in life and that the resource-less Singapore should transform itself into a vibrant adventuring nation:

> As a small country with limited natural resources, we have to punch above our weight in many areas in order to survive and succeed. To be a vibrant nation, we need creativity, passion and an adventurous spirit to scale the many mountains facing us. Singaporeans must have the guts and skills to face whatever challenges and to overcome them. Goh Chok Tong, Singapore Prime Minister (Reutens 2001: Foreword)

By this, and in less metaphorical terms, Goh and his party mean the constitution of the kind of "flexible" subjects Coe & Kelly (2002: 362) describe:

> The flexibility to accept lower wages when necessary to assist in employers' continued profitability . . . the flexibility to embrace changes in career directions; to acquire new skills and especially computer literacy and technical competencies; to accept retrenchment and eventually re-employment as a fact of life; and finally the flexibility to think creatively and innovatively in order to further add value to a technologically dynamic economy.

Goh's comments originated from a foreword he penned for the Singapore Antarctica expedition team's commemorative publication. This adventure picture book is instructive. Sponsored by the Northeast Community Development Council, an administrative and town management arm of PAP, it promotes a specific position, and one modified from what Rose (1992) calls the "enterprising self" or, in terms of this paper, what may be more specifically termed the "adventurer-citizen," to cope with new capitalist workplace aspirations. By the "enterprising self," Rose (1992: 146) infers a subject that will:

> . . . make a venture of its life, project itself a future and seek to shape itself in order to become what it wishes to be . . . a calculating self, a self that calculates about itself and that works upon itself in order to better itself.

This is a subject that internalises neo-liberal ideals and are those "who are governed through their freedom and aspirations of subjects rather than in spite of them" (Rose 1992: 147). In the case of Singapore, the tension between its promotion of "Asian Values" (which characterizes Singaporean workers as docile and disciplined workers) and that of the current neo-liberal notions of enterprise and creativity, seemed resolved in the kind of "adventurer-citizen" Goh promoted. The Antarctica adventurers' incredible feat — which originated as personal pursuits — has been extrapolated as national successes. Singapore's workers/citizens are to look up to these new breed of "adventurer-citizens" and to employ the same kind of "guts and skills" to negotiate the terrains of their new workplace struggles and challenges. The adventurer-citizen is one who is creative, passionate and always ready and welcoming of uncertainties and difficulties. They are also high-performing workers capable of not just "getting the job done," but hyper-productive ones willing to "punch above our weight in many areas in order to survive and succeed." Yet this notion of an adventurer-citizen is appealing in that it does not require a complete overhaul or an abolishment of past rhetoric of "Asian Values" which was the key to "disciplining" the Singapore worker. The adventurer-citizen and the adventurer on which it is modelled are not unpredictable and anti-social/subversive individuals. Discipline and submission to team ideals are key attributes of contemporary adventurers who venture in closely knitted teams.

This section has elaborated the "production of a new form of governmentality that privileges that mass production of knowledgeable and enterprising subjects who can simultaneously optimise their relationship to themselves and to work" in contemporary Singapore (Olds & Thrift forthcoming: 18) and related this to what Rose (1992: 146) observes as "the enterprising self." It has discussed a thesis of "adventurism" and the "adventurer-citizen" which have been observed to have been promoted by the PAP. This, it is argued, possesses the potential to resolve the tensions and conflicts between the neo-liberal strands in the "new" capitalist economy and that of the Singaporean brand of Confucian ethics that inspired "Asian Values" responsible for generating and shaping docile and disciplined workers.

These ideals are embodied in the Singaporen adventurer, Khoo Swee Chiow — a new Singaporean ideal commanding glowing testimonial from the PAP and the adventure community. A former employee of Singapore Airlines, Khoo was invited to give a motivation/career talk to National University of Singapore's undergraduates alongside two PAP Members of Parliament. The topic of the talk is particularly relevant to the concerns of this paper: "Global Waters: Will You sink or Swim?" The selection of Khoo, an adventure guru in a seminar with seemingly economic themes, is first evidence of his stature as a new economy Singaporean role model and as an embodiedment of adventurism. Second it points explicitly to the adoption of adventure values in the ERC's "globalised knowledge economy." The converse happens too because Khoo's narration of his enterprising ways of securing expedition sponsorship, amongst others, aligns workplace ideals with adventure tourism.

What is most intriguing is Khoo's promotion of the use of adventure landscapes, particularly treacherous and sublime foreign spaces, as "outdoor gymnasiums" for actualising the "adventurer-citizens" capable of surviving in "soft" capitalism. Khoo claimed, with a touch of humour, that "Singaporeans cannot think out of the box because we live in boxes." By boxes he meant the state-built apartments that shelters 85% of Singapore's population (Housing and Development Board, http://www.hdb.gov.sg/ accessed 9 Sept 2003). While Khoo never made this connection, it is suggested here that such "boxed-up" landscape subjectivities include Singapore's routine urban planning, safe and peaceful landscape sheltered from industrial action and even opposition politics. The success of PAP in creating a docile and disciplined workforce and the endurance of the landscape Singaporean workers and their state jointly configured constitute such subjectivities. Such subjectivities, Khoo and the PAP will agree, created the unimaginative worker problematised today in the new economy rhetoric. Thus, Khoo urges Singaporeans to venture into the sublime so as to realise themselves, just as he did.

Adventure Tours or the "Scheduled Workouts" in "Outdoor Gymnasiums"

This section reports participant observation of Singaporean scuba divers and adventure trainees on their adventure tours in Peninsula Malaysia to illustrate the adoption of workplace ethics in adventure tours, thereby reconfiguring them into "schedule workouts" in "outdoor gymnasiums." The Singaporean scuba divers are an important group because it forms a large and growing community. Scuba diving is increasingly popular with the affluent 20–45 group professionals according to interviews with scuba dive operators. Statistical sources are not available but from interviews, it is estimated that there are a total of 45,000 certified scuba divers in Singapore and of these 10,000 are active divers. Adventure training is crucial in that most Singaporean adventure tourists have undergone at least one adventure course to provide them with the skills needed. These courses are often conducted by adventure experts and constitute real expeditions beyond Singapore's borders.

Ideals and ethics of adventure, such as risk-taking and competency, have been widely invoked by tourism researchers and practitioners in explanations of adventure tourism motivations. Ewert (1989), Meier (1978) and Martin & Priest (1986) relate adventure to competency and risk taking and assumed that experiencing risk is an integral part of adventure tourism motivation. Walle (1997) points to the existence of both risk taking adventure and the pursuit of self-knowledge or insight. From the wider tourism literature, the seminal works of Cohen (1972; 1973; 1974) point to the existence of the non-institutionalised "explorer" or "drifter" tourists whose primary shared values during their tours are characterised by novelty, spontaneity, risk, independence and counter-culture. From institutes of education to individuals conducting their own adventure tours, these practices of backpacking, climbing, scuba-diving and trekking and other adventures are bound up with a conception of adventure tourism as a remedy for the supposedly socio-psychologically undesirable effects of living in a "sheltered" city. For the NUS MIR programme mentioned in the first part of the chapter, climbing the peaks of the world is seen as a cure for the "soft student-citizen" or "couch potato" youths formed by the air-conditioned comfort of its lecture theatres. It is a means of re-conditioning them into adventurous leaders and citizens. The desired Singaporean citizens, according to the NUS think-tank, can only be formed in rugged environments. Such concepts are consistent with the view of adventure tourism as a development of self (Loker-Murphy 1996; Ross 1993; Vogt 1976), rites of passage (Adler 1985) and secular pilgrimages (Bell 2002).

Having said that, how are adventure landscapes reconfigured into "outdoor gymnasiums" and how are adventure tours re-engineered into "scheduled workouts"? The underwater environments are deemed dangerous spaces by the scuba diving community. Divers acknowledge the risk and danger involved in their underwater adventures but believe that with adequate training, one will acquire the competency to explore the underwater landscape safely. This training is provided by cultural/adventure authorities such as the Professional Association of Diving Instructors (PADI) and National Association of Underwater Instructors (NAUI). Besides training scuba divers, these authorities also certify scuba dive tour operations based on the operator's competency in managing the scuba diving risk. Because of this real and perceived danger, the underwater world becomes an ideal outdoor gymnasium to realise flexible and adaptable adventurer-citizens. Scuba diving is not inherently dangerous. Neither are scuba-dives necessarily adrenaline-pumping activities. However, to scuba dive, one needs to acquire an entrepreneurial mindset, one that is open to contingencies in a fast changing landscape (of changing visibility, lost guides and encounters with dangerous marine forms) and the ability to adapt in a new environment. Humans are not configured to survive underwater. It is common for scuba divers, particularly beginning divers and trainees, to quit scuba diving for they have problems, psychologically and/or bodily in adapting to the underwater environment. By venturing into a landscape we are not bodily designed for and for some, not psychologically prepared for — and however safely and easily we do it — is a feat beyond our "comfort zones." Divers, like workers in a workplace shaped by adventurism and soft capitalism, need to "upgrade" their skills constantly and are encouraged to go for a myriad of scuba courses so as to upgrade their underwater proficiency. The underwater world is a fast changing and unpredictable terrain, not dissimilar to the workplace in "soft" capitalism.

Adventure training is an important component of adventure tourism as it equips adventure tourists with the skills and confidence to embark on their tours. As part of this research, the author participated in an adventure course conducted by a PAP affiliated community club in Singapore and underwent 3 months of basic outdoor adventure training. The instructors and trainees derive mainly from tertiary educated executives and professionals aged 22–32. The course requires trainees to meet and practice at least twice a week for the duration of the course for expedition planning, physical training, lectures and other forms of adventure training. Adventurism, it was observed — while rappelling down the cliffs of Changi "Commando" Cliff or pitching a tent on Mount Ophir, Malaysia — shapes the imagination, conduct and experience of the course. Most trainees feel guilty about the sedentary and safe lifestyle young Singaporeans lead and aspire to acquire adventure skills so they can go on expeditions in rugged and sublime places in foreign and "exotic" lands. Trainees aspire to leave the "comfort" zones of their office and apartments and thus sign up for a course which seeks to equip them with essential outdoor skills. There are two adventure tours to Peninsula Malaysia for them to test these new-found skills.

Many of the adventure ideals and ethics promoted and "taught" in the course are actually extrapolations from workplace environment, notably, the "new" economy workplace anticipating or coping with "soft" capitalism. Teamwork, perseverance and the ability to deal with contingencies are among the recurring themes in the course. Contrary to explanations that adventure tourists are seekers of freedom, participants actually paradoxically surrender this. They "escape from freedom" (Fromm 1941) and are governed by ideals of team-building and self-improvement/competency to realise themselves according to course objectives, requirements and deliverables. In choosing to realise themselves in this way, they are governed through their freedom (Rose 1999) and never really achieve the pursuit of freedom and escape they aspire to.

There is also an emphasis on abilities to handle "accidents," "crisis" and other things one cannot "pre-plan" during expeditions. This resonates with the tensions between the PAP top-down policy planning and the party's promotion of autonomy and contingency in the adventurer-citizen. The fast changing adventure terrains, like the new capitalist workplace in "soft" capitalism, are places where disciplined but enterprising adventurer-citizens are desired. Landscapes of adventures are outdoor gymnasiums for Singaporean scuba divers and adventure trainees. These outdoor gymnasiums require not just a bodily and "touristic" engagement with the landscapes of adventure but also an alignment of workplace and adventure, in line with the ways that Prime Minsiter Goh, the PAP and the ERC desire.

The researcher has investigated the manifestation of adventurism in the embodied practices of adventure tourism by Singapore adventure tourists in their attempts to realise themselves as "adventurer-citizens" and demonstrated how leisure time and space away from Singapore are no longer mere avenues for "rest and relax" but are transformed to include scheduled "work-outs" in "outdoor gymnasiums" in Singapore adventure tourists' travels. Adventurism, it is suggested, transformed adventure landscapes across Singapore's political borders into "outdoor gymnasiums" and vacations into "scheduled work-outs" for their realisation as "adventurer-citizens" capable of (ad)venturing in "soft" capitalism.

Conclusion

This chapter has considered a discourse termed, "adventurism" by examining Singapore's adventure tourists in the discursive and material terrains of "soft" capitalism. The text has demonstrated that adventurism has been aligning Singapore workplace ideals and conduct with that of an established and increasing practice of adventure tourism by these adventure tourists. Singapore-specific workplace aspirations and conduct have been shown to have been shaped by international business, particularly the notions of "knowledge-based" economy and "soft" capitalism. There has been a transforming governmentality of Singaporean workers and the chapter highlights the recent alignment of adventure and workplace aspirations in the government of Singapore's workers. The examples of Singaporen adventure tourists (scuba divers and adventure trainees) travelling in the leisure spaces of Peninsula Malaysia have shown that adventurism and the new forms of governmentality has necessitated new "adventurer-citizens" — enterprising but disciplined subjects capable of coping with the unpredictable terrains of "soft" capitalism. Adventurism has transformed adventure landscapes across Singapore's borders into "outdoor gymnasiums" and vacations into "scheduled work-outs" for their realisation as rugged "adventurer-citizens" capable of (ad)venturing in "soft" capitalism.

Implication

It is thus argued that Singaporean adventure tourists' freedom is shaped by adventurism and they are not totally free from Singapore and their workplace ethics when they (ad)venture. They are governed through a constrained freedom and never achieving a freedom that is unrelated to the necessities of contemporary "soft" capitalism. The paradox exists that whereas adventure tourism has often been seen as pursuits of escape from work and its ethics, in practice it better shapes the "escapee" for the rigours of the contemporary work place. The actualization of adventurer-citizen selves in the geography of outdoor gymnasiums positions adventure tourism as a crucial part of a new phase of capitalism, or perhaps of the anticipation of such a new avatar of capitalist developments.

Thrift (1998) points out that "dancing" and "surfing" best describe the nature of capitalism in this new phase, for they suggest "weightlessness, lightness and facility of movement" (Bauman 2000: 221). Singapore's adventure tourists have a role to play in our understandings of "soft" capitalism for if metaphors for life in such a capitalist phase or an anticipation of it are needed, we need not look to Thrift's "dancers" and "surfers," as equally good metaphors can be found in the Singaporean adventure tourists studied. The trekker, diver and other adventure tourists need to be disciplined, enterprising and flexible since the environments they realise themselves in are as fast-changing and treacherous as the managerial spaces Thrift describes in his seminal essays. Lastly, and returning to the discourse of adventurism, for all the supposed empowering rhetoric of self-actualisation, as Thrift observes of "soft" capitalism, adventurism must also be considered as a way for the elite to potentially maintain and legitimise their privileged position. The unemployed, retrenched and other segments marginalised in "soft" capitalism have been problematised as "dependent," "soft" and "unimaginative" and their situations deemed results of their inability or unwillingness to realise themselves appropriately in "soft" capitalism. Finally, it may additionally be argued that just, as in the past, mass tourism represented an extension of Fordist society, so the new forms of tourism are also not independent of, or challenging of the structures of economic structures, but are indeed determined by and shaped to operate in the service of those structures.

Acknowledgments

This paper is not possible without the advice of Tim Bunnell, Kelvin Low, Albert Wai and my friends in the field but the errors are mine. I am grateful to The National University of

Singapore (NUS) and the Singapore Tourism Board (STB) for the award of the NUS-STB Research Scholarship and to the Faculty of Arts and Social Sciences, National University of Singapore (NUS) for financial support rendered to fieldwork under the Graduate Research Support Scheme which provided avenues for my "realisation" as an "enterprising" fieldworker. I am also indebted to the Department of Geography, NUS for providing an excellent research environment.

Section 4

Dark Tourism

Chapter 17

Dark Tourism — An Introduction

Chris Ryan

Following the publication of the work of Lennon & Foley (2000) entitled *"Dark Tourism: The Attraction of Death and Disaster"* a significant level of interest was expressed in the subject matter. To avoid duplication of the chapters that follow it can simply be stated that Lennon and Foley sought to distinguish between, on the one hand, a "simple" curiousity with past events that involved visitation to sites of past battles, disasters and places of possibly morbid interest and, on the other hand, a phenomenon that was arguably more meaningful because the sites of death, disaster and man's inhumanity toward man raised questions about the nature of modernity. Such sites were also of global importance and comprised events that had occurred within living memory.

The case studies that Lennon and Foley examined included those associated with the Third Reich and especially those associated with the holocaust (but including the military hospital built by slave labour in Jersey), the war sites of the First and Second World Wars and the Dallas site of President Kennedy's assassination. The role of technology and globalization and the meanings in contemporary society to which they in conjunction with dark tourism give rise are further examined in a chapter in the U.S. Holocaust Museum, which also represented a case of spatial displacement in that the museum commemorates past events that took place in another continent. The presence of the holocaust museum in Washington D.C. however represents specific political realities as they existed in the United States for the period 1946–1993 when the museum opened. Yet along with these major examples Lennon and Foley cite other cases including the site of Princess Diana's death and the tomb of Jim Morrison. These arguably represent instances of fame derived from popular culture which may be of less enduring importance. Indeed, they comment that Jim Morrison's grave "questions the whole Victorian bourgeois cultural view of the cemetery as a place of dignity and mourning" (Lennon & Foley 2000: 77), given that, as Deutsche Welle radio reported on 28 July 2004:

> Unfortunately, Morrison worshippers have been disturbing the peace of the cemetery, damaging neighbouring graves and holding drinking binges. Now managers of the graveyard have introduced barricades and surveillance cameras in an attempt to stamp this out.

Taking Tourism to the Limits: Issues, Concepts and Managerial Perspectives
© 2005 Published by Elsevier Ltd.
ISBN: 0-08-044644-2

Morbidity in this instance thus becomes thus an act of celebration of a past life and a social reconfirmation of participants' current life styles. Additionally Lennon and Foley record other commodifications of past deaths that include recreating the dining experiences of the *Titanic* and the possibility of taking a ride in a Lincoln Continental along the route followed by President Kennedy in Dallas. Perhaps even more bizarre is the commercial exploitation of sites of "the fantastic" that include those concerned with the "real events" at Roswell.

Consequently "dark tourism" can seemingly encompass a wide range of any questioning of modernity. These examinations would appear to range from the serious to the apparent frivolous. They include:

(a) a questioning as to whether human society has advanced given its continuing ability to inflict harm on its own members and to exhibit cruel behaviours;
(b) whether current behaviours are sustainable or indeed threaten the very bio-system upon which we depend;
(c) to, at another extreme, exhibitions of credulity that perhaps Elvis Presley is alive, that Jim Morrison's ghost has been seen or that the American government did dissect aliens at Roswell.

Given that all of these activities to greater or lesser extent have become the subject of commercial practice, then a further aspect of modernity is that associated with an ability to create product for monetary profit, and to do so on a global scale.

It thus appears that while "dark tourism" initially is focused upon sites of horror and destruction, its extension toward the bizarre, the morbid and the strange begins to either dilute the original concept, or to change the nature of the original concern of death to one of a form of tourism whose importance is that it queries the nature of contemporary society. However, it can be observed that many forms of tourism possess this feature without having to incorporate death, destruction or morbidity. For example Boniface has argued that new, emergent forms of tourism represent significant shifts in people's understanding of society that rejects many of the core ethical understandings of modernity that reduces people to being cyphers in productive processes. She writes that:

> ... it does seem that we are seeking more depth to our tourism, whatever form it may take. We are no longer so much sight-*seeing* as sight-*involving*. We want to know, feel and understand what we visit and perceive. We want to measure the significance of these perceptions to our own lives (Boniface 2001: 36).

For his part, Wang comments in his work, *Tourism and Modernity: A Sociological Analysis* that:

> ... an understanding of the social construction of tourism helps us to appreciate modernity in general. The sociology of tourism is, in a sense, a sociology of modernity and its associated experiences. In this book postmodernity has been treated as part of modernity, namely a dimension of late modernity ....

... Tourism is a mirror in which many of the "secrets" of modern life and modern existential conditions become visible and clear (Wang 2000: 218).

Therefore, on closer examination it might be argued that Lennon and Foley's thesis of "dark tourism" is but a specific component of the wider touristic phenomenon. In consequence it is not without surprise that some authors who concentrate upon the experience of visitation to sites of death, destruction, war, battles, torture and genocide tend to concentrate upon the meanings of those visits and the ways in which sites are interpreted for their visitors. For example Seaton (2000) examines how visitors interacted with the sights associated with a tour of the battlefields of the First World War. His findings indicated three different groups among the tour party, and that "The Landscape of the battlefields held different meanings for, and occupied a different place in the life spaces, of the three groups" (Seaton 2000: 69). Of importance to some respondents was a collective memory and understanding of events, and thus group members would reinforce and add to the meanings of the experiences to create a holistic identification with sites, group members and self understanding. Seaton describes the acquisition of technical expertise and specific language of one of the groups to provide evidence for this interpretation.

Hall (2002) provides evidence of how events of past years create new meanings for contemporary generations in his examination of the commemoration of ANZAC day at Gallipoli in Turkey for young Australians and New Zealanders who attend in increasing numbers each 25th April. He notes that:

> Such travelers are locating identity in a symbolic pilgrimage to the birthplace of an important set of national myths including Australian and New Zealand nationshood and certain essences of national identity. This travel thereby continues to reproduce such myths which are themselves being increasingly encouraged by the Australian and New Zealand governments ... (Hall 2002: 86).

Much of this interest in sites of grim realities or absorptions of being is not, as Seaton (2002) points out, a new phenomenon. He notes the popularity of cemeteries and churchyards as attractions, and the fact that guidebooks to such locations in Paris were being printed early in the nineteenth century. In London, Highgate Cemetery had its first guidebook published in 1865. He similarly notes that such locations have been visited for many motives, including not only those of paying respect to the dead, but using such sites for a range of activities such as brass rubbing, epitaph gathering and sculptural studies as well as simply enjoying peace and quiet. In short, the sites of Lennon and Foley's dark tourism can meet many needs and the visits themselves represent a many-layered pattern of understanding of modernity and the human fascination with death. It is also evident that time also plays a role, as the recent events that are vivid in one generation's mind become the increasing distant past for subsequent generations.

In the chapters that follow, these themes are developed in some detail. For example Preece and Price examine Port Arthur, a site in Tasmania. The site began as a small timber station in 1830, but quickly assumed importance as a penal colony. Initially in the 1830s it developed a series of manufacturing enterprises with penal labour, but in the 1840s it increasingly took on the character of a prison and in 1848 a separate stone prison was constructed. A new "model prison," it was built on the thesis that a man should have silence to reflect upon the nature of his crimes. The reality for many was isolation, the reduction to being but a number and the practice of prisoners wearing head masks when taking exercise in the exercise yards. In 1877 the last convict was shipped to the settlement and it primarily became a secondary economic site. However, tourism to the site commenced in the early twentieth century and by the 1920s three hotels existed to provide accommodation. It thus represents a site iconic to a sense of "Australianess" that incorporates a convict past as a desirable element of its "larrikin" nature and colonial history.

The site then gained additional notoriety from the Port Arthur "massacre" of 28th April, 1996, when a gunman killed 35 people over the space of several hours in a series of random shootings which led to the conviction of Martin Bryant and the subsequent passing of anti-gun laws by the Australian government. Preece and Price in their chapter show how the nineteenth century history attracts several people, some of whom subsequently become more involved emotionally with the later events of 1996.

This "personalisation of experience" becomes a major theme in the work of Smith and Croy in their writing of the Buried Village in New Zealand. This site became almost literally a scene from hell when, on 10th June 1886 Mount Tarawera exploded in volcanic fury and buried the village of Te Wairoa under tons of rocks, ash and boiling mud in New Zealand's greatest natural disaster of the modern era. Approximately 150 people lost their lives and the tourist site of the Pink and White Terraces, acclaimed as one of the greatest "natural marvels," also vanished from sight. Today, a museum and excavations remind visitors of those events, but the location is primarily peaceful and scenic, one that is completed by trout streams and waterfalls. Smith and Croy describe this juxtaposition between past and present and argue that distant events can still amount to a challenge to modernity as required by Lennon and Foley's definition of "dark tourism" by the way events are interpreted and presented to visitors.

The final piece in this section of the book is a chapter by Richard Sharpley. Sharpley notes the wide range of products that today are being characterized as "dark tourism" sites and like others notes the fascination that such sites have for human beings. He attempts to model the diversity of dark tourism products by arguing that products can be demand or supply led, and suggests that dark tourism is one extreme of a "continuum of greyness" that can be discerned from a four cell matrix.

As a collection of three pieces the chapters all illustrate the nature of the debate about dark tourism and tend to the perspective that the works of Lennon and Foley, Seaton and other commentators have all correctly identified a specific type of tourism experience, no matter how it might have fuzzy boundaries and ill-defined limits. Each is therefore a proponent of the view that "dark tourism" exists; and in consequence suggest yet again new opportunities for entrepreneurs and new understandings of the social phenomenon of tourism.

Chapter 18

Motivations of Participants in Dark Tourism: A Case Study of Port Arthur, Tasmania, Australia

Tanaya Preece and Garry G. Price

Introduction

Why do people travel to sites associated with tragic and violent events? Are the tourists who congregate at sites that depict death, disaster and atrocity perverted "ghouls" or just manifesting a normal human curiosity in the unusual? (Ashworth, 2002: 191). The answers to these and other questions are sought within this study.

"Dark tourism" is a relatively new area of research, unrecognised by scholars until the mid-1990s (Dann & Seaton, 2001: 17), and many aspects of dark tourism still require further investigation to reveal the intricacies of the phenomenon. This chapter contributes to greater understanding of dark tourism by providing insight into the reasons why people choose to visit a particular dark tourism site. Port Arthur in Tasmania, Australia meets the authors' criteria for classification as a dark tourism site and was chosen as the focus for the study. Not only does Port Arthur possess an historical convict past with much brutality and death in the nineteenth century, but it also endured a massacre in 1996 which tragically claimed the lives of 35 people.

The Literature of Dark Tourism

Lennon & Foley (2000: 155) defined dark tourism as ". . . the visitation to any site associated with death, disaster and tragedy in the twentieth century for remembrance, education or entertainment." They confined their definition to the twentieth century for two main reasons. Firstly, the constricted definition is based on the belief that earlier events did not take place within the memories of those still alive to validate them and therefore are not worthy of further attention. Secondly, they argue that these earlier events do not posit questions or introduce anxiety and doubt about modernity and its consequences (Lennon & Foley, 2000: 12).

Taking Tourism to the Limits: Issues, Concepts and Managerial Perspectives
Copyright © 2005 by Elsevier Ltd.
All rights of reproduction in any form reserved
ISBN: 0-08-044644-2

Dann & Seaton (2001: 24) asserted that dark tourism should not be restricted to events which occurred in the twentieth century and should be seen as "staged around attractions and sites associated with death, acts of violence, scenes of death and crimes against humanity," events which might or might not have occurred in the twentieth century. Ashworth (2002: 191) also disagreed with the assertion of Lennon & Foley (2000) that dark tourism should only include twentieth century events, arguing that this restriction is defining away very important examples of dark tourism. This contention is supported by Seaton (1999: 130) who argued that the place of the murders at Glencoe, Scotland in 1692 and the location of the Battle of Waterloo in 1815 should be classified as examples of dark tourism sites.

The authors also assert that dark tourism should include visitation to sites of relevant events which have not occurred within the twentieth century. As a consequence, in this study dark tourism is defined as *travel to sites associated with death, disaster, acts of violence, tragedy, scenes of death and crimes against humanity*. Use of this definition does not imply that motivations to visit dark tourism sites remain constant over time. Perhaps as tragic events recede into history, tourist motivations tend more towards visitation out of historical interest. In contrast, perhaps tourists visit the sites of more recent tragedies because of their interest in the macabre nature of the event. Such speculation needs to be addressed.

Although the term "dark tourism" is used by the authors of this study, various synonyms are used in the literature. For example, dark tourism has been referred to as "thanatourism" (Seaton 2001), "milking the macabre," the "dark side of tourism" (Dann 1998, cited in Dann & Seaton, 2001), "tragedy tourism" and "*mea culpa* tourism" (Richter 1999, cited in Dann & Seaton, 2001). Whatever this type of tourism is called, it should be recognized that there are tourists who choose to include dark and pensive experiences in their holiday itineraries. Such tourism includes visitation to concentration camps in Poland and Germany, to sites of mass or individual deaths such as Jim Morrison's grave, the site of the Valentine's Day Massacre, or even more recently the site of the former World Trade Centre in New York City where a viewing platform had to be erected to cater for the large number of people who visited the site (Dent, 2002). A recent macabre exhibition presented in Europe and Japan depicts a collection of perfectly preserved human bodies in various poses (Wilson, 2002). This display has drawn more than 8 million customers paying close to 189 million dollars, evidence of fascination with aspects of the macabre among some people. According to Lennon & Foley (2000: 169), the key to understanding this phenomenon lies in the study of tourists' motivations.

Several possible motivations for visiting dark tourism sites are referred to in the relatively sparse dark tourism literature. Those identified by Ashworth (2002: 191) include the desire for a learning experience and for satisfying curiosity about the abnormal or bizarre. On the other hand, Lennon & Foley (2000: 3) suggest that participants are motivated by pilgrimage, homage and remembrance desires. Further research is required before more definitive conclusions can be drawn with validity.

According to Seaton (1999: 131), "thanatourism" or "dark tourism," comprises five broad categories of tourism behaviour; *viz*:

• travel to witness public enactments of death;
• travel to see the sites of mass or individual deaths after they have occurred;
• travel to internment sites of, and memorials to, the dead;

- travel to view the symbolic representation or material evidence of particular deaths, often in locations unconnected with their occurrence;
- travel for re-enactments or simulation of death.

Research Aim and Objectives

The aim of this research was to determine the characteristics and motivations of visitors to Port Arthur, an example of a dark tourism site. The research purpose encompassed several specific objectives:

- To gain an understanding of the motivations of tourists visiting Port Arthur.
- To determine whether motivations to visit Port Arthur are influenced more by the recent tragedy or by the destination's historical convict past.
- To identify whether the tourists' motivations have changed due to the events of the 28th April, 1996 in which 35 people, both residents and tourists, were brutally gunned down.

Method

A qualitative approach using semi-structured interviews to gather data was selected as the most appropriate technique in this study, given the exploratory nature of the investigation and the objectives of the research. The Port Arthur Historic Site was selected as the data collection location due to the ease of access to the site and its proximity to where the massacre occurred on the 28th April, 1996. According to the authors' definition of dark tourism, the location possesses two distinct sites of dark tourism, *viz*, the site of nineteenth century prison brutality and death and the site of the 1996 massacre. Motivations connected to each were explored.

The population for this study included all tourists at least 18 years of age, visiting Port Arthur at the time of the investigation. The sampling method utilised for this study was "next to pass" or "incidental sampling" (Minichiello *et al.*, 1995: 161). The data were collected via twenty-four audio-recorded in-depth interviews over a period beginning in early September in 2002. The interviews were semi-structured to ensure that the interview remained focused on the research objectives while at the same time allowing participants to explore their motivations in greater depth than a structured interview would allow. The range of issues addressed within each interview included past and current motivations for visiting the site, the influence of the area's convict history upon respondents and the influence of the recent tragedy upon respondents, including those who had visited in the past and those who were first time visitors. The interviewees' responses were transcribed and grouped into the common themes which emerged. These themes were then further investigated as discussed below.

Results and Discussion

From the in-depth interviews conducted, three main themes emerged, *viz,*: *learning, historical interest* and *fascination with the abnormal or bizarre*. From these emergent themes several sub-categories were identified, although it should be recognized that there was overlap between the categories.

Learning

The need to visit for reasons of learning was a clear theme in the interviews. This was particularly apparent when individuals were asked why they had visited the area, and furthermore what they knew about the history of Port Arthur. This motivation was evident in statements made by fourteen of the twenty four participants (58%). The learning theme was characterised by the participants' need to gain a general or specific knowledge and insight and understanding from their visit (either for themselves or for family members).

The desire to learn was often placed in a particular context by participants according to their major interests. A majority of the respondents who were motivated by a desire to learn indicated a specific desire to learn more about the convict history of the area. An attempt was made by the authors to differentiate learning into cognitive and affective domains. That is, distinction between the acquisition of factual information and the formation of personal value judgements and emotional responses was made.

The results indicated that of the 14 respondents who indicated learning as a motivational factor for visiting Port Arthur, 8 (57%) participants were largely motivated by the need to learn factual information while 6 (43%) respondents indicated that affective learning was also an important motivational factor. The results also showed that, of the respondents who claimed a desire to learn as the major motivational factor for their visit to Port Arthur, 5 (62.5%) were also motivated by a need to *sympathise with the underdog*. This motivation was indicated by the respondents' articulation of what they perceived as the terrible injustice and brutality associated with the convict era.

It was also found that, of the participants who indicated a desire to learn, 4 (29%) indicated a need to pay *homage to the departed* at the site of the 1996 massacre. The need to pay their respects to those affected by the tragedy became stronger once participants were actually on site, an outcome of affective learning.

The need to travel for *re-enactments or simulation of death or brutality* was indicated by the respondents' need to identify to some extent with the atrocities of the convict past. Of the respondents who indicated a desire to learn about the convict past, 3 (21%) wanted to *sympathise with the underdog*. It is reasonable to conclude that learning about the conditions that the convicts endured led these participants to display empathy with the convicts.

Historical Interest

The concept of historical interest was the most often cited reason given for visiting this dark tourism attraction. This was evident in statements made by 19 (79%) of the 24 participants who took part in the interviews. Often this interest related to a specific element such an interest in convict history or the pursuit of possible ancestral links.

The desire to gain knowledge concerning family history and family roots was a motivation for at least 5 (29%) of those participants who mentioned historical interest as a motivating factor. This result aligns with the pilgrimage motive suggested by Lennon & Foley (2000) and provides support for Seaton's (1996) contention that motivations to visit dark tourism sites can include pilgrimage. While a pilgrimage is often viewed in a religious context, the participants who claimed family history as a motivating factor in this study indicated that their visit had ideological or spiritual significance.

In a small number of cases (3), participants indicated a general interest in the history of Port Arthur. Often the interest expressed tended to be casual, rather than an interest that was pursued with any conviction or further elaboration. This interest was often demonstrated by comments such as "just because of its historical value," "we were influenced by the history of the place," "I came for the history" and "I was just intrigued as to the history of Port Arthur."

Fascination with the Abnormal or Bizarre

While not as strong as the two previously discussed motivations, a fascination with the abnormal or bizarre was still evident in 6 (25%) of the interviews recorded. The appeal was demonstrated by the respondents' articulation of a need to obtain greater insight into the harsh treatment endured by prisoners and to think about what they came to see as the dark side of human nature. This motive was expressed by the individuals in terms of both the recent tragedy (67%), and the historical convict history (33%) of the site. References to this motivation often showed respondents simply stating that they had a morbid curiosity and thus the identification of this motive became unproblematic. However, in a few cases it was difficult to determine whether this was in fact a strong motivation for some individuals, primarily due to the fact that some participants were unwilling to acknowledge this fascination although this motivation might have been revealed inadvertently in individual narratives.

Further investigation of the results indicated that 60% of the participants who expressed having a *morbid curiosity*, were also motivated by a desire to *sympathise with the underdog*. This result shows that fascination with the abnormal or the bizarre does not necessarily preclude sensitive reactions such as sympathy for the underdog.

Are the Motivations to Visit Port Arthur Influenced More by the Recent Tragedy Compared to the Destination's Historical Convict Past?

During the interviews, respondents were asked to describe the level of influence both the historical convict past and the more recent tragedy had on their initial motivations to visit Port Arthur. A substantial majority of respondents (87.5%) indicated that Port Arthur's convict history provided a strong influence on their decision to visit. However, it was also found that the recent tragedy had a profound effect on the emotions of visitors once they had reached the site. This is not to claim that the recent tragedy did not influence some participants prior to arriving. In fact, 37.5% of respondents who were visiting the site for the first time indicated that the more recent tragedy had also influenced their motivations.

The above results suggest that Port Arthur is an example of a dark tourism destination despite the fact that its major dark tourism attraction, the convict history, did not occur in the twentieth century. Lennon & Foley (2000: 12) have argued that the dark tourism phenomenon should be confined to the twentieth century because events prior to this period do not posit questions or induce anxiety and doubt about modernity and its consequences. In this study all participants who mentioned a need to *sympathise with the underdog* empathised with Port Arthur's convict past. This result suggests that the historical element does in fact evoke strong feelings and emotions concerning both the brutality of the past and its relevance to the present day, lending support to Ashworth's (2002: 191) contention that Lennon & Foley (2000) are defining away very important examples of dark tourism.

Have the Motivations of Tourists who have Travelled in the Past Changed Due to the Events of the 28th April, 1996?

During the interview process, participants were asked whether they had travelled to Port Arthur in the past. Respondents were then questioned about motivations for visiting the area in the past in order to compare these accounts with the respondent's current motivations. Of those who had visited the area in the past, all mentioned the Port Arthur Historic Site as being a point of interest in their stay. Obviously only those participants who had visited in the past and could recall these reasons were taken into account. Of the seven participants to whom this applied, five (57%) indicated that the recent tragedy had influenced their decision to return. While this event was an influential factor on some respondents' desire to return to the area it was a secondary motivation for the majority.

The major themes identified in this study, *learning, historical interest* and *fascination with the abnormal or bizarre*, have been incorporated into a model (see Figure 18.1) which has been developed to suggest possible areas of interest for further investigation. The possible connections between them and their subsets have been suggested.

Conclusion

Why do people travel to sites associated with tragic and violent events? For this particular group of participants, a major motivation to travel was for the purpose of *learning*, in both cognitive and affective domains. The results of the study showed that a majority of the participants were travelling in order to obtain some form of factual knowledge about the area. In many cases this obtained knowledge led to the participants placing some judgement upon the information provided through the tour guides and through interpretive material provided throughout the site. This value judgement can also be closely connected to the desire to *sympathise with the underdog*. A substantial proportion of the participants was also influenced by an *historical interest* in the site. This interest has a close link to the learning theme in that participants were motivated to learn about the history of the site. The third theme identified in the respondents' accounts was that of *fascination with the abnormal or bizarre*. Other motivations identified by the respondents included the desire to investigate *ancestry links*, to experience *re-enactment of death or brutality* and to express *reverence*.

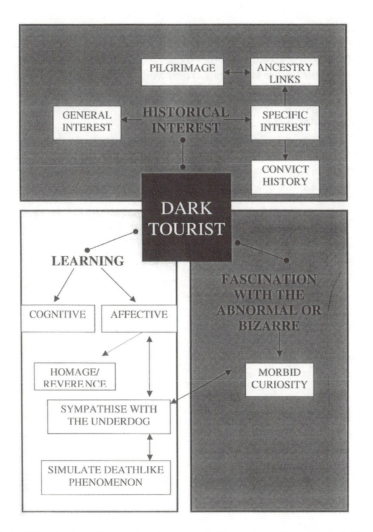

Figure 18.1: Model of tourist motivations to a dark tourism site; a Port Arthur example.

This study has explored the complex area of tourist motivations in connection with a dark tourism destination. However, given the limitations on sample size, time and money available for this study and the unique nature of Port Arthur it is recognised by the authors that the conclusions drawn must be restricted to this study's subjects. The conclusions cannot be applied to other visitors to Port Arthur or to visitors to other dark tourism destinations. Consequently, further research is warranted. Specifically, similar research should be conducted at other dark tourism sites and comparisons between findings should be made. Judgement about the applicability of the model (Figure 18.1) to tourists' motivations to visit other dark tourism destinations might then be made.

An opportunity also exists to research dark tourism attractions with respect to each of the five categories identified by Seaton (1999). The motivations of visitors at each site could be compared in order to determine whether these are common to all forms of dark tourism. There is also a need for further investigation into whether the time period in which an event occurred actually has an impact on the motivations of dark tourists. For example, are the tourists who congregate at the sites depicting recent mass murder motivated for similar reasons as those visiting war sites?

The further research suggested would provide more insight into the conclusions drawn that tourists to a dark tourism destination are motivated by a desire to learn about the dark events, by historical interest and by a fascination with the abnormal or bizarre. The outcomes could have profound implications for the marketing and management of dark tourism sites.

Chapter 19

Presentation of Dark Tourism: Te Wairoa, The Buried Village

Nell Smith and W. Glen Croy

Introduction

The appeal of visiting "dark" sites is not new and indeed such sites have drawn tourists from far and wide for centuries. Ancient Greeks and Romans visited Egyptian pyramids in part because they were the tombs of dead pharaohs. Pompeii is another example of an ancient dark tourism site, the city buried alive. Numerous cases have been presented all around the world, recently none more so than Ground Zero, the site of the September 2001 terrorist attacks in New York City, which is now simultaneously both a personal/public memorial and dark tourist attraction. These anecdotal accounts are not a new field for tourism research, though it is only recently that the interest in the field by researcher and tourist alike has grown significantly. It has been strongly argued that tourist interest in sites associated with death, disaster and depravity has recently grown significantly (Lennon & Foley 2000). Lennon & Foley (1999; 2000) have labelled this phenomena "dark" tourism, however it has also been referred to in the literature as "fatal attraction" tourism (Rojek 1993), "disaster" and "conflict" tourism (Warner 1999) and "thanatourism" (Seaton 1998). It appears however that in contemporary tourism literature the field is most commonly referred to as dark tourism.

In tourism literature, until as late as 1999, the term dark tourism was used interchangeably and synonymously with another prominent term, thanatourism. Both "dark tourism" and thanatourism were defined in a fairly broad manner. Dark tourism has been defined as "sites associated with death, disaster and depravity" (Lennon & Foley 1999: 46) and thanatourism as "travel to a location wholly, or partially motivated by the desire for actual or symbolic encounters with death" (Seaton 1996: 240). Perhaps due to the imagery and connotation so simply and graphically illustrated through the use of a single everyday word, the term dark tourism appears to have become the most commonly used word in describing the concept of travel to sites associated with death, disaster and depravity (Warner 1999). More recently, however, Lennon & Foley (2000) have tightened the reins on what they consider to be suitable for inclusion as part of the dark tourism concept. Lennon & Foley (2000) now maintain that events (for example

Taking Tourism to the Limits: Issues, Concepts and Managerial Perspectives
© 2005 Published by Elsevier Ltd.
ISBN: 0-08-044644-2

the death or disaster) should have taken place within the memories of those still alive to validate them (they suggest 100 years), and the events should posit questions or introduce anxiety and doubt about modernity and its consequences (for example the infallible science and technology at the sinking of the Titanic). The authors of this chapter argue, however, that this definition of dark tourism is too restrictive in that it essentially excludes sites that have previously been referred to as dark by tourists and the literature, such as the site of the Battle of Waterloo which took place in 1815 (Seaton 1996). Ashworth (2002) in a review of Lennon & Foley (2000) also acknowledges these two criticisms or concerns with their revised definition of dark tourism. Ashworth (2002: 19) argues that even within Lennon and Foley's own selected cases that the framework surrounding modernity is "distinctly stretched" and he goes on to disagree with their claim that only recent events can generate dark tourism — "living memory helps but it is not the *sine qua non* of the attractive power of dark events."

Beyond this controversy of definition much literature in the field of dark tourism is largely case based, and like Lennon & Foley's book (2000) it tends to focus more on the "what" than on the "why" (Ashworth 2002). There has been a tracing of the history of dark tourism or thanatourism (Seaton 1996), and many case examples of dark tourism, for example Waterloo (Seaton 1998), Vietnam (Henderson 2000), Northern Ireland (Anson 1999), North Cypress (Warner 1999), and the Jewish Holocaust (Lennon & Foley 1999; 2000). There is little mention in the literature however, of dark tourism in relation to motivation of tourists to visit these sites. In fact the literature has identified that dark tourism is often de-marketed and may be more about the perceived "immoral" promotion of death and disaster. Lennon & Foley (2000) do comment on the lack of marketing, or de-marketing of holocaust related tourism attractions by some European towns. The tourist brochure for the town of Oswieczim for example, resists mentioning nearby Auschwitz by name, illustrating it with a photograph or giving directions despite the fact that Auschwitz generates 750,000 visitors for the town annually (Lennon & Foley 2000). Conversely Warner (1999) discusses the merits of possibilities of "using" dark tourism (and other special interest tourism) as part of a strategy to develop alternatives to the traditional "sun, sand and sea" tourism image of North Cypress. Despite these examples an extensive search of relevant literature has found no specific reference to dark tourism and the concept of image marketing or tourist motivation research.

Based on such discussion this chapter presents a re-extended definition of dark tourism that incorporates both the supply and demand sides of dark tourism. From the literature debate there are two primary elements that are integral to the definition of dark tourism, The first is the touring of a site of death or disaster (as per Lennon & Foley 1999; Seaton 1996; 1998; Warner 1999). Maintaining this definition to touring the sites of death or disaster would be a valid supply side interpretation of the term dark tourism. Nonetheless, the authors would stress that tourists would have to identify the significance and meaning of the site — specifically have knowledge of the death or disaster and interpret the site as dark — for it to be a dark tourism site. The second element derived from this, which will be expanded below, is the personalisation of that death or disaster. This focuses on tourists' emotive responses of anxiety, nervousness or doubt to the sites as stressed by Lennon & Foley (2000). This also incorporates the delimiting parts of the Lennon and Foley definition of living memory and modernity.

The authors' interpretation of living memory is to be in the mind of the living, not as has been presented, or previously interpreted, as those that experienced the disaster are still alive. This draws from the emotive responses stressed in the Lennon & Foley (2000) definition. These responses are not limited to those people that have actually experienced these disasters. Through interpretation tourists, mindful of the context they are visiting, are able to personalise death and disasters and internalise a response to the situation (Moscardo 1996). Therefore, if there were a personalisation of the anxiety, nervousness or doubt associated with touring a place of death, then within this extended definition one can state that a particular location is a dark tourism site. This also draws the point of agreement with Ashworth's (2002) comments, and the authors would further stress that a specific time is an inconsequential element of the definition. Rather it is the personalisation of response that is consequential.

A further extension to Lennon & Foley's (2000) definition is to the factor of modernity. Generally modernity is the era since the period of enlightenment and often refers to humankind's scientific and mechanical developments (as per Lennon & Foley's 2000 definition). This delimits the definition of dark tourism to "modern" human induced disasters and inherently precludes non-human induced disasters. Not wishing to extend the definition for the sake of fitting the phenomena, but rather stressing the two main factors and relegating this point again as inconsequential, it is here argued that touring a site of death or disaster and personalising the death or disaster to produce an emotive response to the site are the primary elements of the definition advocated in this paper.

Therefore dark tourism comprises both supply and demand elements. The supply element is that the site is that of death or destruction. The demand element is that the site is identified as a site of death or destruction, and within this that the site is personalised, as is shown in Figure 19.1.

The defining of sites as dark tourism from the supply side is relatively simple. If the site was one of death or disaster it is a dark tourism site. The difficulty in defining dark tourism site is distinguishing if the tourists identify the significance and meaning of the site as being "dark" in nature. This may be difficult due to the sensitive nature of many sites and problematic issues in questioning tourists about the motivations and experiences of perceived socially "immoral" activities (Oppermann 1999). Therefore, this paper focuses on the interface between the supply side of a possible dark tourism site and the demand

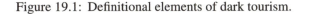

Dark Tourism

- Supply

  A site of death or destruction

- Demand

  Identify and personalize the site of death or destruction

Figure 19.1: Definitional elements of dark tourism.

Management Area	Recreation phase	Experience	
		Organic Images	
	Anticipation ▬	↓	Push and Pull
PRE-SITE	↓	Motivations Awareness	Motivations
		↓	*Induced Images*
		Expectations	
		↓	**DECISION**
		Evoked Set	**MAKING**
		↓	**PROCESS**
		Site Selection	
		↓	
	Travel to	Travel to	*Induced Images*
	↓	↓	↓
ON-SITE	On-Site ▬	Realisation or non-realisation of experience motivations and setting expectations	Perceived *Images* compared to *Real Images*
	↓		
		↓	
POST SITE	Travel back ↓	Identification of Benefits or Dis-benefits ↓	Importance and Perception of *Image* components to holistic *Image*
	Recollection ▬	Satisfaction Or Satisfaction Gap	

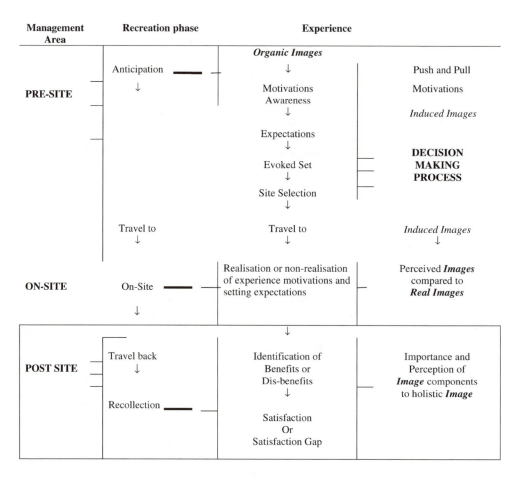

Figure 19.2: Image as the basis to the satisfying experience. *Source:* Croy & Kearsley 2002.

for it. This interface is the images used to present the attraction and to interpret tourist opportunities. The research question thus becomes one of primarily assessing the portrayal of such sites for tourists and the degree to which it is identified as a dark site and the meanings attached to that classification. This chapter nonetheless is not about assessing what the case study site aimed to portray, or if the managers wanted to promote the site as a dark tourism site. Instead the text seeks to systematically review the possible organic, induced and experiential images available for this site. This process focuses on the creation of demand to visit dark tourism sites through images. The analysis is based on Croy & Kearsley's (2002) framework for analysis, *Image as the Basis to the Satisfying Experience* as shown in Figure 19.2. Images, it is argued, determine at least in part, whether a site would be identified as a dark tourism site on the part of the visitor. In turn this would determine if tourists would be motivated to visit the site by the dark nature of the location.

Formation Agent	Examples	Control	
Overt Induced I	Direct destination advertising	Destination	I n c r e a s i n g
Overt Induced II	Travel agency information	Destination	
Covert Induced I	Direct but use third party (celebrity)	Destination	
Covert Induced II	Familiarisation tours	Destination	
Autonomous	News and popular culture	Third party	c r e d i b i l i t y
Unsolicited Organic	Volunteered by unbiased others	Third party	
Solicited Organic	Requested from unbiased others	Third party	
Organic	Past experience of destination	Self	

Figure 19.3: Image generation (after Gartner 1993).

The original model was developed out of a deconstruction of satisfaction gaps of backcountry users in New Zealand (Croy & Kearsley 2002). It has, it is argued, direct relevance to tourist attractions other than just outdoor recreation or the backcountry. It incorporates Hammitt's (1980) recreation multiphase experience, Gartner's (1993) image formation typologies, Woodside & Sherrel's (1977) destination choice process, an experiential satisfaction model, and benefit based management approaches (Burns *et al.* 1994). The model was built from the deconstruction of overall satisfaction into the five phases of the visitor experience, namely anticipation, travel-to, on-site, travel-back, and recollection phases and additionally introduces the images specific to each phase. It then re-constructs the experience. The image agents identified in Figure 19.3 were shown to be the basis of motivations to visit (the organic), decision-making (induced), experiential satisfaction (real) and benefits of the five-phase experience.

The process of image formation has been presented in the tourism literature (Baloglu & McCleary 1999; Fakeye & Crompton 1991; Gunn 1972; Jenkins 1999; MacKay & Fesenmaier 1997; Stabler 1985). Nonetheless the sources in the process generally conform to personal organic, destination generated induced, and experience real agents (Figure 19.3), as per Gartner's (1993) typologies used in the Figure 19.2 model.

Organic image is that which is formed through general life experiences, not specific to tourism destinations or attractions. Sources of organic images include the media, movies, newspaper reports, the internet, television, magazines, and personal sources, such as friends and family. Induced images are tourism destination or attraction specific and usually denoted by an active promotion by the site and an active search for information regarding a possible destination by possible tourists. Sources of induced images include travel and tourism advertising, brochures, the internet, television, magazines, newspaper reports, and travel agents. Real images are those formed through experience of the destination. All the above sources modify destination image to a degree, and the sources of image are deemed at differing levels of credibility in the modification process as indicated by the arrow in Figure 19.3.

To summarise, the pre-site stage of the experience is made up of motivations and expectations, largely or consciously, of an expected experience. The two phases of the experience that make up the pre-site stage are those of anticipation and travel-to the destination. The anticipation phase is based on organic or general images that create our individual perception of our environment. From this environment motivations are developed, created through a range of supply and demand or push and pull motivational factors. Once the motivation for experience has been identified a decision making process is implemented in an effort to satisfy this motivation. A set of sites that could be a setting for the experience are identified, this may be supplemented by obtaining specific information about sites; that is, induced images. Expectations of each of the sites settings are created, and the small number of sites that have the important range of factors are then put into the evoked set, the set from which a final decision will be made. From the evoked set a site is selected that would provide the important setting factors that will in turn satisfy the experience motivations. Whilst travelling to the selected site further images specific to the site (induced images) are identified. These modify, or reinforce the perceptions the user already has of the location. When the site is reached, real images are experienced in the on-site phase. This phase compares the images created through motivations, expectations and experience, that is, there is a comparison between measures of perception and actual images. This evaluation is based upon the organic and induced images perceived by the user compared to the images actually experienced, the real images. This is the also the basis of on-site or experiential satisfaction.

Contextualising this within the growing interest in the phenomena of dark tourism this chapter presents an analysis of a site where death and destruction has occurred to assess if tourists would identify and personalise the site as dark, as per Figure 19.1. More specifically, the objectives of the research were to examine the "darkness" of the motivational (solicited organic), expectations (induced — overt 1) and experience (real) images portrayed, and to examine the level of personalisation of the images of dark tourism sites that result. This paper further seeks to address a limitation in the literature by improving understanding of the concept of image in relation to dark tourism with implications for tourism planners, managers, and marketers especially in the field of heritage.

In order to achieve the above objectives an in-depth analysis was undertaken of a case study, Te Wairoa, the Buried Village. The case was analysed utilising the *Image as the Basis to the Satisfying Experience* model. The model acts as a framework to illustrate the interaction between an attraction and visitor including pre-site and on-site images and experiences. A background to the case study is provided, followed by the analysis of its organic, induced and real images as attributed to each of the phases discussed above.

Te Wairoa, the Buried Village

In New Zealand most disasters have been the result of natural occurrences. This text presents one of these natural occurrences and the resulting death and displacement. This case is Te Wairoa, the Buried Village, about fifteen minutes drive from the North Island tourism centre of Rotorua, New Zealand. In 1886 Te Wairoa was New Zealand's premier tourist village which hosted tourists to the nearby Pink and White Terraces that were commonly described as the "Eighth Wonder of the World." The village boasted two hotels, the 26-room Rotomahana Hotel and the unlicensed Terrace Hotel. Villagers guided, entertained and transported tourists across Lake Tarawera to the Pink and White Terraces in return for an access fee, and interestingly a fee for permission to take photographs. As well as being a relatively busy tourist destination the village was founded by Christian missionaries and there was a strong European influence. Probably due to this, photography was commonplace in the village in the 1880s. In addition to the visual history a detailed, eloquent, and thoughtful written history survives. The village was then buried in ash and mud from the Tarawera volcanic eruption in 1886 that claimed almost 200 lives of residents and guests around Lake Tarawera (which is consequently a site of death and destruction). The combination of Maori, European, tourist, missionary, and rural village at Te Wairoa has resulted in a well documented, imaginable, and interpreted history which appears to successfully minimise any simplistic chronological distance feared by Lennon & Foley (2000). The village is now a tourist attraction in itself, and is marketed as *The Buried Village*. The contemporary attraction is that the village was buried alive, and has now been partially excavated to show what life was like at the time of the eruption.

Referring back to Lennon & Foley's (2000) definition limitations, the question of the relationship between Te Wairoa, the Buried Village and modernity is also interesting and was considered by the authors to be worthy of further examination. It would appear that there is ample opportunity for Te Wairoa, the Buried Village to posit questions about modernity and its consequences, especially developing a "modern" life in the shadow of such a potential disaster. For millions of people around the world the threat of geothermal or volcanic disaster is very real (Kreck 1981; Taylor 2002; Wycherly 2002). Indeed, in New Zealand the biggest single source of fatalities from natural disasters during the last 150 years has been, either directly or indirectly, volcanic activity, and it is generally said to be not a case of if the next big eruption will occur, but when (Harbutt 1995). This has also been related to tourism, as when Harbutt, for example, was visiting a New Zealand volcanic area and a siren went off she, and her companions feared "the prospect of becoming a lava-encrusted Pompeii-style tourist attraction" (Harbutt 1995: 50). However, to fit Te Wairoa, the Buried Village into Lennon and Foley's most recent definition would be "stretching it" in the way described by Ashworth (2002). Volcanic and other natural disasters do induce emotive responses that are personalised, as per Harbutt (1995). In addition to the above example the personalisation of nature induced death, disaster and destruction has been exemplified on a mass scale in a range of recent natural disaster movies, for example, *Armageddon*, *The Perfect Storm*, *Dante's Peak*, *Twister*, *Volcano* and *Deep Impact*.

The following analysis, in the first instance, will focus on images portrayed in guide material (solicited organic images), external promotions (overt induced images), and the images portrayed on site (real images). These images will be compared to the model of *Image as the Basis to the Satisfying Experience* introduced above.

Solicited Organic Images

This section will focus on the solicited organic images of Te Wairoa, the Buried Village as may be requested from unbiased others. In this case, specifically those images presented in tourist guidebooks and on general New Zealand tourism websites. These are identified as unbiased as it is commonly regarded that guidebooks are written by independent experts, and the future success of their publications are dependent on their relative objectivity. The

Table 19.1: Guidebooks and websites used.

Guidebooks and Websites	Year
Nelles Guides: New Zealand	1992
At Cost: New Zealand	1995
Fielding's New Zealand	1996
Fodor's New Zealand	1998
Lonely Planet Cycling New Zealand	2000
Eyewitness Travel Guides: New Zealand	2001
Let's Go: New Zealand	2002
Purenz.com	2002
Rotoruanz.com	2002

websites are also regarded as independent as they cannot promote one attraction over another within the area covered without raising the ire of other attractions. Tourist guidebooks and the internet are also identified as primary sources of travel planning information, particularly in what to do and what to see sources of images for long- haul travellers, which are most of New Zealand's international tourists (Tourism New Zealand 2000; undated). The guidebooks and websites used in this section are presented in Table 19.1, (all included Te Wairoa, the Buried Village).

Two of the older guidebooks, *At Cost: New Zealand* and *Fielding's New Zealand* do not contain words that describe the area as a place of death and destruction. In the other guidebooks and websites Te Wairoa, The Buried Village is introduced as similar to other areas destroyed by volcanic eruptions around the world. The buried Village is described as "Rotorua's Pompeii" (Nelles Guide: New Zealand 1992: 90), and "a Pompeii like site" (Lonely Planet Cycling New Zealand 2000: 156). Though the Buried Village is of a much smaller scale and has an inhabited history much shorter than that of Pompeii, they are both nonetheless tourist sites of death and destruction due to volcanic eruption. The volcano in this case is that of Mount Tarawera. This death and destruction is also described in the tourist guidebooks, and in many cases the focus of the description of the attraction. A content analysis of the text in the tourist guidebooks and websites that reflect the death and destruction are presented in Table 19.2.

The Buried Village is presented as a dark site in the solicited organic images. Nonetheless, the other point from the definition of dark tourism as presented above was the ability of tourists or possible tourists to personalise these events. In this vein, a number of the guidebooks and the Rotoruanz.com website included stories of Te Wairoa, The Buried Village and the Mount Tarawera eruption. Eyewitness's (2001) story entitled *Tarawera Eruption*; Rotoruanz.com's (2002) story titled *Tarawera Te Maunga Tapu . . . Tarawera A Scared Mountain — Disaster: The Tarawera Eruption*; Lonely Planet's (2000) *Disaster on Lake Tarawera*; and Let's Go's (2002) story *Prophet of Doom*, all portrayed the dark presence of the area in personalised stories. The themes and details of these boxed stories are also included in the text of the other guides.

Table 19.2: Content of the guidebooks reflective of death and destruction.

• Blasted	• As if hit by a huge cleaver	• Buried
• Cataclysmic	• Blew and rent the mountain asunder	• Died
• Death toll	• Deafening roar	• Destroyed
• Devastated	• Destruction	• Die
• Disaster	• Completely destroyed	• Doom
• Exploding	• Excavated	• Fear
• Grief	• Great balls of flaming rock	• Killed
• Remains	• Ripping a 17km wound	• Obliterated
• Terror	• Sliced and opened	• Violent

The telling of the story of the area and the eruption personalises Te Wairoa, the Buried Village to possible visitors on a number of levels — tourists site, tourist guides, priests, volcanic eruptions. As well as the presentation of Te Wairoa, the Buried Village as a past site of death and destruction, a number of the guidebooks include stories of the eruption, particularly focusing on Te Wairoa being the staging post for tourists trips to the Pink and White Terraces, and guide Sophia Hinerangi and tohunga (priest) Tuhoto Ariki. The personalised link is created as those reading these books are themselves tourists, or possible tourists, and many would have seen or wanted to see great and amazing natural features. In many cases the readers would have also been guided around sites, just as guide Sophia would have done, and most would have, at some time, encountered a tohunga or priest.

The solicited organic images of Te Wairoa, the Buried Village, though not all focussed on death and destruction, were nonetheless considered to be dark. There was also much personalisation in the interpretation with links between the readers and the site made available at many different levels.

Overt Induced Images

This section will analyse the overt induced images portrayed in Te Wairoa, the Buried Village brochure and website that are produced in efforts to market the attraction by site management. The cover of the brochure *History Alive Today* (2002) mixes the contemporary imagery of the village (a waterfall and bush walking) with that of the eruption of Mt. Tarawera. On the inside the first words are "we are in the midst of a terrible convulsion of nature" and it goes on to reflect the theme of death and destruction at the site although there is little personalisation as such in the interpretation portrayed either in the brochure, or indeed on their website (www.buriedvillage.com).

The Buried Village is presented as a dark site through the overt induced images (Table 19.3). Although some personalisation of interpretation is evident, for example, reference to the village being a tourist "staging post," the induced images are not as personalised in their portrayal of the darkness as the solicited organic images. The exception to this is a separate brochure targeted at children. This brochure in addition

Table 19.3: Content of the brochure and website (induced images) reflective of death and destruction.

• Shattered	• Hot, heavy ash and mud	• Violent and unexpected
• Outpouring of the Earth's fury	• Killing	• Volcanic devastation
• Remained buried for 100 hours	• More than 150 lives were lost	• New Zealand's greatest natural disaster
• In the midst of a terrible convulsion of nature	• The wreckage … brought awe and dismay to the rescuers	• Events deep in the ground were menacingly unfolding
• Fiery glow in the night sky	• The thunderous roar of the explosions	• In the gloom of the day
• For more than four terrifying hours rocks, ash and boiling hot mud bombarded the peaceful village		• The place where nature displayed her most fierce and unforgiving forces

to including some quite general activities, for example, "Name two mountains you can see," also attempts to draw a personal link in its portrayal of the village as a dark site. For example, "On June 10, 1886 Tarawera erupted burying villages in mud and ash. Write a poem or story, or draw a picture about how you would feel if it happened to you."

In summary the pre-site images of Te Wairoa, the Buried Village portrayed through both the solicited organic and overt induced imagery are reflective of the death and destruction that occurred on the site in 1886 (see Figure 19.4). This imagery was also in many cases personalised. This indicates that tourists to Te Wairoa, the Buried Village, would, to a degree, be motivated by the darkness of the site, and they would also have expectations of a dark experience. These two points are illustrative of the application of the re-extended definition introduced by the authors above. This further indicates that Te Wairoa, the Buried Village,

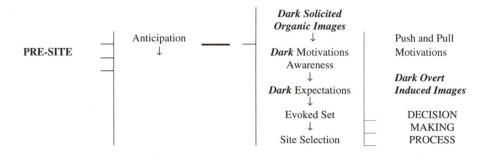

Figure 19.4: Image produced dark motivations and expectations.

is a dark tourism site. Nonetheless, it needs to be asked if tourists can identify the site as dark through their on-site experience.

Experiential Images

This section will briefly analyse the travel-to phase of the experience and then discuss the on-site experience phase in more detail. The majority of visitors to Te Wairoa, the Buried Village travel along Tarawera Road, which is the only road access (Lake Tarawera can also be accessed by boat from Lake Rotomahana). The road takes tourists past the Blue (Tikitapu) and Green (Rotokakahi) Lakes, where a look-out briefly introduces the sacredness of the Green Lake to local Maori. There is no mention however, of the fact that the road being travelled by the tourists was the same road that rescuers, survivors and then tourists used to get to and from Rotorua after the volcanic eruption in 1886.

Once past the Blue and Green Lakes the appearance of Te Wairoa, the Buried Village as a tourist attraction when visitors arrive is quite understated and not overtly dark. The main building area is in keeping with an 1880s style building and it houses the reception, café and inside interpretation area (museum). The reception area itself is conventional and very much a souvenir shop. There is a broad range of souvenirs available and while most are general in nature (Kiwiana merchandise such as sheep and Buzzy Bees) there are some specific, mainly contemporary, volcanic images. Imagery also abounds in books and on display as postcards displaying Mount Tarawera, the Pink and White Terraces and the eruption. On the counter there are some references to the darkness of the site with a history book of the area and a mock-up of an 1886 newspaper, *The New Zealand Chronicle*, with the headlines "Terrible Volcanic Disturbance in Rotorua Area: Mount Tarawera in Violent Eruption: Heavy Loss of Life Feared."

Entrance to the museum area is through the reception area and souvenir shop. Visitors have the option of a self-guided or a guided tour, which departs at no extra cost every hour. The museum employs multi-media interpretation devices such as photographs, signs, models, videos, touch screen computers, and displays. Much of the interpretation is personalised through first person stories with accompanying photographs, maps and graphics. The flow of the museum takes the visitor through the history of the village and sets the scene for life in the village in the 1880s. The interpretation then moves on to the volcanic eruption and follows individual victims and survivors through the actual event and the days that followed. The museum ends with a memorial to the dead that lists the names of those people that the tourist has been introduced to by the earlier interpretation.

The museum is reflective of the aims of the interpretation which is to "give visitors an authentic appreciation of the people of Te Wairoa, both Maori and European and how they lived and died." There is also a children's section that revolves around the stories of two children from the village in 1886. The stories and activities of the children, Amy and Tamati, are told in such a way that relates them to the children of today, for example, "Hello, my name is Tamati. I am ten years old . . .."

The common theme in the museum is that of how a serene tourist village was suddenly faced with terrible death and devastation. This theme of death and devastation is told primarily through a collection of personalised interpretation using multi-media devices.

The victims' words are recollected and are illustrated with photographs and drawings. For example, a female survivor, Kimihia writes:

> presently we came to a part of the road where we (her husband and children) discussed to which way we should go. My husband wanted to go to the right, I to the left so we fell out about it and he went off his way and I mine. I travelled on slowly, for the ashes were becoming deep, and the stones falling so that I seemed to lose my senses. I don't know what happened after that for many days I was in the mud.

Even when the words are not in the first person the resulting interpretation can be personal and moving:

> Tragedy struck Penetito Hawea as he and his wife and two children struggled to reach the Hinemihi Wharenui.
>   Penetito carried one child on his back and the other under his arm. He was knocked down and in spite of frantic searching both children were lost. Penetito and his wife reached Hinemihi.

The stories told in the words of the survivors are often quite moving and graphic as well as personalised. The village teacher, Amelia Hazard, for example explains what happened to her and her family as they gathered around her on the night of the eruption.

> Mona cried to me to give her more room, as I was pressing her against the (fallen) beam, but the loud of the volcanic mud pouring down on me prevented me from being able to render any assistance and the child was crushed and smothered in my arms and died. My little boy who had been standing by me said 'We can't live can we?' and I replied 'No dear, we will die together'. While the debris and mud were falling in, one of my little girls gave a glad cry of 'Papa' and spoke no more. All throughout the night, the roar of the volcano, the sound of the falling mud and the heat of the flames continued. I could not move or make anyone hear and but for the corrugated iron on the building I'm sure I should have been burnt.

The guides to the site, on the day visited by the authors, both had relatives that were victims of the 1886 eruption of Mt. Tarawera. They imparted personal knowledge and added a sense of reflectiveness to the interpretation especially during the karakea (prayer) to the dead.

The exit from the museum leads the visitor outside where they are free to take a self-guided tour around the village and its surrounds — "You've experienced the story . . . now visit the sites" states a sign. The visitor at this point is left with only limited interpretation panels — although more are currently under construction and have been put in place since the initial research was conducted (and no option of a guide). There is little personalisation in the existing interpretation panels and after the relative ease of the museum in terms of being "carried through" the stories the visitor now must effectively work harder to imagine, and to make connections. The language used in the interpretation panels is relatively unemotive and is reminiscent of traditional museum interpretation. The "Chimney Across the Road" panel, for example, simply states that:

> On the hill across the road, identified by a white marker, you can see the chimney (built of locally quarried perlite) of a large house buried by the eruption. The house belonged to Tuhourangi Paramount Chief Keepa Te Rangipuawhe a magistrate in the District, and respected by the people of Te Wairoa.

Spread throughout the remains of the village are general New Zealand wildlife park features such as a deer enclosure, pigs and Rainbow Trout. The inclusion of these features helps to further remove the focus of the visitor from the darkness that was so prominent and emotive in the museum. The juxtaposition of the inside and outside experiences at the Buried Village sat uneasily with the authors who were attempting to relate the personalisation of the museum interpretation with the archaeological remains outside (who lived where? where did they escape to?).

In summary, the travel-to Te Wairoa, the Buried Village was not dark, nonetheless the museum experience was a very personalised interpretation of the village and the dark destruction that the Mount Tarawera eruption caused (see Figure 19.5). Many links were also drawn between individual accounts of victims and the tourist furthering the personalisation. Whilst the outside experience was relatively impersonal and reliant on self-linking of stories from the museum to the contemporary environment the burying of the village could be imagined through the re-created *whares* (houses). Therefore, the on-site experience did, to relative degrees, reflect the darkness of the natural disaster and was presented in such a way that it could be personalised by all tourists to the site.

Future research in this area could be conducted to assess if tourists actually are motivated by the dark nature of a site (especially in terms of the organic and induced images) as this would further our understanding of the typology of tourists to such sites. A better understanding of experiential emotive responses to dark tourism sites would aid in the management and presentation of these sensitive stories. Another area of dark tourism that would expand upon our understanding of the emotive and personalised experience of dark sites by tourists is research into the post-site phases of the experience. Thus, Te Wairoa, the buried Village can be defined as a dark tourism site as exemplified in Figure 19.6.

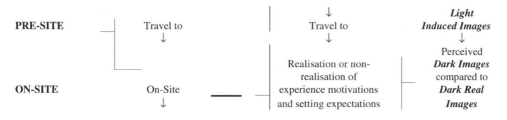

Figure 19.5: Dark real images.

Te Wairoa, the Buried Village
A Dark Tourism Site?

• Supply	• Demand
A site of death or destruction	Identify and personalise the site of death or destruction
• A site where nearly 200 people were killed	• Identifiable as a site of death and destruction in organic imagery
• Presented as a site where nearly 200 people were killed	• Personalisable through stories in organic imagery
• A site where a volcano erupted causing massive destruction	• Identifiable as a site of death and destruction in induced imagery
• Presented as a site where a volcano erupted causing massive destruction	• Personalisable through stories in overt induced imagery
	• Identifiable as a site of death and destruction in real imagery
	• Very personalisable through stories in real imagery

Figure 19.6: Dark tourism at Te Wairoa, the buried village.

Conclusion

Dark tourism is an increasingly popular research topic although, from a definitive viewpoint, it is still in infancy. This paper was intended to direct and develop discussion regarding the definition. The authors have advocated an extension of the current definition put forward by Lennon and Foley, based on two primary elements of supply and demand — a site of death and destruction, and identified and personalised as a site of death or destruction. It has been argued that through the organic, induced and real images portrayed a site can be distinguished as a dark tourism site. To illustrate this further a case study was introduced, Te Wairoa, the Buried Village, which was analysed from the images available. These were identified as dark organic images, dark induced images, and dark real images. Darkness was identified in the organic images produced and it was interpreted by all authors as a dark tourist site. The induced images produced by the Buried Village also portrayed darkness (in the brochure and website). While the experiential images (travel to and on-site) were occasionally impersonal and relatively neutral in feeling (in the reception and outside areas) the image, especially from the museum, was predominantly dark and personalised.

This presentation of Te Wairoa, the Buried Village indicates that it is an excellent illustration of a dark tourism site based on the re-extended definition. Future research opportunities have been identified in assessing tourist motivations and analysing the post-site phases of the experience. Overall this chapter makes a contribution to the understanding the dark tourism phenomena, particularity in the understanding of the concept of image in relation to dark tourism with implications for tourism planners, managers, and marketers especially in the field of heritage. These implications for heritage and attraction managers will now be discussed.

Implications

Images presented or portrayed of a site create motivations and expectations. These images are a principal component of the tourist decision making process and consequently a prime component of the management of tourist sites. It is critically important that site management identify that this image is in their control and it is crucial that it is managed accordingly. The manager has to be aware that all imagery representing their site plays a role in this holistic image formation. This research indicates that the perceived socially immoral darkness of a site does not detract from the holistic image, although it must be noted that the darkness must be presented in a sensitive manner. The presentation of darkness should also be in a manner that can be personalised by tourists. This can be achieved through multi media interpretation techniques, incorporating individual accounts and first person stories, although this has to encompass the whole site. Overall managers of sites must be aware that the motivations and expectations created through a range of image sources must be provided during the on-site experience to satisfy tourists. This creation of the holistic image through organic and induced images can be managed for dark sites and it is especially important that tourists identify the significance and meaning of the site for a personalised understanding of the past death and destruction.

Chapter 20

Travels to the Edge of Darkness: Towards a Typology of "Dark Tourism"

Richard Sharpley

Introduction

August 2002. In the small Cambridgeshire town of Soham, local people appealed for an end to the so-called "grief tourism" that was bringing tens of thousands of visitors to their town. Many of these visitors, travelling from all over Britain, had come to lay flowers, to light candles in the local church or to sign books of condolence. Others had simply come to "gaze" at the town — indeed, it was reported that tourist buses en route to Cambridge or nearby Ely Cathedral were making detours through the town (O'Neill 2002). All, however, had been drawn to Soham by its association with a terrible (and highly publicised) crime — the abduction and murder of schoolgirls Holly Wells and Jessica Chapman.

September 9th 2002. One year after the attacks on World Trade Centre in New York, Ground Zero was being visited by thousands of people each day and had become one of the most popular tourist attractions in the city. Whereas prior to "9/11" about 1.8 million visitors used to ride up to the Centre's observation deck each year, it was expected that the ruins would have attracted double that number over the twelve months following the destruction of the twin towers (Blair 2002). Along with the visitors had come numerous street vendors "selling trinkets that run the gamut of taste" (Vega 2002); souvenirs on sale ranged from framed photographs of the burning towers to Osama Bin Laden toilet paper, his picture printed on each square.

November 20th 2002. At an art gallery in the east of London, five hundred members of the public, each of whom had paid £12.00 for a ticket, witnessed the first public autopsy in Britain for 170 years. Performed by Professor Gunther von Hagens, creator of the *Bodyworlds* exhibition that had attracted large numbers of visitors both in London and elsewhere (half a million people visited the exhibition in Tokyo in 1997), the autopsy was highly controversial. Many claimed it was both unethical and illegal yet, in addition to the crowd of more than 1,000 people who competed for tickets to the event, the subsequent screening of the film of the autopsy on national television also attracted a large audience (Paterson 2002).

Taking Tourism to the Limits: Issues, Concepts and Managerial Perspectives
© 2005 Published by Elsevier Ltd.
ISBN: 0-08-044644-2

To some, these events may be simply a reflection of people's inherent morbid or ghoulish interest in the suffering or death of others — in a sense, extreme examples of "rubbernecking"; to others, they may be "expressions of a form of postmodern tourism" (Blom 2000) or tourism that, as Lennon & Foley (2000: 21) claim, "introduces anxieties and doubts . . . about the key tenets of the project of modernity such as progress, rationality, science, technology, industrialisation and liberal democracy."

Irrespective of these positions, however, it is evident that the above are extreme, contemporary examples of a phenomenon that, in the context of tourism, has occurred as long as people have been able to travel. That is, tourists have long been drawn, purposefully or otherwise, towards sites, attractions or events that are associated with death, violence or disaster. For example, early pilgrimages were to places associated with the death of particular individuals (the expected emotional or spiritual experience being, perhaps, no different to those of contemporary travellers to "death" sites such as Hiroshima or Auschwitz — see Reader (2003)). Similarly, Boorstin (1964) alleges that the first guided tour in England in 1838 was a train trip to witness the hanging of two murderers whilst MacCannell (1989) notes that, perhaps as a 19th Century precursor to the *Bodyworlds* exhibition referred to above, visits to the morgue were a regular item on tours of Paris.

It is also a phenomenon that, over the last century, has become both widespread and diverse. Smith (1998), for example, suggests the sites associated with war probably constitute "the largest single category of tourist attractions in the world" (see also Henderson 2000), supporting specialised tour operators such as Holts Tours and Midas Tours in the U.K. Yet war-tourism attractions, though themselves diverse, are a subset of the totality of tourist sites associated with death and human suffering (Dann 1998). Reference is frequently made, for example, to the Sixth Floor in Dallas, Texas (Foley & Lennon 1996a), visits to graveyards (Seaton 2002), prison tourism (Strange & Kempa 2003) or slavery-heritage tourism (Dann & Seaton 2001). But, as will become evident throughout this paper, there is a wide variety of other tourism sites or attractions that are associated with death, although this may not always be the dominant motivating factor for tourists — it is likely, for example, that the draw of the Taj Mahal is its beauty as a building that epitomises India rather than its function as a tomb (but, see Edensor 1998).

Despite this long history, however, it is only recently that academic attention has focused upon what has been collectively referred to as "dark tourism" (Foley & Lennon 1996b; 2000). In particular, attempts have been made to define or label death-related tourist activity, such as "thanatourism" (Seaton 1996), "morbid tourism" (Blom 2000), "black spot tourism" (Rojek 1993) or as Dann (1994: 61) alliterates, "milking the macabre"; to analyse specific manifestations of dark tourism, from battlefields to "hyper-real" experiences; and, to explore the popularity amongst tourists of such sites and experiences. In the case of the latter, the suggested "drivers" of dark tourism vary from morbid curiosity to a collective sense of identity or survival "in the face of violent disruptions of collective life routines" (Rojek 1997).

However defined, it can be said that the dark tourism literature remains eclectic and theoretically fragile, raising more questions than it answers. For example, is dark tourism generally a tourist-demand or attraction-supply related phenomenon? More specifically, has there been a measurable growth in "tourist interest in recent death, disaster and atrocity . . . in the late twentieth and early twenty-first centuries" (Lennon & Foley 2000: 3) or are there simply more sites/attractions on offer to ever-increasing numbers of tourists? Does the popularity of "dark sites" result from only an interest or fascination with death or are there more powerful motivators? Are there degrees or "shades" of darkness that can be related to either the nature of the attraction or the intensity of interest in death or the macabre on the part of tourists? Is there, in a sense, a "pure" dark tourism as opposed to the generic label attached to the almost infinite variety of death-associated sites and attractions?

The purpose of this paper is to address (though not necessarily answer) a number of these and other questions by considering the phenomenon of dark tourism from both a demand and a supply perspective. In so doing, it will propose a typology of dark tourism that is constructed around differing motives on the part of both the providers and consumers of such experiences and that, in turn, suggests that the term "dark tourism" — as will be interpreted here — can only be applied to a limited set of tourist experiences. First, however, it is necessary, through a brief review of the literature, to draw together extant concepts and knowledge of dark tourism as a framework for the subsequent discussion.

Dark Tourism: Definitions and Perspectives

The term "dark tourism" was first coined by Foley & Lennon (1996a, b) in a special issue of the *International Journal of Heritage Studies* and, subsequently, as the title of a book that arguably remains the most widely cited study of the phenomenon (Lennon & Foley 2000). Their work was not, however, the first to focus on the relationship between tourism attractions and an interest in death, whether violent, untimely or otherwise. In particular, Rojek (1993) had considered the concept of "Black Spots," or "the commercial developments of grave sites and sites in which celebrities or large numbers of people have met with sudden and violent death" (1993: 136), as tourist attractions. Interestingly, Rojek introduces his analysis by making reference to the hordes of sightseers flocking to the sites of disasters, such as the shores of Zeebrugge in 1987 (the capsizing of the ferry *Herald of Free Enterprise*) and Lockerbie in Scotland (the crash site of Pan Am 103) in 1988, before going on to discuss three different examples of Black Spots — the annual pilgrimage to the place where James Dean died in a car crash in 1955, the (again) annual candlelight vigil in memory of Elvis Presley at Graceland in Tennessee and the anniversary of JFK's assassination in Dallas, Texas. These he refers to as postmodern spectacles, repeated reconstructions that are dependent on modern audio-visual media for their continued popularity (as we shall see below, also a fundamental underpinning of Lennon and Foley's thesis). Other attractions, such as national and metropolitan cemeteries, are categorised as "nostalgic" sites and it is only later that he goes on to distinguish disaster sites as being "analytically distinct from Black Spots as sensation sites" (Rojek 1997: 63). A similar distinction is made by Blom (2000) who defines "morbid tourism" as, on the one hand, tourism that "focuses on sudden death and which quickly attracts large numbers of people" and, on the other hand, "an attraction-focused artificial morbidity-related tourism." Thus, the concept of dark tourism is at once rendered more complex by a number of variables, including:

• the immediacy and spontaneity of "sensation" tourism to dark sites of contemporary death and disaster compared with premeditated visits to organised sites or events related to near and/or distant historical occurrences;

- the distinction between purposefully constructed attractions or experiences that interpret or recreate events or acts associated with death, and "accidental" sites (that is, those sites, such as churches, graveyards or memorials that have become tourist attractions "by accident");
- the extent which an "interest" in death (to witness the death of others, to dice with death in dangerous places (Pelton 2003), to learn about the death of famous people, etc.) is the dominant reason for visiting dark attractions; and
- why and how dark sites/experiences are produced or supplied — for example, for political purposes, for education, for entertainment or for economic gain.

These issues are addressed below but, to return to the work of Foley & Lennon (1996a), their use of the term relates primarily to "the presentation and consumption (by visitors) of real and commodified death and disaster sites." This rather broad definition is later refined by their assertion that dark tourism is "an intimation of post-modernity" (Lennon & Foley 2000: 11). That is, firstly, interest in and the interpretation of events associated with death is to a great extent dependent on the ability of global communication technology to instantly report and, subsequently, repeat them *ad infinitum* (hence time-space compression). Secondly, it is claimed that most dark tourism sites challenge the inherent order, rationality and progress of modernity (as does the concept of postmodernity) and, thirdly, at most sites, the boundaries between the message (educational, political) and their commercialisation as tourist products has become increasingly blurred. As a result of these rather strict, self-imposed parameters, attractions based on events that neither took place "within the memories of those still alive to validate them" (Lennon & Foley 2000: 12) nor induce a sense of anxiety about modernity do not qualify as dark tourism. Thus, for these authors, dark tourism is a chronologically modern (i.e. twentieth century onwards), primarily western phenomenon based upon (for reasons they do not justify) non-purposeful visits due to "serendipity, the itinerary of tour companies or the merely curious who happen to be in the vicinity" (2000: 23). As Reader (2003) suggests, this lack of attention to motivation in general and an evident reluctance to accept that tourists may positively desire "dark" experiences overlooks an essential dimension of the study of dark tourism.

In contrast to Lennon and Foley's somewhat restricted focus, Seaton (1996) argues that dark tourism has a long history, emerging from what he refers to as a "thanatoptic tradition" (i.e. the contemplation of death) that dates back to the Middle Ages but that intensified during the Romantic period of the late eighteenth and early nineteenth centuries. He cites a number of attractions, including graves, prisons, public executions and, in particular, the battlefield of Waterloo to which tourists flocked from 1816 onwards and Pompeii, "the greatest thanatoptic travel destination of the Romantic period" (Seaton 1996). He goes on to argue that dark tourism is the "travel dimension of thantopsis" (hence thanatourism), defined as "travel to a location wholly, or partially, motivated by the desire for actual or symbolic encounters with death, particularly, but not exclusively, violent death." Importantly and, again, challenging Lennon and Foley's position, Seaton also proposes that:

- dark tourism or thanatourism is essentially a behavioural phenomenon, defined by the tourist's motives as opposed to the particular characteristics of the attraction or destination, and

- thanatourism is not an absolute form; there exists a "continuum of intensity" dependent upon the motive(s) for visiting a site and the extent to which the interest in death is general or person-specific. Thus, visits to disaster sites such as Ground Zero are a "purer" form of thanatourism (as long as the visitor was not related to a victim) than, say, visiting the grave of a dead relative.

Based on this behavioural perspective, Seaton suggests five categories of dark travel activities:

(i) Travel to witness public enactments of death — though public executions now occur in relatively few countries, Rojek's (1997) sensation tourism at disaster sites may fall under this heading.
(ii) Travel to see the sites of individual or mass deaths after they have occurred. This embraces an enormous variety of sites, from battlefields (e.g. Gallipoli), death camps (e.g. Auschwitz) and sites of genocide (e.g. Cambodia's "killing fields") to places where celebrities died (such as the site of James Dean's death in a car crash referred to above), the sites of publicised murders (e.g. the California house where Nicole Simpson, the estranged wife of O. J. Simpson, was found stabbed to death in 1994), or the homes of infamous murderers.
(iii) Travel to memorials or internment sites, including graveyards, cenotaphs, crypts and war memorials. The reasons for such visits are diverse, from an interest in brass-rubbing or epitaph collection (see Seaton 2002) to pilgrimages to the resting place the famous, the Père Lachaise cemetery in Paris being an oft-quoted example.
(iv) Travel to see evidence or symbolic representations of death at unconnected sites, such as museums containing weapons of death (e.g. the Royal Armouries in Leeds, U.K.) or attractions that reconstruct specific events or activities. As Dann (1998) observes, these "morbid museums" may focus on selected themes and, thus, be "less concerned with historical accuracy."
(v) Travel for re-enactments or simulation of death. As Seaton (1996) suggests, this originally took the form of plays or festivals with a religious theme though, over the last century, "secular derivations," such as the re-enactment of famous battles by groups or societies, have become increasingly popular.

Seaton also notes that, although "thantourism" has a long history, it has become increasingly popular over the last two centuries — certainly, Dann's (1998) comprehensive review of the "dark side of tourism," in which he presents a multitude of examples under five principal headings (perilous places, houses of horror, fields of fatality, tours of torment and themed thanatos) and eleven sub-headings, reveals the diversity of contemporary sites, attractions and experiences that can be referred to as dark tourism. Importantly, Seaton (reflecting Lennon & Foley's (2000) position) suggests that the role of the media has been central to this growth in tourism to sites and attractions associated with death, principally through increasing the geographical specificity of murder and violent death and, more recently, through global communication technology that transmits events almost as they happen into people's homes around the world.

As discussed shortly, this role of the media is a crucial element in the consumption and supply of dark tourism experiences. However, a third perspective on dark tourism in the literature that, although not of direct relevance to this paper nevertheless deserves mention here, is that of dissonant heritage (Tunbridge & Ashworth 1996). Whilst Lennon & Foley's (2000) analysis focuses on the ethical aspects of dark tourism, in particular the dilemmas associated with managing, preserving or reconstructing an often contentious history, the challenge of heritage dissonance is, perhaps, most starkly evident in the context of dark tourism, particularly that associated with the heritage of atrocity (Ashworth 1996). Dissonant heritage is concerned with the way in which the past, when interpreted or represented as a tourist attraction, may, for particular groups or stakeholders, be distorted, displaced or disinherited. As Ashworth (1996) states, "atrocity heritage is both a highly marketable combination of education and enjoyment and a powerful instrument for the transference of political or social messages." Inevitably, then, conflicts arise between interested groups, representing significant challenges for the managers of atrocity-tourism sites — for Ashworth, the dramatic increase in tourism to the Kazimierz district of Kraków in Poland (importantly, directly related to the 1993 film "Schindler's List") is a powerful example.

To summarise, then, a variety of perspectives and, indeed, terminology, with respect to dark tourism exists within the literature, although some commonality on a broad definition (the one that is adopted for the purposes of this paper) is in evidence. That is, dark tourism is tourism motivated by a fascination/interest in death and/or tourism to sites associated with death, whether individual, mass, violent, natural, untimely or otherwise. This at once points to two distinctive bases of analysis of dark tourism, namely, the tourist as a consumer (the "dark" tourist?) and the site/attraction as the object of consumption (the "dark" attraction?). At the same time, the scope and diversity of dark tourism (from both the behavioural and product supply perspectives) as exemplified in the literature not only raises a number of questions, such as those posed in the introduction to this paper, but also suggests that an all-embracing and, perhaps, fashionable and emotive, term such as "dark tourism" oversimplifies a complex, multi-faceted and multi-dimensional phenomenon. Therefore, as this paper now suggests, a clearer understanding of what is referred to as dark tourism may be provided by the development of a typology of the phenomenon.

Dark Tourism: Towards a Typology

As discussed above, dark tourism or thanatourism may be considered a behavioural phenomenon, the contemporary tourism-related manifestation of thanatopsis (Seaton 1996). There is also, according to Seaton, a "continuum of intensity" reflecting the extent to which an interest in death is general (rather than person specific) and the only or dominant motive. That is, there quite evidently exists an almost infinite variety of forms of consumption of dark tourism, from the morbid curiosity of visitors to Rojek's (1997) "sensation" disaster sites to tourism to sites where the interest in death is minimal or non-existent. For example, it may be argued that the thousands of visitors who annually gaze upon William Wordsworth's grave at Grasmere in the English Lake District are more interested in his life, not his death. Moreover, there may, of course, be a variety of motivations amongst different tourists to the same site. Therefore, there may exist different "shades of darkness" with respect to tourists' consumer behaviour.

At the same time, there is also an enormous diversity of tourist sites, attractions and experiences which exist or have been developed for different reasons or purposes, which may intentionally or unintentionally be tourist attractions and which also convey, in a sense, a "continuum of intensity." For example, some attractions, such as "House of Horrors" wax museums, are little more than centres of (admittedly gruesome) entertainment, whereas other sites, such as war cemeteries or memorials to specific events/atrocities (e.g. the Nanjing Memorial in China, commemorating the 1937 Nanjing Massacre), convey a more intense sense of "darkness." In the extreme, perhaps, the $65 per person "Flight 93 Tour" to the Pennsylvania crash site of the United Airlines Flight 93 — one of the highjacked aircraft on "9/11" — established and run by a by a local farmer, is a most intense form of dark tourism product (Bly 2003). The point is, however, that dark tourism is a function of both demand and supply and, therefore, it is important to consider both in attempting to construct a typology of the phenomenon.

The Consumption of (Dark) Tourism

A variety of reasons or motives for participating in dark tourism are proposed in the literature, ranging from morbid curiosity to expressions of national grief (e.g. the death of Princess Diana), the achievement of some mental purification through the confrontation of unpleasant events (Blom 2000), the sense of identity and "intense collectivity" or survival in the face of disruptions to the normality of everyday life (Rojek 1997) or, more simply, nostalgic yearnings. These are usefully summarised and added to by Dann (1998) who identifies eight motivating factors. These include the "fear of phantoms" (i.e. overcoming childlike fears), the search for novelty/difference, a more basic "bloodlust," the desire to reaffirm the benefits of progress and, at a more practical level, "dicing with death" — that is, undertaking journeys or "holidays in hell" (O'Rourke 1988) that challenge tourists or heighten their own sense of mortality.

As Dann (1998) accepts, these categories are largely descriptive and may be related to specific attractions, destinations or activities. Therefore, it is more useful to explore the consumption of dark tourism within a framework of consumer behaviour in general and according to a "typology of consumption practices" (Holt 1995) in particular. In other words, postmodern societies have come to be defined by consumption; not only has the practice of consumption become simplified, but the significance of consumption (and, hence, the meaning of goods and services) has increased (Lury 1996). A given object (including a tourism experience) may be consumed in a variety of ways by different people according to the cultural meaning they attach to it and, therefore, a focus on consumption practices, or how people consume goods and services, transcends the characteristics of specific objects of consumption.

As considered elsewhere (Sharpley 1999; 2000), Holt's (1995) typology of consumption practices provides an effective framework for analysing the consumption of tourism in general. The four "metaphors" of consumption he proposes also represent a useful basis for considering the notion of dark tourism and, as is now discussed, suggest that "dark" sites or attractions may be consumed in a variety of ways, pointing in turn to a continuum of "shades of darkness" of tourism consumption.

Essentially, Holt (1995) proposes that, in terms of purpose, consumption may be an end in itself (autotelic) or a means to an end (instrumental); structurally, consumption may be focused directly upon the object of consumption (object actions) or, conversely, the object of consumption may serve as a focal point for interpersonal actions. Within these two dimensions (purpose and structure) of consumption, therefore, lie four possible "metaphors" of consumption. These may be summarised briefly as follows:

(a) *Consuming tourism as experience* (autotelic-object action) — consumption objects, including tourism, are embedded in a social world which provides the framework for their definition or understanding. Thus, the way in which people consume tourism depends upon their interpretation of tourism within that social world — it may, for example, be interpreted as "festival, liminal time" (Belk *et al.* 1989), a sacred or spiritual experience. Conversely, it may be framed by the experiential aspect of modern consumption, namely, the pursuit of "fantasies, feelings and fun" (Holbrook & Hirschman 1982) or the hedonistic satisfaction of romantic day-dreams (Campbell 1987).

(b) *Consuming as play* (autotelic-interpersonal) — this perspective suggests that people utilise objects as a resource or focus for interaction with other consumers; the consumption object becomes a vehicle for the achievement of broader, interpersonal goals. In the tourism context, this may be manifested in the communal consumption of tourism experiences where tourists play a "performative, reciprocal" role (Holt 1995), or the sharing of unusual, extraordinary or dangerous experiences (Arnould & Price 1993).

(c) *Consuming as integration* (instrumental-object action) — consumers "integrate self and object, thereby allowing themselves access to the object's symbolic properties" (Holt 1995). The object becomes a constituent element of their identity either by merging external objects into their self-concept or by adapting their self-concept to match the socially or institutionally defined identity of the object. For tourists, the process may occur by, for example, integrating particular experiences into the self-concept (the experience of adventure tourism being a common example) or by adapting the self to particular destinations, modes of travel or experience.

(d) *Consuming as classification* (instrumental-interpersonal) — the role of consumption in identity creation is widely considered in the literature, as is its applicability to tourism. However, as Munt (1994) observes, "while travel has remained an expression of taste since the eighteenth century, it has never been so widely used as at present." Thus, tourists are increasingly seeking forms of travel and tourism that, in some way or another, are status symbols.

Although any particular object (including specific types of tourism) may be consumed in any one of these four ways, different forms of dark tourism may be related to these consumption metaphors. Moreover, adhering to Seaton's (1996) notion of a "continuum of intensity," different modes of consumption may be accorded different "shades" of darkness. In other words, although it is not suggested that specific forms of dark tourism consumption can be explained by only one metaphor, different types of dark tourism can nevertheless be categorised under each consumption mode and consequently may be placed on a continuum from "pale" to "darkest."

Dark Tourism as Experience

A wide variety of dark tourism consumption practices may be seen as being defined by or related to the social world of the tourist; that is, dark tourism experiences may be consumed in order to give some phenomenological meaning to tourists' own social existence. Included in this category are visits to: war cemeteries/memorials; battlefields; other war-related museums or attractions, such as the Death Railway and Khwae (Kwai) Bridge at Kanchanaburi in Thailand; holocaust sites; the sites of assassinations — Dallas (JFK) or Sveavägen in Stockholm, where Olof Palme was shot dead in 1986; and, the sites of disasters (though some time after the event). In each of these cases, it is a fascination not with the manner, but the meaning or implication of individual/mass death that is fundamental to the experience. Thus, such forms of dark tourism consumption fall, arguably, around a central to "darker" position on the continuum. This category also embraces implicitly paler "fantasy" experiences, such as the "Graveline" tour in Holywood where the interest is more in the lifestyle (and death) of celebrities.

Dark Tourism as Play

Representing "paler" experiences, consumption as play focuses upon the shared, communal consumption of dark tourism sites or experiences. That is, although it is the death of an individual or group of people that is the initial driver, it is the collective celebration, remembrance or mourning that is the dominant factor. Thus, dark tourism becomes pilgrimage, or a journey followed by the experience of "communitas" (Turner 1973), either at "one-off" events such as the funeral of Princess Diana or at annual celebrations (for example, the anniversary of Elvis Presley's death at Graceland). Such play may also be sensed rather than actual, in as much as an individual pilgrimage to, say, the grave of a celebrity is given extra meaning by the knowledge that many others have shared, and will share, the same experience.

Dark Tourism as Integration

There are two levels (and shades) of dark tourism as integration. On the one hand, and with evident links to the notion of consumption as fantasy, tourists may integrate themselves into the object of consumption, the fascination not being in death itself but the broader context within which death occurs. Henderson (2000), for example, cites the example of the Cu Chi tunnels near Ho Chi Minh city in Vietnam, where it is possible to crawl through the tunnels used to great effect by the Viet Cong and to fire replica AK-47 rifles on a nearby firing range, enabling tourists to "become," temporarily, a soldier. On the other hand, the darkest or most intense form of dark tourism is where tourists seek to integrate themselves with death, either through witnessing violent or untimely deaths (travelling to the scene of disasters, murders, etc.) or, in the extreme perhaps, travelling in the knowledge or expectation of death. In the former case, Dann (1998) refers to tours organised to Sarajevo during the Balkan conflict, the motivation for which may have been status enhancement (see below) or, perhaps, witnessing the death and destruction associated with war. (Modern technology that brings warfare "as it happens" into our homes through television — as with the recent war in Iraq — representing dark "armchair" tourism). In the latter case, recent reports of terminally ill people travelling to Switzerland to take advantage of the services offered by Dignitas, an organisation that assists legal euthanasia, could be regarded as the most intense form of dark tourism (Bunyan 2003).

Dark Tourism as Classification

Travel has long been a marker of social status — the history of tourism is little more than the story of how tourists have sought (and continue to seek) social status through emulating the touristic practices of others. In context of dark tourism, such status may be sought through travelling to places or undertaking forms of travel (and, in either case, surviving to tell the tale) that are dangerous for the tourist. For example, some years ago, El Salvador was considered a particularly perilous destination for backpackers, with those having been there anxious to wear "I survived El Salvador" T-shirts. Equally, visits to dark tourism sites or attractions in more exotic destinations, such as the "burning ghats" at Varanasi in India or the "killing fields" of Cambodia, may be motivated more by the potential status of having visited such locations rather than any specific fascination with death. Thus, this form of consumption falls towards the paler end of the dark tourism continuum.

Inevitably, the above analysis is open to criticism, particularly as any dark tourism site may be consumed in different ways by different tourists. Nevertheless, it serves to demonstrate that a fascination with or interest in death — the defining element of dark tourism — may often not be the principal factor driving the consumption of such experiences.

The Supply of Dark Tourism

As suggested above, in proposing a typology of dark tourism it is important to consider the supply as well as the consumption of dark tourism experiences. That is, it can be theorised that the "purest" form of dark tourism is a function of not only an intense fascination with death on the part of the tourist but also an attempt to exploit or profit from this fascination on the part of the supplier. In other words (and accepting the implicit motive of commercial gain), there is quite evidently an enormous variety of purposes underpinning the supply of dark tourism, varying from the unintentional (i.e. sites that were not originally intended as tourist destinations) to those that are purposely established to exploit people's thanatopsis. This, in turn, points to a "continuum of purpose" of supply linked to potential consumers' assumed interest in or fascination with death, at one end of which are located sites such as burial sites, churches or battlefields that have, frequently, become tourist attractions by

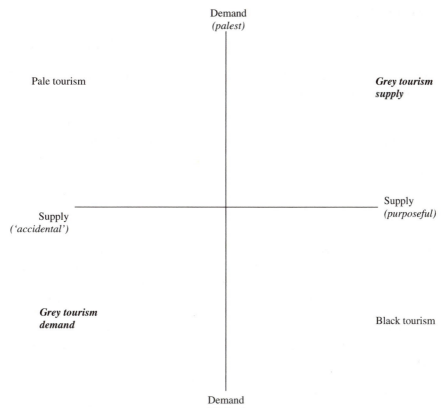

Figure 20.1: Shades of grey tourism.

accident; at the other end lie experiences such as the "Flight 93 Tour" referred to earlier. Within these extremes, it is possible to suggest a wide range of cultural, political, historical or commercial purposes that underpin the development of dark tourism attractions and, to a lesser or greater extent, are more powerful than simply representing or interpreting the death of one or more people.

A full exploration of these purposes is beyond the scope of this paper. The important point is, however, that by combining the consumption/supply continuums it is possible to place different types or intensities of dark tourism on a matrix (see Figure 20.1). Within this matrix, dark tourism attractions or experiences are measured by the extent to which both a fascination with death is a dominant consumption factor and the supply is purposefully directed towards satisfying this fascination. As a result, it is possible to identify four "shades" of dark tourism:

- *Pale tourism* — minimal or limited interest in death when visiting sites unintended to be tourist attractions.

- *Grey tourism demand* — tourist with a fascination with death visiting unintended dark tourism sites.
- *Grey tourism supply* — sites intentionally established to exploit death but attracting visitors with some, but not a dominant, interest in death.
- *Black tourism* — in effect, "pure" dark tourism, where a fascination with death is satisfied by the purposeful supply of experiences intended to satisfy this fascination.

Within these shades, it is possible to locate specific attractions or experiences. For example, the live autopsy referred to in the introduction is most appropriately placed in the "black" quadrant, whilst visits to the graves of well-known people (motivated by an interest in their lives rather than their death) would be categorised as pale tourism.

Conclusion

Though tourism to sites and attractions linked with death has been in evidence throughout history, academic interest in the subject is relatively recent. Moreover, as demonstrated here, the literature addressing dark tourism is both limited and eclectic, perhaps raising more questions than it answers. This paper has, therefore, attempted to advance understanding of the phenomenon by focusing on the varying modes of both the demand for and supply of dark tourism experiences. In so doing, it has proposed a matrix of dark tourism intensities from which a number of conclusions may be drawn. Firstly, dark tourism as defined here (i.e. motivated by a fascination with death) is a relatively rare phenomenon; moreover, it is most likely to be manifested in the context of one-off events, such as disasters or murders, with interest in the site or event trailing off rapidly. Secondly, and related, both the demand for and supply of many attractions referred to as dark tourism sites is driven by factors other than a fascination with death; that is, many forms of alleged dark tourism experience are, in fact, alternative experiences. Finally, it is evident that there is a significant lack of understanding with respect to the behavioural perspective of dark tourism. There is, therefore, a pressing need for further research into the motivations of visitors to such sites in order to establish whether there indeed exists an identifiable "dark" sector of tourism.

Section 5

The Accommodation Sector

Chapter 21

Trends in the Accommodation Sector — An Introduction

Chris Ryan

With reference to the hotel and hospitality sector a cliché is that the standard of accommodation is a significant component in the generation of satisfying travel experiences. A poor standard of hotel room or poor service in a restaurant may not in itself necessarily impede enjoyment of a holiday, but equally the potential for complaint and loss of satisfaction with the total trip remains high. A full literature exists with reference to the role of hotel accommodation and reference can be made to concepts such as the critical incident, confirmation-disconfirmation models of satisfaction and, from a service perspective the importance of emotional labour and the creation of a theatre of service. A second cliché is that the demand for accommodation is a derived demand; that is it is the wider appeal of a destination that may be the major determinant for a trip and the requirement for accommodation is a consequence of that initial decision to travel. While this may still be true for the greater part, increasingly caveats have to be stated that modify the cliché.

The emergence of urban stays and short break holidays have made a feature of the accommodation as a reason for travel away from home. The weekend break is a long established form of holidaying, having a modern history that commenced, at least in the U.K. with offers such as those of Grand Metropolitan Hotels and British Rail in 1964 that were marketed under the "Stardust" Holiday brand. This was subsequently taken up by various chains with growing success so that by 1973 at least 750 hotels in the U.K. were associated with such schemes (Ryan 1980).

An extension of this concept has been the emergence of the boutique hotel that reaffirms the concept of the hotel being the reason for a trip. The promise is often a combination of high quality service, excellent cuisine, small and intimate settings offering high levels of furnishings and different styles that exemplify good taste often set in attractive surroundings. These hotels may be in either rural or urban settings, and can be associated with a secondary product such as wineries, theatre stays, literary activities or rural pursuits such as fly fishing.

While the boutique sector has been one of the faster growing hotel sectors in the early part of the twenty-first century, for much of the latter years of the previous century demand has primarily concentrated upon the 3-star sector. While nearly very major city will have its deluxe 4 and 5 star hotels, their clientele is primarily that of the major business

Taking Tourism to the Limits: Issues, Concepts and Managerial Perspectives
© 2005 Published by Elsevier Ltd.
ISBN: 0-08-044644-2

corporates, high profile events such as governmental conferences or those associated with the entertainment and fashion industries and of course with those possessing above average incomes or people wishing for a once in a life time experience. Similar resort complexes can be found on the shores and islands of scenic places that possess accessibility to major air routes through one means or another. For the most part however, dictates of time, income and changing patterns of travel nodes have emphasised the need for value for money but good quality accommodation. New hotels have tended to be located at motorway junctions, within access of airports or sited on new ring roads around towns and cities. Such hotels tend to cater for business users, but not exclusively so. They will feature in holiday brochures and additionally seek to cater for local demands such as banqueting, weddings and social gatherings as well as perhaps a convention and conference business. Similarly new resort complexes aimed at a middle class and professional market have emerged to meet a demand for more but shorter duration breaks. The cost realities of such travel patterns reinforces a demand for good quality 3-star accommodation as additional travel costs associated with more journeys have to be met from an income now being stretched to meet a demand for perhaps as many as four short holiday breaks a year.

Given these changes in demand patterns hoteliers have responded in varying ways. One approach is summarised by the advertising slogans of the Holiday Inn franchise in the 1980s, which was that no surprises awaited the traveller. Based upon a good standard of room design, furnishings and reception service, the traveller, particularly the business traveller, who might arrive tired from a "red eye" flight that had landed in the early hours of the morning would be met with a standardised offering that required little if any adaptation to new procedures. Conformity meant familiarity, and in travel situations such as that described, this was perceived as an asset. Combined with the security of a room booking confirmed through the use of new computerised central reservations the traveller had no concerns about where to stay and what might be found. Such an approach still has its advantages today, especially in the chains of lower priced accommodation. The F1 motel formula of Accor is one example of a branding exercise that carries conviction because it provides a good standard of room with minimal fuss over check in procedures with the traveller having the security of knowing that in spite of paying a highly competitive price no short cuts will exist in room provision as to the standard of the bed and room fittings.

However, for the most part competition and an appreciation of the importance of both "word of mouth" recommendation and repeat visitation has meant that hotels and motels have tended to upgrade facilities while seeking to control costs through the use of technology and good design. Computerised booking systems have permitted the adoption of yield management to maximise revenues from differential pricing, while better stock control and allocation of staff to meet demand permits cost saving without sacrificing quality of service provision. A corollary has been that hotels have had to develop staffing policies that:

(a) retain flexibility of labour provision where possible; while
(b) retaining increasingly skilled staff within operating procedures; where
(c) staff empowerment has been perceived as a necessity inherent in the nature of the industry.

The hospitality industry has sought to achieve this in a truly 24 hour a day, 7 days a week, 52 weeks a year industry cycle that, traditionally, has not been matched by many other occupations. That it has been able to do this is in part due to the rise of tertiary training and education and the industry's espousing the importance of such training, although evidence still exists of a loss of young people to the industry, and high labour turnover.

The academic literature is replete with examples of both good and bad practice, but what has emerged as possessing importance is the establishment of cultures that value staff and their contribution. Carlson's work is much cited and in this section of the book Sharon Kemp provides further evidence of the importance of organisational culture by describing the attitudes of management and staff within hotels belonging to the Regency group.

While staffing practices are undoubtedly important, better design of the new generation of hotels has made possible the provision of staff services due to cost savings elsewhere. Bedroom, corridors, meeting rooms and restaurants are designed in such a way so that cleaning equipment can be effectively used and time (and hence money) is saved. Energy savings have become an important component of cost savings and rooms are designed to avoid wasteful use of air conditioning, heating and lighting by the use of key cards that turn these services off when the occupant is out of the room. Proper insulation helps retain comfortable ambient temperatures with minimal energy use. Kitchen practices are carefully monitored to avoid waste and recycling is increasingly being practiced by hotels. Guests are also encouraged to play their part by being given opportunities to minimise laundry needs and the energy and detergent use by opting to retain towels after use and by not requiring their beds to be made up with clean sheets each day of their stay. Just how effective these practices are is a matter of some debate, but evidence exists of at least a section of the market that is sensitive to these practices and will adopt them.

There is thus a congruence between cost saving, design and the provision of better facilities for guests — and the common factor that underlies each of these three components is the ability to generate investment funds. Poor profitability undermines any capacity for such investment and of course inhibits the ability to remain competitive. It is here, arguably, that large multi-national chains have some advantages. They possess risk diversification by operating in different markets, and their size provides access to lower cost capital, including an ability to raise monies through debenture or share issues. Such strategies are not open to family based owner-managed smaller motels and hotels; yet they too must provide facilities acceptable to the market place where the criteria of what is acceptable is, to a large extent, determined by travellers' experiences of the rooms and services provided by major hotel groups.

In their chapter Roberts and Jago discuss the needs of Australian moteliers and the means they possess of remaining competitive. They note the low financial returns and the danger of a slowly degrading accommodation stock as units do not receive the re-investment that is required. Ryan (1991) noted that increasingly the advertising of satellite or cable television did not promise more than the guest had at home, but simply a reassurance that favourite programmes would not be missed. Roberts and Jago adopt a similar argument in that they suggest that whereas in the past the hotel stay represented an opportunity to experience luxury not found in the ordinary home, today guests come from better furnished homes with electronic entertainment that combines internet and television, and thus the accommodation sector has to provide similar facilities just to sustain a lifestyle that guests expect as the norm.

Several implications arise. A more affluent market may travel more, but increased travel costs mean that the market is still to a high degree price sensitive with reference to accommodation and so requires "value for money." The ability of the industry's distribution chain to package "good deals" of flight and accommodation is one reason why the travel agents and tour operators continue in business inspite of prophecies that the guest would increasingly create their own deals through the internet directly with the service provider. Accommodation providers thus have different options. Standardise and provide carefully cost controlled services of an acceptable but minimal level is one approach — but while the F1 formula is successful, lower priced motels and hotels are increasingly facing competition from upgraded hostels and backpacker accommodation providers. A second alternative is to provide three-star accommodation that represents "good value for money"; is cost controlled but nonetheless providing a good range of services and facilities that at least equal those of middle class family homes. The third alternative is to provide the extra not normally found in such homes, and charge higher prices still. Such is the approach of the 4- and 5-star hotels, the boutique hotels and the luxury resorts.

Mohsin and Lockyer here suggest a possible fourth approach; namely the accommodation unit as an entertainment centre. While this is not wholly new — for example Las Vegas hotels have been operating for more than three-quarters of a century, the extension of entertainment in many forms is arguably an emergent trend. Hotels are no longer simply providers of accommodation. For some, in theme park type environments, the style of accommodation is part of the entertainment. Others provide cabaret style bars; others are spa resorts or provide sporting facilities that might include water-based sports to gymnasia, jogging tracks, golf etc.

Together the three chapters provide illustrations of how the accommodation sector is not simply an ancillary to tourism as is perhaps often contended, but increasingly a tourism product in its own right. Additionally Kemp's chapter in particular draws attention to the culture of organisations, which arguably is just as important as the more usual concern in tourism that describes culture as a tourism product. In this instance guests do consume the culture in as much as their experiences are shaped by the culture of the accommodation provider they choose to patronise.

Chapter 22

Organisation Culture as a Method of Shaping and Planning Behaviour in a Hospitality Organisation

Sharon Kemp

Introduction

The choice of strategies that are utilised by hospitality organisations can have a significant impact on their performance. An organisation's culture has an important influence on strategies adopted and their success. Managers often overlook or ignore organisation culture as a tool in their strategic armoury (Dwyer, Teal & Kemp 1999; Dwyer, Teal, Kemp & Wah 2000; Kemp & Dwyer 2000).

The utilisation of strategic management and planning is useful to organisations in general because it provides an identified direction in which the organisation is heading or heralds forthcoming changes in direction. Such directions are often expressed in strategic plans, missions, objectives, vision statements and goals. These expressed directions are highly visible to employees, customers/clients and to the public. The expectation is that "good" valued employees will adhere to management's expressed directives. From this perspective, it can be argued that operationalised in this way strategic management is mechanistic in nature (Morgan 1997). Consequently this style of strategic management relies on power and decision-making residing at the top level of the organisation and a reliance on authority legitimised by hierarchical position. The use of policies, procedures and rules ensures that action in the organisation is regulated by the "grand master plan." In such a regulated environment, most organisation members are "doers" expected to implement determined policies rather than "thinkers." One advantage of such a structured way of managing an organisation is that its members' actions are controlled and predictable. Employee roles, and therefore appropriate responses and actions, are defined by their position in the organisation. Those who crave additional responsibility and avenues of growth are barred from what is considered to be the province of senior management.

The costs of this approach are its potential negative consequences for employee motivation and commitment to the organisation (Lorsch 1986). Employees are likely to be more motivated and productive if they feel they can make a valuable contribution to the

Taking Tourism to the Limits: Issues, Concepts and Managerial Perspectives
Copyright © 2005 by Elsevier Ltd.
All rights of reproduction in any form reserved
ISBN: 0-08-044644-2

organisation through contributing new ideas, better ways of doing things and participating in decision-making. Employees are more receptive to change in the organisation if they feel they have had their views taken into consideration, even if the organisation does not implement employees' preferred options.

In particular, this traditional approach to strategy ignores an important and powerful element of organisations, that of culture. Not only do organisations operate within a cultural/social context, but they are also culture-bearing entities. There is no one, uncontested, definition of culture. Sathe (1983: 6) suggests that it is a set of important understandings that members of a community share in common. Culture here is viewed as an integrating, unifying phenomenon, in the sense that it is shared by all organisational members and in the sense that various cultural phenomena are consistent with each other. Culture integrates and binds; it is a normative glue — "the way we do things around here" (Deal & Kennedy 1982). While this view has its critics (e.g. Nord 1985; Uttal 1983), most organisation researchers agree that an analysis and recognition of the surface culture should be the initial step in strategy formulation and implementation, and that it is a crucial element in an evaluation of organisation performance (Brown 1998).

An organisation's culture is often characterised as the personality of an organisation (Oswick & Grant 1996). The organisation's personality (culture) is the total pattern of its representative ways of thinking, feeling and behaving that constitute the organisation's distinctive method of relating to its environment (Kagan & Haverman 1976). There are very few examples in the management literature of this direct metaphorical connection being made. Bridges (1992) is a notable exception who describes organisations as "having character" which appears to equate to culture. Bridges (1992: 10) explains that:

> Character is the typical climate of the organizational country; it is the personality of the individual organization; or it is the DNA of the organizational life form. It is the organization's character that makes it feel and act like itself.

Other writers such as Robbins, Waters-Marsh, Cacioppe & Millett (1994) have drawn similar inferences regarding the personality metaphor. They suggest that organisations are more than a rational means by which to co-ordinate and control a group of people. "Organisations have personalities, as do individuals. They can be rigid or flexible, unfriendly or supportive, innovative or conservative" (Robbins *et al.* 1994: 466). Both personality and organisation culture are inextricably linked. The demands of a "strong"[1] culture can lead to the suppression of particular personality characteristics via a process of socialisation, and nuture the expression of others through the use of coercive measures. Therefore, there is a dynamic interplay between an organisation's culture and the personality of employees.

It is the author's conviction that the existence of a strong culture can be a powerful enabling force in strategy formulation. The positive effects of increased employee identification and

---

[1] A strong culture is where the core values are intensely held and widely shared. The more members who accept the core values and the greater their commitment to those values, the stronger the culture is. Strong cultures have a greater impact on employee behaviour and are more directly related to reduced turnover, increased loyalty and cohesiveness.

commitment highlight the importance of linking culture and strategy, to achieve change, thought necessary for the pursuit of heightened organisational performance. Culture can be used strategically to elicit unified and consistent responses and the expression of shared values in an organisation.

Using illustrative examples from a study of organisational culture of four properties in an international hotel group, this chapter discusses the usefulness of the concept of the "cultural onion" for understanding the organisational culture of hospitality organisations. The text also raises a number of issues for further research on the links between organisation culture, strategic change and performance of hospitality organisations.

The chapter has three specific aims:

(1) To define organisational culture, identify the main elements of what is called the "cultural onion," and to highlight the role which elements of this "cultural onion" play in strategy formulation and organisational performance.
(2) To employ the concept of the "cultural onion" to study the organisational culture of four Regent International Hotel' properties.[2] The extent to which different elements of the "cultural onion" are present in the hotel group and the ways in which they have an influence on organisational performance are discussed.
(3) To discuss the usefulness of the concept of the "cultural onion" for assessing strategy formulation and organisational performance in hospitality organisations generally and to identify issues for further research.

The "Cultural Onion"

A coherent culture is important for the effective functioning of an organisation. A distinctive organisational culture can ensure that the various parts of the organisation are all working to a common end and provide the very basis of competitive advantage in markets because it proves so difficult to imitate. However, organisational cultures can be very resistant to change and may therefore impair the development of business strategies that are essential responses to changes in the external environment, including competitor actions.

Organisational culture is the "deeper level of basic assumptions and beliefs that are shared by members of an organisation that operate unconsciously and define, in a basic taken-for-granted fashion, an organisation's view of itself and its environment" (Schein 1986). The understanding of the culture of an organisation is not a straightforward task but often the strategy and values of an organisation can be found in documents such as its strategic plans and annual reports. The underlying assumptions that comprise the paradigm of the organisation are commonly observed in conversations and discussions between people in the organisation; or it may be that assumptions are so deeply embedded in the organisation and its members that they can be observed only in people's actions. As culture often goes unquestioned by organisational members its "taken-for-granted-ness"

---

[2] It is important to highlight that the author is referring to the study of four Regent International Hotels properties (Sydney, Bangkok, Singapore and Kuala Lumpur) and further research would be needed to establish if the organisational culture discussed here is common to all hotels in the Regent International Hotels group.

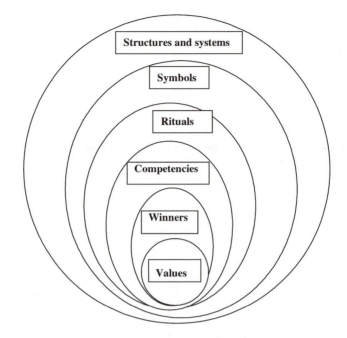

Figure 22.1: The cultural onion. *Source:* Jackson, D. (1997: 66) Dynamic Organisations: The Challenge of Change, Macmillan Business Press, London, p. 66.

means that any discovery of an organisation's culture requires being sensitive to signals from a wider culture — that is, the public perception of the organisation (Figure 22.1).

Perceptions of an organisation's culture are shaped by its image, people and style of doing business. Customers often choose to deal with one supplier rather than another for many reasons other than price, quality or availability. The choice of company or firm is partly to do with what is thought of them and how they relate to personal values. Purchases are made on the basis of what the company stands for as much as the quality of their products or services. Even when specific value stances have not been taken by organisations, culture still plays a large part in the purchase decision. Organisations often fail to recognise the pervasive nature of culture and values. Processes are reflections of a company's culture, and its systems, structures and communications are the framework of that culture. As noted, culture can be viewed as an onion (Jackson 1997). It is important to consider each layer, peeling it back to progressively reveal successively deeper layers of organisational culture. The individual's and organisation's core values are at the heart of the onion. An organisation's founders are often responsible for setting the initial values of an organisation.

Winners and their competencies are explored in the next two layers. Winners are the people who are successful in the organisation and competencies refer to their behaviour. Winners are often seen as role models for others in the organisation. The organisation's management style is derived from the inner three layers whilst the outer three layers represent the more overt signs of culture.

Rituals are repetitive sequences of activities that express and reinforce the key values of the organisation: the annual awards dinner, the corporate planning retreat, and dress-down casual days are important elements of an organisation that are repeated on a regular basis.

Symbols convey to employees and those external to the organisation who, within the organisation is important, the kinds of behaviour that are appropriate and the corporate image that is desired. The public face of the organisation is communicated by dress attire, the elegance of furnishings and the style and quality of the annual report.

The organisation's structures and systems are the final layer of the cultural onion. This layer comprises reporting lines, how activities in the organisation are grouped and who has control and responsibility over certain groupings of activities.

Managers often mistakenly target the "outside layer" of the organisation, its structures and systems, in order to introduce change into an organisation. However, Jackson (1997: 67) states that "real change must cut right through the onion — and of course that often leads to tears!" Change must be introduced into all layers of the organisation's culture. Changing the organisation's systems and structures will have little positive influence on the organisation if organisational members values — the unwritten rules of the organisation that encourage people to behave in a particular way — remain unchanged. Strong values often become deeply embedded over time, and can prove resistant to change and act as a counterculture impervious to any surface-based change program.

The layers of Jackson's onion are now detailed.

Values

Values are part of the cognitive sub-structure of an organisational culture. Values are intimately connected with moral and ethical codes of conduct, and determine what organisational members think *ought* to be done. According to Brown (1998: 26), individuals and organisations which value honesty, integrity and openness consider that they (and others) should act honestly, openly and with integrity because it is the right thing to do. Other authors have defined values as particular sorts of belief. For example, Rokeach (1973: 5) has suggested that "a value is an enduring belief that a specific mode of conduct or end-state of existence is personally or socially preferable to an opposite or converse mode of conduct or end-state of existence." It therefore seems tempting and logical to speak of belief-value clusters. Schein (1985) tends to reinforce this view, suggesting that an organisational leader's beliefs can be transformed into collective beliefs over time through the medium of values. If the leader of the organisation proposes a solution to a problem, organisational members hear this view not as a statement of belief (to which they may not subscribe) but as an assertion of the leader's values. If the proposed solution brings about the desired outcome then organisation members may gradually accept the value as an accurate description of how the world works. It is suggested by Brown (1998) that, as the value comes to be taken for granted and is seen to work reliably, then social validation transforms it into a rarely questioned belief.

Winners

Winners or corporate heroes were initially identified in the early 1980s by Peters & Waterman (1982) and Deal & Kennedy (1982). Winners and corporate heroes were claimed to be the key to the success of their organisations. Deal & Kennedy (1982: 138) stated that:

> The hero [winner] is a great motivator. The magician, the person everyone will count on when things get tough . . . Heroism is a leadership component that is all but forgotten by modern management.

Heroes (winners) are seen as important by Brown (1998) as they make success seem attainable, they provide role models who set high standards of performance for others to follow, they encourage greater commitment and they motivate employees.

Competencies

Competencies provide both an example and an expectation of appropriate behaviour from organisation members. These may cover matters as diverse as style of dress, appropriate ways of addressing and attending to a guest's needs, and the levels of effort or output regarded as proper.

Organisation members who fail to observe and adopt the standards of behaviour or competencies run the risk of being sanctioned for their actions. Dunford (1992) suggests that typically the deviant is likely to have the particular qualities and behaviour of organisational heroes brought to their attention. This acts as a reminder of the example that has been set by others and is now expected of all. Action may escalate if appropriate standards of behaviour are not forthcoming. Heroes' (winners') competencies and their adoption as an expectation of behaviour promotes conformity and predictability, and enhances a manager's control over organisational members (Feldman 1984).

Rituals

Recurrent patterns of behaviour are a feature of organisational life. The *routine* ways that members of the organisation adopt towards each other and those outside the organisation comprise "the way we do things around here." The *rituals* of organisational life are the special events through which the organisation emphasises what is particularly important and reinforces "the way we do things around here." Rituals can be "relatively elaborate, dramatic, planned sets of activities that consolidate various forms of cultural expression into organised events, which are carried out through social interaction usually for the benefit of an audience" (Beyer & Trice 1988: 142).

Symbols

Symbols are words, objects, conditions, acts or characteristics of persons that signify something different or wider from themselves, and which have meaning for an individual or group. *Symbols* cover a range of different elements; logos, titles or the type of language and terminology commonly used become a shorthand representation of the nature of the organisation. They include physical layouts, e.g. how hotel space is used (open or closed plan, shared or individual working spaces, relative location of different departments) and the quality and functionality of furnishings. Berg & Kreiner (1990) suggest that the architecture of corporate buildings has a significant influence on employee behaviour in terms of how they interact, communicate and perform their work tasks. Buildings can become part of the organisation's product such that a visit to them is distinctive for hotel guests. Hotel buildings can be symbols of opulence, status, potency and good taste, and can even be regarded as "landmarks" in big international cities.

Structures and Systems

Organisation structure refers to the organisation's formal framework by which job tasks are divided, grouped and co-ordinated. Conceptually, it is defined as the degree of centralisation, formalisation, span of control, chain of command, departmentalisation and work specialisation in the organisation (Robbins *et al*. 1994). It encompasses the formal hierarchy as well as the informal structures and networks of the organisation. The organisational structure is likely to reflect *power structures*, delineate important relationships and emphasise what is important in the organisation (Johnson & Scholes 1997).

Power structures in an organisation are likely to be closely associated with groupings (often managerial) within the organisation and influence the formulation and observance of a set of core assumptions and beliefs, since these underlie the "perceived wisdom" of how to operate successfully.

Systems indicate what is important to monitor in the organisation, and what to focus attention and activity upon.

Method

The use of multiple investigators, multiple sources of data, or multiple methods, otherwise known as triangulation, allows researchers to confirm their emerging findings (Miles & Huberman 1994). The aim of triangulation is to establish validity through pooled judgement. This study used multiple sources of data, semi-structured face-to-face interviews; document analysis of in-house publications, staff bulletin board notices and flyers, and advertising material; and a series of observations of interactions between both hotel staff and hotel staff and guests.

The fieldwork for the first Regent International Hotels' property in this study (Sydney) was undertaken in late 1997 to early 1998 and reported in Kemp & Dwyer (2000). The Sydney hotel site was used as a pilot study. The fieldwork for the other three Regent International Hotels' properties in Bangkok, Singapore and Kuala Lumpur was completed in early 2000. The richest source of data was the interviews. The issues covered in the interviews are listed in Appendix. The interviews, ranging from 25 to 45 minutes, were conducted with section managers and with a range of employees, from each key section at each of the four hotel sites.

Twenty-five respondents were interviewed at each of the four Regent International Hotels' properties. Forty percent of the respondent sample was established using the organisation charts for each site to identify section managers who were approached for interview. The other 60% of the respondent sample was obtained by researcher invitation. Whilst the researcher was on site at each hotel carrying out observations, staff were randomly selected and approached before commencing their shift, so that an interview could be secured immediately after the end of their shift. The researcher carried out observations at different times of the day and night and on different days of the week so that a wide variety of staff would be recruited from all sections of each hotel site.

The respondents' length of service at the Regent Hotel was taken into account in the selection of interviewees. It was considered that those respondents who had spent a lot longer period of service with Regent International Hotels were more likely to have accepted the culture of Regent International. Some respondents with over 10 years of service had fully adopted the Regent International culture and were proud to be a "Regent person." Respondents with less than 6 months service were also interviewed and their responses suggested that they were still undergoing the socialisation process, in that they were deciding on the extent to which they believed in and wanted to embody "The Regent Experience."

The actions of members of a culture and the actions and writings of the researcher both construct and signify meaning. Ricoeur (1971) and Geertz (1973) argue that the ways in which meanings are constituted in a culture must be read or interpreted by the researcher in much the same manner as one would read or interpret a complicated text. *What* it is that the researcher reads and *how* this activity of reading should be construed is highlighted by Geertz's (1973) view that there is no world of social facts "out there" waiting to be observed, recorded, described and analysed by the inquirer. Rather, the inquirer constructs a reading of the meaning-making process of the people he or she studies. What the researcher has done in this study of culture at four Regent International Hotels' properties is to trace the curve of social discourse and fix it to a framework or paradigm in order to derive the meaning, the gist, the thought of a speech event, not the event itself. In doing so the researcher has re-contextualised the activity of participants' meaning-making, changing it from a passing event, which exists only in its own moment of occurrence, into an account, which exists in its inscriptions and can be consulted. An analysis from the elements of culture — that is, the cultural onion — was conducted and then an account was developed.

The four hotel properties were revisited in mid-2000 and brief interviews were conducted with previous interview respondents to assess if they were still a "Regent person." The aim of the interviews conducted during the revisit, combined with a re-examination of the hotels' literature and advertising materials, and a further series of observations of interactions between staff members as well as interactions between staff and guests, was to determine whether there had been any drift in the culture and strategy of the four hotel properties.

Organisational Culture of Regent International Hotels

The organisation culture of four Regent International Hotels' properties can be examined with reference to each element of the cultural onion.

Values

Statements of philosophy such as "exceed your guests' expectations", and "attempt to surprise and delight your guests" highlight the underlying values that are historically embedded in the "Regent Experience." Staff at Regent International Hotels are encouraged to surpass guests' expectations consistently by being creative, showing initiative, and reasoned risk-takers who demonstrate their dedication to making every guest feel "special."

Winners

Accounts about winners and their feats told by members of the organisation to each other, to outsiders, to new staff members, etc. locate the present in its organisational history and highlight important events and personalities. They typically deal with success, disasters, heroes, villains and mavericks that deviate from the norm. Accounts of winners' actions distil the essence of an organisation's past, legitimise types of behaviour and are devices for telling people what is important in the organisation (Ott 1989). The management at the selected Regent International Hotels properties regularly express the view that they reward innovation and risk taking. It is then not surprising to hear the frequently recounted stories of the guest who decided to go to the hotel gym and spa after surviving an exhausting day of business meetings. The guest was extremely disappointed to find that they had forgotten to pack their sports shoes and rang the concierge to enquire about the location of the nearest sports store to the hotel. The concierge not only lent the guest a pair of sports shoes but joined the guest on the hotel's rooftop running track, providing the guest with some company and "going just that little bit further to provide a valuable personal touch." Then, there is the story of the hotel guest who faced embarrassment when their luggage, containing a business suit, was misplaced by the airline, with only 2 hours before an important business meeting. The guest was surprised and delighted when a hotel employee, recognising the guest's dilemma, arranged for a high fashion men's wear store in the city to come to the hotel and fit one of their basic-stock suits to the guest's physique. The day was saved and the deal was signed. The actions of these "Regent people" were seen as so innovative and unique that Regent International Hotels decided to introduce the "No Luggage Required" program. Guests who lose luggage or are missing personal belongings can take advantage of the program, which goes beyond replacing essential items, to replacing a missing tie or outfitting guests with a suit for that all-important meeting.

Even when the details become blurred, accounts about winners and their activities are important indicators of cultural values and beliefs, formal and informal rules and procedures, the consequences of deviation from and compliance with, the rules, and thus the power structure of an organisation. Accounts of winners act as guardians of cultural values and beliefs. They are an effective control mechanism because they facilitate recall of information, they tend to generate belief, and they encourage attitudinal comment by appealing to legitimate values (Wilkins 1983). Recalling winners in the organisation is also a means by which organisations make claims to *uniqueness*, often incorporating distinctive personalities and specific organisationally relevant avenues and activities (Martin, Feldman, Hatch & Sitkin 1983; Robbins *et al.* 1994). Stories regarding a staff member's meteoric rise in the organisation highlight the rewards for subscribing to and practising the desired ways of thinking and acting at Regent International Hotels. Statements of philosophy such as "exceed your guests' expectations" and "attempt to surprise and delight your guests" identify the path adopted by those who have made legendary success at Regent International. Staff members' attempts to excel in all aspects of their work are regularly recounted in organisation success stories to guests, the public and new staff with a degree of pride in "The Regent Experience."

Competencies

Competencies of friendliness, creativity, initiative, confidence and enthusiasm are expected of "Regent people." Staff are selected on the basis of possessing these personality traits that are considered by Regent International Hotels to be essential for achieving their desired level of customer focus and quality. Other competencies such as effective team membership, guest service skills, company knowledge and specific standards of appearance and grooming are acquired through training and reinforced with a range of rewards and behavioural controls.

Reward systems are important influences on behaviour, but can also prove to be a barrier to the success of new strategies. Therefore, an organisation with individually based bonus or reward schemes related to volume could find it difficult to promote strategies requiring teamwork and an emphasis on quality rather than volume. Non-financial rewards also figure in Regent International Hotels' management systems. For example a prominently placed "guest board" contains words of praise from satisfied guests on one side and guest criticisms on the other: both sides of the board are updated frequently. Teams work hard to identify how they can ensure those guest criticisms are rectified and not repeated.

Behavioural control is exerted through Regent International Hotels' training. Staff are taught how to enjoy their job and that they should greet guests at all times with a smile. In the attitude workshop staff are told that "smiles are what count." These smiles need to be impeccable and almost as crisp as their daily dry-cleaned uniforms. "Nothing is to be too big a chore." Their well-rehearsed behaviour has led to staff being referred to as "sophisticated McDonaldites" and Regent International Hotels has been dubbed "The Smile Factory" and "Home of the Plastic Smile." This is not just a select few staff members practising their public relations. The Regent International style of doing things is the American style of human relations with all its gimmicks: "Smile and the whole world smiles with you." A general manager in his interview reinforced the need for uniform behaviour with guests stating that:

> Competition in the hotel industry is aggressive and the only true differentiator is our people. Our commitment to The Regent Experience is more than just an attitude. It must be a way of life at work!

Rituals

The greeting of guests on arrival and the checkout procedure in a hotel are examples of routines. Rituals include *relatively formal organisational* processes — training programs, appointment, promotion and assessment procedures, induction programs and so on, and relatively informal processes such as "Thank God It's Friday" drinks after work, the awarding of outstanding service awards, etc. (Robbins *et al.* 1994: 752).

The use of jargon as a form of communication shorthand emphasises the embeddedness of terms and phrases in the routines of the hotels. At Regent International Hotels, jargon such as "experience expansion" (moving staff to other areas of the hotel) and "buddying" (being nice to a new member of staff) emphasise the distinctive culture and shared understandings which emphasise the notion of everyone working together as a team to meet guests' needs.

Rituals are routinised activities that maintain cultural beliefs and values. At Regent International Hotels, rituals such as the weekly section meeting ensure that all staff are kept informed of important events, decisions and changes. The meetings are also an occasion at which staff can express ideas and participate in decision-making for their section as well as for the hotel. The information discussed at the meetings is posted on staff bulletin boards to reinforce important points of the meeting and decisions that are made.

Rituals can also take the form of formal celebrations of cultural values; such events are often referred to as ceremonies. Ceremonies may be thought of as celebrations of organisational culture, or collective acts of cultural worship that remind and reinforce cultural values (Brown 1998: 17). At Regent International Hotels, staff who exceed expectations in some aspect of guest service, are rewarded through formal recognition of their outstanding performance in front of their peers. These ceremonies are extremely motivating and serve to ensure a repeat of the superior performance by the staff member. The ceremony serves to reinforce for other staff members the importance of not only respecting the organisational culture, but also taking an active part in demonstrating commitment to the espoused features of the culture at Regent International Hotels. At each hotel, awards are given to outstanding "Regent people" each month, the awards being presented to the employees at a gathering of their section peers. The monthly awardees are also rewarded with an accommodation package that is inclusive of meals and entertainment. The "reward night" can be shared with their spouse or partner. Employees are expected to complete a written evaluation of their night, commenting on the standard of housekeeping, the conduct of the concierge and hotel reception, and the standard of restaurant food and service and porterage on checkout. The aim of requesting employees' evaluations of their "reward night" is to ensure that a guest's stay with the hotel is "truly rewarding." The identification of flaws in service delivery and criticism are encouraged more than praise. The view often expressed by managers is that if Regent International and its staff do not know that problems exist, then how can solutions be found? When guests raise a concern, it is to be viewed an opportunity. A duty manager in reception stated during his interview, "We want to find opportunities to define and redefine "The Regent Experience" so that our guests experience the highest standards of luxury hospitality, so that their stay with us is a truly rewarding experience."

Symbols

Companies use symbols, role models, ceremonial occasions and group gatherings to tighten the strategy-culture fit. Buildings can serve as totems or unity symbols of company identity for employees (Brown 1998: 12). This is evidenced by the tendency for many organisations to use pictures of their buildings in advertising and in annual reports. Symbols also include types of technology used and dress codes (formal/informal). The type of language and terminology used by staff to address each other, or to refer to customers and clients, can also reflect and symbolise those values that are seen as important, and which impact on strategy and performance. Abstractions such as "inspirational spaces," "exquisite service" and "excellent locations" are commonly used at Regent International to promote strategic and operational objectives in organisations. However, such terms can (and do) mean different things in different organisational cultures (Schein 1984). Managerial reliance on a common understanding needs to be balanced with an awareness that serious communication problems can arise if different people, or sections, in the same organisation interpret those and other ideas in different ways.

The image of elegance is symbolised in the grey capital "R" that scrolls across the front of menus, is woven into the carpet in the hotel groups' properties and is embroidered on the lapels of employees tailored and starched uniforms. The "R" symbol of the Regent brand name is recognised internationally and is used to constantly reinforce in the minds of guests and the public in general that the Regent International Hotels chain and its "Regent people" provide "the discerning business and leisure travellers with the highest standards of luxury hospitality by providing understated elegance and a guarantee of quality in every aspect of guest service."

Within Regent International Hotels, staff are encouraged to provide service that is personalised, genuine and caring. Guests are greeted by name and staff are to be friendly and warm in their approach, but never over-familiar with guests. Attention is to be paid to guests' needs; in fact, a Regent International staff member should anticipate guests' needs where possible but not be intrusive. As mentioned by a banqueting manager during an interview, "it is the less obvious and unseen actions of Regent International staff that can make a guest feel truly welcome." The policy of twice-daily maid service reinforces this point. Quality is symbolised by the way staff are required to pay particular attention to their dress and grooming. The expectations of staff in this aspect of their performance are detailed in the silver-embossed staff handbook. Staff are told to "shower daily." It can be offensive to guests and fellow colleagues if you do not smell pleasant. Perfumes, deodorants, aftershave and men's colognes are to be very light and subtle-smelling. Any jewellery worn is to be stylish but subdued and mainly confined to small dress rings, stud-style earrings, and a watch. Staff are to be friendly and helpful. The "selling of strawberries" to guests refers to satisfying the guest's request and then adding a little more, a special touch over and above what would normally be expected by the guest. The hotel staff are to adopt a professional approach in all guest contact, the expectations here being presented to staff in courtesy and attitude workshops. These workshops are provided to all new appointees and staff are rostered for regular refresher sessions.

Structures and Systems

Organisations such as hotels are increasingly relying on work groups to monitor their own performance, and generate new ideas and better ways of "delighting" guests. The competition between work groups to excel and improve their work place has been found to be far more effective in generating both guest and worker satisfaction than a structure that relies on hierarchy, rank, rules and procedures. At Regent International Hotels, hierarchical structures have been dispensed with in favour of a flatter structure with few levels of reporting. In fact, control comes from the team structure. This structure emphasises that, whilst individuals can be successful at Regent International Hotels, the real synergy comes from team members working together to support each other and to act as "quality controllers" on other team members' behaviour and work quality. The team approach promotes the free flow of ideas and suggestions of how to operate better and provide a quality experience for guests.

Within organisation structures are embedded structures of power. A number of researchers have pointed to the links between the focus of power in organisations and the perceived ability of such powerful individuals or groups to reduce uncertainty (Hickson *et al.* 1971). Since the core set of assumptions and beliefs underlies the perceived wisdom of how to operate successfully, it is likely that those most associated with it will be the most powerful in the organisation. Human resources — that is, the staff of Regent International Hotels — are seen as being the most important resource to the organisation, without which the desired culture of quality could not be achieved. In an organisation where guest service and satisfaction are priorities, the human resources department can wield a lot of power. They play a crucial role in organisations such as hotels by ensuring that only service-oriented people are employed and remain in the organisation.

A primary source of new appointees is introductions provided by staff already working for Regent International Hotels. The management of Regent International Hotels have found that personal links reduce social variability in the applicant pool. All final appointees have two personal interviews with Human Resources staff. The emphasis is placed on identifying people who conform to Regent International Hotels' highly specific standards of appearance, grooming, behaviour and personality. Staff in the Human Resources section have their interview questions carefully planned, and interviewers are highly trained and experienced so they distinguish between "job seekers" and "career seekers." Personality is what counts; prospective "Regent persons" must be confident and enthusiastic but not overly so. Preservation of the Regent International Hotels' culture and "The Regent Experience" is dependent on the Human Resources section and their selection skills. At the Regent International Hotels in Sydney, Bangkok, Singapore and Kuala Lumpur, it was recognised that a culture that was customer-focused and fixated on quality had to be maintained. Regent International Hotels explicitly recognised that the quality of service that it offers is only as good as the staff that it employs. Recruitment and selection are taken extremely seriously, with applicants undergoing a detailed selection process to discover not just if they have the required analytical abilities but are enthusiastic, motivated, dedicated, extrovert and hard-working. Unsurprisingly, the overriding factor to assess is their commitment to customer service. Regent International Hotels recognise that it is vital that all of their staff project a positive and professional image of the organisation. It is also important for raw recruits to be socialised into the dominant culture, with its heavy emphasis on quality, service and guests.

Once appointed, new employees undergo entry socialisation that is formal, collective and serial. Incoming identities are not so much dismantled as they are set aside as employees are schooled in their new identities. New employees are immersed in the company's history dating back to 1970 in Hong Kong when Regent International Hotels was founded, and instructed in the Regent philosophy and the standards of guest service that are expected of a "Regent person." One important point to note is that training does not finish once basic induction is complete: all interactions, phone and face to face, are monitored and observed, and regular feedback is provided to staff concerning the appropriateness and effectiveness of both their conversation and accompanying interactions in terms of style and tone.

Power also resides with each and every "Regent person." As all staff are encouraged to contribute to the decision-making process in the hotel properties, staff are empowered to use their initiative and determine the best way of providing a quality experience for each guest they come into contact with. Some theorists, such as Pickard (1993), have expressed scepticism about the labels that management use for this empowering process. He claims that labels such as "democratising the work-force" and "worker participation" are means to an end, not an end in themselves, and that it is a form of exploitation by another name. Whether Regent International Hotels is using staff empowerment or exploitation cannot be answered here; however, it can be said, using the information collected by observation and interview, that the use of a cultural approach had the positive effects of reducing staff turnover substantially, reducing guest concerns and heightening public and guest awareness of the distinctive, quality service provided by Regent International Hotels and their teams.

It might be said that the literature has been less concerned with cultural processes and rather more focused on "strong cultures" and how they can be created. Control can be achieved either through cultural strategies that generate the consent of the workforce through the diffusion and popularisation of the culture of senior management, or by a culture which senior management popularise without actually sharing (Bate 1994). In both cases, according to Kirkbride (1983), values and norms are first disseminated; then there may be some denial and censorship of alternate or opposition views; finally there will be some attempt to define and limit the parameters of what is able to be discussed, and eventually people will internalise this and just avoid certain topics and lines of critique. Control is increasingly being exercised over sensory, aesthetic and emotional responses — employees are being told what to feel as well as what to think, and these feelings are played on by culture manipulators. Increasingly, employees are required to artificially generate sincere feelings. This process is also identified by Oswick, Lowe & Jones (1996: 111) who state, "The job of the leader is not just the management of meaning (Smircich & Morgan 1982), but also the management of feeling (Bate 1994)."

In service oriented organisations it can also be observed that while quality of service, and exceeding guest expectations, may be closely controlled and monitored to ensure that the organisation and its members attain high levels of service and guest satisfaction, one possible consequence is that financial controls and reporting may be relegated to a lower priority. The uniformity of staff behaviour that is demanded provides management with greater predictability and therefore control of their very important people, and implicitly therefore, cost structures. Management state that staff are considered to be "the most important ingredient in the hotel's success." Critics might therefore maintain that staff thus appear to be considered as another economic component in the cogs that turn in the hotel group and they become the keys to increasing profits. However, staff who have accepted the Regent International culture take a different view. As one wait staff member put it, "The most important thing is to sell yourself to the guests. Once we get them in, we can keep them coming back." This view was emphasised by a guest relations manager in her interview who stated, "A loyal guest provides the basis of successful financial results. We know that loyal employees are the key to that success." Once trained, Regent International employees come to believe they are "Regent persons" and the ease with which they glide into their guest-friendly roles is, in large measure, a feat of social engineering.

Recruiting only the type of people that identify with the corporate objectives further ensures ease of organisation control by management. At Regent International Hotels, all of the front of house staff are under 30, they are youthful and have pleasant, out-going, but not overly confident personalities. The ultimate "Regent person" displays ambition and "will leap tall buildings in a single bound when they feel that they are wanted and that they can contribute to the organisation."

The use of overt controls is avoided at the Regent as too tight a control discourages daring and initiative, the precise qualities that "The Regent Experience" and the "Regent person" value and thrive on. Hotel employees are encouraged to be creative in devising solutions to challenges presented by guests. Management realise and value the fact that better ways of operating can grow from employees' creativity. Employees are engaged in solution finding rather than problem solving.

Human Resources and their Impact on Organisation Performance

From the above discussion it can be seen that culture permeates every aspect of operations at Regent International Hotels. Culture shapes the employees' responses to guests and also management's responses to their most important asset, their human resources. As suggested by Robbins *et al.* (1994), culture conveys a sense of identity for organisational members, it facilitates the generation of commitment to something larger than one's individual self-interest and provides a "social glue" that helps hold the organisation together, and thereby acts as a control mechanism that shapes the attitudes and behaviour of employees.

Yet the hotels' external environment creates many pressures for change. Changes occur on economic, social, legal, environmental and technical dimensions, requiring appropriate and timely responses (Dwyer & Kemp 1999). Internally the hotel has an equally demanding environment. Employees needs for achievement, recognition, responsibility, advancement and satisfying work must be recognised and appropriately responded to. Guests' needs and what they see as important are constantly changing and once demands are met future expectations are increased. The supremacy of guests' desires is further emphasised by the competitive pressure for guests by rival hotels.

The ability to adapt and respond to this range of pressures is largely determined by the role human resources play in the organisation's culture. A strong organisational culture increases behavioural consistency; efficiency and effectiveness are achievable. In fact, a strong culture can act as a substitute for formal, mechanistic approaches to strategy. The point being made here is that a strong culture, such as that exemplified by the Regent International Hotels, achieves the same end without the need for expressed written strategies.

Formal strategy, and culture as a tool of strategy, can be viewed as two different roads to a common destination. The stronger an organisation's culture, the less management need to invoke formal rules and intervene to guide employee behaviour. Those guides will be internalised in employees when they accept the organisation's culture. It is possible therefore to identify some key components that emerge from the case study, and these include:

> If human resources are deemed to be important and are nurtured through an organisation's culture, the benefit to the organisation is that employees will enable the organisation to adapt and respond to changes in its internal and external environment, whilst enjoying the benefits of employee commitment to the organisation and its cultural strategy.

> It is important for managers not to view organisational culture as elusive, intangible and insignificant, but rather as an important component of strategic planning and management. Culture-based strategy is the key to governing day-to-day behaviour in the workplace and in the longer term, sustaining the organisation and its members on its strategic mission.

> Regent International Hotels are very culturally driven. The inherent benefit of understanding and effectively using a cultural approach to management is that it extends the benefits of collective participation into the lower levels of the hotel group in order to secure commitment to the organisation's goals and strategies throughout the organisation. In essence, top management set the game plan and communicate the direction in which the hotels should move, but then give individuals the responsibility of determining the details of how to execute the plan.

> Regent International Hotels' culture is based on 'soft' control. This is a subtle and potentially powerful means of influencing behaviour, through shaping the norms, values, symbols and beliefs that managers and hotel staff use in making day-to-day decisions.

> The difference between managers using a cultural approach, and those simply involved in participative management, is that the managers at Regent International Hotels understand that corporate culture should serve as the handmaiden to corporate strategy, rather than adopting the new faith of empowerment and the like, for its own sake.

The cultural approach at Regent International Hotels has involved personnel practices such as less-specialised career paths, job rotation and consensus decision-making, an expectation of full involvement of hotel staff in decisions, both in their formulation and implementation stages. Managers have more interaction with their subordinates who they now see as team members. At Regent International Hotels, the cultural approach has resulted in breaking down the barriers between "the thinkers" and "the doers." The staff at the Hotel group share a strong awareness of the corporate mission and philosophy. They all know that "The Regent Experience" encourages "Regent people" to be innovative. Creativity, new ideas and initiative are encouraged at every level and in each location within the hotel group. The most visible cost of this approach is also its primary strength: the consensus decision-making and other culture reinforcing activities consume large amounts of time. However, the major return is that a new initiative can be speedily implemented; there is less gamesmanship between managers and less time and effort spent on fighting any negative feelings held by staff.

Discussion and Conclusion

In this study the anthropologist's concept of societal cultures has been taken and applied to a business organisation. The main thesis has been that employees of an organisation develop common perceptions, which, in turn, affect their attitudes and behaviour. The strength of that effect, however, depends on the strength of the organisation's culture. It is recognised that national differences — that is, national cultures — must be considered if accurate predictions are to be made about organisational behaviour in different countries. Research investigating this issue has been ongoing since 1986. Notably Adler (1986) and Adler & Ghadar (1990) contend that national culture has a greater impact on employees than does their organisation's culture. Indeed, in a global chain of hotels such as Regent International Hotels, management may have to address the possibility of national culture overriding an organisation's culture. To counter this effect the management of Regent International Hotels place a special focus on combining the culture and way of life of the local community, in which the hotel is sited, with the globally applied Regent International Hotels culture. Regent International Hotels are clearly attempting to appreciate national culture whilst guarding against dilution of their distinctive Regent International Hotels culture.

It is recognised that there may be gaps between what is done and what is said to be done, and so the espoused culture and the actual culture become loosely coupled. The formal culture is a blueprint for action that may or may not be followed. The strategies in place may provide for a "desired" reality that conforms to the formally espoused culture guidelines rather than an actual reality. However, the effort put into implementing or changing a culture in an organisation is not only politically motivated to create an illusion. For whilst the preparation of plans and documentation of policies and strategies does not entail great costs, the implementation and process of creating new ways of working and developing a culture can create substantial costs for the organisation. For the culture to be implemented there have to be deliberate decisions taken and human agency involved. It would be illogical to decide that structures should be in place and costs incurred if there was not a belief that some positive benefits would accrue. Compliance can be signalled by changes in "appearance" and behaviour that signify commitment to action. The actions do not have to be successful as the focus is not on actual results and outcomes but on conformity of action and subscription to the desired culture.

As employees in the organisation have a choice as to whether they adopt the elements of the desired culture, what is clearly at issue here is the differences in intensity and vigour that each employee uses in adopting the organisational culture. It is also suggested that a manager's capability and competence in implementing strategies to support the organisation culture, as perceived by the employees he/she is attempting to lead and influence, will also have an important influence on the degree of success of the cultural strategies, the amount of change that can be achieved and the survival and success of the organisation.

The distinctive features of Regent International Hotels that appear to explain the success of the cultural approach as an instrument of strategy are decentralised power structures, shared goals of the organisation and its employees, organisational stability and growth, and planning that includes sufficient organisational slack (that is, unused resources) to absorb the costs of implementing and maintaining the culture of the hotel group. This cultural approach, as judged by the managers and the staff that were interviewed for this study, has been successful. Yet the cultural approach to strategically managing an organisation does possess some limitations. First, the approach works well only with informed and enthusiastic people. Second, it consumes large amounts of time to implement, as highlighted earlier. Finally, it can foster such a strong sense of organisational identity among employees that it becomes almost a handicap. It can be difficult to bring in "outsiders" at the top levels of the organisation and acceptance of new blood may present an ongoing problem. Organisations such as Regent International Hotels that have strong cultures often suppress deviance, find that attempts to introduce change outside of agreed boundaries are resisted, and that homogeneity and inbreeding can occur. For Regent International Hotels to avoid these problems, management need to be aware that a doctrinal air can accompany a strong culture. Instead of achieving increased performance and satisfaction, the cultural approach to strategy may end up being just another variant of the management-centred approach and consequently runs the risk of maintaining a barrier between "thinkers" and "doers" in the organisation. Properly executed, the cultural approach to strategy can achieve a firm commitment from management and staff to the organisation's goals and strategies by capitalising on natural inclinations to want to develop opportunities in a reasoned way, without the impediment of management feeling threatened and drawing in the reins of control.

Regent International Hotels have achieved much with their cultural approach to strategy. The Regent International culture has fostered in employees a personal belief in and commitment to the hotel group's values. The work environment is guest and employee-centred. Both management and employees are open to learning and adopting change. The hotels in the group have a structure that provides a framework of agreed tasks, priorities and performance standards, and lines of clear authority, achieved through cross-functional teamwork and effective peer relationships. Dispersed decision-making is aided by the provision of timely, relevant and simple information linked to the task, enabling employees to have self-control. Motivation of employees is achieved through the development of all of their competencies, through meaningful rewards, and clear promotion and career plans designed for each employee in partnership with management. Regent International employees have a clear view of the link between their role and the corporate goals and strategy, and they have the opportunity to contribute to the direction of the hotel group. The strategic use of a culture that reinforces the notion of employees not only planning for their future with the hotel group but also having a key involvement in planning the future of the hotel group ensures increased performance.

This study of four Regent International Hotels' properties has focused on the integrating nature of culture and its use as a "driver" of strategy. This view of culture is highly desirable, particularly to the hotel group's management. Numerous advantages accrue to the organisation, more complex tasks are easily undertaken that otherwise could not be achieved by individuals; a wider range of new ideas is possible and mutual stimulation increases creativity; groups present an easier co-ordination task; inputs from a range of perspectives provides distinct benefits to problem-solving situations; and finally culture can be used as a means of socialisation, where a common message can be given and a common perspective reinforced through group pressure.

Linstead & Grafton Small (1992) argue that a distinction can be made between "corporate culture" and "organisational culture." The former is devised by management and transmitted and, marketed, sold or imposed on the rest of the organisation, with both internal and external images yet also including action and belief — the rites, rituals, stories and values which are *offered* to organisational members as part of the seductive process of achieving membership and gaining commitment. The latter is that which "grows or emerges within the organisation and which emphasises the creativity of organisational members as culture-makers, perhaps even resisting the dominant culture." The researcher recognises that the culture of Regent International Hotels may be best identified as a "corporate culture" rather than an "organisational culture" if we accept the argument of Linstead & Grafton Small (1992). However, it is highlighted that Linstead and Grafton Small refer to a culture that is "offered" and therefore a Regent International Hotels' employee has a choice to accept or reject the prevailing culture. However, acceptance is more likely as the lengthy hiring process reduces the likelihood that "misfits" will have been selected into the organisation.

Additionally it must be acknowledged that the researcher in this study of the culture of Regent International Hotels may have found what Louis (1985: 79) describes as "for-public-consumption culture" — that is, a portrayal of the character of the organisation that top management would like to see presented, rather than one that truly reflects the existing culture. Thus, further investigation of the culture of the Regent International Hotels group and a re-examination of the evidence should be undertaken in order to find evidence that points to differentiation in the hotel group's culture. The focus needs to be on the existence of subcultures, the "islands of clarity in a sea of ambiguity" (Martin 1992). The notion of "shared meaning" is still likely to be present, however. Rather than seeing it as shared across the organisation, for a more comprehensive examination of the culture present in the Regent International Hotels group, it is more fruitful to view culture as shared with subcultures.

Although dimensions of organisational culture permeate all functional areas of business it seems fair to say that much of the management literature has neglected its importance for strategy implementation. It is no easy task to uncover the cultural artefacts and those more basic values and beliefs that comprise organisational culture but they can represent some of the more important strengths and weaknesses of any hospitality organisation bearing on its performance. As such, they are deserving of further study in different organisations and in different locations.

A major challenge of strategic management today is to bring about changes in organisational culture and individual mind sets necessary to support the formulation, implementation and evaluation of strategies to enhance a firm's competitive advantage. Further research particularly relevant to the hospitality industry would include identification and analysis of subcultures within hospitality organisations, exploration of the influence of deep culture on strategy formulation and implementation, and the role of individual elements of culture on organisation performance of hospitality organisations.

Chapter 23

The Role of Innovation in Enhancing Sustainability: A Case Study on the Motel Sector

Linda Roberts and Leo Jago

Introduction

In recent years there has been increasing interest in the value of innovation, particularly in relation to entrepreneurship and the creation and maintenance of sustainable competitive advantage (Drucker 1985; Johannessen *et al.* 2001). There are few industries where this is more important than tourism. According to the CRC for Sustainable Tourism, Australia's tourism industry comprises well over 100,000 enterprises, many of which are small in size. This type of situation is not unique to Australia and would be common in many countries of the world. Both globally and locally tourism is a highly competitive industry and it is therefore crucial that entrepreneurship and innovation are encouraged. Indeed, in a mature market, innovation is required for a business to gain market share or to differentiate itself from competitors (Jones 1996).

By definition, tourism cannot exist without a stay of at least 24 hours away from home, which means that the accommodation sector is a fundamental component of the industry. In Australia, much of this accommodation is provided by the motel sector (Australian Bureau of Statistics (ABS) 2003). According to the ABS (2003), there are over 3,000 motels, guesthouses and apartments in Australia and many of these were built in the 1960s and 1970s and now require substantial upgrading. In regional areas in particular, some of the motel accommodation on offer is well below the expectation of tourists and leads to many written and verbal complaints (personal communication with Tourism Tasmania staff), which may lead to low repeat visitation and poor word of mouth publicity. Tourism forecasts suggest that much of Australia's increase in tourism visitation will be in regional areas where motels provide the vast majority of tourist accommodation. If accommodation does not meet consumer expectations in these regions, it works directly against the marketing campaigns that are being developed at great expense by national and state marketing organisations, and will have a negative impact on the tourism industry and broader economy as a whole.

Although much of the promotion in relation to regional accommodation in recent years has been directed towards the boutique end of the market, such as Bed and Breakfasts (B&Bs) and Farm Stays, motels still provide the vast majority of tourist beds on offer. However, sub-standard motel accommodation is a major problem, and it is well recognised by state and territory tourism organisations and peak accommodation bodies such as the HMAA (Hotel, Motel and Accommodation Association). Thus, as it is the standard of motels that influences most consumers' views of the accommodation on offer and it is motels that provide the greater proportion of available accommodation within a region, substandard accommodation may play a significant role in influencing consumers' choice of destination.

This chapter describes results derived from a Cooperative Research Centre (CRC) for Sustainable Tourism project that was initiated by Tourism Tasmania and the Hotels Motels and Accommodation Association (HMAA) and sought to explore the ways in which innovation could be used to enhance the performance of mid-range motels (three to four star rating). The key objectives of the entire project "Reinventing 3 and 4 star motel accommodation in regional Australia: the identification of innovative strategies to meet visitor needs" are to:

(1) Assess visitor needs in terms of infrastructure;
(2) Assess operator attitudes towards, and the constraints which impact upon, their ability to renovate/refurbish or rebuild;
(3) Assess the standards of motel accommodation on offer in regional Australia;
(4) Develop a model, based on building typology, for assessing the capacity and potential costs of renovating, redeveloping or rebuilding motel accommodation in line with the previous three objectives;
(5) Develop strategies for innovatively addressing the infrastructure requirements of existing regional motel accommodation to more closely meet the needs of the market;
(6) Develop a conceptual framework for the motel-renovation-innovation process.

In this chapter, the first stage in this project will be addressed. The results of an assessment of the available secondary data and preliminary qualitative exploratory research involving focus groups with key industry stakeholders and motel visitors will be presented and the major research issues identified.

What is Innovation?

In the literature there are many alternative definitions of innovation and, as Kotabe & Swan (1995) note, this is indicative of the difficulty of measuring innovation. Drucker (1985) also acknowledged that it is difficult to develop a theory of innovation but he added that the practice of innovation can be described in terms of the systematic searching for novel or creative opportunities and subsequent judgement of their potential for success or failure. He described innovation as a "diagnostic discipline" that exploits change. Hence:

> Systematic innovation therefore consists in the purposeful and organised search for changes, and in the systematic analysis of the opportunities such changes might offer for economic or social innovation (Drucker 1985: 31).

More recently Johannessen, Olsen & Lumpkin (2001) have addressed the question of a definition, developing Zaltman, Duncan & Holbek's (1973: 10) early definition of an innovation as "any idea, practice, or material artefact perceived to be new by the relevant unit of adoption." Johannessen *et al.*'s (2001) attention focused on the concept of newness by asking the questions: "What is new?; How new?; and New to whom?" They operationalised *what is new* into four categories; new products or services, new organisational structures or administrative systems, new process technologies and new plans or programs. *How new* was identified using a continuum from radical innovation to incremental innovation and this was linked to *new to whom* via an examination of "the relevant unit of adoption," whether industry, company or the market.

Innovation and New Product Development

In contrast, Jones (1996: 87), when writing about managing hospitality innovation defined innovation as "anything new a firm does, irrespective of whether it is new to the world, copied from competitors or adapted from existing products and services." This definition is much more limited and appears to be restricted to the firm's view of innovation and its management. Further, Jones (1996) equates the innovation process to the new product development process and identifies 15 steps for managing innovation. Crawford & Di Benedetto (2000) have discussed this relationship at length and note that the process of innovation begins with a strategy, for example how to overcome competitive threats and return to a growing market. Like Drucker (1985), they stress the importance of systematic activity and the identification of opportunities, whether they arise from an under-utilised resource, a new resource, an external mandate like a stagnant market or an internal mandate where a gap in sales needs to be filled through innovation. Thus Crawford & Di Benedetto (2000) apply the new product development process to the systematic activity associated with innovation.

Innovation and Competitive Advantage

In a recent study of new product development in British small and medium enterprises (SMEs), Woodcock, Mosey & Wood (2000) observed that, in order to compete with Eastern European and the Asian "Tiger" economies, three strategies have been used including enhancing differentiation from the competition by more innovation. However, despite the need for new product development, the firms in this study still deprioritised it because of short-term pressures. The findings also indicated that few firms recorded information systematically about the new product development process with the result that they had difficulty comparing their performance with that of their competitors.

In the hospitality industry there have been similar findings in relation to hotel renovation. Hassanien & Losekoot (2002), in their study of 3, 4 and 5 star hotel properties in Cairo, Egypt, found that hotel managers believed in the importance of hotel renovation but there was little evidence to show that they actually thought of it in a strategic way. In their description of hotel renovation these authors linked new product development to business performance in terms of competitiveness, efficiency and image.

Hotel renovation can be seen as those activities associated with the development and/or modification of the hotel's tangible assets used to produce services in order to extend the useful life of the property, to stay competitive, improve the operational efficiency of the property, and/or build up a better image for the property within the market place (Hassanien & Losekoot 2002: 232).

Further, Hassanien & Losekoot (2002) found that customer opinion was an important factor affecting the decision to renovate a hotel and hotel managers believed that there was a strong relationship between new product development/innovation and renovation. This view is also expressed by Hassanien & Baum (2002: 145) who note that "property renovation is considered as one of the most, if not the most essential, tool for product innovation in the hotel business."

The Motel Sector

According to Dunstan (1991), the first motel opened in California in December 1925. In Australia, it was not until 1955 that the first motel opened in Canberra, followed shortly afterwards by one opening in Oakleigh, Melbourne. By 1960, the number of motels in Australia had grown to 94 (Dunstan 1991) and during the 1960s, 1970s and 1980s, the numbers of motels skyrocketed. The rapid growth in the number of motels and the profits that were being made during this period attracted many newcomers to the industry who paid increasingly inflated prices for their motel businesses. In Australia, a large percentage of the motels are leased, which means that people with smaller financial assets are able to enter the industry. In these situations, the business is sold by the owner of the freehold to a lessee usually for a period of between 15 and 20 years in the first instance. The lessee is also charged a monthly rent that usually runs at between 20 and 25% of gross turnover. Many of the people who entered the industry during the 1980s and 1990s had little business experience and found that they had paid too much for their motels.

With the advent of cheaper domestic airfares over the last decade, many more tourists are now travelling by air on their vacations. This has meant that travel by car between key destinations has reduced, which has adversely impacted on the motel sector. For example, until a decade ago, the vast majority of Melbournians holidaying on the Gold Coast would drive up the Newell Highway usually spending one or two nights staying in motels on the way up and on the return trip. Nowadays, many more people take advantage of the more frequent flights and reduced airfares and thus do not require accommodation enroute.

In the recession of the early 1990s, the Australian tourism industry experienced a large downturn and the motel sector, in particular, was very severely affected. Many motels went into receivership; indeed, the banks were reported to have become the largest owners of motels in Australia at this time as a result of the many motels that they re-possessed. Although the motel sector has stabilised since the mid-1990s, there has been a much smaller annual growth in the number of motels being built. A large number of the motels that still operate date back to the 1960s and 1970s, and many of these are not able to meet the increasing level of consumer expectations. Australia's second motel that was built before the 1956 Olympics in Melbourne still operates. The fact that so many motels are run by lessees has meant that the refurbishment that has been undertaken in these properties has involved little more than a coat of paint and some modernisation of the fittings. In most motel leases, the lessee is responsible for the maintenance of the motel and because business has not been as buoyant as in the halcyon days of the motel industry, lessees do not have the surplus funds to invest in substantial upgrades of the motel. For some, rents have not declined in line with the decline in revenue, which puts an additional strain on operators. In a lease situation, many lessees are concerned about spending large sums of money on a property that they do not actually own. These factors have all conspired to reduce the likelihood of motels staying in tune with consumer expectations.

In the early days of motels in Australia the amenities offered were often in advance of the facilities that the visitors had in their homes. Over the past five decades, motels have introduced televisions, then colour televisions, video equipment and more recently spas, ahead of domestic purchases of similar equipment and fittings (Stancliffe 1996). This is illustrated in Table 23.1, which shows how motel facilities have been developed over the past five decades from the 1950s to the 1990s (Dennis 1991, cited in Stancliffe 1996). Further, it is clear from the literature that, more recently, the focus in hotels has been on offering improved services rather than improved facilities. The question now is what will be the next stage for innovation in motels? The trend towards all-suite hotels and apartments is still not meeting demand in the USA as, according to Walsh (2003), "25–30% of all lodging guests would prefer a suite, but fewer than 10% of properties in the industry are all-suite hotels." Could this be the direction that motels must take in order to stay competitive?

Analysis of Secondary Data

Much attention has been paid in the literature to the gathering of data on customer attitudes to their stay in hotels but little has been done for motels. The early work of Lewis (1984) on the basis for hotel selection examined the attributes of hotels that were; *salient* when they (customers) select a hotel, *determinant* when they choose a hotel, *important* when they stay in a hotel and *used* to differentiate between hotels. They also investigated how the hotels in the survey were perceived at the time in terms of satisfaction/dissatisfaction. Their focus was on attributes of the existing hotel product. Gleaned from the literature and from interviews with travellers and a questionnaire survey of hotel staff, the hotel attributes identified by Lewis (1984) for his major survey were those for the selected, existing properties. Other studies have taken similar approaches to the identification and assessment of hotel attributes (Callan 1998; Knutson 1988; Lewis 1987; Lockyer 2002). The findings of such research have been used to direct marketing strategies for hotels. Lewis (1984) stressed that a different group of factors/attributes determines choice as opposed to keeping customers satisfied. The results of his study also showed that attributes varied depending upon the individual hotel and also on the customer's reason for travelling.

Many researchers have focussed on hotel attributes in relation to particular market segments including: business both from the business traveller's point of view (Lockyer 2002; McCleary, Weaver & Hutchinson 1993) and the corporate travel departments

Table 23.1: Development of Australian motel facilities.

Facilities	1950s	1960s	1970s	1980s	1990s
First Australian Motel solid brick	✓				
One storey with views	✓				
Parking at the door	✓				
Slots for razors	✓				
Shoe-cleaning racks	✓				
Bottle openers	✓				
Good carpet	✓				
Writing desk	✓				
Curtains, wireless	✓				
Double beds	✓				
Sanitising strips on toilet seats	✓				
Two storey honeymoon suites		✓			
Inter-connecting rooms		✓			
Colour TV		✓			
Electric radiators		✓			
Telephone		✓			
Large rooms		✓			
Luggage racks		✓			
Pet accommodation		✓			
Recreation areas		✓			
On-premise laundries			✓		
Air conditioning			✓		
Electric blankets			✓		
Refrigerators			✓		
Queen size beds			✓		
Dining setting			✓		
Guest laundry			✓		
Swimming pool			✓		
Toll-free residential lines				✓	
Room service				✓	
Bedside lamps				✓	
STD/IDD phones				✓	
Clock radios, videos				✓	
In-room spas				✓	
King-size beds				✓	
Lounge suites				✓	
Floor to ceiling mirrors				✓	
Wall to wall carpet				✓	
Fire sensors				✓	
Bidets				✓	
Two car parks				✓	

Table 23.1: (*Continued*)

Facilities	1950s	1960s	1970s	1980s	1990s
Solarium/heated indoor pool				✓	
Tennis court				✓	
Free ice				✓	
Conference areas				✓	
Good quality linen					✓
Mini bars					✓
Computer points					✓
Iron/ironing board					✓
Remote controlled TVs					✓
Reverse cycle air conditioning					✓
Kitchenettes					✓
Better beds					✓
Franchised restaurants					✓

Source: Stancliffe (1996).

(Bell & Morey 1996); frequent travellers for both business and leisure (Knutson 1988); female travellers (McCleary, Weaver & Lan 1994) and older people (Wei, Ruys & Muller 1999).

In a recent study undertaken by Colmar Brunton Research for AAA Tourism (2000) in Australia, of the 232 respondents in the study the majority chose to stay in hotels or motels for an overnight stay (29 and 27% respectively) or for a short break (23, 26% respectively). However, when they took a holiday (for a week or more) 47% stayed in self-catering accommodation, 24% in caravan parks and 19% in on-site cabins, while only 19% stayed in motels. This indicates that, for longer stays like holidays, motels appear to be competing directly with the alternative self-catering options. Thus, a study is now needed to examine what the visitor will seek in the future in order to assist moteliers in making decisions about the nature of refurbishing and renovating their properties to differentiate them from the competition and so gain competitive advantage.

A number of studies exist in the literature that seek to understand the factors that prompt tourists to select particular hotels and many that seek to explore the levels of satisfaction that tourists have with their accommodation. However, few have been found that take a more proactive stance and seek to understand the factors that tourists look for in an accommodation facility that may not be provided at this point in time. That is, most of the work undertaken to date in this field tends to focus on the facilities that currently exist in hotels and motels rather than trying to identify the dimensions that are missing. These studies relate largely to satisfaction with existing facilities rather than trying to collect information on what consumers are likely to require in the future.

An exception to this is a study that looked at motels from the motelier's perspective undertaken in regional Victoria (Stancliffe 1996). The owners/managers of nineteen motels, with a minimum of a 3 star rating (most were 3.5 star) and located in the regional centres of Ballarat, Horsham, Stawell and Ararat, were interviewed. Data were collected on the changes that had been made to the physical facilities of the motel since the owner/manager had taken over the property and respondents were asked what they would like to add to make their property more competitive and to provide reasons for their suggestions. They were also asked what "sorts of things" they would like to see in motels in the future. From the results of this research it was clear that the facade of the motel was a concern for most moteliers, both in terms of work already completed and predicted changes for the future (8 and 11 of the 19 moteliers respectively). However, in terms of what additional (changed) features would most likely improve competitiveness, upgraded bathrooms were mentioned by 17 of the 19 moteliers, almost twice as many as for the second most mentioned feature. While the study did show that moteliers were concerned to upgrade their facilities, Stancliffe (1996) did not extend this exploratory study to verify whether their concerns matched those of their guests.

Given the paucity of literature adopting a proactive stance in terms of the future requirements for motel facilities, it was decided to conduct a focus group with key stakeholders in the accommodation sector in order to obtain a better understanding of the future direction of the sector and to undertake two preliminary focus groups with consumers who stay in 3–4 star motels.

Methods

In the first stage of the project, qualitative exploratory research was undertaken. This involved a focus group with key industry stakeholders and two focus groups with motel patrons.

As was noted in the literature review, there is a lack of secondary data available in the public domain relating to the factors that tourists will look for in an accommodation facility in the future. This was identified as one of the key issues for discussion in the focus group comprising key industry stakeholders, together with other questions exploring industry needs, their perceptions of consumer issues and cost effective methods of collecting data from motel visitors. Findings from this focus group then assisted in planning for the preliminary collection of data from motel visitors.

Focus Group with Key Stakeholders

A 90-minute focus group was conducted in June 2003 involving five key industry stakeholders in the accommodation sector as participants. Invited participants included senior staff from two major motel cooperatives, AAA Tourism, Hotel and Motel Accommodation Association (HMAA), and Tourism Tasmania. The key aims for the focus group were:

(1) To identify important secondary data, including industry market research reports that should be consulted and/or incorporated when refining the methodology for this project.
(2) To identify the specific issues that should be addressed in seeking to assess consumers' needs in relation to motel accommodation.

The topic was deemed by the group members to be "very important" in meeting their needs and this ensured an extremely lively discussion. Whilst all of the organisations represented at the focus group were very interested in understanding the future needs of consumers in terms of their accommodation requirements, little had been done to date by their organisations to explore such issues. Those past studies that had been undertaken by the various groups tended, as was the case with the academic literature, to focus on satisfaction with existing facilities. Participants at the focus group stressed the need to be more proactive in seeking to identify future accommodation requirements.

Focus Groups with Motel Visitors

Two additional one-hour focus groups were conducted in September 2003 with participants who had some experience in staying in different types of motels. Participants included both males and females, represented a broad age range from 20+ years to 60 years and were employed in a wide range of positions. Whilst some participants were quite regular users of commercial accommodation, others were infrequent users. Some stayed in motels when travelling for leisure, while others stayed for both business and leisure. The focus group interviews were recorded and the tapes transcribed.

Results and Discussion

As the findings from the focus group with key industry stakeholders informed the planning of the two focus groups with motel visitors these will be addressed first.

Focus Group of Key Stakeholders

Secondary data   Participants identified a number of market research reports that had been commissioned by the organisations represented at the focus group and it was agreed that researchers could view these reports even though they were not available in the public domain. It was clear, however, that none of these studies addressed the issue of what physical facilities visitors will need in the future when staying in motels. The nearest report had been market research into visitor expectations of hotel and motel properties.

Visitor expectations   It was noted that visitor expectations will vary according to the type of traveller, whether business or leisure, whether transient or destination-based. The participants noted that there is a need to identify why people are choosing motels, what preferences they have, and what their needs are. Results will likely vary by target market segment, which means that the needs of different key segments will have to be taken into account.

In the light of these findings, two preliminary consumer focus groups were conducted to obtain the motel visitors' perspectives.

Focus Groups with Motel Visitors

In these focus groups the participants discussed their perceptions of what a motel is and the image of 3–4 star motels before describing how they use the physical facilities. Expanding on this, they explained what they thought would enhance their stay for both short and for longer periods. Finally they discussed their dislikes and likes about motels and outlined their ideal motel in terms of its physical facilities.

As noted by Ulwick (2002: 92), "customers only know what they have experienced. They cannot imagine what they don't know about emerging technologies, new materials and the like." It is, therefore necessary to ask customers "only for outcomes — that is, what they want a new product or service to do for them." Thus, by asking the focus group participants to explain how they use the physical facilities and then to ask what would enhance their stay, they are thinking about outcomes rather than trying to imagine new technologies or products that they have not yet heard about.

Facilities that motel visitors use   In discussing the facilities that respondents use during their normal motel stays and their attitudes towards such facilities, the key aspect upon which there was substantial agreement was in terms of the overall ambience of the room, especially as it related to spaciousness. The motel room having a modern appearance and bright décor was seen as important as well as the room being of an acceptable size. First impressions were deemed to be very important. As stated by one respondent:

> Size of the room is important. If you feel the room is crowded then I think
> that creates a really bad impression. It doesn't necessarily have to be a small
> room (to create a bad first impression), it just has to be inappropriate décor.

Facilities that would enhance the visitor's stay   In this part of the discussion the participants continued to think about how they would use the facilities in terms of what would enhance their stay. *For short stays* the emphasis was on space with a request for bigger rooms with comfortable facilities for eating meals and the provision of chairs and a table, small kitchen facilities or kitchenette. Tea/coffee-making facilities were considered essential. An outside seating area, attached to the unit, that is partially secluded and/or with a pleasant outlook was also seen as desirable.

The bed should be comfortable and at least Queen sized. Most participants regarded suitable floor space as a most important issue and many motels were criticised for having more beds in a room than was suitable. Sufficient luggage racks to store cases were also considered essential. Provision of a bath was an issue with different opinions on what type of bath. The older generation expressed a preference for a standard bath (especially for females), while others said they would prefer a spa-bath. There was substantial criticism of the radios in many motels in that so many failed to pick up a range of stations. A television with a selection of free to air and movie channels was seen as important and for families, a video or DVD player was perceived as desirable.

Availability of breakfast and also a good restaurant were mentioned. The provision of recreational facilities for families in the public areas of the motel was seen as highly desirable.

For business travellers, the important facilities or services were thought to be an internet connection in the room, ISD/STD dialling, being able to park at the door, a good TV and radio and in-room dining.

For longer stays, participants definitely wanted a "miniature home." This incorporates many of the facilities already mentioned including a kitchenette with a range of utensils, toaster, pots and pans, a refrigerator, a microwave oven, a meals area with chairs and a table for dining, good radio, TV, video/DVD and comfortable chairs to watch TV. In-room ironing facilities were also seen as highly desirable. Reflecting the fact that few participants smoked, the general view was that guest rooms should be genuinely non-smoking and be larger. The following comments summarise expectations:

> I think your expectations change the more you stay there. You sort of almost start to think of it like this should be a replacement home.

> The expectation level increases the longer you stay there; I think because you almost get a sense of "ownership" about the place because you're there. But if it's just overnight it doesn't matter, you can rough it for a night.

There should also be some recreational facilities, like a table tennis/games room and pool, for children.

Likes and dislikes and the ideal motel   Essentially, the aspects that were liked included the convenience; being able to park in front of the unit, and the anonymity/privacy that motels offer. Respondents did not like having uncomfortable beds or cramped rooms with dated furnishing, fittings and furniture. Further, "cold" exposed brick walls inside were not considered homely enough.

> . . . everything crammed into too tight a space within the room. And it may have all the list of facilities but from an ergonomic (perspective), and visually, it's just chaos and you can't function because you're bumping into things the whole time.

From the discussion it was clear that the ideal motel should have comfortable beds and be suitably spacious, or at least not have a cramped appearance. There should be storage for at least two suitcases, a table at which meals can be eaten as well as some comfortable chairs for reading or talking. There should be an outdoor seating area attached to the unit that is secluded. The unit should have fresh, clean, bright paintwork, clean carpets, plastered walls, lighting that is subtle but bright enough to read. In fact it should be something like the visitor's own home. It should be clean and comfortable. It should be quiet with double-glazing or some sort of sound barrier, or be off the main road and it should be secure. Car parking should be secure and be near the guest rooms for easy transfer of luggage. There should be external facilities like a pool, a grassed area and play area. Dinner should be available either in the motel or nearby.

In a respondent's own words "I think the message is something more akin with your own home."

However, the location and surrounding must also be taken into consideration.

> ... but in regional areas we are often looking for large grounds, trees, and sometimes even an outdoor eating area, a BBQ facility ... Like it might be an old motel but if its got nice gardens which you can go wander around, smell the flowers ...

For business travellers, more lighting is needed and the TV and radio should be in good working order. There will be recreational things for when business is done and breakfast provided and/or a bar to enable travellers to talk to others.

In summary, therefore, the participants tended to choose motels because of their convenience and generally only for a short stay, although several respondents indicated that they would be satisfied with a motel for a week. However, for longer stays, most participants expressed a preference for apartments that are modern, spacious, and self-contained or caravan parks or on-site cabins that offer outdoor space and activities for families.

Conclusion

Key industry stakeholders confirmed that most of the consumer research in the motel sector focused on the level of satisfaction of consumers with the existing product on offer; little had been done to explore consumers' future needs in relation to their use of commercial accommodation. These stakeholders strongly endorsed the need for research that takes a more proactive stance in this area.

Even though the researchers went to great lengths to probe participant responses in the consumer focus groups in order to take a forward looking perspective, most responses referred to satisfaction with the existing motel product. This supports Ulwick's (2002) view that people have great trouble in moving beyond what they have already experienced.

Coming through strongly in the consumer focus groups was the importance of space in the motel rooms and a modern ambience. Participants were seeking the comforts of home, especially during longer stays. As one motel visitor commented; Now people seem to want more luxury, they want suites, they want better facilities." In other words, "it's the difference between staying somewhere just overnight and like a miniature home."

Until recent years, motels tended to provide opportunities for customers to try things that they would not normally have at home; motel facilities tended to be ahead of facilities available in the standard home and many people would go to motels to experience these new trends. For example, this happened with the introduction of black and white television, then colour television, videos and spa-baths. There do not appear to have been many substantial advances in recent years and most homes have facilities at least as good as motels. It was interesting that participants in the focus groups suggested that a motel stay should provide comfort as good as one gets at home. Some years ago, motels would have been seen as a treat and able to offer an experience not available at home.

Although nothing specifically new emerged from the focus groups in terms of new trends, it did identify the elements that seem to be the most important in the eyes of consumers. Additional research is currently being planned that includes discrete choice modeling to assess the relative importance of these characteristics. Having prioritised the different dimensions in the consumer decision process, it will be possible to then progress the project to identify innovative approaches to solving these issues.

Implications

It is clear that, for motels to remain competitive, especially with the increasingly popularity of apartments, on-site cabins and caravan parks, innovative solutions to the desire for spaciousness and a "mini-home," particularly for longer stay travellers, are needed. For this, "systematic innovation" (Drucker 1985) and a new approach to motel renovation and refurbishment is required. The degree of "newness" (Johannessen *et al.* 2001) may not necessarily involve new technologies beyond internet provision for business travellers and DVD facilities for entertainment. However, innovative ways of creating a spacious and modern feel to the accommodation in order to emulate the visitors' own homes, albeit on a smaller scale, will be required in order to encourage longer stays and return visits. These issues remain to be addressed. Readers interested in the subsequent stages of the research are invited to e-mail the authors for details.

Acknowledgments

The researchers wish to thank the participants in the focus groups and, in particular, the CRC for Sustainable Tourism for awarding the grant to make this project possible.

Chapter 24

Accommodation — The New Entertainment Centre

Asad Mohsin and Tim Lockyer

Historically the accommodation industry has been referred to as "a home away from home" and throughout its development there have been many changes in the facilities and attractions offered to guests. Many of these developments have taken place since the beginning of the nineteenth century. For example in 1846 central heating was introduced, 1859 saw the introduction of elevator, the electric light was introduced in 1881 and the in-room telephone in 1907. The first in-room entertainment became available to guests in 1927 with the introduction of the in-room radio. In many parts of the world the introduction of air-conditioning in 1940 made a very significant impact on guests' level of comfort. This was followed by the introduction of free television, a very popular entertainment feature (Bardi 2003: 6). Each of these developments has changed and enhanced the experience of guests.

The facilities and attractions offered by accommodation providers closely follows changes in the community at large, with growth in the entertainment sector of the economy today having a direct impact on the service industry as a whole and in particular the accommodation sector. The U.S. Department of Commerce (1992) showed that the consumer expenditure on entertainment and recreation increased rapidly from US$ 91.3 billion in 1980 to US$ 256.6 billion in 1990 (Figure 24.1).

Consequently, as well as hotels and other accommodation providers providing their guests with televisions, hair dryers and a large number of similar appliances, there is a growing need and expectation among guests for other forms of entertainment. Accommodation providers can learn from the current developments in large shopping centres for example, where entertainment is increasingly becoming an integral part of the marketing strategy used to entice customers (Sit *et al.* 2003). Quality and variety of entertainment is fast becoming a potential means of differentiation, and for example large shopping centres are trying to project distinctive images by providing a mix of entertainment and shopping. The entertainment in shopping centres potentially includes a mixture of movie theatres, fashion shows, food outlets, live music and even fun fairs as is the case of the Metro Centre in Newcastle, United Kingdom (Sit *et al.* 2003). The availability of such entertainment greatly increases the motive for a customer to visit, while also widening the appeal and increasing

Taking Tourism to the Limits: Issues, Concepts and Managerial Perspectives
© 2005 Published by Elsevier Ltd.
ISBN: 0-08-044644-2

Personal comment by Mr Robert Lagerwey, General Manager Ritz Carlton Singapore (23rd
June 2004):

Our guests are watching large screen plasma televisions at home, when they come to stay
with us we must offer them at least as good as they would have at home.

Figure 24.1: Changing requirements — the hotel competes with home.

the number of repeat visitors. Sit *et al.* (2003) identifies the following "big four" attributes
of shopping centre image:

(1) Merchandising — this has an important image attribute because it represents the "core
    product" of a shopping centre. Merchandising and tenant variety serves as a stimuli that
    induces excitement in a shopping experience and thus influences the consumers' image
    of the shopping mall or centre.
(2) Accessibility — Accessibility can be further divided into macro-accessibility and micro-
    accessibility. Macro-accessibility concerns access road conditions to the centre and the
    proximity of the centre from customers' place of work or residence. Unlike macro-
    accessibility, micro-accessibility refers to parking facilities within the centre and ease
    of navigation within the shopping centre. It is recommended that in order to increase
    patronage, a shopping centre should be easily accessible to minimize the searching time
    and psychological costs of consumers, including stress and frustration.
(3) Services — the third of the "big four" attributes of the shopping centre image. The
    authors suggest in the literature shopping centre services are confined to behaviour
    of retail employees, such as courtesy, knowledge and friendliness. These could be
    classified as personal services. However, beside personal service, shopping centres also
    provide communal services in terms of ambulance, escalators, lifts, restrooms, etc. The
    combination of personal and communal services is central to the shopping centre image
    and adds value to the total shopping experience of customers.
(4) Atmosphere — the fourth of the "big four" attributes of shopping centre image concerns
    the atmosphere of a shopping centre. Five common atmospheric features measured are
    ambience, colour, décor, music and layout. Atmosphere is critical because it acts as an
    environmental cue that consumers use to assess the quality of a shopping centre.

Though significant work has been done in studying the attributes of shopping centre
image, only a few shopping centre studies have identified entertainment as a distinctive
attribute of a shopping centre. Yet it can be contended that in contemporary shopping
centre marketing, entertainment is promoted as a distinct attribute that is operationalised by
multiple items of entertainment (Sit *et al.* 2003) and is continuously growing to become an
integral part of shopping centres providing excitement and fun in the shopping experience
for its customers.

In the example of a shopping centre the characteristics and outcome of enhancing
customer satisfaction and continued patronage can be clearly identified. For similar reasons
the accommodation industry passes through continuous changes. In the very broadest sense

the accommodation industry is in the business of selling space, and in some parts of the industry this is just what they do; for example in the case of backpacker accommodation. But for many other parts of the industry extra facilities and attractions have been added including, food and beverage facilities, gymnasiums, computer facilities, and many other forms of entertainment along with facilities that enhance the general appeal of the accommodation, as is discussed below.

While often the room is the main product being sold, a sale dependent on room only, is unlikely to generate a growth in sales and without such a growth a business may not sustain profitability. Accommodation industry business operators continually study customer needs and contemporary trends to increase sales by developing appropriate product-service bundles and value-adding systems. However, it is important to ensure that the availability of the facilities does not just simply add to the cost of providing accommodation to the guest; the return on the investment needs to also be clearly identified. This is done through the identification of the attraction as a profit centre. Many of the enhancements to the accommodation experience carry with them considerable cost, and it is can be difficult to justify such expenditure unless a guest values the enhanced service and is prepared to pay more for it. As a result, management are put in the situation where they not only need to provide a growing level of attraction and entertainment but also be able to measure the return on the investment. For example in many countries the availability of cable or satellite television, which offers news programmes, movies etc, is an essential part of the accommodation. When it was first introduced it was viewed as an important marketing tool to encourage guests to stay, but over time this has changed to where the availability of such stations is simply an essential part of the product and no longer is viewed as a marketing advantage (Lockyer 2005; Ryan 1991). The accommodation provider therefore has additional costs upon which it is difficult to generate a return on investment.

A restaurant can be clearly identified as a profit centre. It is possible to measure the costs and revenues of each of the products sold on the menu; it is also possible to determine labour and other operating costs, but what is harder to determine is the impact that a restaurant has on the average room occupancy and average room rate. Value adding becomes easier if systems and capacity exist on the premises. A food and beverage outlet which offers a variety and quality in meal experience can not only add a feature to main product (rooms) but also may add to revenue generation, and hence a growth in sales, the sustaining of cash flow and perhaps marginally contribute to profits. A continual growth in sales is like a never-ending challenge for the business world and the accommodation industry is no different. Providing entertainment with rooms and food and beverage is therefore seen as another feature to entice customers and achieve growth in sales and profitability.

The factors that influence the selection of accommodation is a complex question with many researchers looking at this question. It is clear from recent research (Lockyer 2005) that seemingly simple issues such as price are in reality much more complex than anticipated, with multiple "trigger" points that influence the selection process. Emotional factors can impact on the selection process. Research recently conducted in the United States of America involved the interviewing of 35,000 frequent travellers using the MMHI (the Market Matrix Hotel Indicator) which includes measures of brand loyalty and an emotion index for 133 hotel chains. It was reported that luxury hotels ranked the highest in providing positive emotional experiences (Barsky 2001). Barsky (2001) suggests a close relationship exists between the emotions that are felt by a potential purchaser of accommodation and their brand loyalty. What was of particular interest was that additional to the existence of a relationship between emotion and brand loyalty, there was also a willingness to pay on average an additional US$13 per night more. An example of the lengths that hoteliers go to influence the purchase decisions of potential guests can be seen in the Ritz-Carlton in Naples. The owners, Host Marriott Corp, spent more than US$100 million to upgrade and expand the property (Landro 2002). These developments include a 51,000 square foot luxury spa with marble locker rooms, with every possible amenity. Developments such as this add significantly to the facilities offered by an accommodation provider. This is further developed into what is referred to as "The all-under-one-roof" notion at the Gaylord Texan Hotel which opened in April 2004 (Chittum 2004). This development by Gaylord Entertainment is a further development of an earlier hotel opened in Nashville, the Opryland Resort and Convention Centre that opened in 1977. It includes 2,800 rooms and 6,000,000 square feet of meeting space, making it the biggest hotel and convention centre outside of Las Vegas. The Opryland Resort and Convention Centre includes a large glass-covered area which is air conditioned which includes mature trees and a river. The major objective of such large developments are not only to further develop the types of facilities available for guests but also, as reported by Colin V. Reed, president and chief executive of Gaylord, "If you stay at the Texan, you're not leaving" (Chittum 2004: B.1.). This example exemplifies the concept of the development of the hotel complex as a "total destination," with areas such as shopping malls and other forms of entertainment all designed to retain the hotel guest's expenditure within the company owned facilities rather than in competitors' facilities. The recently announced Sheraton Shenzhen hotel will include the normal expected facilities plus a retail centre (Strauss 2004) (Figure 24.2).

Not only do these developments focus on such areas as shops and related facilities but also on a large variety of other facilities. The entertainment industry over the last decade has grown significantly (Dosher & Kleiner 1997). Holiday makers/tourists, commercial travellers, young and old; all seek some enjoyment while travelling either on holiday or business. The leisure service operators, being a part of entertainment business themselves, offer more entertaining sales promotions than other types of service operators (Wakefield & Bush 1998). Wakefield & Bush (1998) further state that leisure services may offer price deals, but also frequently offer non-price sales promotions which may add entertainment value for customers. Large hotels as a part of their marketing strategy promote a variety of entertainment available for the enjoyment of their guests. Some means of adding entertainment value for the accommodation industry customers (usually referred as guests) include:

- Live music band (usually in restaurant/coffee shop/lobby);
- Solo performances (usually in restaurant/coffee shop/lobby);
- Live shows (usually poolside): magic, dance etc;
- In-house latest movies including adults only choices (usually in rooms);
- Selection of a variety of in-house TV entertainments (usually in rooms);
- Gambling (in-house casinos);
- Night club/bars;
- Spas — massage, mud etc.;
- PC with internet, play station;
- Themed rooms/areas/restaurants.

The grandest hotel in the great Southwest

Surrounded by rolling pastureland and overlooking beautiful Lake Grapevine, the magnificent new Gaylord Texan pays tribute to everything Texas as only Texas can: on a grand scale.

As a guest of the resort, you'll experience the best of the Lone Star State under our signature glass atrium where you can dine, shop, socialize, and be entertained among four-and-a-half acres of lush indoor gardens. Take a stroll around and soak in the festive atmosphere of Riverwalk, explore the vast canyons of Texas Hill Country, and taste the Nuevo Latino creations of award-winning Texas chef Stephan Pyles.

For rest and relaxation, enjoy our luxurious 25,000-square-foot world-class spa and fitness center with indoor pool, 18-hole championship golf at the adjacent Cowboys Golf Club, outdoor pool, and exclusive on-site entertainment including live music nightly at the Glass Cactus overlooking Lake Grapevine, opening Fall 2004. We can also arrange for bass fishing, water skiing and other watersports through the nearby marina. Whether you're here for a weekend or a week, youíll never run out of things to see and do.

After retiring for the evening to your beautifully appointed room, you can unlock your safe to find your laptop and mobile phone fully recharged, relax with an in-room movie, plug into high-speed Internet, or check messages and make calls using a standard or cordless phone. Youíll find all the comforts of home and then some.

We look forward to meeting you and giving you a warm Texas welcome with our brand of superior hospitality, service and entertainment.

Figure 24.2: New facilities — new entertainments.

Berkley & Thayer (2000) in discussing the policing of entertainment districts state that retailing and urban development are now driven by entertainment thereby creating the perception of economic vitality. The authors further state that all new large-scale commercial developments have significant entertainment components and entertainment businesses have revitalized many abandoned downtowns. Sceptics who thought that entertainment available in a hotel may not be the determinant of hotel choice may well have to reconsider this view.

A study of visitors to Blackpool U.K., undertaken by Hughes & Benn (1997) reveals entertainment as the single most important factor in the decision to visit a resort.

So — What Does Entertainment Mean to the Modern Accommodation Industry?

Entertainment is emerging as possessing value for customers of all ages. Parents who travel with children seek entertainment for children, the aged seek light entertainment, and the young seek that which is "fast and funky." If the accommodation industry considers the role entertainment has played in the retail industry it clearly reflects a contemporary trend and is a feature that entices customers. Entertainment is proving its role in promoting accommodation and attracting customers and will be seen as adding value to the other attributes of the industry. Figure 24.3 shows a variety of entertaining features used in hotels. However, the choices of such features usually depend on size and affordability of hotels. Providing live music for the entertainment of the guests throughout the week or on certain days of the week, the use of solo vocal or musical instrument performers, organising live shows for example magic shows, dance shows, etc create an energetic and busy atmosphere in the hotel. A different entertaining experience particularly for the younger generation comes through night clubs in the hotels. A "thrilling" experience is provided by casinos within the hotels. Las Vegas is an excellent example of a very popular destination where "casino thrills" and live shows are well integrated with the accommodation. Large hotels are continually competing to create a unique entertaining environment within the hotel. The hotel seeks a situation wherein guests spend most of their time and money within the

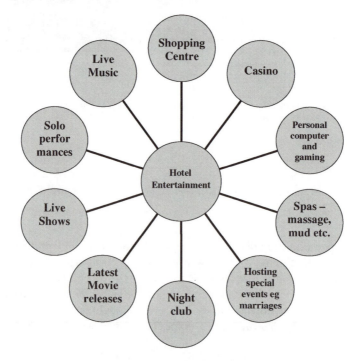

Figure 24.3: The entertainment portfolio.

complex and the variety of entertainment features facilitates such an approach whether the guest chooses to spend most of his or her time out of, or in the room. In-room entertainment provides not only a variety of television channels to watch but also most recent movie releases. Some hotels contract to show movies not yet released in theatres (Figure 24.4).

Many hotels through marketing promote a claim of providing an everlasting experience through entertaining and organising special events like marriages, birthdays etc in their premises. The shopping experience is another entertaining feature used by hotels and many large complexes provide shopping centres under the same roof. Many Asian cultures use

Aladdin Hotel Las Vegas

Located midway on the Vegas Strip, the Aladdin boasts convenience and luxury. The hotel features: gourmet restaurants, world-class shopping at Desert Passage and great entertainment. Themed after several stories from the Arabian Nights, the Aladdin feels like another world. Ebony Horses stampede from the race and sports book and a giant Djinni's lamp smokes in the casino center. And there are other, more practical kinds of magic at the Aladdin -- the rain that falls gently from the "sky" of the mammoth **Desert Passage shopping mall**, and an innovative, multi-floor casino layout that allows guests to access their rooms from check-in without trekking through the gaming areas.

- **Number of rooms:** 2,567.
- **Casino:** Yes, 100,000-square-foot main casino with 2,800 slot machines and 87 table games. Plus The London Club, 35,000-square-foot European-style gaming salon operated in partnership with London Clubs International. Casino games include Blackjack, Caribbean Stud Poker, Craps, Keno, Let It Ride, Pai Gow Poker, Poker, Roulette, Slots, Baccarat, Wheel of Fortune, Megabucks and Super Megabucks.
- **Race & Sports Book:** Yes, more details.
- **Restaurants**: For a complete list of dining options in the Aladdin and Desert Passage, click here. In the Aladdin are: P.F. Chang's China Bistro, Elements, Tremezzo, Spice Market Buffet, Zanzibar Cafe, Starbucks and Towering Palms Cafe and Bar. Desert Passage restaurants include: Lombardi's, Cheeseburger at the Oasis, La Salsa Cantina, Oyster Bay Seafood & Wine, Commander's Palace, Todai Seafood & Sushi Buffet, Aromi D' Italia, Blondies Sports Bar & Grill and Ben & Jerry's.
- **Entertainment**: Steve Wyrick performs in the Steve Wyrick Theater. Headliner acts show up at the 7,000-seat Aladdin Theatre. Click here, for a schedule of this week's entertainment.
- **Pools:** Yes, more details.
- **Health Club:** Yes.
- **Spa**: Yes, more details.
- **Shops:** More than 130-world class and one-of-a-kind retail shops and 14 unique restaurants can be found in the Desert Passage mall.
- **Wedding chapel:** Yes, more details.
- **Convention rooms:** Yes, A total of 75,000 square-feet of meeting space including a 37,000 square-foot grand ballroom.
- **Business center:** Yes.
- **In-room computer data port**: Yes. Also all of the guest rooms offer a computer with high-speed Internet access.
- **Room service:** Yes.

Interesting facts about Aladdin: The Aladdin Theater for the Performing Arts boasts the largest proscenium arch stage in the country. The 35,000-square-foot London Club at Aladdin is Las Vegas' only European-style luxury gaming salon. The world's largest indoor light board creates a 130-foot "Enchanted Garden," with a constantly changing display of blooming flowers.

Figure 24.4: The Casino Hotel entertainment complex.

retailing not only as a source of entertainment but also as a means to meet the need to take back home gifts for friends and relatives.

One of the major advantages that hotel complexes have is that of security. In many parts of the world hotels can be considered to be soft targets. It used to always be that a hotel was considered by many as a public facility. Anyone who has travelled recently in many parts of the world finds quite a different atmosphere in hotels. It is evident, in a very connected and information world, that concerns about safety, security and other issues of terrorism have an impact on the choices that guests and accommodation organisers make. Although at times various world events such as SARS, Iraq, the Madrid bombing and terrorism in Israel clearly impact on businesses, many travellers are still looking forward to travel and feel safe while doing so (Steinhauer 2004). This changes the nature of the hotel business — where at one time international companies would bring hundreds of their employees together for a conference all at one time, there are now concerns over security that have resulted in smaller conferences and a growing use of technology.

There are other interesting trends developing internationally that include health awareness, which has led hotels to promote gymnasium; spas facilities like mud baths, massage etc; and using personal computers with internet facility and play station (comments by Mr. Steve Kirkpatrick — Area General Manager, Rydges Hotels, New Zealand). The traditional hotel or motel accommodation is subject to constant change, with a number of other developments challenging the traditional hotel type accommodation in various ways: all attempting to fulfill the different requirements of a diverse market. For example, residential hotels were introduced for those persons looking for the service and convenience of a hotel stay but over an extended period. The introduction of time share accommodation was developed to give flexibility and to spread the cost of accommodation. A growing trend based on the time share principle is that of "Fractionals" (Verburg 2003). Although fractionals are similar to time share accommodation they differ in a number of ways: (1) They are built to the standard of a 5-star resort; (2) They offer amenities such as concierge service, room service and housekeeping; and (3) They provide owners with access to hotel facilities — spas, tennis courts, and golf courses.

Thus this review indicates that the accommodation industry is going through continued periods of change. The introduction of the many and varied types of attractions and facilities assist management in the development of measurable profit centers that add to the attractiveness of the facilities and satisfaction of the guests. In what is a continuing troubled world these facilities also provide hotel guests those in other forms of accommodation the ability to stay in a controlled environment. Over the next years as the industry continues to change and identify needs and requirements these trends will continue. Hotels thus extend the range of tourist choice. They offer alternatives to "adventure" and adrenalin chasing activities described elsewhere in this book, but often those who seek adventure will also seek comfort, luxury and fun. In a post-modern world market segments that define tourists by typologies miss an essential truth; which is that the market comprises tourists who play roles (Ryan 2004); and it is this role playing that facilities the extension and need for entertainment in hotels, while additionally extending its market to all types of tourists, regardless of age, ethnicity or disposition.

References

Abbott-Cone, C. (1995). Crafting selves: The lives of two Mayan women. *Annals of Tourism Research*, *22*, 314–327.

Acevedo, A. (1991). Interactions between boats and bottlenose dolphins, Tursiops truncatus, in the entrance to Ensenada de la Paz, Mexico. *Aquatic Mammals*, *17*, 120–124.

Adler, J. (1985). Youth on the road: Reflection on the history of tramping. *Annals of Tourism Research*, *12*, 335–354.

Adler, N. J. (1986). *International dimensions of organisational culture*. Boston: Kent Publishing, pp. 46–48.

Adler, N. J., & Ghadar, F. (1990). Strategic human resource management: A global perspective. In: R. Pieper (Ed.), *Human resource management: An international comparison* (pp. 235–260). Berlin/New York: de Gruyter.

Agar, M., & McDonald, J. (1995). Focus groups and ethnography. *Human Organization*, *54*(Spring), 78–86.

Akis, S., Peristianis, N., & Warner, J. (1996). Residents' attitudes to tourism development: The case of Cyprus. *Tourism Management*, *17*(7), 481–494.

Amante-Helweg, V. (1996). Ecotourists' beliefs and knowledge about dolphins and the development of cetacean ecotourism. *Aquatic Mammals*, *22*, 131–140.

Amsden, A. (1990). Third World industrialization: 'Global fordism' or a new model? *New Left Review*, *182*, 5–32.

Anonymous (1996). *Learning to care for our environment – perspectives on environmental education: A discussion document*. Wellington: Ministry for the Environment.

Anonymous (1997). *The educational values of whale watching*. The International Fund for Animal Welfare.

Anson, C. (1999). Planning for peace: The role of tourism in the aftermath of violence. *Journal of Travel Research*, *38*(August), 57–61.

Arnberger, A., & Brandenburg, C. (2002). Visitor structure of a heavily used conservation area: The Danube Floodplain National Park, Lower Austria. In: A. Arnberger, C. Brandenburg, & A. Muhar (Eds), *Conference Proceedings of the Monitoring and Management of Visitor Flows in Recreational and Protected Areas* (pp. 7–13). Bodenkultur University, Vienna, Austria.

Arnould, E., & Price, L. (1993). River magic: Extraordinary experiences and extended service encounter. *Journal of Consumer Research*, *20*(June), 24–45.

Ashworth, G. (1996). Holocaust tourism and Jewish culture: The lessons of Kraków-Kazimierz. In: M. Robinson, N. Evans, & P. Callaghan (Eds), *Tourism and cultural change* (pp. 1–12). Sunderland: Business Education Publishers.

Ashworth, G. J. (2002). Book review. *Tourism Management*, *23*(2), 190–191.

Attwell, D. (2003). Telling stories: Whites seeking home in Africa. *Journal of Southern African Studies*, *29*(1), 307–309.

Auger, T. (2001). *Eyewitness travel guides: New Zealand*. London: Dorling Kindersley.

Australian Bureau of Statistics (ABS) (2003). *Tourist accommodation in Australia* (8635.0), March 2003.

Ballantine, J. L., & Eagles, P. F. J. (1994). Defining Canadian ecotourists. *Journal of Sustainable Tourism, 2*, 210–214.

Baloglu, S., & McCleary, K. W. (1999). A model of destination image formation. *Annals of Tourism Research, 26*(4), 868–897.

Bardi, J. A. (2003). *Hotel front office management* (3rd ed.). New Jersey: Wiley.

Barr, K. (1997). *The impacts of marine tourism on the behaviour and movement patterns of dusky dolphins (Lagenorhynchus obscurus), at Kaikoura, New Zealand.* Master of Science Thesis, University of Otago, Dunedin, New Zealand.

Barr, K., & Slooten, E. (1999). *Effects of tourism on dusky dolphins in Kaikoura.* Wellington: Department of Conservation.

Bate, S. P. (1994). *Strategies for cultural change.* London: Butterworth Heinemann.

Bauman, Z. (1996). From pilgrim to tourist: Or a short history of identity. In: S. Hall, & P. du Gay (Eds), *Questions of cultural identity* (pp. 18–36). London: Sage.

Bauman, Z. (1998). *Globalization: The human consequences.* Cambridge: Polity.

Bauman, Z. (2000). *Liquid modernity.* Cambridge UK: Polity Press.

Beach, D. W., & Weinrich, M. T. (1989). Watching the whales: Is an educational adventure for humans turning out to be another threat for an endangered species? *Oceanus, 32*, 84–88.

Beckerman, W. (1994). Sustainable development: Is it a useful concept? *Environmental Values, 3*, 191–209.

Beinart, W. (1998). Men, science, travel and nature in the eighteenth and nineteenth century Cape. *Journal of Southern African Studies*, Special Issue on Masculinities in Southern Africa, *24*(4), 775–799.

Beinart, W., & Coates, P. (1995). *Environment and history: The taming of nature in the USA and South Africa.* London: Routledge.

Bejder, L. (1997). *Behaviour, ecology, and impact of tourism on Hector's dolphins (Cephalorhynchus hectori) in Porpoise Bay, New Zealand.* Master of Science Thesis, University of Otago, Dunedin, New Zealand.

Bejder, L., & Dawson, S. M. (1998). *Responses by Hector's dolphins to boats and swimmers in Porpoise Bay, New Zealand.* (Report SC/50/WW11). International Whaling Commission Scientific Committee.

Bejder, L., Dawson, S. M., & Harraway, J. A. (1999). Responses by Hector's dolphins to boats and swimmers in Porpoise Bay, New Zealand. *Marine Mammal Science, 15*, 738–750.

Belk, R., Wallendorf, M., & Sherry, J. (1989). The sacred and the profane in consumer behaviour: Theodicy on the odyssey. *Journal of Consumer Research, 16*(June), 1–38.

Bell, C. (2002). The big 'OE': Young New Zealand travellers as secular pilgrims. *Tourist Studies, 2*(2), 143–158.

Berg, P. O., & Kreiner, K. (1990). Corporate architecture: Turning physical settings into symbolic resources. In: P. Gagliardi (Ed.), *Symbols and artifacts: Views of the corporate landscape* (pp. 41–67). New York: Aldine de Grutyer.

Berger, J. (2003). From ways of seeing. In: A. Jones (Ed.), *The feminism and visual culture reader* (pp. 37–40). London: Routledge.

Berger, P., Berger, B., & Kellner, H. (1973). *The homeless mind.* Harmondsworth: Penguin.

Berger, P. L., & Luckmann, T. (1967). *The social construction of reality: A treatise in the sociology of knowledge.* London: Allen Lane and Penguin Press.

Berkley, B. J., & Thayer, J. R. (2000). Policing entertainment districts. *International Journal of Police Strategies & Management, 23*(4), 466–491.

Berno, T., Moore, K., Simmons, D., & Hart, V. (1996). The nature of adventure tourism experience in Queenstown, New Zealand. *Australian Leisure*, *7*(2), 21–25.

Beyer, J. M., & Trice, H. M. (1988). The communication of power relations in organizations through cultural rites. In: M. D. Jones, M. D. Moore, & R. C. Sayder (Eds), *Inside organizations: Understanding the human dimension* (pp. 141–157). Newbury Park, CA: Sage.

Bird, E. C. F. (1993). *The coast of Victoria — the shaping of scenery*. Carlton, Vic.: Melbourne University Press.

Black, J. (1985). *The British and the grand tour*. Dover: Croom Helm.

Blair, J. (2002). Tragedy turns to tourism at Ground Zero. *New York Times* at www.theage. com.au/articles/2002/06/28/1023864657451.html.

Blank, U. (1989). *The community tourism industry imperative: The necessity, the opportunities, its potential*. Pennsylvania: Venture Publishing.

Bloch, P. H., & Bruce, G. D. (1984). Product involvement as leisure behavior. *Advances in Consumer Research*, *11*, 197–202.

Bloch, P. H., Sherrell, D. L. *et al*. (1986). Consumer search: An extended framework. *Journal of Consumer Research*, *13*(1), 119–126.

Bly, L. (2003). Disaster strikes, tourists follow. *USA Today*. www.usatoday.com/travel/vacations/ destinations/. . ./2002-08-30-disaster-tourism.html.

Boo, E. (1990). *Ecotourism: The potentials and pitfalls*. Washington, DC, USA: World Wildlife Fund.

Boorstin, D. (1964). *The image: A guide to pseudo-events in America*. New York: Harper & Row.

Bottrill, C. G. (1995). Ecotourism: Towards a key elements approach to operationalising the concept. *Journal of Sustainable Tourism*, *3*, 45–54.

Bramwell, B. (1994). Rural tourism and sustainable rural tourism. *Journal of Sustainable Tourism*, *2*(1), 1–6.

Bramwell, W. (Ed.) (2003). Special issue Mediterranean tourism. *Journal of Sustainable Tourism*, *11*(2/3), 95–294.

Bramwell, B., & Lane, B. (2000). Collaboration and partnerships in tourism planning. In: B. Bramwell, & B. Lane (Eds), *Tourism collaboration and partnerships: Politics, practice and sustainability* (pp. 1–19). Clevedon: Channel View Publications.

Brannan, L., Condello, C., Struckum, N., Vissers, N., & Priest, S. (1992). Public perception of risk in recreational activities. *Journal of Applied Recreation Research*, *17*(2), 144–157.

Bridges, W. (1992). *The character of organizations*. Palo Alto, CA: Consulting Psychologists Press.

Brockington, D. (2002). *Fortress conservation*. Oxford: James Currey.

Brohman, J. (1996). New directions in tourism for Third World development. *Annals of Tourism Research*, *23*, 48–70.

Brown, A. (1998). *Organisational culture* (2nd ed.). London: Pitman Publishing.

Brown, L. D. (1991). Bridging organizations and sustainable development. *Human Relations*, *44*(8), 807–831.

Brown, T. C., & Daniel, T. C. (1987). Context effects in perceived environmental quality assessment: Scene selection and landscape quality ratings. *Journal of Environmental Psychology*, 233–250.

Bryant, A. T. (1949). *The Zulu people as they were before the white man came*. Pietermaritzburg: Shuter and Shooter.

Buckley, R. (2000). Neat trends: Current issues in nature, eco and adventure tourism. *International Journal of Tourism Research*, *2*, 437–444.

Buckley, R. (Ed.) (2003). *Case studies in ecotourism*. Wallingford: CABI Publishing.

Buhalis, D. (1999). Limits of tourism development in peripheral destinations: Problems and challenges. *Tourism Management*, *20*(2), 183–185.

Bulbeck, C. (2005). *Facing the wild: Eecotourism, conservation and animal encounters*. London: Earthscan.

Bunnell, T. (2002). Kampung rules: Landscape and the contested government of urban(e) Malayness. *Urban Studies, 39*(9), 1685–1701.

Bunyan, N. (2003). Paralysed man pays £40 to die legally. *Daily Telegraph*, 21st January.

Burns, D., Driver, B. L., Lee, M. E., Anderson, D., & Brown, P. J. (1994, June 8). *Pilot tests for implementing benefits-based management*. The Fifth International Symposium on Society and Resource Management: Advances in Amenity Resource Management, Colorado.

Burr, S. W. (1991). Review and evaluation of the theoretical approaches to community as employed in travel and tourism: Impact research on rural community organisation and change. In: A. J. Veal, P. Johnson, & G. Cushman (Eds), *Leisure and tourism: Social and environmental change* (pp. 540–553). Papers from the World Leisure and Recreation Association Congress, Sydney, Australia.

Butler, R., & Boyd, S. (Eds) (2000). *Tourism and national parks*. Chichester: Wiley.

Buzard, J. (1993). *The beaten track: European tourism, literature and the ways to culture: 1800–1918*. Oxford: Oxford University Press.

Callan, R. J. (1998). Attributional analysis of customer's hotel selection criteria by UK grading scheme categories. *Journal of Travel Research, 36*(3), 20–34.

Campbell, C. (1987). *The romantic ethic and the spirit of modern consumerism*. Oxford: Blackwell.

Campbell, J. (2001). *Map use and analysis* (4th ed.). New York: McGraw-Hill.

Canard, H. (2001). Tourism, conservation and recreation. Paper presented at the Managing New Zealand's Wildlands Conference, Rotoiti Lodge.

Cano, V., & Prentice, R. (1998). Opportunities for endearment to place through electronic 'visiting': WWW homepages and the tourism promotion of Scotland. *Tourism Management, 19*(1), 67–73.

Carson, R. (1962). *Silent spring*. London: Hamish Hamilton.

Cater, C. (2004, June). Looking the part: The relationship between adventure tourism and the outdoor fashion industry. Paper presented for the conference, *Tourism – the State of the Art*. Proceedings of the Conference, The Scottish Hotel School, The University of Strathclyde, Glasgow.

CEDA (1991). *Calgary: Host, consultant & educator to the world*. Calgary, Alberta: Calgary Economic Development Authority.

Celsi, R. L., Rose, L. R., & Leigh, T. W. (1993). An exploration of high-risk leisure consumption through skydiving. *Journal of Consumer Research, 20*, 1–23.

Central Coast Consulting (2002). *Nicola tribal association eco-tourism study*. Merritt, BC.

Charles, G. (1996). *New Zealand whitewater*. Nelson: Craig Potton Publishing.

Chatwin, B. (1988). *The songlines*. London: Picador.

Chittum, R. (2004, August 11). *What's not big at the Texan hotel*? Tourists (Eastern ed.). New York, NY. p. B.1.

Clark, G. (1998). *Muskwa-Kechika advisory board terms of reference*. Victoria, BC: Government of British Columbia.

Clarkson, M. B. E. (1995). A stakeholder framework for analysing and evaluating corporate social performance. *Academy of Management Review, 20*, 92–117.

Cloke, P., & Perkins, H. C. (1998). Cracking the canyon with the awesome foursome: Representations of adventure tourism in New Zealand. *Environment and Planning D: Society and Space, 16*(2), 185–218.

Cloke, P., & Perkins, H. C. (2002). Commodification and adventure in New Zealand tourism. *Current Issues in Tourism, 5*(6), 521–549.

Coccossis, H. (1996). Tourism and sustainability: Perspectives and implications. In: G. Priestly, J. A. Edwards, & H. Coccossis (Eds), *Sustainable tourism? European experiences* (pp. 1–21). Oxford: CAB International.

Coccossis, H. (2002). Island tourism and sustainable development: Caribbean, Pacific and Mediterranean experiences. In: Y. Apostolopoulos, & D. Gayle (Eds), *Island tourism development and carrying capacity* (pp. 131–143). Westport: Praeger.

Coe, N., & Kelly, P. (2000). Distance and discourse in the local labour market: The case of Singapore. *Area, 32*(4), 413–422.

Coe, N., & Kelly, P. (2002). Language of labour: Representational strategies in Singapore labour control regime. *Political Geography, 21,* 341–371.

Cohen, E. (1972). Towards a sociology of international tourism. *Social Research, 39*(1), 164–182.

Cohen, E. (1973). Nomads from affluence: Notes on the phenomenon of drifter tourism. *International Journal of Comparative Sociology, 14,* 89–103.

Cohen, E. (1974). Who is a tourist?: A conceptual clarification. *The Sociolological Review, 22,* 527–555.

Cohen, E. (1979). A phenomenology of tourist experience. *The Journal of the British Sociological Association, 13*(1), 179–201.

Comaroff, J., & Comaroff, J. (2002). Naturing the nation: Aliens, apocalypse and the postcolonial state. *Journal of Southern African Studies, 27*(3), 627–651.

Connell, R. (1990). A whole new world: Remaking masculinity in the context of the environmental movement. *Gender and Society, 4*(4), 452–478.

Constantine, R. L. (1995). *Monitoring the commercial swim-with-dolphin operations with the bottlenose (Tursiops truncatus) and common dolphins (Delphinus delphis) in the Bay of Islands, New Zealand.* Master's Thesis, University of Auckland, New Zealand.

Constantine, R. L. (1999). *Effects of tourism on marine mammals in New Zealand.* Science for Conservation 106, Department of Conservation, New Zealand.

Constantine, R. L. (2001). Increased avoidance of swimmers by wild bottlenose dolphins (*Tursiops truncatus*) due to long-term exposure to swim-with-dolphin tourism. *Marine Mammal Science, 17*(4), 689–702.

Constantine, R. L., & Baker, C. S. (1997). *Monitoring the commercial swim-with-dolphin operations in the Bay of Islands.* Science for Conservation 56, Department of Conservation, New Zealand.

Cooper, C. (1995). Strategic planning for sustainable tourism: The case of the offshore islands of the UK. *Journal of Sustainable Tourism, 3*(4), 191–209.

Corkeron, P. J. (1995). Humpback whales (*Megaptera novaeangliae*) in Hervey Bay, Queensland: Behaviour and responses to whale-watching vessels. *Canadian Journal of Zoology, 73,* 1290–1299.

Cosgrove, D. (1984). *Social formation and the symbolic landscape.* London: Croom Helm.

Costa (2001). An emerging tourism planning paradigm? A comparative analysis between town and tourism planning. *International Journal of Tourism Research, 3*(6), 425–441.

Crawford, C. M., & Di Benedetto, C. A. (2000). *New products management.* Boston: Irwin & McGraw-Hill.

Crotty, M. (1998). *The foundations of social research: Meaning and perspective in the research process.* St Leonards: Allen & Unwin.

Croy, W. G., & Kearsley, G. (2002). Motivating and satisfying images of back country areas. Presented at Ecotourism: Wilderness and Mountains. University of Otago, Dunedin. 27–29 August.

Cumes, D. (1998). *Inner passages, outer journeys: Wilderness, healing and the discovery of self.* St. Paul Minnesota: Llewellyn Publications.

Curran, S., Wilson, B., & Thompson, P. (1996). Recommendations for the sustainable management of the bottlenose dolphin population in the Moray Firth. *Scottish Natural Heritage Review,* Issue 56.

Dann, G. M. S. (1981). Tourist motivation: An appraisal. *Annals of Tourism Research, 8*(2), 187–219.

Dann, G. (1994). Tourism: The nostalgia industry of the future. In: W. Theobald (Ed.), *Global tourism: The next decade*. Oxford: Butterworth Heinemann.

Dann, G. (1998). The dark side of tourism. *Etudes et Rapports*, série L. Aix-en-Provence: Centre International de Recherches et d'Etudes Touristiques.

Dann, G. S., & Seaton, A. V. (2001). Slavery, contested heritage and thanatourism. *International Journal of Hospitality and Tourism Administration*, 2(3–4), 1–29.

Dann, G. S., & Seaton, A. (Eds) (2001). *Slavery, contested heritage and thanatourism*. Binghampton, HY: Haworth Hospitality Press.

Dann, M. S., & Seaton, A. V. (2001). Slavery, contested heritage and thanatourism. *International Journal of Hospitality and Tourism Administration*, 2(3/4), 1–29.

Deal, T. E., & Kennedy, A. A. (1982). *Corporate cultures*. Reading, MA: Addison-Wesley.

Dean, D. L. (1994). How to use focus groups. In: J. S. Wholey, H. P. Hatry, & K. Newcomer (Eds), *Handbook of practical program evaluation* (pp. 338–349). San Francisco: Jossey-Bass.

Dean, M. (1999). *Governmentality: Power and rule in modern society*. London: Sage.

Dent, J. (2002, May 6). Ever interested in the dark side, tourism embraces the World Trade Centre. <www.bulletin.ninemsn.com.au/bulletin>.

Department of Rural Sociology (n.d.). *Building our Future: A guide to community visioning*, http://www.drs.wisc.edu/visinf.htm, accessed 18/04/02.

Devall, B., & Sessions, G. (1985). *Deep ecology: Living as if nature mattered*. Salt Lake City: Gibbs Smith.

Dobson, A. (1996). Environmental sustainabilities: An analysis and typology. *Environmental Politics*, 5(3), 401–428.

Dodson, K. J. (1996). Peak experiences and mountain biking: Incorporating the bike into the extended self. *Advances in Consumer Research*, 23, 317–322.

Donnelly, P., & Young, K. (1988). The construction and confirmation of identity in sport subcultures. *Sociology of Sport Journal*, 5, 223–240.

Dosher, B. K., & Kleiner, B. H. (1997). Practices of excellent companies in the entertainment industry. *Managing Services Quality*, 7(3), 127–131.

DOTARS (2002). *Stronger regions: A stronger Australia*. Canberra: Commonwealth Department of Transport and Regional Services.

Draper, M. (1998). Zen and the art of garden province maintenance: The soft intimacy of hard men in the wilderness of KwaZulu-Natal (1952–1997). *Journal of Southern African Studies*, Special Issue on Masculinities in Southern Africa, 24(4), 801–828.

Draper, M. (2003). Going native: Trout and settling identity in a rainbow nation. *Historia*, 48(1), 55–94.

Draper, M., & Maré, G. (2003). Going in: The garden of England's gaming zookeeper and Zululand. *Journal of Southern African Studies*, 29(2), 551–569.

Dredge, D. (2001). Local government tourism planning and policy-making in New South Wales: Institutional development and historical legacies. *Current Issues in Tourism*, 4(2), 355–380.

Dredge, D., & Jenkins, J. (2003). Destination place identity and regional tourism policy. *Tourism Geographies*, 5(4), 383–407.

Dror (1973). The planning process: A facet design. In: A. Faludi (Ed.), *A reader in planning theory* (pp. 323–343). Oxford: Pergamon Press.

Drucker, P. F. (1985). *Innovation and entrepreneurship*. Oxford: Butterworth-Heinemann.

Duffy, R. (2005). The politics of ecotourism. In: C. Ryan, S. Page, & M. Aicken (Eds), *Taking tourism to the limits: Issues, concept and managerial perspectives* (pp. 99–112). Amsterdam: Elsevier.

Dunford, R. W. (1992). *Organisational behaviour*. Sydney: Addison-Wesley.

Dunstan, K. (1991). *Flag; The first 30 years*. Box Hill: Jenkin Buxton Printers Pty Ltd.

Dwyer, L., Bushell, R., Sherringham, C., Kemp, S., & Knowd, I. (1995). *A tourism action plan for Greater Western Sydney*. Produced for the Greater Western Sydney Economic Development Board.

Dwyer, L., Edwards, D., & Valerio, P. (1997). *A tourism strategy for Campbelltown*. Produced for Campbelltown City Council.

Dwyer, L., & Kemp, S. (1999). Strategy formulation and environmental assessment: A study of Fiji's Hidden Paradise. *Proceedings of the Fifth Annual Asia Pacific Tourism Association Conference*. 23–25 August, Hong Kong Addison-Wesley, SAR, China.

Dwyer, L., Teal, G., & Kemp, S. (1999). Organisational culture and strategic management in a resort hotel. *Asia Pacific Journal of Tourism Management*, *3*(1), 27–36.

Dwyer, L., Teal, G., Kemp, S., & Wah, C. Y. (2000). Organisational culture and human resource management in an Indonesian resort hotel. *Tourism Culture and Communication*, *2*(1), 1–11.

Eadington, W. R., & Redman, M. (1991). Economics and tourism. *Annals of Tourism Research*, *18*(1), 41–56.

Eagles, P., & McCool, S. (Eds) (2002). *Tourism in national parks and protected areas*. Wallingford: CABI Publishing.

Echtner, C. M., & Ritchie, J. R. B. (1991). The meaning and measurement of destination image. *Journal of Travel Studies*, *2*(2), 2–12.

Eden, S. E. (1994). Using sustainable development: The business case. *Global Environmental Change*, *4*, 160–167.

Edensor, T. (1998). *Tourists at the Taj: Performance and meaning at a symbolic site*. London: Routledge.

Elsrud, T. (2001). Risk creation in travelling. *Annals of Tourism Research*, *28*(3), 597–617.

Escobar, A. (1995). *Encountering development: The making and unmaking of the Third World*. Princeton: Princeton University Press.

Ewert, A. W. (1985). Why people climb: The relationship of participant motives and experience level to mountaineering. *Journal of Leisure Research*, *17*(3), 241–250.

Ewert, A. W. (1989). *Outdoor adventure pursuits: Foundations, models and theories*. Columbus, Ohio: Publishing Horizons.

Ewert, A., & Hollenhurst, S. (1989). Testing the adventure model: Empirical support for a model of risk recreation participation. *Journal of Leisure Research*, *21*, 124–139.

Ewert, A., & Jamieson, L. (2003). Current status and future directions in the adventure tourism industry. In: J. Wilks, & S. J. Page (Eds), *Managing tourist health and safety in the new millennium* (pp. 67–83). Sydney: Pergamon.

Fabian, J. (2000). *Out of our minds. Reason and madness in the exploration of Central Africa*. London, Berkeley: University of California Press.

Fakeye, P. C., & Crompton, J. L. (1991). Image differences between prospective, first-time and repeat visitors to the lower Rio Grande Valley. *Journal of Travel Research*, *30*(2), 10–16.

Farrell, B. H. (1986). Cooperative tourism and the coastal zone. *Coastal Zone Management Journal*, *14*(1–2), 113–130.

Faulkner, B. (2003). Rejuvenating a maturing destination: The case of the Gold Coast. In: L. Fredline, L. Jago, & C. Cooper (Eds), *Progressing tourism research – Bill Faulkner* (pp. 34–86). Clevedon: Channel View Publications.

Faulkner, B., & Noakes, S. (2002). *Our Gold Coast: The preferred tourism future*. Gold Coast: CRC for Sustainable Tourism.

Feifer, M. (1985). *Going places*. London: Macmillan.

Feifer, M. (1986). *Tourism in history: From imperial Rome to the present*. New York: Stein and Day.

Feldman, D. C. (1984). The development and enforcement of group norms. *Academy of Management Review*, *9*, 47–53.

Fennell, D. (1999). *Ecotourism: An introduction*. London: Routledge.

Fennell, D. (2002). *Ecotourism programme planning*. Wallingford: CABI Publishing.

Fennell, D., & Dowling, R. (Eds) (2003). *Ecotourism policy and planning*. Wallingford: CABI Publishing.

Fennell, D. A. (1996). A tourist space-time budget in the Shetland Islands. *Annals of Tourism Research*, *23*(4), 811–829.

Fluker, M. R., & Turner, L. W. (2000). Needs, motivations, and expectations of commercial white-water rafting experience. *Journal of Travel Research*, *38*(4), 380–389.

Fodness, D. (1994). Measuring tourist motivation. *Annals of Tourism Research*, *21*(3), 555–581.

Foley, M., & Lennon, J. (1996a). JFK and dark tourism: A fascination with assassination. *International Journal of Heritage Studies*, *2*(4), 198–211.

Foley, M., & Lennon, J. (1996b). Editorial: Heart of darkness. *International Journal of Heritage Studies*, *2*(4), 195–197.

Foley, M., & Lennon, J. (1997). Dark tourism – an ethical dilemma. In: M. Foley, J. Lennon, & G. Maxwell (Eds), *Hospitality, tourism and leisure management: Issues in strategy and culture* (pp. 153–164). London: Cassell.

Forer, P. C. (1995). Geometric approaches to the nexus of time, space and microprocess: Implementing a practical model for mundane socio-spatial systems. In: M. Egenhofer, & R. Colledge (Eds), *Spatial and temporal reasoning in GIS*. New York: OUP.

Forestell, P. H., & Kaufman, G. D. (1990). The history of whalewatching in Hawaii and its role in enhancing visitor appreciation for endangered species. *Proceedings of the 1990 Congress on Coastal and Marine Tourism* (Vol. 1). National Coastal Resources Research Institute, Corvallis.

Foster, G. M. (1986). South seas cruise: A case study of a short-lived society. *Annals of Tourism Research*, *13*, 215–238.

Foucault, M. (1978). *The history of sexuality: An introduction*. London: Random House.

Fox, K. J. (1987). Real punks and pretenders: The social organization of a counterculture. *Journal of Contemporary Ethnography*, *16*(October), 344–370.

Frankline, A. (1999). *Animal and modern cultures: A sociology of human-animal relations in modernity*. London: Sage.

Freeman, R. E. (1984). *Strategic management: A stakeholder approach*. Boston: Pitman.

Fromm, E. (1941). *Escape from freedom*. New York: Avon Books.

Fukuyama, F. (1989). The end of history? *The National Interest*, *16*, 3–16.

Fukuyama, F. (1992). *The end of history and the last man*. New York: Avon.

Gartner, W. C. (1993). Image formation process. *Journal of Travel and Tourism Marketing*, *2*, 191–215.

Geertz, C. (1973). *The interpretation of cultures: Selected essays*. New York: Basic Books.

Getz, D., & Jamal, T. B. (1994). The environment-community symbiosis: A case for collaborative tourism planning. *Journal of Sustainable Tourism*, *2*(3), 152–173.

Gonzalez, A. M., & Bello, L. (2002). The construct "lifestyle" in market segmentation: The behaviour of tourist consumers. *European Journal of Marketing*, *36*(1–2), 51–85.

Goodchild, M., Klinkenberg, B., & Janelle, D. (1993). A factorial model of aggregate spatio-temporal behaviour: Application to the diurnal change. *Geographical Analysis*, *25*(4), 277–294.

Goossens, C. (2000). Tourism information and pleasure motivation. *Annals of Tourism Research*, *27*(2), 301–321.

Government of British Columbia and Kaska Dena Council (1997). *Letter of understanding*. Victoria, BC: Government of British Columbia.

Grant, D. (2001). Adventure tourism: A journey of the mind. In: L. Roberts, & D. Hall (Eds), *Rural tourism and recreation: Principles and practice* (pp. 166–170). New York: CABI Publishing.

Gray, B. (1989). *Collaborating: Finding common ground for multiparty problems.* San Francisco: Jossey-Bass Publishers.

Gray, B., & Wood, D. J. (1991). Collaborative alliances: Moving from practice to theory. *Journal of Applied Behavioural Science, 27*(1), 33–44.

Green, D. C., & Chalip, L. (1988). Sport tourism as the celebration of subculture. *Annals of Tourism Research, 25*(2), 275–291.

Griffiths, J. (1999). *Pip pip: A sideways look at time.* Flamingo: Harper-Collins.

Griffiths, J. (2003). Sex, drugs, rock 'n' roll: Play, nature, and the sacred. *Utne magazine* January/February 2003 Issue http://www.utne.com/pub/2003_115/.

Gunn, C. (1972). *Vacationscapes: Designing tourist regions.* Austin, TX: Bureau of Business Research, University of Texas at Austin.

Gunn, C. (1988). *Tourism planning* (2nd ed.). New York: Taylor & Francis.

Gunn, C. (1994). *Tourism planning: Basics, concepts, cases.* Philadelphia: Taylor & Francis.

Hadley, D., Grenfell, R., & Arrowsmith, C. (2003, September 23–25). Deploying location-based services for nature-based tourism. *Conference proceedings for the Spatial Sciences Coalition Conference.* Canberra.

Hall, C. M. (1992). Adventure, sport and health tourism. In: B. Weiler, & C. M. Hall (Eds), *Special interest tourism* (pp. 141–158). London: Belhaven.

Hall, C. M. (1994). *Tourism and politics: Policy, power and place.* Chichester and New York: Wiley.

Hall, C. M. (1998). The politics of decision making and top-down planning: Darling Harbour, Sydney. In: D. Tyler, M. Robertson, & Y. Guerrier (Eds), *Tourism management in cities: Policy, process and practice* (pp. 9–24). Chichester: Wiley.

Hall, C. M. (2000). *Tourism planning: Policies, processes and relationships.* Harlow: Pearson Education.

Hall, M. (1995). The legend of lost city or, the man with golden balls. *Journal of Southern African Studies, 21*(2), 179–199.

Hammitt, W. E. (1980). Outdoor recreation: Is it a multi-phase experience? *Journal of Leisure Research, 12*(2), 107–115.

Hammitt, W. E. (1984). Cognitive processes involved in environmental interpretation. *Journal of Environmental Education, 15*(4), 11–15.

Harbutt, J. (1995). The mountain has spoken. *New Zealand Geographic, 28*(October–December), 48–66.

Harris, R., & Leiper, N. (1995). *Sustainable tourism: An Australian perspective.* Chatswood, NSW: Butterworth-Heinemann.

Harrison, D. (Ed.) (1992). *Tourism and the less developed countries.* London: Belhaven Press.

Harrison-Hill, T. (2005). Getting into the spirit: Using internet information search to heighten emotions in anticipation of the sport tourism experience. In: S. Ryan, S. J. Page, & M. Aicken (Eds), *Taking tourism to the limits.* Oxford: Pergamon.

Hassanien, A., & Baum, T. (2002). Hotel repositioning through property renovation. *Tourism and Hospitality Research, 4*(2), 144–157.

Hassanien, A., & Losekoot, E. (2002). The application of facilities management expertise to the hotel renovation process. *Facilities, 20*(7–8), 230–238.

Haviland, W. (1999). *Cultural anthropology.* Orlando, Florida: Harcourt Brace.

Hawkins, D. T. (1996). Hunting, grazing, browsing: A model for online information retrieval. *Online* (January–February), 71–73.

Haywood, K. M. (1988). Responsible and responsive tourism planning in the community. *Tourism Management, 9*(2), 105–118.

Henderson, J. (2000). War as a tourist attraction: The case of Vietnam. *International Journal of Tourism Research, 2*(4), 269–280.

Henry, W., & Western, D. (n.d.). Carrying capacity, ecological impacts and visitor attitudes: Applying research to park planning and management. In: *The challenge of wilderness, an introduction to wilderness philosophy, concepts and practice*. The Wilderness Action Group, The Centre for Environment and Development (University of Natal) and The Wild Foundation.

Heywood, I., Cornelius, S., & Carver, S. (1998). *An introduction to geographical information systems*. Harlow, UK: Pearson Education.

Hibbert, C. (1987). *The grand tour*. London: Methuen London.

Hickson, D. J. et al. (1971). A strategic contingencies approach of intra-organisational power. *Administrative Science Quarterly, 16*(2), 216–229.

Hill, L., & Marshall, G. (1989). *Stalking trout: A serious fisherman's guide*. Auckland: Media House.

Hirschman, E. C., & Holbrook, M. B. (1982). Hedonic consumption: Emerging concepts, methods and propositions. *Journal of Marketing, 46*, 92–102.

Hitchcock, M., & Teague, K. (Eds) (2000). *Souvenirs: The material culture of tourism*. Aldershot: Ashgate.

Hoffman, D. L., & Novak, T. P. (1996). Marketing in hypermedia computer-mediated environments: Conceptual foundations. *Journal of Marketing, 60*, 50–68.

Holbrook, M. B., & Hirschman, E. C. (1982). The experiential aspects of consumption: Consumer fantasies, feelings and fun. *Journal of Consumer Research, 9*, 132–140.

Holt, D. (1995). How consumers consume: A typology of consumption practices. *Journal of Consumer Research, 22*(June), 1–16.

Holstein, J. A., & Gubrium, J. F. (1997). Active interviewing. In: D. Silverman (Ed.), *Qualitative research: Theory, method and practice* (pp. 113–129). London: Sage.

Holyfield, L. (1999). Manufacturing adventure — The buying and selling of emotions. *Journal of Contemporary Ethnography, 28*(1), 3–32.

Hoogvelt, A. (2001). *Globalization and the post-colonial world: The new political economy of development* (2nd ed.). Baltimore: John Hopkins University Press.

Housing and Development Board (2003). Welcome to HDB InfoWeb. Accessed on 9 September 2003.

Huang, Y. H., & Stewart, W. P. (1996). Rural tourism development: Shifting basis of community solidarity. *Journal of Travel Research, 34*(Spring), 26–31.

Hudson, S. (1999). Consumer behaviour related to tourism. In: A. Pizam, & Mansfeld (Eds), *Consumer behaviour in travel and tourism*. New York: Haworth Hospitality Press.

Hughes, H. L., & Benn, D. (1997). Entertainment in tourism: A study of visitors to Blackpool. *Managing Leisure, 2*, 110–126.

Hulme, D., & Murphree, M. (Eds) (2001). *African wildlife and livelihoods*. London: Heinemann.

Hungerford, H. R., & Volk, T. L. (1990). Changing learner behaviour through environmental education. *Journal of Environmental Education, 21*(3), 8–21.

Huntington, S. P. (1971). *Political order in changing societies*. New Haven: Yale University Press.

Hussey, D. (1999). *Strategy and planning: A manager's guide*. Chichester: Wiley.

Inskeep, E. (1991). *Tourism planning: An integrated and sustainable development approach*. New York: Van Nostrand Reinhold.

Inskeep, E. (1994). *National and regional tourism planning*. London: Routledge.

International Fund for Animal Welfare (1997). *Report of the international workshop on the educational values of whale watching*. East Sussex, UK: IFAW.

Iozzi, L. A. (1989). What research says to the educator – Part one: Environmental education and the affective domain. *Journal of Environmental Education, 20*(3), 3–9.

Itami, R. M., & Gimblett, H. R. (2001). Intelligent recreation agents in a virtual GIS world. *Complexity International* (Vol. 8).

Itami, R., MacLaren, G., Hirst, K., Raulings, R., & Gimblett, R. (2002). RBSim 2: Simulating human behavior in National Parks in Australia. *4th International Conference on Integrating GIS and Environmental Modeling (GIS/EM4)*, Banff, Alberta, Canada.

Jaakson, R. (1987). Exploring the epistemology of ecotourism. *Journal of Applied Recreation Research, 22*(1), 33–47.

Jackson, D. (1997). *Dynamic organisations: The challenge of change*. London: Macmillan Business Press.

Jackson, L. E. (1986). Outdoor recreation participation and attitudes to the environment. *Leisure Sciences, 5*(1), 1–7.

Jackson, L. E. (1987). Outdoor recreation participation and views on resource development and preservation. *Leisure Sciences, 9*, 235–250.

Jamal, T. B., & Getz, D. (1995). Collaboration theory and community tourism planning. *Annals of Tourism Research, 22*(1), 186–204.

Janelle, D. (1997). Communication/Information technologies and diurnal change in the social geographies of cities: The case for periodic space-time activity surveys on uses of telecommunications. Paper presented to the *E*Space 3: Digital Cities/Analog Worlds Workshop*, Singapore/Kuala Lumpur.

Janik, V. M., & Thompson, P. M. (1996). Changes in surfacing patterns of bottlenose dolphins in response to boat traffic. *Marine Mammal Science, 12*, 597–602.

Janowsky, D., & Becker, G. (2002). Recreation in urban forests: Monitoring specific user groups and identifying their needs with video and GIS-support. In: A. Arnberger, C. Brandenburg, & A. Muhar (Eds), *Conference proceedings of the monitoring and management of visitor flows in recreational and protected areas* (pp. 296–301). Vienna, Austria: Bodenkultur University.

Jenkins, O. (1999). Understanding and measuring tourist destination images. *International Journal of Tourism Research, 1*(1), 1–15.

Johannessen, J., Olsen, B., & Lumpkin, G. T. (2001). Innovation as newness: What is new, how new and new to whom? *European Journal of Innovation Management, 4*(1), 20–31.

Johnson, G., & Scholes, K. (1997). *Exploring corporate strategy*. London: Prentice-Hall.

Johnson, J. D., & Snepenger, D. J. (1993). Application of the tourism life cycle concept in the Greater Yellowstone region. *Society and Natural Resources, 6*, 127–148.

Jones, J. D. F. (2001). *Storyteller: The many lives of Laurens van der Post*. London: John Murray.

Jones, P. (1996). Managing hospitality innovation. *Cornell Hotel and Restaurant Administration Quarterly, 37*(5), 86–95.

Jones, P., & Wan, L. (1993). Innovation in the UK food service industry. *International Journal of Contemporary Hospitality Management, 5*(2), 32–38.

Kagan, J., & Haverman, E. (1976). *Psychology: An introduction* (3rd ed.). New York: Harcourt Brace Jovanovich.

Kane, M. J. (2002). Niche image: The touchstone to destination image. In: W. G. Croy (Ed.), *International tourism student conference: New Zealand tourism hospitality research*. Rotorua: School of Tourism and Hospitality, Waiariki Institute of Technology.

Kay, J., & Laberge, S. (2002a). The 'new' corporate habitus in adventure racing. *International review for the sociology of sport, 37*(1), 17–36.

Kay, J., & Laberge, S. (2002b). Mapping the field of "AR": Adventure racing and Bourdieu's concept of field. *Sociology of Sport Journal, 19*(1), 25–46.

Keen, T. (2002). Tomorrow its heli-shark ski-racing. *For Him Magazine*, May, 174–176.

Kelly, J. R., & Freysinger, V. J. (2000). *21st century leisure: Current issues*. Boston: Allyn & Bacon.

Kemp, S., & Dwyer, L. (2000). An examination of organisational culture. *International Journal of Hospitality Management, 20*(1), 77–93.

Keough, B. (1990). Public participation in community tourism planning. *Annals of Tourism Research, 17*, 449–465.

Kerr, W. (2003). *Tourism in Scotland*. Oxford: Pergamon.

Keßel, A., Klüpfel, H., Meyer-König, T., & Schreckenberg, M. (2002). A concept for coupling empirical data and microscopic simulation of pedestrian flows. In: A. Arnberger, C. Brandenburg, & A. Muhar (Eds), *Conference proceedings of the monitoring and management of visitor flows in recreational and protected areas* (pp. 199–204). Vienna, Austria: Bodenkultur University.

Kiiskilä, K. (2001, August 23–24). Attitude as interpreters of travel behaviour – A cluster analysis approach. *4th KFB Research Conference: Cities of Tomorrow*.

Kirkbride, P. S. (1983). *Power in the workplace*. Unpublished Ph.D. Thesis, University of Bath, UK.

Knutson, B. J. (1988). Frequent travellers: Making them happy and bringing them back. *Cornell Hotel and Restaurant Administration Quarterly, 29*(2), 83–87.

Koolhaas, R. (1995). Singapore songlines: Or thirty years of tabula rasa. In: J. Siglar (Ed.), *Small, medium, large, extra large: Office for metropolitan architecture*. Rotterdam: 010 Publishers.

Korac-Kakabadse, N., & Kakabadse, A. P. (1998). Vision, visionary leadership and the visioning process: An overview. In: A. Kakabadse, F. Nortier, & N. B. Abramovici (Eds), *Success in sight: Visioning* (pp. 1–34). London: International Thomson Business Press.

Kotabe, M., & Swan, K. S. (1995). The role of strategic alliances in high technology in new product development. *Strategic Management Journal, 16*(8), 621–636.

Kreck, L. A. (1981). When Mt. St. Helens blew its top. *Journal of Travel Research, 19*(4), 16–22.

Krippendorf, J. (1984). *The holiday makers*. Oxford: Heinemann Professional.

Krippendorf, J. (1987). *The holiday makers* (2nd ed.). Oxford: Heinemann.

Kroh, D. P., & Gimblett, R. H. (1992). Comparing live experience with pictures in articulating landscape preference. *Landscape Research, 17*, 58–69.

Kruse, S. (2000). The interaction between killer whales and boats in Johnstone Strait, B. C. In: J. Mann, R. C. Connor, P. L. Tyack, & H. Whitehead (Eds), *Cetacean societies — field studies of dolphins and whales* (pp. 335–346). Chicago: University of Chicago Press.

Kull, C. A. (1996). The evolution of conservation efforts in Madagascar. *International Environmental Affairs, 8*(1), 50–86.

Kull, C. A. (2005). *The isle of fire: The political geography of grassland and woodland burning in the highlands of Madagascar*. Berkeley: University of California.

Land Use Coordination Office, Province of British Columbia (1997a). *Fort St. John land and resource management plan*. Victoria, BC: Government of British Columbia.

Land Use Coordination Office, Province of British Columbia (1997b). *Fort Nelson land and resource management plan*. Victoria, BC: Government of British Columbia.

Land Use Coordination Office, Province of British Columbia (1997c). *Oil and gas exploration and development in the Muskwa-Kechika*. Victoria, BC: Government of British Columbia.

Land Use Coordination Office, Province of British Columbia (1997d). *Mineral exploration and mine development in the Muskwa-Kechika*. Victoria, BC: Government of British Columbia.

Land Use Coordination Office, Province of British Columbia (2000). *Mackenzie land and resource management plan*. Victoria, BC: Government of British Columbia.

Landro, L. (2002). The pearl of Naples. *Wall Street Journal* (Eastern ed.). New York, NY: Dec 20, 2002. p. W.1.

Lash, S. (1990). *Sociology of postmodernism*. London: Routledge.

Latham, A. (1991). *The frozen leopard: Hunting my dark heart in Africa*. London: HarperCollins.

Lawson, S., Manning, R., Valliere, W., Wang, B., & Budtruk, M. (2002). Using simulating modelling to facilitate proactive monitoring and adaptive management of social carrying capacity in Arches National Park, Utah, USA. In: A. Arnberger, C. Brandenburg, & A. Muhar (Eds), *Conference proceedings of the monitoring and management of visitor flows in recreational and protected areas* (pp. 205–210). Vienna, Austria: Bodenkultur University.

Leach, M., & Mearns, R. (Eds) (1996). *The lie of the land: Challenging received wisdom on the African environment*. Oxford: James Currey.

Leiper, N. (1990). *Tourism systems*. Department of Management Systems, Occasional Paper 2, Auckland: Massey University.

Lemke, T. (2001). The birth of bio-politics: Michel Foucault's lecture at the College de France on neo-liberal governmentality. *Economy and Society, 30*(2), 190–207.

Lennon, J., Foley, M., & Washington, D. C. (1999). Interpretation of the unimaginable: The U.S. Holocaust Memorial Museum, and "Dark Tourism". *Journal of Travel Research, 13*(August), 46–50.

Lennon, J., & Foley, M. (2000). *Dark tourism: The attraction of death and disaster*. London: Continuum.

Lewis, R. (1984). The basis of hotel selection. *Cornell Hotel and Restaurant Administration Quarterly, 25*(2), 54–69.

Lindberg, K., Enriquez, K. J., & Sproule, K. (1996). Ecotourism questioned: Case studies from Belize. *Annals of Tourism Research, 23*, 543–562.

Linstead, S. A., & Grafton Small, R. (1992). On reading organizational culture. *Organization Studies, 13*(3), 331–355.

Lockyer, T. (2002). Business guests' accommodation selection: The view from both sides. *International Journal of Contemporary Hospitality Management, 14*(6), 294–300.

Lockyer, T. (2005). The perceived importance of price as one hotel selection dimension. *Tourism Management, 26*(5), TBA.

Loker-Murphy, L. (1996). Backpackers in Australia: A motivation-based segmentation study. *Journal of Travel and Tourism Marketing, 5*(4), 23–45.

Lorsch, J. W. (1986). Managing culture: The invisible barrier to strategic change. *California Management Review, 28*(2), 95–109.

Louis, M. R. (1985). An investigator's guide to workplace culture. In: P. J. Frost, L. F. Moore, M. R. Louis, C. C. Lundberg, & J. Martin (Eds), *Organisational culture* (pp. 73–93). Beverly Hills, CA: Sage.

Lury, C. (1996). *Consumer culture*. Cambridge: Polity Press.

Lusseau, D., & Higham, J. E. S. (2004). Managing the image of dolphin-based tourism through the definition of critical habit: The case of the bottle nose dolphins (Tursiops spp.) in doubtful sound. *Tourism Management, 25*(6), 657–667.

Lynn, W. (1992). Tourism in the people's interest. *Community Development Journal, 27*, 371–377.

MacCannell, D. (1989). *The tourist: A new theory of the leisure class* (2nd ed.). New York: Schocken Books.

MacCannell, D. (1999). *The tourist*. New York: Schoken.

MacInnis, D. J., & Price, L. L. (1987). The role of imagery in information processing review and extension. *Journal of Consumer Research, 13*, 473–491.

MacKay, K. J., & Fesenmaier, D. R. (1997). Pictorial element of destination image formation. *Annals of Tourism Research, 24*(3), 537–565.

Maitland, R. (2002). Partnership and collaboration in destination management: The case of Cambridge, UK. In: K. W. Wober (Ed.), *City tourism 2002, Proceedings of the European Cities Tourism International Conference*. Vienna, Austria. New York: Springer Wien.

Malloy, D., & Fennell, D. (1998). Ecotourism and ethics: Moral development and organisational cultures. *Journal of Travel Research, 36*(4), 47–56.

Mamdami, M. (1998). *When does a settler become a native? Reflections on the colonial roots of citizenship in equatorial and South Africa.* Inaugural lecture, University of Cape Town: University of Cape Town Press.

Manfredo, M. (Ed.) (2002). *Wildlife viewing: A management handbook.* Corvallis: Oregon State University Press.

Manning, R. E. (1999). *Studies in outdoor recreation, search and research for satisfaction.* Oregon State University Press.

Marsky, J. (2001). Hotels with higher emotion scores can obtain higher rates. *Hotel and Motel Management, 216*(20), 23.

Martin, J. (1992). *Cultures in organisations.* New York: Oxford University Press.

Martin, J., Feldman, M. S., Hatch, M. J., & Sitkin, S. B. (1983). The uniqueness paradox in organisational stories. *Administrative Science Quarterly, 28*(3), 438–453.

Martin, P., & Priest, S. (1986). Understanding adventure experience. *Adventure Education, 3*(1), 18–21.

Masoud, O. (2000, March). *Tracking and analysis of articulated motion with an application to human motion.* Doctoral Thesis, University of Minnesota.

Matless, D. (1998). *Landscape and englishness.* London: Reaktion Books.

Matthews, H. G., & Richter, L. K. (1991). Political science and tourism. *Annals of Tourism Research, 18*, 120–135.

Maykut, P., & Morehouse, R. (1994). *Beginning qualitative research: A philosophic and practical guide.* London: Falmer Press.

Mayo, E. J., & Jarvis, L. P. (1981). *The psychology of leisure travel.* Boston, MA: CBI.

McCleary, K. W., Weaver, P. A., & Hutchinson, J. C. (1993). Hotel selection factors as they relate to business travel situations. *Journal of Travel Research, 32*(2), 42–48.

McCleary, K. W., Weaver, P. A., & Lan, L. (1994). Gender-based differences in business travelers' lodging preferences. *Cornell Hotel and Restaurant Administration Quarterly, 35*(2), 51–58.

McGrew, A. G. (1992). Conceptualising global politics. In: A. G. McGrew, & P. G. Lewis (Eds), *Global politics* (pp. 1–28). Cambridge: Polity Press.

McGrew, A. G. (2002). Liberal internationalism: Between realism and cosmopolitanism. In: D. Held, & A. G. McGrew (Eds), *Governing globalization: Power, authority and global governance* (pp. 267–289). Cambridge: Polity Press.

McIntosh, R. W., & Goeldner, C. R. (1986). *Tourism: Principles, practices, philosophies* (5th ed.). New York: Wiley.

McKenzie, J., & Katic, E. (2002). Recreational use and wildlife movement near mountain park communities: Integrating social and ecological management objectives in Banff National Park. In: A. Arnberger, C. Brandenburg, & A. Muhar (Eds), *Conference proceedings of the monitoring and management of visitor flows in recreational and protected areas* (pp. 429–435). Vienna, Austria: Bodenkultur University.

Meier, J. F., Morash, T. W., & Welton, G. E. (1980). *High-adventure outdoor pursuits: Organisation and leadership.* Ohio, USA: Publishing Horizons.

Meyersohn, R. (1981). *Tourism as a socio-cultural phenomenon: Research perspectives.* Waterloo: Otium.

Miles, M. B., & Huberman, A. M. (1994). *Qualitative data analysis: An expanded sourcebook* (2nd ed.). Beverly Hills, CA: Sage.

Mill, J. S. (1863). *Utilitarianism* (Reprint 1987). London: Everyman.

Miller, C. A. (2000). The dynamics of framing environmental values and policy: Four models of societal processes. *Environmental Values, 9*, 211–234.

Miller, J. (1993). *The passion of Michel Foucault.* New York: Anchor Books.

Millington, K., Locke, T., & Locke, A. (2001). Adventure travel. *Travel and Tourism Analyst, 4*, 65–97.

Milman, A. (1993). Maximizing the value of focus group research: Qualitative analysis of consumers' destination choice. *Journal of Travel Research, 32*(Fall), 61–63.

Minca, C., & Getz, D. (1995). Planning, environment and policy making, public and private-sector cooperation in destination planning: A comparison of Banff and Niagara Falls. *The Tourist Review, 4,* 49–59.

Minichiello, V., Aroni, R., Timewell, E., & Alexander, L. (1995). *In-depth interviewing: Principles, techniques, analysis.* Sydney, Australia: Longman.

Minister of Environment, Lands and Parks (1998). *Bill 37-1998.* Muskwa-Kechika Management Area Act. Victoria, BC: Government of British Columbia.

Mintzberg, H. (1990). The design school: Reconsidering the basic premises of strategic management. *Strategic Management Journal, 11,* 171–195.

Miossec, J. M. (1976). Un modele de l'espace touristique. Quoted in: *Tourist Development* (D. Pearce, 1981). Harlow: Longman.

Mitchell, D. (2000). *Cultural geography: A critical introduction.* Oxford: Blackwell.

Mitchell-Banks, P. J. (1999). *Tenure reform for facilitating community forestry in British Columbia.* Unpublished Ph.D. thesis at the University of British Columbia.

Morgan, D. (1998). *The adventure tourism experience on water: Perceptions of risk and competence and the role of the operator.* Unpublished masters thesis, Lincoln University, Canterbury, New Zealand.

Morgan, D. (2000). Adventure tourism activities in New Zealand: Perceptions and management of client risk. *Tourism Recreation Research, 25*(3), 79–89.

Morgan, D. L. (1988). *Focus groups as qualitative research.* Newbury Park, California: Sage.

Morgan, G. (1997). *Images of organization.* Beverly Hills, CA: Sage.

Moscardo, G. (1996). Mindful visitors: Heritage and tourism. *Annals of Tourism Research, 25*(2), 376–397.

Mowen, A. J. (2002). Estimating visitor occasions and recreational visits at an urban park district. In: A. Arnberger, C. Brandenburg, & A. Muhar (Eds), *Conference proceedings of the monitoring and management of visitor flows in recreational and protected areas* (pp. 436–438). Vienna, Austria: Bodenkultur University.

Murphy, P. E. (1983). Perceptions and attitudes of decision making groups in tourism centres. *Journal of Travel Research, 21*(3), 8–12.

Murphy, P. E. (1985). *Tourism: A community approach.* London: Routledge.

Murphy, P. E., & Cooper, C. (2002). *Communities as regional destinations: A development potential index.* Gold Coast: Cooperative Research Centre for Sustainable Tourism.

National University of Singapore Press Releases (2002, 26 November). *Launch of make it real 2003 student mountaineering programme.*

Neil, D. T., Orams, M. B., & Baglioni, A. (1996). Effects of previous whalewatching experience on participants knowledge of, and response to, whales and whale watching. *Encounters with Whales 1995 Proceedings.* Australian Nature Conservation Agency, Canberra.

Neumann, D. R. (2001). *The behaviour and ecology of common dolphins in New Zealand.* Massey University: Ph.D. Thesis.

Newsome, D., Moore, S., & Dowling, R. (2000). *Natural area tourism.* Clevedon: Channel View Publications.

New Zealand Tourism Board (2001). *A framework of needs and motivations for understanding the long haul travel market.* Auckland: New Zealand Tourist Board.

New Zealand Tourism Online (2002). *NZ guidebooks.* New Zealand Tourism Online. http://www.tourism.net.nz/new-zealand-guidebooks.html#guide.September.

Nord, W. R. (1985). Can organisational culture be managed? In: P. J. Frost, L. F. Moore, M. R. Louis, C. C. Lundberg, & J. Martin (Eds), *Organisational culture* (pp. 187–196). Beverly Hills, CA: Sage.

Nowacek, S. M. (1999). *The effects of boat traffic on bottlenose dolphins, Tursiops truncatus, in Sarasota Bay, Florida*. Master of Science thesis, University of California, Santa Cruz.

O'Brien, R., Goetz, A., Scholte, J., & Williams, M. (2000). *Contesting global governance: Multilateral economic institutions and global social movements*. Cambridge: Cambridge University Press.

O'Neill, S. (2002). Flood of tourists worsens pain. *Daily Telegraph*, 27th August.

O'Rourke, P. (1988). *Holidays in hell*. London: Picador.

Oil and Gas Commission (1999). *First annual report*. October 23, 1998–March 31, 1999. Fort St. John, BC: Oil and Gas Commission.

Oil and Gas Commission (2001). *Activity levels and processing timelines* on website. Fort St. John, BC: Oil and Gas Commission.

Olds, K., & Thrift, N. (2004). Cultures on the brink: Re-engineering the soul of capitalism – On a global scale. In: A. Ong, & S. Collier (Eds), *Global assemblages: Technology, politics, and ethics as anthropological problems*. Malden, MA: Blackwell.

Olson, E. C., Bowman, M. L., & Roth, R. E. (1984). Interpretation and non-formal environmental education in natural resource management. *Journal of Environmental Education, 15*(4), 6–10.

Opperman, M. (1999). Sex tourism. *Annals of Tourism Research, 26*(2), 251–266.

Opperman, S. (2003). African grey. *Student Life*, December 2002/January 2003.

Orams, M. B. (1993). The role of education in managing marine wildlife-tourist interaction. *Proceedings of the 7th Annual Marine Education Society of Australasia Conference*, 6–11. Marine Education Society of Australasia, Brisbane, Queensland.

Orams, M. B. (1995). Towards a more desirable form of ecotourism. *Tourism Management, 16*(1), 3–8.

Orams, M. B. (1996a). A conceptual model of tourist-wildlife interaction: The case for education as a management strategy. *Australian Geographer, 27*(1), 39–51.

Orams, M. B. (1996b). Using interpretation to manage nature-based tourism. *The Journal of Sustainable Tourism, 4*(2), 81–94.

Orams, M. B. (1997). The effectiveness of environmental education: Can we turn tourists into "greenies"? *Progress in Tourism and Hospitality Management, 3*(4), 295–306.

Orams, M. B., & Hill, G. J. E. (1998). Controlling the ecotourist: Is education the answer? *Journal of Environmental Education, 29*(3), 33–38.

Orams, M. B. (1999). *Marine tourism: Development, impacts and management*. New York: Routledge.

Orams, M. B., & Page, S. J. (2000). Designing self-reply questionnaires to survey tourists: Issues and guidelines for researchers. *Anatolia: An International Journal of Tourism and Hospitality Research, 11*(2), 125–139.

Oswick, C., & Grant, D. (Eds) (1996). *Organisational development: Metaphorical explanations*. London: Pitman.

Oswick, C., Lowe, S., & Jones, P. (1996). Organisational culture as personality: Lessons from psychology? In: C. Oswick, & D. Grant (Eds), *Organisational development: Metaphorical explanations* (pp. 106–120). London: Pitman.

Ott, J. S. (1989). *The organisational culture perspective*. Brooks Cole, CA: Pacific Grove.

Page, S. J. (2000). Tourism and natural areas. In: C. Ryan, & S. J. Page (Eds), *Tourism management in the new millennium* (pp. 273–278). Oxford: Pergamon.

Page, S. J. (2003). *Tourism management: Managing for change*. Oxford: Butterworth Heinemann.

Page, S. J., & Dowling, R. (2002). *Ecotourism*. Harlow: Prentice-Hall.

Page, S. J., & Hall, C. M. (2002). *Managing urban tourism*. Harlow: Prentice Hall.

Page, S. J., & Thorn, K. (1997). Towards sustainable tourism planning in New Zealand: Public sector responses. *Journal of Sustainable Tourism*, 5(1), 59–77.

Page, S. J., & Thorn, K. (2002). Towards sustainable tourism planning in New Zealand: Public sector response revisited. *Journal of Sustainable Tourism*, 10(3), 222–238.

Palmer, A., & Bejou, D. (1995). Tourism destination marketing alliances. *Annals of Tourism Research*, 22(3), 616–629.

Parinello, G. L. (1993). Motivation and anticipation post-industrial tourism. *Annals of Tourism Research*, 20(2), 233–249.

Parks Victoria (2002). *2001–2002 parks Victoria annual report* [Online] http://www.parkweb.vic.gov.au/resources/03_0806.pdf accessed June 2003.

Parks Victoria (1998). *Port Campbell National Park and Bay of Islands Coastal Park management plan.*

Paterson, M. (2002). Hundreds pay to see human body being cut open. *Daily Telegraph*, 21st November.

Pattullo, P. (1996). *Last resorts: The cost of tourism in the Caribbean*. London: Cassell.

Pearce, D., Barbier, E., & Markandya, A. (1990). *Sustainable development*. Aldershot: Edward Elgar.

Pearce, P. L. (1982). *The social psychology of tourist behaviour*. Oxford: Pergamom Press.

Pelton, R. (2003). *The World's most dangerous places* (5th ed.). London: Harper Resource.

Peters, T., & Waterman, R. (1982). *In search of excellence*. New York: Harper & Row.

Peterson, R. A., & Merino, M. C. (2003). Consumer information search behavior and the internet. *Psychology & Marketing*, 20(2), 99–121.

Phillips, J. (1987). *A man's country? The image of the Pakeha male: A history*. Auckland: Penguin Books.

Player, I. (1997). *Zululand wilderness: Shadow and soul*. Cape Town: David Philip.

Porter, M. (1990). *The competitive advantage of nations*. London: Macmillan.

Potts, T. D., & Harrill, R. (1998). Enhancing communities for sustainability: A travel ecology approach. *Tourism Analysis*, 3, 133–142.

Pratt, M. L. (1992). *Imperial eyes: Travel writing and transculturation*. London: Routledge.

Province of British Columbia (1997). *Muskwa-Kechika management plan*. Victoria, BC: Government of British Columbia.

Przeclawski, K. (1985). The role of tourism in contemporary culture. *The Tourist Review*, 40, 2–6.

Reader, I. (2003). Review of 'dark tourism; the attraction of death and disaster'. http://cult-media.com/issue2/Rreade.htm.

Reutens, L. (2001). *Southbound: The Singapore Antarctica expedition*. Singapore: Epigram.

Richins, H. (1995). Decision making and community commitment in a coastal tourism region. In: *Proceedings of the national tourism and hospitality conference* (pp. 177–187). St. Kilda, Melbourne.

Ricoeur, P. (1971). The model of the text: Meaningful action considered as a text. *Social Research*, 38, 529–562.

Ring, H. (Ed.) (2002). *Let's go: New Zealand*. Cambridge, MA: Let's Go Publications.

Ritchie, J. R. B. (1988). Alternative approaches to teaching tourism. In: *Presented to the international conference, teaching tourism into the 1990s*. University of Surrey, UK.

Ritchie, J. R. B. (1993). Crafting a destination vision: Putting the concept of resident-responsive tourism into practice. *Tourism Management*, 14(5), 379–389.

Ritchie, J. R. B. (1999). Crafting a value-driven vision for a national tourism treasure. *Tourism Management*, 20, 273–282.

Ritchie, J. R. B., & Crouch, G. I. (2000). The competitive destination: A sustainability perspective. *Tourism Management*, 21(1), 1–7.

Robbins, S. P., Waters-Marsh, T., Cacioppe, R., & Millett, B. (1994). *Organisational behaviour*. Sydney: Prentice-Hall.

Roberts, L., & Simpson, F. (2000). Developing partnership approaches to tourism in central and eastern Europe. In: B. Bramwell, & B. Lane (Eds), *Tourism collaboration and partnerships: Politics, practice and sustainability* (pp. 230–246). Clevedon: Channel View.

Rogers, E. M. (2003). *Diffusion of innovation* (5th ed.). New York: Free Press.

Rojek, C. (1993). *Ways of escape*. Basingstoke: Macmillan.

Rojek, C. (1995). *Decentering leisure*. London: Sage.

Rojek, C. (1997). Indexing, dragging and the social construction of tourist sights. In: C. Rojek, & J. Urry (Eds), *Touring cultures: Transformations of travel and theory* (pp. 52–74). London: Routledge.

Rokeach, M. (1973). *The nature of human values*. New York: Free Press.

Rose, K., & Webb, C. (1998). Analysing data: Maintaining rigour in a qualitative study. *Qualitative Health Research, 8*(4), 556–562.

Rose, N. (1992). Governing the enterprising self. In: P. Heelas, & P. Morris (Eds), *The values of the enterprise culture: The moral debate*. London: Routledge.

Rose, N. (1999). *Powers of freedom: Reframing political thought*. New York: Cambridge University Press.

Rosenau, J. (1990). *Turbulence in World politics: A theory of change and continuity*. New York: Harvester Wheatsheaf.

Rosenau, J. (1992). Governance, order, and change in world politics. In: J. Rosenau, & E. Czempiel (Eds), *Governance without government: Order and change in World politics* (pp. 1–29). Cambridge: Cambridge University Press.

Ross, G. (1993). Ideal and actual images of backpacker visitors to northern Australia. *Journal of Travel and Research, 32*(2), 54–57.

Russell, C. A., & Puto, C. P. (2000). Exploring the relationship between popular culture and consumer behavior: Insights from multiple perspectives. *Advances in Consumer Research, 27*, 254–254.

Russell, C. L. (1994). Ecotourism as experiential environmental education? *The Journal of Experiential Education, 17*(1), 16–22.

Russell, C. L. (2002). Whalewatching as critical science education? *Canadian Journal of Science, Mathematics and Technology Education, 2*(4), 485–504.

Ryan, C. (1980). *Weekend breaks*. Unpublished M.Phil Thesis. Nottingham: Nottingham Trent University.

Ryan, C. (1995). *Researching tourist satisfaction: Issues, concepts, problems*. London: Routledge.

Ryan, C. (1998). The travel career ladder – An appraisal. *Annals of Tourism Research, 25*(4), 936–957.

Ryan, C. (2002). Tourism is the edge: An essay in margins and liminalities, '12th International Research Conference of CAUTHE' "Tourism and Hospitality on the Edge". Fremantle, WA 6th to 9th February 2002.

Ryan, C. (2002). Equity, management, power sharing and sustainability — issues of the 'new tourism'. *Tourism Management, 23*(1), 17–26.

Ryan, C., Hughes, K., & Chirgwin, S. (2000). The gaze, spectacle and ecotourism. *Annals of Tourism Research, 27*(1), 148–163.

Ryan, C., & Trauer, B. (2004). Involvement in adventure tourism: Toward implementing a fuzzy set. *Tourism Review International, 7*(3–4), 143–152.

Ryan, C., Trauer, B., Cave, J., Sharma, A., & Sharma, S. (2003). Backpackers — what is the peak experience? *Tourism Recreation Research, 28*(3), 93–96.

Ryan, G. W., & Bernard, H. R. (2000). Data management and analysis methods. In: N. K. Denzin, & Y. S. Lincoln (Ed.), *Handbook of qualitative research* (2nd ed., pp. 769–802). Thousand Oaks, CA: Sage.

Saayman, G. (Ed.) (1990[1986]). *Modern South Africa in search of a soul: Jungian perspectives on the wilderness within.* Boston, MA: Sigo.

Sagoff, M. (1994). Four dogmas of environmental economics. *Environmental Values, 3,* 285–310.

Sathe, V. (1983). Implications of corporate culture: A manager's guide to action. *Organisational Dynamics, 12,* 5–23.

Sautter, E. T., & Leisen, B. (1999). Managing stakeholders: A tourism planning model. *Annals of Tourism Research, 26*(2), 312–328.

Savage, V. (1997). Singapore's garden city: Translating environmental possibilism. In: O. Giok Ling, & K. Kwok (Eds), *Singapore's built environment revisited.* Singapore: Institute of Policy Studies: Oxford University Press.

Savage, V., & Kong, L. (1993). *Symposium on environment and culture with emphasis on urban issues.* Bangkok: Siam Society.

Schein, E. H. (1984). Coming to a new awareness of organisational culture. *Sloan Management Review, 25*(4), 3–16.

Schein, E. H. (1985). How culture forms, develops and changes. In: R. H. Kilmann, M. J. Saxton, & R. Serpa (Eds), *Gaining control of the corporate culture* (pp. 17–43). San Francisco, CA: Jossey-Bass.

Schein, E. H. (1986). *Organisational culture and leadership.* San Francisco: Jossey-Bass.

Scheyvens, R. (2002). *Tourism for development.* Harlow: Prentice Hall.

Schmidt, C. J. (1979). The guided tour: Insulated adventure. *Urban Life, 7*(4), 441–467.

Scott, D., & Scott-Shafer, C. (2001). Recreational specialization. *Journal of Leisure Research, 33*(3), 319–343.

Scottish Local Authority Economic Development (SLAED) Group (2002). *The role of councils in tourism.* Edinburgh: SLAED.

Seaton, A. V. (1996). Guided by the dark: From thanatopsis to thanatourism. *International Journal of Heritage Studies, 2*(4), 234–244.

Seaton, A. V. (1998). War and thanatourism: Waterloo 1815–1914. *Annals of Tourism Research, 26*(1), 130–158.

Seaton, A. V. (1999). War and thanatourism. *Annals of Tourism Research, 26*(1), 130–158.

Seaton, A. (2002). Thanatourism's final frontiers? Visits to cemeteries, churchyards and funerary sites as sacred and secular pilgrimage. *Tourism Recreation Research, 27*(2), 73–82.

Selby, M., & Morgan, N. J. (1996). Reconstruing place image — A case-study of its role on destination market research. *Tourism Management, 17*(4), 287–294.

Selwyn, T. (Ed.) (1996). *The tourist image: Myths and myth making in tourism.* Chichester: Wiley.

Shackley, M. (1996). *Wildlife tourism.* International Thomson Business Press.

Sharpley, R. (1999). *Tourism, tourists and society* (2nd ed.). Huntingdon: Elm.

Sharpley, R. (2000). The consumption of tourism revisited. In : M. Robinson *et al.* (Eds), *Reflections on international tourism: Motivations, behaviour and tourist types* (pp. 381–391). Sunderland: Business Education Publishers.

Sharpley, R. (2005). Travels to the edge of darkness: Towards a typology of "dark" tourism, presented at '*Taking Tourism to the Limits*'. The University of Waikato, Hamilton, New Zealand, 8–11 December, 2003.

Sheller, M., & Urry, J. (2004). *Tourism mobilities: Places to play and places in play.* London: Routledge.

Shim, S., & Eastlick, M. A. (2001). An online pre-purchase intentions model: The role of intention to search. *Journal of Retailing, 77,* 397–416.

Sit, J., Merilees, B., & Birch, D. (2003). Entertainment seeking shopping centre patrons: The missing segments. *International Journal of Retail & Distribution Management, 31*(2), 80–94.

Smircich, L., & Morgan, G. (1982). Leadership: the management of meaning. *Journal of Applied Behavioural Science, 18*(2), 257–273.

Smith, A. (1776). *The wealth of nations* (Reprinted 1970). London: Pelican Books.

Smith, F. (1995). *At cost: New Zealand.* Crows Nest, NSW: Little Hills Press.

Smith, L. G. (1984). Public participation in policy making. *Geoforum, 15,* 253–259.

Smith, R. (1992). Beach resort evolution. *Annals of Tourism Research, 19*(2), 304–322.

Smith, V. (1998). War and tourism: An American ethnography. *Annals of Tourism Research, 25*(1), 202–227.

Society of American Foresters (n.d.). *Report of the society of American Foresters' Wilderness Management Task Force.* Bethesda, MD: Society of American Foresters.

Solomon, M. R. (1992). *Consumer behavior.* New Jersey: Prentice-Hall.

Sorensen, A. (2003). Backpacker ethnography. *Annals of Tourism Research, 30*(4), 847–867.

Stabler, M. J. (1985). The image of destination regions: Theoretical and empirical aspects. In: B. Goodall, & G. Ashwood (Eds), *Marketing in the tourism industry: The promotion of destination regions* (pp. 133–161). London: Routledge.

Stancliffe, H. L. (1996). *The motel: Past and future trends.* Victoria University, Melbourne: School of Hospitality Tourism and Marketing.

Stanford, P. (2002). *Heaven: A traveler's guide to the undiscovered country.* London: HarperCollins.

Stebbins, R. A. (1982). Serious leisure: A conceptual statement. *Pacific Sociological Review, 25,* 251–272.

Stebbins, R. A. (1992). *Amateurs, professionals, and serious leisure.* Montreal: McGill-Queen's University Press.

Stebbins, R. A. (1999). Serious leisure. In: E. L. Jackson, & T. L. Burton (Ed.), *Leisure studies: Prospects for the twenty-first century* (pp. 69–79). State College, PA: Venture.

Steinhauer, J. (2004, 5 August). Foreigners shun New York, keeping hotel rates down. *New York Times,* p. B4.

Straits Times (Various issues). Singapore.

Strange, C., & Kempa, M. (2003). Shades of dark tourism: Alcatraz and Robben Island. *Annals of Tourism research, 30*(2), 386–403.

Strauss, K. (2004). Starwood to open 18th hotel in China. *De Plaines, 38*(6), 30.

Sung, H. H., Morrison, A. M., & O'Leary, J. T. (1997). Definition of adventure travel: Conceptual framework for empirical application from the providers' perspective. *Asia Pacific Journal of Tourism Research, 1*(2), 47–67.

Swarbrooke, J., Beard, C., Leckie, S., & Pomfret, G. (2003). *Adventure tourism: The new frontier.* Oxford: Butterworth Heinemann.

Swarbrook, J., & Homer, S. (1999). *Consumer behaviour in tourism.* Oxford: Butterworth Heinemann.

Taylor, C. (2002). Taupo crater erupts. *The Daily Post,* 18 September, 1.

The Knowledge Enterprise: A Publication of National University of Singapore, January 2003. Singapore: National University of Singapore.

Thoreau, H. D. (1995 [1854]). *Walden or life in the woods.* New York: Dover.

Thrift, N. (1998). The rise of soft capitalism. In: A. Herod, G. O. Tuathail, & S. M. Roberts (Eds), *An unruly world? Globalization, governance and geography* (pp. 25–71). London: Routledge.

Thrift, N. (2000). Performing cultures in the new economy. *Annals of the Association of the American Geographers, 90*(4), 674–692.

Timmermans, H., Van Er Heijden, R., & Westerveld, H. (1982). The identification of factors influencing destination choice: An application of the repertory grid methodology. *Transportation, 11,* 189–203.

Timur, S. (2002). Applying stakeholder theory to the implementation of sustainable urban tourism In: K. W. Wober (Ed.), *City tourism 2002, proceedings of the European Cities Tourism International Conference*. Vienna, Austria. New York: Springer Wien.

Tosun, C., & Timothy, D. (2001). Shortcomings in planning approaches to tourism development in developing countries: The case of Turkey. *International Journal of Contemporary Hospitality Management, 13*(7), 352–359.

Tourism New Zealand (2000). *Growing New Zealand's share of the UK travel market*. Tourisminfo. http://www.tourisminfo.govt.nz/documents/UKLonghaulMarket.pdf. 24th September.

Tourism New Zealand (undated). *Product development opportunities for European and North American markets*. http://www.tourisminfo.govt.nz/documentsfEuropeNorthAmerica ProductOps.pdf. 24 September 2002.

Tremblay, P. (2000). An evolutionary interpretation of the role of collaborative partnerships in sustainable tourism. In: B. Bramwell, & B. Lane (Eds), *Tourism collaboration and partnerships: Politics, practice and sustainability* (pp. 314–332). Clevedon: Channel View.

Tucker, H. (2003). *Living with tourism: Negotiating identities in a Turkish village*. London: Routledge.

Tucker, L. (2001). *Children of the sun god: A journey with the white lions into the heart of human evolution*. Milpark: Earthyear.

Tucker, M. (1994). A proposed debit-for-nature swap in Madagascar and the larger problem of LDC debt. *International Environmental Affairs, 6*(1), 59–68.

Tulloch, S. (Ed.) (1995). *The Oxford dictionary and thesaurus*. Oxford: Oxford University Press.

Tunbridge, J., & Ashworth, G. (1996). *Dissonant heritage: The management of the past as a resource in conflict*. Chichester: Wiley.

Turk, J. (1998). *Cold oceans: Adventures in kayak, rowboat, and dogsled*. New York: Harper Collins.

Turner, L., & Ash, J. (1975). *The golden hordes*. London: Constable and Company Limited.

Turner, V. (1973). The centre out there: The pilgrim's goal. *History of Religions, 10*, 191–230.

Ulwick, A. W. (2002). Turn customer input into innovation. *Harvard Business Review, 80*(1), 91–97.

United States Congress (1964). *The wilderness act*. Washington, DC.

United States Department of Commerce (1992). Statistical abstracts of the United States 112th United States Department of Commerce, *235*, 245–246.

Urry, J. (1990). *The tourist gaze. Leisure and travel in contemporary societies*. London: Sage.

Urry, J. (2002). *The tourist gaze*. London: Sage.

Uttal, B. (1983). The corporate culture vultures. *Fortune, 17*(October), 66–70.

Uysal, M., & Jurowski, C. (1994). Environmental attitude by trip and visitor characteristics. *Tourism Management, 15*(4), 284–294.

Valentine, P. S. (1990). Nature-based tourism: A review of prospects and problems. In: M. L. Miller, & J. Auyong (Eds), *Proceedings of the 1990 Congress on Coastal and Marine Tourism* (Vol. 2, pp. 475–485).

Van den Berghe, P. (1995). Marketing Mayas: Ethnic tourism promotion in Mexico. *Annals of Tourism Research, 22*, 568–588.

Van der Post, L. (1955). *The dark eye in Africa*. London: Hogarth Press.

Van der Post, L. (1977). The other side of silence. In: I. Player (Ed.), *Voices of the wilderness: Proceedings of the First World Wilderness Congress* (pp. 1–16). Johannesburg: Jonathan Ball.

Van der Post, L. (1990). Address by and extract from a film interview with Robert Hinshaw and Peter Ammann. *Quadrant: The Journal of Contemporary Jungian Thought, 23*(2), 9–19.

Van der Post, L. (1996). A conversation with the African bush. In: L. Van der Post, & I. Player (Eds), *Wilderness and the human spirit* (pp. 26–39). Cape Town: Ian Player and The Wilderness Foundation.

Vega, C. (2002). Fast trade at ground zero. *The Press Democrat*. http://nl.newsbank.com.

Verburg, P. (Sep. 29, 2003). Luxury by factions. *Toronto, 76*(10), 81.

Vestner, H. (1992). *Nelle's guides: New Zealand*. Germany: Nelle's Verlag.

Vogel, R. K., & Swanson, B. E. (1988). Setting agendas for community change: The community goal-setting strategy. *Journal of Urban Affairs*, *10*(1), 41–61.

Vogt, C. A., & Fesenmaier, D. R. (1998). Expanding the functional information search model. *Annals of Tourism Research*, *25*(3), 551–578.

Vogt, C. A., & Stewart, S. I. (1998). Affective and cognitive effects of information use over the course of a vacation. *Journal of Leisure Research*, *30*(4), 498–520.

Vogt, J. (1976). Wandering: Youth and travel behaviour. *Annals of Tourism Research*, *4*, 25–40.

Wagner, P. L. (1996). *Showing off: The Geltung hypothesis*. Dallas: University of Texas Press.

Wahab, S., & Pigram, J. J. (1998). Tourism and sustainability: Policy considerations. In: S. Wahab, & J. J. Pigram (Eds), *Tourism, development and growth: The challenge of sustainability* (pp. 277–290). London: Routledge.

Wakefield, K. L., & Bush, V. D. (1998). Promoting leisure services: Economic and emotional aspects of consumer response. *Journal of Services Marketing*, *12*(3), 209–222.

Walle, A. H. (1997). Pursuing risk or insight. *Annals of Tourism Research*, *24*(2), 265–282.

Walsh, A. (2002a). Hot money and daring consumption in a northern Malagasy sapphire mining town. *American Ethnologist*, *30*(2), 290–305.

Walsh, A. (2002b). Preserving bodies, saving souls: Religious incongruity in a northern Malagasy mining town. *Journal of Religion in Africa*, *32*(3), 366–392.

Walsh, J. (2003). Hotel & motel management. Available www.hotelmotel.com, July, 2003.

Walzer, N. (1996). *Community strategic visioning programs*. Westport: Praeger.

Wang, Y., & Fesenmaier, D. R. (2003). Towards understanding members' general participation in and active contribution to an online travel community. *Tourism Management*, *25*(6), ???.

Wang, Y., Yu, Q. *et al.* (2002). Defining the virtual tourist community: Implications for tourism marketing. *Tourism Management*, *23*(4), 407–417.

Warner, J. (1999). North Cypress: Tourism and the challenge of non-recognition. *Journal of Sustainable Tourism*, *7*(2), 128–146.

Weaver, D. (Ed.) (1998). *Ecotourism in the less developed world*. Wallingford: CABI.

Weaver, D. (Ed.) (2003). *Encyclopaedia of ecotourism*. Wallingford: CABI.

Weaving, S., & Neil, J. (1999). *Ecotourism impacts, potentials and possibilities*. Melbourne: Butterworth Heinemann.

Weber, K. (2001). Outdoor adventure tourism: A review of research approaches. *Annals of Tourism Research*, *28*(2), 360–377.

Wei, S., Ruys, H., & Muller, T. E. (1999). A gap analysis of perceptions of hotel attributes by marketing managers and older people in Australia. *Journal of Marketing Practice: Applied Marketing Science*, *5*(6–8), 200–212.

Wells, N., Irvine. N., & Duckworth, I. (2000). *Lonely planet: Cycling New Zealand*. Victoria, Australia: Lonely Planet.

Westley, F., & Mintzberg, H. (1989). Visionary leadership and strategic management. *Strategic Management Journal*, *10*, 17–32.

Wheaton, B. (2000). "Just do it": Consumption, commitment, and identity in the windsurfing subculture. *Sociology of Sport Journal*, *17*, 254–274.

Whipp, R. (1993). The real meaning of empowerment. *Personnel Management*.

Wigglesworth, Z., & Wigglesworth, J. (1996). *Fielding's New Zealand*. California: Fielding Worldwide.

Wilkins, A. L. (1983). The culture audit: A tool for understanding organisations. *Organisational Dynamics*, *12*, 24–38.

Williams, P. W., Penrose, R. W., & Hawkes, S. (1998). Shared decision-making in tourism land use planning. *Annals of Tourism Research*, *25*(4), 860–889.

Williams, R. (1973). *The country and the city*. London: Chatto & Windus.

Willis, C. (1999). *Wild: Stories of survival from the world's most dangerous places*. Edinburgh: Adrenaline Mainstream.

Wilson, P. (2002). Artist's dead body of work a new take on still life. http://www.theaustralian. news.com (1 June 2002).

Winpenny, J. (1991). *Values for the environment*. London: HMSO.

Wolf, S. (1998). *Fodor's: New Zealand*. New York: Fodor's Travel.

Woodcock, D. J., Mosey, S. P., & Wood, T. B. W. (2000). New product development in British SMEs. *European Journal of Innovation Management*, *3*(4), 212–221.

Woodside, A. G., & Sherrell, D. (1977). Traveler evoked, inept, and inert sets of vacation destinations. *Journal of Travel Research*, *16*(1), 14–18.

World Bank (1994). *World development report*. Oxford: Oxford University Press.

World Tourism Organisation Business Council (2001). *Internet poised to take a quarter of tourism sales*. WWW. [http://www.interactive-tourism.com].

Wycherley, G. (2002). Thar she blows, all over tourists. *New Zealand Herald* (18 September).

Yeoman, J. (2000). Achieving sustainable tourism: A paradigmatic perspective. In: M. Robinson, J. Swarbrooke, N. Evans, P. Long, & R. Sharpley (Eds), *Reflections on international tourism: Environmental management and pathways to sustainable tourism* (pp. 311–327). Sunderland: Business Education Publishers.

Yeung, H. W. C. (1998). The political economy of transnational corporations: A study of the regionalisation of Singaporean firms. *Political Geography*, *17*, 389–416.

Yeung, H. W. C. (1999). Regulating investment abroad: The political economy of the regionalization of Singaporean firms. *Antipode*, *31*, 245–273.

Yeung, H. W. C. (2003). Managing economic (in)security in the global economy: Institutional capacity and Singapore's developmental state. A revised paper presented at the conference on *Globalisation and Economic Security in East Asia: Governance and Institutions*. 11–12 September, 2003, Institute of Defence and Strategic Studies, Nanyang Technological University, Singapore.

Young, B. (1983). Touristization of traditional Maltese fishing-farming villages. *Tourism Management*, *4*(1), 35–41.

Young, G., Richins, H., & Rugimbana, R. (1993). New directions for tourism planning, *Proceedings of the National Conference on Tourism Research*. University of Sydney, Australia.

Zaltman, G., Duncan, R., & Holbek, J. (1973). *Innovations and organizations*. New York: Wiley.

Zell, L. (1991). Ecotourism of the future – The vicarious experience. *Ecotourism, Incorporating The Global Classroom*. 1991 International Conference Papers. Bureau of Tourism Research, Canberra.

Ziener, K. (2002). Types of conflicts between recreational use and nature conservation in national parks and biosphere resources. In: A. Arnberger, C. Brandenburg, & A. Muhar (Eds), *Conference proceedings of the monitoring and management of visitor flows in recreational and protected areas* (pp. 467–473). Bodenkultur University, Vienna, Austria.

Subject Index